TACITUS
GERMANIA

BCP Classic Latin and Greek Texts in Paperback

Current and forthcoming titles in this new series are listed below:

Calpurnius Siculus: The Eclogues, C. Keene
Cicero: The Poems, W. Ewbank
Empedocles: The Extant Fragments, M. Wright
Euripides: Helen, A. Dale
Euripides: Troades, K. Lee
Nicander: Poems & Fragments, A. Gow & A. Schofield
Seneca the Elder: Suasoriae, W. Edward
Tacitus: Dialogus, W. Peterson
Tacitus: Germania, J. Anderson

TACITUS
GERMANIA

Edited with Introduction
and Notes by
J.G.C. Anderson

Bristol Classical Press

Cover illustration: from *Gemma Augustea*, showing a German wearing trousers and shoes.

First published at the Clarendon Press, Oxford

Reprinted by arrangement with Oxford University Press in 1997
by Bristol Classical Press
an imprint of
Gerald Duckworth & Co. Ltd
The Old Piano Factory
48 Hoxton Square, London N1 6PB

© 1938 Oxford University Press

A catalogue record for this book is available
from the British Library

ISBN 1-85399-503-7

Available in USA and Canada from:
Focus Information Group
PO Box 360
Newburyport
MA 01950

Printed in Great Britain by
Booksprint, Bristol

PREFACE

'THIS edition is designed to take the place of that published forty-four years ago by H. Furneaux, which has long been out of date. Its aim is to provide an historical–archaeological as well as linguistic commentary on a scale suitable for the needs of English-speaking students and teachers, for whom the *Germania* should have an abiding interest, second only to that which it has for the Germans themselves. I have accordingly sought to maintain a balance between the more or less dogmatic brevity of a school-book and the overloaded fullness of an exhaustive edition. The work began as a revision of Furneaux's commentary, but it soon became clear that revision would mean almost complete rewriting. The original plan has, however, left traces in the incorporation (with alterations, or additions, or both) of a fair number of the shorter notes, chiefly of the ordinary explanatory kind needed by less-advanced students. Apart from these, the commentary is new, as are also the introductory sections.

Since 1894 knowledge has made a great advance, thanks partly to the labours of Classical and Germanic scholars, but even more to the steady progress of archaeological investigation, which has served not only to confirm and to correct the statements of Tacitus, but also to amplify the information that he gives and partially to lift the veil that shrouded the prehistory of the Germanic peoples and the process of their expansion over Central Europe. The output of work bearing directly and indirectly on the treatise has been enormous, and to attempt to take complete stock of it is a formidable task; but I hope I may have succeeded in gathering together the more assured results of criticism and research.

Use has naturally been made of recent commentaries, especially those of the eminent Germanist K. Müllenhoff

(*Deutsche Altertumskunde*, iv, new ed. 1920), Ed. Schwyzer (3rd revision of Schweizer–Sidler, 1923), A. Gudeman (whose American edition of 1928 varies some of the views expressed in his German edition of 1916), and W. Reeb (with some appendixes by K. Schumacher, 1930). E. Fehrle's *Germania* (1929, 2nd ed. 1935) contains some useful information on folklore and survivals of ancient customs; and Ed. Wolff's small edition (1915) has furnished occasional suggestions. I have also consulted on particular points the older works of A. Baumstark, *Erläuterung . . . der Germania* (1875) and *Urdeutsche Staatsalterthümer* (1873), which are still not negligible. When the volume was ready for the printer in the spring of 1937 there was published a lengthy commentary by the late R. Much, a distinguished Germanist, of whose previous work I had made large use. The book appeared too late to be fully utilized, but it was possible to run hastily through it, with some advantage to my commentary. It is a closely reasoned and sober (though not always convincing) exposition, in which readers will find fuller information on matters appertaining to Germanic antiquities.

The other works and articles used in the preparation of this edition are too numerous to detail: some are cited in the body of the book. But special mention must be made of one acute and stimulating work, *Die germanische Urgeschichte in Tacitus' Germania* (3rd ed., 1923), by Ed. Norden, who has done brilliant service by establishing beyond doubt the literary character of the treatise and the dependence of its author on the tradition of ethnographical composition, and by exploring with extraordinary acumen the sources of his information.

For the *apparatus criticus* the recent critical edition of R. P. Robinson (1935) has been of great use. His comprehensive collation is likely to hold the field for a long time to come; and as I have cited the evidence not only of the five manuscripts hitherto used as the basis of the text but also of three codices to which he assigns an independent value and of two others, I have deemed it advisable to follow his notation, while regretting that he has not retained the symbols that have generally been used since Halm's time for four of the five 'canonical' manuscripts.

I have to acknowledge with gratitude the aid I have received from several scholars: C. F. C. Hawkes, whose knowledge of prehistoric Europe, freely placed at my service, enabled me to improve the fourth section of the Introduction; H. Mattingly, who helped in numismatic matters; S. G. Owen and C. Bailey, who gave their opinion on some points of Latinity; Sir G. Macdonald, who read the proofs and made helpful suggestions; and R. Syme, who did a like service, especially in respect of the second part of the treatise. I have also to thank E. B. Birley for some useful notes on the illustration following page 64. I must add an acknowledgement of the service rendered by the proof readers at the Clarendon Press, who made various useful suggestions.

J. G. C. A.

Oxford,
March 1938

CONTENTS

LIST OF ILLUSTRATIONS

Figs. 7, 14, 15, 18, 20, 21, *and* 25, *and* 8, 17, *and* 22 *are reproduced from photographs kindly supplied by the Röm.-
german. Zentral-Museum, Mainz, and Herr Geheimrat
Neeb, Mainz, respectively.*

MAPS

INTRODUCTION
Section I
THE LITERARY CHARACTER AND THE PURPOSE OF THE WORK

THE *Germania* was published, soon after the *Agricola*, in A.D. 98.[1] What particular reasons led Tacitus to write it is a question that has often been asked and variously answered.

(1) It was once commonly believed that his purpose was to hold up a moral mirror to his compatriots by painting a picture of the virtues of unspoilt barbarism in such a way as to throw these into strong relief against the blemishes of contemporary Roman civilization. This view was based on the impression conveyed by the first twenty-seven chapters, where in almost every line there is a comparison, direct or implicit, between Germany and Rome, and where the laudable features of German social customs and institutions are emphasized and pointedly contrasted with Roman ways, the contrast often taking the negative form that this or that Roman practice is not to be found beyond the Rhine. The Germans, we read, are a free people who strictly limit the power of their rulers in peace and war; who care no more for silver plate than for earthenware; who bury their dead without pomp, and do not deify mortals; who have no professional artists or hireling gladiators to amuse them, but only the pure pastime of the sword-dance; among whom the intrigues of the wife, her love-letters, her corruption by licentious shows and banquets find no place, the marriage tie is indissoluble, and unchastity is rare and meets with ruthless punishment; who neither expose their children to die nor hand them over to foster-nurses, but rear them up to a youth of hardihood and purity, and pay no court to childless old

[1] See note on c. 37, 2. The life of Tacitus is sketched in the Introduction to the *Agricola*, pp. xix ff.

age—and more in the same strain. That, however, is not the whole picture. If the virtues of the Germans are emphasized, their failings are not veiled: they are undisciplined, impulsive in battle, indolent and quarrelsome in peace, predatory, drunken, absorbed by the passion for gambling. Moreover, if it were merely a moralizing homily that Tacitus set out to write, the second part of the treatise (cc. 28–46), which contains little of ethical import, would be an irrelevance such as could not be imputed to a great literary artist. Plainly the theory of a purely ethical purpose does not cover all the facts, and those which it does cover are capable of a simpler explanation. Every writer who describes foreign peoples naturally tends to compare their civilization with his own and consequently to concern himself more with the differences between the two than with the resemblances, while the moralizing tone is not only in keeping with the ethical purpose which Tacitus regarded as the chief aim of the historian but is a feature of every age that awakes to a sense of the evils which a highly developed civilization is bound to bring in its train.

(2) Others have held that the *Germania* had a political purpose: it was a political pamphlet written for a particular occasion.[1] It was published in the year when Trajan succeeded to the principate. At the time of his accession he was in charge of the provinces of Upper and Lower Germany, and instead of hastening to Rome, where his arrival was impatiently awaited,[2] he remained for nearly a year and a half on the northern frontier, strengthening and consolidating the defences of the Rhine and Danube and thereby indicating not only that he had no intention of attempting the reconquest of Germany but that he considered the existing position insecure against the danger of German aggression. The Roman public (it is argued) did not appreciate the

---

[1] Müllenhoff's statement of this view is that which is here outlined (*Deutsche Altertumskunde*, iv, 1920, pp. 13 ff.).
[2] Martial, x. 6 and 7; Pliny, *Paneg.* 20, 22.

seriousness of the peril that threatened this frontier, and could not understand why the emperor tarried so long when there was no fighting on hand. There was also a party, or at any rate certain people, who demanded war against the Germans to wipe out the disgrace of Domitian's disasters. In these circumstances Tacitus came forward to enlighten the Roman public about the character and life of the Germans, so that it should realize that the strengthening of the frontier defence was so important as to require the personal attention of Trajan, and at the same time to justify and uphold the emperor's prudent policy against the advocates of war.

In support of this view it is claimed that, although the author gives no direct indication of his purpose, the manner in which German and Roman life are contrasted in the first part of the monograph was calculated to bring home to the Roman mind that abundant man-power, strict morality, untamed passion for freedom, and the warlike spirit fostered by their whole manner of life combined to make the Germans the most redoubtable foes of the Empire. This impression would be strengthened by the description of the individual tribes—their great number, their diversity of character, the vast expanse of country which they covered, stretching away into the misty regions of the unknown. The main purpose of the book, to stress the gravity of the German menace, is made especially clear by the historical retrospect in the thirty-seventh chapter, which can only have been inserted to remind the reader of the repeated blows which this great free people had inflicted on Rome during more than two hundred years.

There can be no doubt that Tacitus was convinced of the seriousness of the German peril, and it may have been this conviction that led him to write the *Germania* (see below). But it is incredible that the author of a treatise planned with a special political purpose should give no plain indication of his purpose and at best only imply it when he has reached his thirty-seventh chapter. If his aim had been to explain and support Trajan's policy, the theme would have been given out in the opening chapters and would have been heard running through the work: Müllenhoff's contention that the concealment of the writer's special purpose would make the treatise all the more effective, when Roman readers knew where Trajan was and what he was doing, is paradoxical. The existence of a party at Rome which favoured war and hoped by its clamour to influence the emperor's policy is pure hypothesis, and there is no likelihood that Tacitus, who, though eminent as an orator, had had a very ordinary public career and had not yet figured as an historian, would think it appropriate to advocate in public a particular line of policy, which was a matter for the emperor to deal with, or would imagine that the emperor needed his support. There are other considerations that are fatal to the theory. Tacitus expresses no opinion on matters of public policy. The form, the contents, and the style of the treatise are all wholly inappropriate to a political brochure. Nor would it have been an easy task to collect and digest the material for the work and put it into careful literary form within the brief time available in the year 98 after the publication of the *Agricola*. The *Germania* was the fruit of study and thought, which may well have dated back to the reign of Domitian, when one might read and think but dared not write.

(3) It is now generally agreed that the *Germania* was intended to be what its form and contents would lead the ordinary reader to suppose—a description of the land and its inhabitants for the enlightenment of the Roman public.[1]

---

[1] This view was first expressed by A. Riese, *Die ursprüngl. Bestimmung der Germ. d. Tac.* (in *Eos*, ii, 1866, pp. 193 ff.), and later by Th. Mommsen (*Sitzb. Preuss. Akad.*, 1886, p. 44; *Reden u. Aufsätze*, 1905, p. 152). It has been established beyond doubt by the studies of K. Trüdinger, *Studien zur Gesch. d. griechisch-römischen Ethnographie* (Basel, 1918), and E. Norden, *Die germanische Urgeschichte in Tacitus' Germania*, 3rd ed., Berlin, 1923, which have proved decisively the literary category to which the *Germania* belongs.

Whether it was written in the spirit of purely scientific inquiry is a separate question which will require consideration (see p. xv). The usual view has been that the work was suggested by the preliminary studies for a history of Domitian's reign which Tacitus had planned when he wrote the *Agricola* in A.D. 98, as he himself tells us (c. 3, 3), and which ultimately appeared in an extended form as the *Histories*. It was the long-established practice of historians, when they reached a point in their narrative where the scene of events changed, to give the reader his bearings by describing the land and the people concerned. Of this practice Tacitus himself has given evidence in the account of Britain in the *Agricola* (cc. 10–17) and of the Jews in the *Histories* (v. 1–13). As Germany was the scene of important events which would find a place in his historical work, a descriptive sketch of the country and its inhabitants would be needed, and such a sketch was probably inserted at an appropriate point in the narrative (the greater part of which has perished). Such an excursus would, however, be comparatively short, whereas the material was abundant and the subject important, and so Tacitus resolved to embody all the results of his investigation in a substantive work.

Whether or not this be the true account of the genesis of the work, there is no doubt about the literary *genre* to which it belongs, and the fact is important for its proper appreciation. Tacitus was heir to an established tradition of ethnographical writing, with definite rules of form, method of treatment, and descriptive style, which had been developed by a long line of Greek authors and which bound their Roman successors. The pioneers in this field were the Ionian Greeks. The germs of geographical and ethnographical description are to be found in the Homeric epics, but the first scientific description of lands and peoples was given by Hecataeus of Miletus, who wrote towards the end of the sixth century B.C. To him was due the fruitful idea, suggested by the peculiar civilization and conditions of Egypt, that an intimate connexion existed between the climate of a country and the character of its inhabitants. His influence is manifest in the history of Herodotus, who in telling the story of non-Hellenic peoples prefaces his narrative by an ordered description of their country, their customs, and their institutions. A little later in the fifth century the doctrine of Hecataeus was developed by a medical writer of the school of Hippocrates of Cos, who wrote a tract περὶ ἀέρων ὑδάτων τόπων,[1] dealing with the influence of the climate, water, and geography of a country on the health, physical type, and mental characteristics of its inhabitants. The leading idea of this treatise found its way into the common stock of knowledge and exercised a great influence on Greek thought in general and on historiography in particular. The work itself was known perhaps to Plato, certainly to Aristotle and his school, who turned their attention to comparative sociology and, by making a comprehensive collection of facts concerning the customs and institutions (νόμιμα) of civilized and uncivilized peoples and applying philosophical method to the study of them, laid the foundations of cultural history. Such sociological investigation naturally appealed to the Stoics, who sought to transcend the national and to discover manifestations of eternal Reason even in the soul of barbarians.

One of their greatest representatives was Posidonius (c. 135–51 B.C.), a Syrian philosopher and historian, about whom more will be said in the next section. He was the first to give some account of the Germans. He was also the last of the great Greek historians. The Romans, who rarely displayed the Greek spirit of inquiry and the Greek love of knowledge for its own sake, had hitherto done nothing for the scientific exploitation of the lands they had conquered. It was Greeks that had seized the opportunities which Roman conquests offered of adding to knowledge. Polybius and Panaetius had done something for Africa; Polybius, Artemidorus, Asclepiades of Myrlea, and Posidonius supplied the

[1] Ed. Gundermann, Bonn, 1911.

materials for the description of Spain and its peoples which
fills the third book of Strabo's *Geography*. The shortcomings
of the Romans in the sphere of science and art had been recognized by Virgil in his famous lines, *Aen.* vi. 847–53 ; and Strabo
was justified in the complaint he made regarding Spain, that
what Roman writers related they took over from the Greeks,
and that they brought to their task little real love of knowledge, so that when the Greeks left gaps they did little to
fill them.[1] When Germany was opened up by the Roman
arms, the spirit of first-hand investigation had declined
amongst the Greeks and, if the new knowledge were to be
marshalled and recorded in literary form, it could only be
done by Romans. What they achieved in this field is embodied in the *Germania*.

But when we have labelled the work an Ethnography we
have not settled the question of the author's purpose in
writing it. Was his interest in the Germans purely scientific ?
Was his object simply to make a contribution to ethnological
and sociological knowledge ?[2] The reader soon perceives
that the whole picture of German institutions, customs, and
beliefs is painted against the background of Roman civilization. That in itself, as has been said, is in no way surprising :
every observer of foreign civilizations naturally takes his
own as the standard by which he observes and judges. It is
quite common for Greeks and Romans to refer to the similari-
ties and differences between foreign customs and their own ;
it is common, too, for them to use their own political, social,
and religious concepts in describing them. But in the *Germania* the comparison goes very much deeper, and with it is
often associated a palpable feeling of sympathy which im-
pels the writer to get down to the mentality, or what he
believes to be the mentality, of which the customs and
ceremonies he describes are an expression, to probe the soul

---

[1] iii. 4, 19, p. 166.
[2] Erwin Wolff's article, 'Das geschichtliche Verstehen in Tacitus'
Germania', in *Hermes*, lxix, 1934, pp. 121–66, is a suggestive study of
this question, which is here laid under contribution.

of the people. The comparative method of exposition is obviously a means of enabling readers to comprehend the meaning of institutions which have a strange appearance, to understand the sentiments, whether political, social, or religious, on which they are based. And the writer's aim clearly is to make them understand. When he comes to describe customs and institutions which he believes to involve important principles or beliefs, his diction becomes elevated and he strives to engage the interest of his readers by the use of all manner of stylistic devices—anaphora (the repetition of an adjective, pronoun, or adverb) to give impassioned emphasis, antithesis, alliteration, asyndeton, poetical (especially Virgilian) colouring, epigrammatic phrase. This is a feature of the *Germania* which distinguishes it from any other ethnographical description. How is it to be accounted for?

It seems clear that Tacitus recognized in the Germans a people who, despite all differences, exhibited qualities that were fundamentally akin to the Roman or, more strictly, to what the Roman had been in older days. Their *mores* were in many respects the *mores antiqui* which had built up the Roman empire: of *deliciae, luxus, opes* they knew nothing, as Seneca had said,[1] whereas in contemporary Rome civilization had brought with it a moral declension. They were a simple people, more primitive than the old Romans, more impulsive, more undisciplined, more inert in time of peace, but with a similar (if more intense) love of freedom, with the same moral sentiments, the same method of government, the same mystical belief in invisible Powers. The correspondence is made most explicit in the ethical sphere. The moral principles on which German marriage customs and married life were based are those of the old Romans.[2] They had the same idea of the seriousness and sanctity of wedlock. Their wedding gifts symbolized the indissoluble partnership of man and wife in peace and war; they had the same

---

[1] *De Ira*, i. 11, 4 (quoted below).   [2] cc. 18–19.

binding force as the *arcana sacra*, the *di coniugales* had for Romans. And just because of their lofty conceptions of matrimony unfaithfulness was very rare and, when it occurred, met with condign punishment. The ceremonies of marriage were a regular ethnographic topic, but Tacitus speaks only of the gifts exchanged, because they were a symbol of the moral forces that inspired the people. The two chapters devoted to this subject are plainly not a purely sociological description, nor are they a blend of moral criticism of contemporary Roman practice, idealization, and romantic longing. They are a selective description of German *mores* in so far as they reveal principles identical in character with those of the Romans of an earlier age. On the political side, the formative forces which produced a method of government by a council of chiefs and an assembly of the people in arms[1] are the same as those which developed the system of government by Senate and Centuriate Assembly under the free Republic. The admission of the young German into the citizen body by investiture with arms[2] is the counterpart of the assumption of the *toga virilis* by the young Roman, *primus iuventae honos*, only that in Germany the military side of life overshadows the civil. With the like difference, training for leadership runs on lines parallel to those which obtained at Rome. Though the *comitatus* is an alien-looking institution, it has grades of rank which furnish opportunity for wholesome rivalry and it provides the young man with the means of rising ultimately to the position of *princeps* with a large and keen following: Tacitus' readers would think of the career of office, the *cursus honorum*, by which the young Roman could gradually rise to the position of a leading man in the State, *princeps civitatis*, with a numerous clientèle. But, unlike the training of the Roman, that of the German is purely military. In the sphere of religion,[3] too, German ideas are those of the old Romans. They make no images of gods—the maintenance of this

[1] c. 11.   [2] c. 13.   [3] cc. 9, 39–40.

practice, said Varro, would have kept Roman worship purer[1]—and to them, as to the Romans even of Tacitus' time, the source of spiritual intuition is the mysterious stillness of lonely woods and groves, those hallowed dwellings (*sedes sacrae*) to which the soul withdraws, there to find her delight.[2] It was on religious belief that German courage was grounded.[3]

The experience of more than two hundred years had shown the military prowess of the race, had proved them (so Tacitus was convinced) to be the most dangerous foe that Rome had ever faced in her long struggle for power, more dangerous than the Carthaginians, in whom Romans were wont to see the most formidable enemy that had ever crossed their path, more dangerous than the Parthian Empire.[4] Hitherto the Germans had been kept at bay because they lacked the Roman virtues of *disciplina* and *ratio*. 'Give them these qualities', Seneca had said,[5] 'and we shall certainly have to go back to the old Roman ways of life.' Some of the western tribes had already attained them:[6] if that development should become general, what would the issue be? It is in the West that the danger-point lies. On the Danube the tribes are friendly or under Roman influence; beyond, in the vast spaces of eastern Europe, they are politically and socially backward : the more remote they are the more backward, until the descending scale of civilization sinks into pure barbarism. Once convinced that the Germans were Rome's most serious foe, Tacitus would seem to have set himself to find out the truth about the people, to discover what made them so dangerous, and to expound the facts to his countrymen in such a way as to drive home their significance and to stir

---

[1] *Ap.* Aug. *Civ. Dei*, iv. 31: *quod si adhuc mansisset, castius di observarentur.*

[2] Tac. *Dial.* 12, 1.   [3] cc. 7–8.   [4] c. 37.

[5] *De Ira*, i. 11, 4: *agedum illis corporibus, illis animis delicias luxum opes ignorantibus da rationem, da disciplinam: ut nil amplius dicam, necesse erit certe nobis mores Romanos repetere.*

[6] cc. 30, 32.

them to serious thought. The picture must be true. It must also be complete. For the Germans have vices as well as virtues, vices which spring from their excessive *libertas* and their bellicose character. Therein lies one ground for hope. Proximity to the Roman Empire, too, is beginning to impair their virtues.[1] A further source of comfort is the chronic disunion of the tribes, in which Tiberius had seen a safeguard against the danger of aggression.[2] 'May there abide, I pray, and endure among the nations, if not love for us, at least hatred of each other; for as the destinies of the Empire drive it on, Fortune can now vouchsafe no greater boon than discord among our foes.'[3] That passionate prayer came from the heart.

Section II
TACITUS' SOURCES OF INFORMATION

Nowhere does Tacitus lay claim to first-hand knowledge of the country and the peoples he describes, and it is practically certain that he had none. It is not beyond the bounds of possibility that when he was absent from Rome during the four years preceding the death of his father-in-law Agricola (Aug. 23, A.D. 93), he held a legionary command on the Rhine frontier or governed the province of Belgica, where his father had been imperial procurator. But on such an hypothesis no conclusion can be based, and we may be sure that, if Tacitus had possessed personal knowledge of the country he would not have concluded the first part of his treatise with words which plainly indicate dependence on the accounts of others: 'haec . . . de omnium Germanorum origine ac moribus *accepimus.*' The sources from which he drew his information were mainly literary.

Among the works from which material was derived,

---

[1] *Iam et pecuniam accipere docuimus*, c. 15, 3; *saepius pecunia-iuvantur*, c. 42, 2.

[2] *Ann.* ii. 26; 62.   [3] c. 33, 2.

ultimately if not directly,[1] were the *Histories* ('Ιστορίαι) of
the Syrian philosopher and historian Posidonius, a native
of Apamea in the valley of the Orontes. After a period of
travel for scientific and historical purposes, in the course
of which he visited Liguria, southern Gaul, and Spain, Posidonius settled at Rhodes, where by his teaching and writing
he exerted a profound influence on both Greeks and Romans,
not only as a philosopher who transformed Stoicism by
fusing with it the mystical doctrines of the Syrian–Babylo-
nian East, but also as an historian and ethnographer. His
Histories in fifty-two books, which continued the work of
Polybius down to about 80 B.C. and were written in a flowing
and richly coloured style, have perished; but the free use
made of them by Strabo, Diodorus, Plutarch, and Athenaeus
enables us to recover something of their contents. Deeply
interested in the doctrine of a causal connexion between
physical environment and national character, a theme which
found a place in the teaching of his master Panaetius,[2] he
developed the doctrine in the light of the new knowledge
available about northern and western Europe and formulated
conclusions (reproduced by Vitruvius)[3] concerning the physical and mental characteristics of northern and southern
races which became the stock-in-trade of subsequent his-

[1] On this point opinion differs. Norden, whose second chapter is
a fine study of the contribution of Posidonius to German ethnography,
believes that Tacitus did not use his *Histories* directly but obtained
his information from Livy's version. Wissowa (*Neue Jahrb.* 1921,
p. 20) holds that distinctive features of Posidonius' style, which
recur (as Norden shows, pp. 459 ff.) in the *Germania*, could not have
been caught by Tacitus from Livy and were not likely to have been
of independent origin—hardly a convincing argument. On Posidonius
cp. also Trüdinger, *op. cit.* (p. xii, note), pp. 80 ff., 146 ff.

[2] It is reproduced in a passage of Polybius dealing with the Arca-
dians (iv. 21): 'By a law of our nature we men become, all of us, per-
force assimilated to our physical environment; to this cause and to
no other are due the great differences that prevail among us, whether
as between nations or over whole regions of the world, in respect of
character, physical form, complexion, and most of our habits of life.'
Cp. Cic. *De divin.* ii. 96 f.

[3] vi. 1, 3–9.

torians; while his descriptions of non-Hellenic lands and peoples, enriched with copious notices of their religious beliefs, social customs, and folk-lore, formed the basis of the accounts given by later writers.

With him the Germans begin to appear in literature: the thirtieth book of his *Histories* contained an account of them, from which Athenaeus quotes a sentence relating to food and drink.[1] These Germans were evidently tribes, occupy ing the right bank of the Rhine, which had been so deeply affected by Celtic influences that they seemed to him hardly distinguishable from their Gallic neighbours, save by their wilder character, their larger frames, and their fairer hair.[2] That he had actually seen them is improbable, but he could easily obtain information about them from the Greeks of Marseilles, who were in close commercial contact with the Rhine lands. The anthropological element in his description of them had a permanent value, and when in the decades following the completion of his work the true nationality of the Cimbri came to be definitely recognized,[3] his account of them and their comrades the Teutoni, which ranked as authoritative, could be utilized for German ethnography.

Owing to the loss of his historical work, the debt which Tacitus owed to him cannot be exactly estimated, but as comparatively little was known of the Germans in the early decades of the first century B.C., it must have been limited to sociological facts of a general type: the more detailed statements about German life and tribal characteristics must have been based on later authorities who wrote when knowledge had grown. To Posidonius may be ultimately traced the legend of the divine descent of the race (c. 2), its ethnological characteristics (c. 4), the so-called shield-song (c. 3), perhaps the legend of Hercules and the beginnings of the process of identifying German deities with gods of

[1] iv. 153 e.

[2] *Ap.* Strabo, iv. 4, 2, p. 196; vii. 1, 2, p. 290.

[3] Posidonius regarded them as neighbours of the Scythians and conjecturally identified them with the Cimmerians (below, p. xxxviii).

Rome and Greece (c. 9), certainly the descriptions of the
retinue (*comitatus*) of the German chief (cc. 13–14) and of
German hospitality, diet, and drink (cc. 21, 23), and perhaps
other customs of public and private life.

There was no other Greek writer on whom Tacitus could
have drawn, as the historical geography of Strabo, whose
description of Germany in Book VII reflects the progress of
geographical knowledge down to the time of Augustus, and
the universal history of Diodorus were both unknown in the
West. His other sources of information were Roman.

The first Roman contribution to knowledge of Germany
was made by Julius Caesar, who devoted three chapters of
his *Gallic War* to a description of the Suebi (iv. 1–3) and four
to an account of German *mores* (vi. 21–4), the latter forming
part of a lengthy comparative sketch of Gauls and Germans
and their manner of life. His information about Germany
was mainly based on reports, and he evidently knew the
account of Posidonius;[1] but his description marked a distinct advance in its clear differentiation between Germans
and Celts, whom Posidonius had found similar to each other
both in physical characteristics and in culture. The *Gallic
War* was well known to Tacitus, who speaks of its author in
c. 28 as *summus auctorum* in respect of his authoritative
knowledge of Gaul, but it could not have been a primary
source for the *Germania*. Where both deal with the same
matters the account of Tacitus sometimes differs (as in the
enumeration of German deities) and is usually much more
detailed than that of Caesar, while on many other points it
gives information which is not contained in Caesar's sketch.
Tacitus must have depended on later authorities who had
largely extended the comparatively slight knowledge of
Caesar's time.

Of these later narratives two were clearly sources of pri-

---

[1] Norden, pp. 99 ff. In connexion with the Hercynian forest, Caesar
refers to 'Eratosthenes and certain Greeks' (vi. 24), whom he had
apparently not read, but found quoted by Posidonius.

mary importance. Both are lost. One was bk. civ of **Livy's**
History, written towards the end of the principate of
Augustus, the first part of which gave a description of Ger-
many and its inhabitants[1] by way of introduction to the
history of Caesar's campaign against Ariovistus (58 B.C.).
In the preceding book the account of the subjugation of the
Helvetii was followed by a description of Gaul, and in the
following book the narrative of Caesar's two expeditions to
Britain was prefaced by a similar but briefer sketch of this
country, to which Tacitus refers in the *Agricola* (c. 10). For
these descriptions Livy's main sources were Posidonius and
Caesar. His indebtedness to the former is a well-established
fact: his narrative of the Cimbric wars was based on the
classic account of Posidonius and his intimate familiarity with
the *Histories* long before he began to use them as a source
is plainly shown by the speech which he puts into the mouth
of Manlius when he addressed his troops before the battle
with the Galatian Tolistobogii in 189 B.C. What we hear is
the voice of Posidonius detailing the characteristics of the
Celts and explaining how their racial character has been
modified by their physical and human environment in
Galatia, just as differences of soil and climate produce
different species in the plant and animal world.[2] But a
description of Germany which merely served up Posidonius
and Caesar would have been antiquated: Livy must have
embodied the new knowledge acquired during the reign of
Augustus as a result of the Roman campaigns in Germany
and of the development of trade. This knowledge was utilized
to some extent by Strabo in his seventh book, but his account
was not one of Livy's sources: the *Geography* was not published before Livy died and it was unknown to Romans.
Whether the new material had been put together by any
other writer whose work Livy used, is unknown.[3]

[1] Perioch. lib. civ.: *prima pars libri situm Germaniae moresque
continet.*
[2] Liv. xxxviii. 17; Norden, pp. 156 ff.
[3] Norden, pp. 152 ff., 350, 502 (developing a theory of A. Klotz in

Another source of primary importance was the lost *Bella Germaniae* of the elder Pliny, a narrative of all the Roman wars with Germany in twenty books, extending perhaps to the close of Claudius' reign.[1] This narrative was continued in his historical work *A fine Aufidii Bassi* (carried down to Vespasian's reign), which has also perished. It was used by Tacitus in the *Annals* and was closely followed by him in his account of the great rebellion on the Rhine (*Hist.* iv–v), but it would naturally furnish much less material for the *Germania*. Pliny was (so far as we know) the most recent authority on Germany available to Tacitus. He had first-hand knowledge of the country, gained during his service as a military officer in Lower Germany under Corbulo (A.D. 47) and in Upper Germany under his friend P. Pomponius Secundus (A.D. 50–1), whose life he wrote.[2] His history of the wars with Germany was begun during his military service.

Pliny's passion for knowledge of every kind, unusual among Romans, made him a very keen observer, and the *Bella Germaniae* was undoubtedly a storehouse of information about the Germans, their mythology and their customs and institutions, political, social, and military. The loss of the work makes it impossible to determine the extent of Tacitus' debt to it, but we may safely believe[3] that Pliny

---

his *Caesarstudien*), thinks that the new material had been put together by Timagenes of Alexandria, who had been brought as a prisoner to Rome and enjoyed for a time the friendship of Augustus. He wrote an historical work, eulogized by Quintilian, from which Ammianus Marcellinus (xv. 9, 2 ff.) quotes an account of the origin of the Gauls. Norden believes that he also wrote about the Germans, but his arguments are inconclusive. Timagenes is a rather shadowy figure, and the scope of his historical work is indeterminable; he may well have played a part in moulding ancient historical tradition, but we cannot prove it. Cp. Laqueur's article 'Timagenes' in Pauly-Wissowa, *Real-Encyc.* (1936).

[1] Pliny, *Epp.* iii. 5, 4.

[2] F. Münzer, 'Die Quelle des Tacitus f. die Germanenkriege', in *Bonner Jahrb.* civ, 1899, pp. 67 ff.

[3] See especially Norden's acute study in c. iv, *Auf den Spuren der Bella Germaniae des Plinius.*

was the eyewitness from whose description were taken the legend of the altar dedicated by Ulixes on the lower Rhine and the account of the memorial barrows inscribed with Greek letters (c. 3); the statements about the small value set on silver vases and the preference shown for *serrati* and *bigati* (c. 5), about the remains of Cimbrian camps (c. 37) and the cavalry manœuvres of the Germans (c. 6); the appreciation of the military qualities of the Chatti (c. 30, unless this was due to a Roman officer who took part in Domitian's campaigns). From Pliny were probably taken also the statements about the ancient abodes of the Helvetii and the Boii and the survival of the latter name in Bohemia (c. 28), about the origin of the Batavi (c. 29) and about the great lakes of the Frisian country now merged in the Zuyder Zee (c. 34). In all probability, too, Tacitus found collected in the *Bella* the material about the *origo Germanorum* (cc. 2-4), although he weighed the evidence for himself and reached a different conclusion about the purity of the race. On the other hand, there are no good grounds for believing that Tacitus ransacked the encyclopaedic *Natural History* for scattered references to Germany.[1]

The sources on which Tacitus drew were not, however, solely literary. Between Pliny's historical work and the year when the *Germania* was published there was an interval of more than twenty years which was not covered by any literary work that we know of, and these were years when knowledge grew. The gap must have been filled by oral information gained partly from Roman officers who served in the campaigns of this period, partly from traders who penetrated deeply into Germany.[2] The accounts of officers and travelling merchants (*Romana arma* and *negotiatores nostri* or *mercatores*, in the phraseology of the elder Pliny) had always been a primary source of knowledge about foreign

---

[1] Gudeman's arguments on this question seem conclusive (most recently stated in his American edition, 1928, pp. 353 ff.).

[2] This kind of evidence is well treated by Norden, pp. 434 ff. Trade relations with Germany are alluded to in cc. 5, 17, 23, 24, 41, 45.

lands and peoples. The former were not infrequently put into literary form: Caesar's *Commentaries*, the memoirs of Domitius Corbulo on Armenia, of Suetonius Paullinus on Mauretania, and of Cornelius Bocchus on Spain (which furnished Pliny with material for his *Natural History*), and Trajan's *Dacica* are well-known examples. Not all the information with which officers filled their note-books saw the light, but it found its way into literature, either by dissemination among their friends or by direct communication to literary men, whether by letter or by word of mouth: Tacitus himself in the *Agricola* acknowledges his debt in this respect to his father-in-law.[1] The knowledge acquired by Roman traders was sometimes given to the world: the *Periplus of the Erythraean Sea*, a commercial handbook to the Red Sea and Persian and Indian waters, written by an Egyptian Greek about the middle of the first century A.D.,[2] cannot have been unique. More frequently, however, their knowledge remained unpublished, but it reached interested people either directly or through intermediaries. On such information Tacitus must have been almost wholly dependent for what he has to tell in the last four chapters about the tribes of the Germanic East and Scandinavia, with hardly any of whom had the Romans ever come into political or military contact. Direct trade with the East Baltic along the amber-route from Carnuntum through Moravia and Poland began in Nero's reign and developed steadily till about A.D. 150;[3] with Southern Scandinavia there was no direct commerce in the time of Tacitus, but some information could be obtained by Roman merchants about the Swedes (*Suiones*), who plied a regular trade between their own country and the delta of the Vistula.[4]

[1] Pliny, *Epp.* vi. 16 is an answer to a request from Tacitus for an account of his uncle's death to enable him to record the facts accurately.
[2] Cp. *Camb. Anc. Hist.* x. 881.
[3] See the notes on c. 45, 2 and 5.
[4] Notes on c. 44, 2.

THE TRUSTWORTHINESS OF THE *GERMANIA*

NOT without justice did scholars of the Renaissance call the *Germania* 'libellus aureus'. It is incomparably the fullest and most valuable monograph of its kind that has come down to us from antiquity. Thanks to it, we know more of the Germans of the first century A.D. than of any other people outside the Roman Empire and, indeed, of many within it. The information available to Tacitus was, of course, much more abundant about western Germany than about remoter parts: as he proceeds northwards and eastwards his knowledge becomes more and more scanty till he reaches the region of fable. It is not to be expected that his description should be free from errors and defects. Among the latter is the extreme condensation of his style, which often leaves obscurities where a little more detail would have let in light. Other weaknesses have tended to impair belief in the objective value of the account. While Tacitus was beyond doubt a searcher after truth, he was also a great literary artist, trained in all the arts of rhetoric; and rhetoric is the foe of truth. He was, moreover, a cultured philosopher of the Stoic school, wont to garnish facts with reflections, and the *Germania* is full of philosophic explanations of German customs and beliefs which could not have emanated from the Germans themselves. Evidence, too, has been perceived of that tendency to idealize primitive peoples which did not begin with Rousseau but runs through ancient literature from the time of Homer; and to idealize is to falsify. It will be found, however, that the rhetoric mostly takes the form of acid epigrams, particularly at the close of a section, or that it is an expression of appreciation and sympathy or of marvel, which does not affect the accuracy of the facts. The philosophic interpretations are easily separable from the statements of fact, and they must be separated in assessing the scientific value of the work. The signs of idealization have been greatly exaggerated: there is no Utopian romanticism, no conscious idealization. The description of the Fenni, which forms the climax in an ascending scale of barbarism, has been taken as the best extant example of fanciful idealization, but the remarks that seem most plainly to bear the stamp of romantic idealization are rather sheer irony. What Tacitus admires in the Germans is not their realization of the Stoic or Epicurean ideal of freedom from wants, but their fresh vitality and their moral purity.[1]

So far as archaeological investigation can check its statements, the objective value of the *Germania* has, on the whole, been vindicated in a remarkable way by the research of recent times. As might have been expected, some mistakes and inexactitudes have been revealed, but in general the result has been to show the marvellous accuracy of the observation of the eyewitnesses to whose reports the information it contains was in the last resort due. In the last two decades, however, many scholars have had their faith in the trustworthiness of the narrative shaken anew by the critical studies of Wissowa, Norden, and others.[2] These have shown that the *Germania* is almost the last of a long series of descriptions of ancient peoples, and that ethnography, like other kinds of literary composition, had not only created a style of its own and established a universally recognized form of treating the subject, but had also gone through a typological development. There are quite a number of striking resemblances and congruences between what Tacitus says of the Germans and what older writers had said of other non-Hellenic peoples—Persians, Scythians, Thracians, Sarmatians, Celts, and others—which (it is held) are only to be explained by the practice of transference. What one observer had said about one definite

---

[1] Cp. Trüdinger, *op. cit.*, p. 166.

[2] Wissowa, *Gött. gel. Anz.* clxxviii (1916), pp. 656 ff., *Neue Jahrb.* xlvii–xlviii (1921), pp. 14 ff.; A. Schroeder, *De ethnographiae antiquae locis quibusdam communibus observationes*, Halle diss., 1921.

people was transferred by another to a different people in a similar stage of cultural development: ancient ethnography is strewn with what have been called 'migratory motifs' (*Wandermotive*), and the *Germania* is no exception. This practice was the result of the growth of a sort of dogma that certain characteristics and customs were typical of all half-civilized peoples and could be predicated of any one of them without positive evidence. This produced a stock of commonplaces (τόποι) which were utilized in describing any given people, such as that primitive peoples make no images or temples of their gods or that precious metals have no attraction for them, which might not be true or might need qualification.[1] Such methods of procedure are calculated to impair belief in the scientific value of the *libellus aureus*.

The existence of certain kinds of commonplace is undoubted. For the doctrine of transferences the more decisive items of evidence adduced are these. The famous phrase which Tacitus uses of the German race, *tantum sui similis gens* (c. 4), was coined by Hecataeus to describe the Egyptians, was echoed by Parmenides, and was transferred first to the Scythians by a writer of the school of Hippocrates,[2] then to the Cimbri and their allies by Posidonius, and finally to the Germans in general by Tacitus.[3] According to Norden, the whole description of the characteristics of the Germans which follows this phrase is to be traced back to Posidonius, whose 'description of the Celts and Scythians has been transferred to the Germans who dwelt between these two peoples'.[4] In fact, as has since been pointed out,[5] the description tallies verbally with that which had been given of the Celts (in Galatia) by Livy; and it is also to be noted that

---

[1] It is exceptional to find the elder Pliny saying of the Cingalese: *ne Taprobane quidem . . . nostris vitiis caret. aurum argentumque et ibi in pretio* (*N.H.* vi. 89).
[2] See above, p. xiv.
[3] See note *ad loc.*   [4] p. 115.
[5] By W. Capelle in *Philologus*, lxxxiv (1929), pp. 349 ff.

the physical features on which Tacitus insists as characteristic of the Germans, 'blue eyes, reddish hair, and large
frames', are precisely those which, according to the elder
Pliny, marked the inhabitants of Ceylon.[1] These are surely
plain instances of the transference of an ethnographic description from one race to another?

Other close correspondences both in thought and in language are found between Tacitus and Herodotus. There is
a striking resemblance between the account of the origin of
the Germans and Herodotus' account of the origin of the
Scythians (iv. 5–15). Herodotus begins with the national
saga of the Scythians, based on a cult legend. They were
descended from Zeus, whose son Targitaos was a man; he
had three sons from whom were descended the three tribal
groups of the Scythians. Besides the group-names there was
a national name by which all the Scythians called themselves. To this Scythian legend corresponds, point by point,
the native German saga in Tacitus. The god Tuisto had a
son Mannus, from whose three sons the three tribal groups
derived their names. Besides the group-names there arose
in later time a national name by which all the Germans
called themselves. Further, in Herodotus the Scythian
legend is followed by that of the Pontic Greeks, who 'say
that Herakles arrived in this country' and had three sons
from whom the people are descended. So in Tacitus the
native legend is followed by the version of foreigners: *fuisse
et apud eos Herculem memorant*, to which there is added the
story about the presence of Ulixes on the lower Rhine.
Herodotus then records a third account which was given by
Greeks and barbarians alike—that the Scythians were a
nomad people who had immigrated from Asia and had driven
out the Cimmerians; by way of proof that the land formerly
belonged to the latter, he mentions a tomb of the Cimmerian
kings and remains of Cimmerian walls which still exist

---

[1] *Ipsos vero excedere hominum magnitudinem, rutilis comis, caeruleis oculis, oris sono truci* (*N.H.* vi. 88).

(καὶ νῦν ἔστι), as well as the fact that there is a district named Cimmeria. This, too, has its counterpart in Tacitus: contacts with Greeks are inferred from remains which still exist, monuments and barrows with Greek letters. Herodotus believes that the third account is correct; Tacitus declares for the first of the views he mentions. Moreover, the plan of the rest of the *Germania* corresponds to that of Herodotus, though the order of the topics varies. Herodotus treats first of the individual tribes (c. 16 ff.), then of the climate (cc. 28–31), and then of the people as a whole, while Tacitus begins with the climate (c. 5), then deals with the people as a whole (cc. 6–27), and then with the individual tribes. So it would seem that Herodotus was Tacitus' model.

Of the other cases of agreement with Herodotus noted by Norden two may be added here. The statement in c. 4, 'their physical type, so far as can be said[1] where the population is so vast, is the same throughout: fierce blue eyes, ruddy hair', etc., recalls that of Herodotus about a Scythian tribe, 'large and numerous as it is, it has as a whole pronouncedly blue eyes and fair hair' (ἔθνος ἐὸν μέγα καὶ πολλὸν γλαῦκόν τε πᾶν ἰσχυρῶς ἐστι καὶ πυρρόν). Is it merely accidental that both introduce the thought of the great size of the people? Again, the statement *deorum maxime Mercurium colunt* (c. 9), which reproduces that of Caesar about the Gauls,[2] agrees verbally with Herod. v. 7, where it is said that the Thracian chiefs σέβονται Ἑρμέην μάλιστα θεῶν, an agreement best explained by supposing that Posidonius was the intermediary (p. 101).

Lastly, the age-old custom of transference is invoked to

---

[1] Norden's translation, 'Daher sind auch alle—und das in Anbetracht einer so zahlreichen Menschenmasse—von einem und demselben Körperschlag', brings Tacitus into closer agreement with Herodotus, but is quite untenable. He explains *tamquam* as = *ut*, as in Hor. *Sat.* i. 6, 79, Ovid *Trist.* i. 1, 17 (pp. 52, 498), but there *ut* means *ut fieri potest*, 'as may well be'. See the note on c. 4. 2.

[2] *Deum maxime Mercurium colunt* (*B.G.* vi. 17).

explain the agreement of Tacitus' account of the German
practice of taking counsel at a feast when drunk and recon-
sidering the decision when sober (c. 22) with the similar
Persian custom described by Herodotus and alluded to in a
scholion on Hom. *Iliad* ix. 70;[1] and to account for the
resemblance between Tacitus' description of German hospitality to strangers (c. 21) and a Homeric scholion on the
Abioi.[2] Here again the intermediary was Posidonius, who
had described these customs in his Celtic ethnography and
given to his description the Homeric colouring which is
discernible in the account of Tacitus.[3]

If the truth of this doctrine of transferences be conceded,[4]
the effect on the question of the trustworthiness of Tacitus
would be serious, if we suppose that the transferences were
made mechanically. That they were so made appears to be
the conclusion to which many of Norden's readers have in-
judiciously leaped. Those who realize the care which Tacitus
took to ensure the accuracy of his facts, *quo verius tradere
posteris posset,*[5] will not readily concur in this view. Norden
himself, though his expressions are not infrequently mis-
leading, has shown much greater prudence. The truth of a
motif which has been taken over, he says, need not in itself
be doubted, although the truth of the picture may have
suffered by the process of progressive transference and
literary elaboration (p. 139). More recently he has defined
his position explicitly.[6] 'In the good ethnographic literature
of antiquity transferences are never made mechanically,
that is, irresponsibly': where, therefore, we find in it the
same language used in describing German characteristics and

---

[1] Διὸ καὶ Πέρσαι μεθύοντες συμβουλεύονται, νήφοντες δ' ἐπικρίνουσιν.

[2] Λέγουσι δὲ αὐτοὺς τοὺς ὁδίτας τρέφοντας ἄλλον ἄλλῳ διαπέμπειν (on
Iliad xiii. 6).

[3] Norden, pp. 127 ff., 130 ff.

[4] There is a good criticism of the doctrine by E. Fehrle in *Schweizer.
Archiv f. Volkskunde,* xxvi (1926), pp. 229 ff.

[5] Pliny, *Epp.* vi. 16, 1 (to Tacitus): *Petis ut tibi avunculi mei exitum
scribam, quo verius tradere posteris possis.*

[6] Preface to ed. 2, p. ix.

customs and those of other peoples, we may depend upon it that the identity of form reflects identity of content, for identical customs are often found among primitive or half-civilized peoples. But in most cases the agreement is not complete, and on close examination we find that, while the groundwork of the picture is the product of old-established technique, the specifically German features are preserved: individual colour-tones and fine shadings reproduce the German element with a fidelity which sets in the most favourable light, not only the high level maintained by this literary *genre* through centuries of development, but also the gift of acute observation possessed by workers in the field, and their fondness for small and what might appear to be unimportant details. A good illustration is furnished by Tacitus' description of German hospitality (c. 21), where above the Homeric colouring, introduced by Hellenistic ethnographers, stand out two individual German features, the truth of which is guaranteed by their survival almost to the present day in some parts of rural Germany.[1]

This goes to the root of the matter. Identity of phraseology and identity in the general method of treating the subject have in truth little bearing on the trustworthiness of the statements. Like his predecessors in this sphere, Tacitus was familiar with the literature of ethnography. When he found in his sources statements similar to those made in another connexion by an earlier writer he did not hesitate to adopt their phraseology when it pleased him, seeking only to make it, if possible, more pointed.[2] Neither Greeks nor Romans

---

[1] These two features are: (1) that the stranger was entertained until the cupboard had been emptied (which is hardly the meaning of *cum defecere epulae*), and (2) that the host accompanied his guest to the house of his nearest neighbour, whose guest he in turn became (Norden, pp. 498, 502). It is to be noted, however, that the parallels quoted from modern Germany refer to the entertainment of neighbours by each other, not to the entertainment of strangers.

[2] An example of this practice is the often-quoted *cum timeret Otho, timebatur* (*Hist.* i. 81), which he took over from the source common to him and Plutarch, who says φοβούμενος ὑπὲρ τῶν ἀνδρῶν

scrupled to appropriate a well-turned phrase. When Tacitus adopted *tantum sui similis gens*, he did so because the phrase struck him and seemed to fit the case, for to him the Germans were unlike any other people. His adoption of it does not imply that the characterization of the Germans which it prefaces was also taken over mechanically. The statements were, in fact, true, although the peculiarities enumerated were not exclusively German, and their truth can be established from other sources.[1] The description which Posidonius had given of the racial characteristics of northern peoples on the basis of his knowledge of Celts and Scythians was known to Romans,[2] but it is gratuitous to suppose that it 'was transferred to the Germans who dwelt between the two peoples'. Such a transference was certainly not made by Tacitus, who appears to be wholly unconscious of the fact that the distinctive marks of Germans, as he defines them, were precisely those which were recognized as characteristic of the Gauls.[3] If transference there was, it was doubtless due to Livy, who was well acquainted with the writings of Posidonius and who described the Germans in his 104th book. But the assumption of a transference is unwarranted. What Livy probably did was to base his description on the account given by Posidonius of the Cimbri and their allies,[4] whose German nationality had long been established when Livy wrote; the correctness of that account could be confirmed in Rome itself, where there was an Imperial bodyguard of Germans till A.D. 68, to say nothing

αὐτὸς ἦν φοβερὸς ἐκείνοις (*Otho*, 3). Here, however, the earlier writer was describing the same events as Tacitus and Plutarch.

[1] See note on c. 4, 2.   [2] Above, p. xx.

[3] See notes on c. 4, 2. So in *Agr.* 11, 2 the ruddy hair and large limbs of the Caledonians are said to mark them off as Germans from the southern Britons, who are like the Gauls.

[4] That the characteristics which Tacitus attributes to the Germans had been noted by Posidonius in the case of the Cimbri is clear from Plutarch's description in his life of Marius (based on Posidonius) and from Florus i. 38 (iii. 3), 5; 13 (based on Livy, who followed Posidonius).

of the available testimony of Romans who had fought in Germany.

Nor would it seem that any special significance is to be attached to the linguistic correspondence with Herodotus mentioned above. In the first example the correspondence is not so close as Norden makes it, and the qualification (*tamquam . . . numero*) is a very natural one, which is also made in *Hist.* i. 8 and which Tacitus was surely capable of making independently of any predecessor. In the second instance *deorum maxime . . . colunt* is a natural enough way of saying that one god was worshipped more than others, and it is not surprising that, where trade was lively,[1] the supreme god should be Hermes—Mercury. The fact is true: Mercury (i.e. Wodan) was the most important deity, at any rate in the West.

In many cases agreement in phraseology was due to the existence of similar customs among uncivilized or half-civilized peoples. When once a writer of repute had described such a custom, a successor finding the same custom elsewhere tended to follow the language of his predecessor. To this cause may reasonably be ascribed the similarity between Tacitus and Herodotus in the matter of deliberation when under the influence of drink and reconsideration when sober.

Agreement in the method of treating a subject is an argument in favour of a transference of form but not of a transference of matter. In the course of a long development ethnography had established a definite form of treatment: it had laid down the sort of questions that should be raised about primitive peoples, the method of proof, and the disposition of topics; and no writer would ever dream of doing anything but follow established tradition. An examination of the correspondence between the Σκυθικά of Herodotus

---

[1] Archaeological discoveries have shown that trade between the Romans and the Germans was much more extensive than Tacitus appears to have realized (p. xxxvii, n. 3).

and the *Germania* in this respect shows plainly that adoption of form does not imply adoption of matter. The method of arrangement agrees closely. There is an exact agreement between the two genealogical trees. But critics seem to forget that in such mythological pedigrees a triad in the third generation was a common feature, and that Tacitus is borne out by the north-Germanic stemma: Buri, Burr, and his three sons Odin, Wili, Wê. Moreover, there is nothing in Herodotus about the divine ancestors being celebrated in songs, a statement confirmed by the alliteration of vowels in the names Ingwas, Istwas, Erminas (or whatever was their exact form), which points unmistakably to a poetical setting.

There remains the question whether the use of common-places has led Tacitus into error. This has been affirmed, for instance, in respect of the passage about the absence of temples and images of the gods (c. 9, 3) and that about German indifference to precious metals (c. 5, 3 ff.).[1] The former passage is held to be irreconcilable with the description of the bath of Nerthus, which implies the idea of a divine image (whatever the actual fact may have been), with the mention of a *templum* of the goddess (c. 40), and with the fact recorded by Tacitus himself that the Marsian temple of Tamfana was razed to the ground by Germanicus in A.D. 14 (*Ann.* i. 51). In these passages, however, *templum* does not mean a temple in the Greek or Roman sense,[2] and the *numen ipsum* which was washed may have been a rude wooden symbol (possibly with a pair of breasts indicated) or a fetish: no image *in humani oris speciem adsimulata* need be meant. It is true that the Germans had already reached an anthropomorphic conception of their gods. That is attested, not only by the identifications with Mercury, Hercules, and Mars in chap. 9, but also by the unequivocal statement that the Alci, identi-

---

[1] G. Wissowa, *Neue Jahrb.* xlvii–xlviii (1921), p. 20; E. Bickel, *Bonner Jahrb.* cxxxix (1934), pp. 3 ff.
[2] See note on c. 40, 4.

fied with Castor and Pollux, were worshipped *ut fratres, ut iuvenes* (c. 43, 4). But the existence of such a conception does not necessarily involve the making of images, and in the last case Tacitus explicitly states that there was no image. There is consequently no reason to believe that here the use of a commonplace has led Tacitus into error. On the other hand, his statement about the small value placed on precious metals (c. 5, 3 ff.), guarded as it is (*haud perinde adficiuntur*), cannot be accepted as valid. In later passages[1] he admits that Germans had learnt from Romans the attraction of money, while elsewhere he recognizes that they were open to bribery by money and gifts.[2] Finds in Jutland show that as early as the Bronze Age gold was highly valued by the Germans of the peninsula, who obtained it by way of trade, chiefly perhaps in exchange for amber; and the numerous finds of coin-hoards, a good many of them buried in the first century, and of gold and silver objects, sometimes far from the Roman frontier, show that his statement is fundamentally unsound. Here he was clearly led astray by the commonplace that the precious metals have no attraction for primitive peoples; he found it supported by the evidence of an eyewitness or eyewitnesses for some particular locality (*est videre*, etc.), but that evidence was insufficient to establish the general conclusion which he enunciates. He does not indeed seem to have been aware of the extent of the trade carried on with Germany.[3] Errors of this and other kinds and misconceptions are not to be denied,[4] but critical investigations have not deprived the *Germania* of its outstanding value as a source of information about the early history of the Germanic race.

[1] c. 15, 3; 42, 2.   [2] *Hist.* iv. 76.
[3] On this subject see now Mrs. Brogan, 'Trade between the Roman Empire and the Free Germans', *J.R.S.* xxvi (1936), pp. 195 ff.
[4] See Index II, s.v. *Germania*.

Section IV
THE EXPANSION OF THE WEST GERMANS

SUCH knowledge as we possess about the Germanic peoples before the first century B.C. is due to archaeological research. Germany was remote from the Mediterranean world and late in coming within its purview. It was the great migration of the Cimbri and their allies (*c.* 120–102 B.C.) that first brought the barbarians of the far North into contact with the Southerners and so into the light of history. Naturally their nationality was then unknown. The geographical science of those days divided northern Europe schematically between the two races which were known to it, the Celts in the west and the Scythians in the east; and Posidonius, whose account of the Cimbric wars ranked as a classic, regarded the Cimbri as neighbours of the Scythians, conjecturally identifying them with the Cimmerii.[1] He had, indeed, some knowledge of Germans: he gave a description of them in the thirtieth book of his *Histories*[2] (which probably contained his narrative of the Cimbric wars), but they were tribes settled near the Rhine, who appeared to him to be ethnically related to the neighbouring Celts of Gaul and to differ little from them either in physical features or in manners and customs.[3] In seeing resemblances between them he was not mistaken, for neither in physical form and appearance nor in dress was there any very substantial difference between Germans and Gauls,[4] and the Rhenish tribes were deeply affected by Gallic influences. Posidonius' work was published about 80 B.C.

The following decades brought more precise and wider knowledge. The gladiatorial war in Italy (73–71 B.C.), in which the rebels fell into ethnically distinct groups of Thra-

---

[1] Strabo, vii. 2, 2, p. 293; Plutarch, *Marius*, 11.
[2] Athenaeus, iv. 153 e.
[3] His view is reproduced by Strabo, iv. 4, 2, p. 196; vii. 1, 2, p. 290.
[4] Cp. Schumacher, *Siedelungs- und Kulturgesch.* ii. 288 ff.; J. Steinhausen, *Arch. Siedlungskunde d. Trierer Landes*, p. 283.

cians, Gauls, and Germans (captives of the Cimbric wars),[1] and Rome's dealings with the Suebic king Ariovistus, who crossed the Rhine about the same time to fight in Gaul, led to the recognition of the real nationality of the Cimbri and the Teutoni and of their ethnical relationship to the Suebic invaders of Gaul and other Transrhenane tribes which had long been known among the Celts of Gaul by the collective name of Germani.[2] Julius Caesar was the first writer to draw a clear distinction between Germans and Gauls, basing it not on physique but on differences of language, religion, and customs.[3] Yet Greek historians continued for centuries to speak of Germans as Celts, adhering to the antiquated idea that northern Europe was inhabited only by Celts and Scythians.

In the earliest period to which we can penetrate the area occupied by Germanic peoples was only a fraction of that which they covered in the time of Tacitus. About 1000 B.C. they were limited to the region around the west Baltic, comprising southern Sweden, the peninsula of Jutland, and the adjoining country bounded roughly by the river Ems on the west, the Teutoburger Wald and the Harz mountains on the south, and the river Oder on the east. To the south-west of them the Celtic peoples were just about this time entering on the most decisive phase of their formation, which had its centre not, as Romans thought, in Gaul, but on the middle Rhine and mainly on the east of the river. The 'urn-field civilization' (so called from its cremation cemeteries) had now reached this district from still farther east, and its bearers were on the move among the 'tumulus people' previously established there, who buried their dead under barrows.[4] The consequent outflow of migration in due course

---

[1] Sallust, *Hist.* iii. fr. 96 (Maurenbrecher); Liv. *Epit.* xcvii; Plutarch, *Crassus*, 9. The mention of Germani in the *Fasti Capitolini* under 222 B.C. (in place of the Gaesatae of Polyb. ii. 22) is a result of the redaction of the list in the time of Augustus.

[2] See below, p. xliii.   [3] *B.G.* vi. 21–4; i. 47.

[4] The 'tumulus people', who had originally for the most part

reached the area of the Lower Rhine, permeating its natives in their turn; and before long the Celts, thus variously moulded, stretched in unbroken range from Central Europe to the British Isles. The history of the Germans thereafter is a story of gradual expansion, eastwards over East Germany and Poland as far as the Vistula (and even beyond it), westwards and southwards over lands held by the Celts, whose displacement caused them to migrate in successive waves towards the south, the west, and the south-east: the last movement carried them beyond the confines of Europe into Asia Minor.

The advance of the western Germans began perhaps in the ninth century, when they pushed across the Teutoburger Wald into the valley of the upper Lippe. By the end of the next century they had arrived in the region of Duisburg at the confluence of Ruhr and Rhine, as is shown by grave-finds with Germanic biconical cinerary urns and Germanic razors. In the seventh century they had settled in large numbers both between the Ems and the Yssel and on both banks of the lower Rhine north of the Ruhr, where their arrival marks the first stage of a cultural blend which, as time went on, became more and more Germanic in character. Late in the sixth century, towards 500 B.C., forward movements continued towards west and south. On the west fresh waves spread gradually across the Maas into southern Holland and eastern Belgium, and more rapidly southwards to the foot of the wooded range of the Ardennes and the Eifel on the left bank of the Rhine and of the Westerwald on the right. Here the advance came to a standstill, and the pause was a long one. The tide of invasion was stemmed by a chain of Celtic hill-forts, surrounded by strong stone walls, of which the best explored is that of Ritterhausen in the Westerwald, some ten miles north of Dillenburg. A similar

inhumed their dead, now mostly practised cremation, depositing the ashes on the ground under a barrow, while the 'urn-field people' placed the ashes in a cinerary urn which they buried in a grave without a barrow.

line of forts belonging to a somewhat later date stretches along the Hunsrück and the Taunus, and a third chain of fourteen forts was subsequently established in French Lorraine to defend the valley of the upper Moselle. In central Germany the Celts adopted the same defensive system.

The result of the Teutonic immigration was the displacement of large numbers of the Celtic inhabitants, who fell back into the region of the river Marne and into south-west France, while a more adventurous section crossed the western Pyrenees into Spain, there to mingle with the Iberians and produce the Celtiberians of historical times. Others crossed the Channel to south and east Britain. The retreat of the Celts did not, however, mean a complete evacuation of the flat lands between the North Sea and the Ardennes and Eifel. The evidence about the material civilization of this region indicates that a considerable proportion of the population remained behind to fuse gradually with the Germanic immigrants and to develop a mixed culture, which remained comparatively barbaric and was affected very little by the La Tène civilization that burst into flower during the fifth century, under stimulating influences both Graeco-Italian and even Scythian, in the country south of the Lower Rhenish mountain belt which shielded it against German penetration.

For more than two centuries the defence of this mountain belt checked the southward advance of the Germans; and this period witnessed a great expansion of the Celtic race, of which an echo survives in Livy's misdated story of the exodus of two vast hosts from Gaul, one under Bellovesus to Italy and the other under Segovesus into the region of the Hercynian Forest.[1] *Hercynia silva* was the old name, already known to Aristotle, of the whole wooded mountain tract of central Germany, which ran eastwards from the Westerwald and encircled Bohemia: sometimes it was made to include the Black Forest, the Jura range that borders the

---

[1] Livy, v. 34.

upper Danube, and the Carpathians.[1] Livy's saga enshrines
the historical fact that towards 400 B.C. two great Celtic
migrations took place, one southwards into Italy, the other
—as archaeological remains testify—eastwards as far as
Bohemia and Moravia, the former at least being occupied by
the Boii.[2] Livy attributes the movement to over-population;
perhaps the impelling motives were the love of adventure
and the hope of plunder; in any case, the cause of the migration cannot have been German pressure, for no Teutonic
advance southwards was made for a long time to come.

It was not until the Middle La Tène period, after about
250 B.C., that the Germans succeeded in breaking through
the Celtic defence of the Lower Rhenish mountain belt.
On the right bank of the Rhine German tribes crossed
the Westerwald and established themselves in the region of
the river Lahn and the Taunus. On the left bank Germanic
elements apparently forced their way over the Eifel into what
was in historical times the country of the Treveri—the basin
of the Moselle and its tributary the Saar and the valley of the
Nahe—which had been the centre of La Tène culture. Their
presence is thereafter shown by the general substitution of
cremation for inhumation burials (which during the Hallstatt period, c. 1000–450 B.C., had come to be the predominant practice among the Celts, although the reversion to
inhumation was never absolutely complete), and by the
appearance of new ceramic forms which are, in part at least,
to be ascribed to Germanic prototypes. The number of the
new-comers was not, however, sufficient to break the continuity of Celtic culture: the La Tène types survive, and the
Treveri remained predominantly Celtic both in language and
in character; yet they claimed to have German blood in
them (c. 28), and their claim is supported by the witness of
a competent observer that they differed little from Germans

---

[1] As by Caesar, vi. 25; cp. also Strabo, iv. 6, 9, p. 207 and vii. 1, 3,
p. 290.
[2] c. 28, 2.

in their mode of life and their fierce character.[1] But the invaders who partially Germanized the Treveri represented only part of an immigrant host which poured over the Rhine and occupied the region behind them on the north. This was the group of tribes, bearing the collective name of Germani, which Caesar found two centuries later sandwiched between the Treveri, the Belgae, and the Rhine. Of these *Cisrhenani Germani* (or *Germani qui cis Rhenum incolunt*)[2] he specifies five tribes with which he came into contact, the Eburones, Condrusi, Caeroesi, Paemani, and Segni,[3] but his enumeration was probably incomplete. Their appearance in this region can hardly be dissociated from the movement which produced the mixed Celto–German civilization of the Treveri. By Caesar's time these German tribes had become Celticized in speech and in nomenclature and they were Celtic in political sympathies, but they still held a middle position between the Belgae and the Treveri and tended to take an independent line. The formidable character of this invasion is plain from the fact that it caused the surrounding Gauls to adopt the group-name of the invaders—*Germani*—as a general designation of all kindred tribes beyond the Rhine.[4]

This inroad was followed by a lull, after which the Low Countries experienced a renewed pressure of immigration. The archaeological evidence indicates a fresh inflow of Germanic elements in the course of the second century, a result of tribal unrest in north-western Germany caused by the growth of population, which came to a head when about 120 B.C. a great encroachment of the sea drove

---

[1] Hirtius, *B.G.* viii. 25: (*Treverorum*) *civitas propter Germaniae vicinitatem cotidianis exercitata bellis cultu et feritate non multum a Germanis differebat, neque imperata umquam nisi exercitu coacta faciebat.* Similarly *feritas* was a characteristic of the Belgic Nervii (Caes. *B. G.* ii. 4 and 15), who had a good deal of German blood (see below).

[2] *B.G.* ii. 3; vi. 2; 32.

[3] ii. 4; vi. 32.

[4] See the notes on c. 2, 5.

the Cimbri, Teutoni, and Ambrones to migrate *en masse* from their homes in Jutland and Schleswig. The overflow of Germans into southern Holland and eastern Belgium dislodged part of the mixed Celtic–Teutonic population of that area and increased the proportion of German blood in the section that stayed behind to amalgamate with the immigrants. The displaced element fell back into the region of the Aisne and Marne, where the old Celtic culture became transformed in a manner which betrays the arrival of a new people. The transformation is seen particularly in the abruptness with which the German custom of cremation interments in flat graves was adopted, and in the appearance of a new type of pottery, in which the old tradition is modified by new influences coming from the north-east and partly also from the middle Rhine. This movement completed the process of fusion which produced the Belgic tribes as they are described by Caesar and Strabo.[1] Their witness attests that the Celtic element, far from being swamped, remained strong, for the Belgae were not noticeably different from the Celts of central Gaul in physical appearance, and they differed but slightly in language and institutions. But they were aware that German blood flowed in their veins, and they were more warlike than the other Gauls and plumed themselves on the fact that they, alone of the Gallic tribes, had kept the Cimbri and Teutoni out of their country.

In central Germany Teutonic expansion southwards was slow. In the fourth century the central mountain chain had not yet been reached. Between it and the Harz—in Thuringia and in the adjoining regions of Saxony and Silesia west of the Oder—a Celtic population still held its ground. It appears to have included the Volcae, whose name was adopted by the neighbouring Germans as a collective designation for all Celts and still survives as *Welsche* in German and *Welsh* in English. The Celtic population had given ground by 300 B.C., but further advance was barred by the mountains,

[1] *B.G.* i. 1; ii. 4. Strabo, iv. 1, 1, p. 177; 4, 3, p. 196.

which the Celts defended by a chain of hill-forts running eastwards from Vogelsberg and Rhön. Of these the largest and strongest was the Steinsburg near Römhild on the south of the Thuringian Forest (between Meiningen and Coburg), which was held for two centuries to come.[1] It was not till towards the opening of the first century that the German advance was resumed. The trek of the Cimbri and their allies, who had passed up the valley of the Elbe, was the prelude to a thrust from that direction which turned the fortified zone. The more westerly of the Suebic group of tribes on the Elbe, of which the most formidable was Caesar's Suebi, crossed the Thuringian Forest and poured through Hessen along the depression of the Wetterau to the junction of Main and Rhine, pressing on the German tribes already settled in the region of the Lahn and spreading across both rivers into Hessen-Starkenburg and Rheinhessen.[2]

On the south of the Main the invaders found the country sparsely occupied. At one time, says Tacitus, the whole region between the Main, the Rhine, and the Hercynian Forest (by which, perhaps, was here meant the Swabian Jura) had been occupied by the Helvetii, who in the first century B.C. were settled in Switzerland. The withdrawal of the Helvetii from their old home was due to the pressure of the advancing Germans. Arrived at the Main and Rhine, the flood of invasion divided into three waves. One, headed by the Triboci, crossed the Rhine and moved southwards up the valley, followed by the Nemetes and Vangiones. In the early first century the Triboci were the only German tribe on the western bank of the upper Rhine: at the time when Posidonius wrote they were in Rheinhessen and the Palatinate (Rheinpfalz).[3] A second wave flowed in a parallel

---

[1] A. Götze, *Praehist. Ztschr.* xiii–xiv, 1921–2, pp. 19 ff.

[2] On this invasion see U. Kahrstedt in *Nachrichten d. Ges. d. Wiss. zu Göttingen*, 1930, pp. 381 ff., and especially his article 'Die Kelten in den Decumates agri', *ibid.* 1933, pp. 261 ff.

[3] Strabo, iv. 3, 4, p. 193; Caes. *B.G.* iv. 10, 3, both reproducing the account of Posidonius.

direction up the right bank of the river into Baden, where in
later time we find the Suebi of the Neckar (Suebi Nicretes)
settled in the region round Heidelberg, and other Suebi
farther south near the sources of the Danube.[1] A third wave
passed along the valley of the Main into Bavaria, leaving
Württemberg high and dry. Before the advancing flood the
Helvetii, already weakened by their losses in the Cimbric
wars, retired southwards across the Rhine upon Switzerland,
the northern part of which (the district of the river Aare and
its gold-bearing tributaries, the two rivers Emme) they
already inhabited before the Cimbric invasion;[2] even here
they were not secure from German attacks.[3] The date of
their retirement is indicated by the Celtic remains of the
region,[4] which include none belonging to the late La Tène
period beginning about 100 B.C. It is usually believed that
the land they evacuated is what Ptolemy describes as 'the
Helvetian Desert' (to the north of the Swabian Jura), a
term no longer applicable in his time and consequently pre-
sumed to have been taken uncritically from an older source.[5]
If this be correct, the phrase is not to be literally interpreted,
for the abandoned land was not completely denuded of in-

---

[1] Strabo, iv. 6, 9, p. 207, confirmed by Tac. *Ann.* i. 44, 6, *imminentes*
(*Raetiae*) *Suebos*.

[2] Strabo, iv. 3, 3, p. 193 (cp. vii. 2, 2, p. 293); Athen. vi. 233 d; see
Norden, *op. cit.*, pp. 230 ff.

[3] At a later date Caesar speaks of the almost daily battles, defensive or aggressive, fought by the Helvetii against the Germans across
the river (i. 1 and 28).

[4] Especially those of Dühren in north Baden on the river Elsenz,
close to Sinsheim (Schumacher, *Altert. uns. heidn. Vorzeit*, v. 73 ff.;
E. Wagner, *Fundstätten u. Funde . . . in Baden*, ii. 332 ff.).

[5] ii. 11, 6, ἡ τῶν Ἐλουητίων ἔρημος. Kahrstedt suggests that the
phrase designates the mountainous region east of the Neckar, lying
in or close to Helvetic territory, which was wooded and uninhabited
until the imperial period (*Nachrichten d. Ges. d. Wiss. zu Göttingen*,
1933, p. 270). He points out that *deserta Syriae* in Plin. *N.H.* vi.
125 is not a region abandoned by Syrians nor is the 'Arabian Desert'
a region abandoned by Arabs. It is, however, to be noted that ἡ Βοίων
ἐρημία (Strabo, vii. 1, 5), Pliny's *deserta Boiorum* (iii. 146), is explained
by Strabo as a region which the annihilation of the Boii left as a
sheep-walk to their neighbours (v. 1, 6).

habitants. Remnants of the Helvetic population probably stayed behind, and in the imperial age we find a corner of the land round the knee of the Main at Miltenberg in the occupation of Toutoni, who were in all probability descendants of a remnant of the Teutoni which had found a refuge there after the destruction of the main body.[1] But the country was thinly inhabited, and that part of it which was apparently not occupied by the German invaders had no compact population: it was *dubiae possessionis solum*, and in the period following Caesar's conquest of Gaul it was occupied by Gallic adventurers, men whom the war had ruined and driven to seek a new home.[2]

The section of the invading host which crossed the Rhine at Mainz found the prospect of establishing themselves permanently in Gaul enhanced by the discord prevailing among the nearer Gallic tribes. About 71 B.C. their chieftain, the Suebic king Ariovistus, was invited by the Sequani and the Arverni to lend his help against the Aedui, and, having done so, he resolved to stay in the rich and pleasant land of Gaul and found a German kingdom there. He forced the Sequani to cede to him the fertile plain of Alsace and brought over further swarms of Germans, until in 58 B.C., when Caesar appeared on the scene, there were 120,000 of them across the river.[3] Caesar drove back the intruders and saved Gaul from the menace of German conquest, but (despite his silence) he allowed three tribes which formed part of the host of Ariovistus—the Vangiones, Nemetes, and Triboci—to settle along the west bank of the Rhine and defend the frontier against their compatriots. There they quickly became Celticized and then Romanized.

With the Suebic immigration the whole country between

[1] Dess. *I.L.S.* 9377. That a remnant of the Cimbri had also found a home near them has been inferred from dedications to Mercurius Cimbrianus (or Cimbrius) at Miltenberg and Heidelberg, but the inference is hardly certain. Most of the traces of a Celtic population probably belong to the later Gallic immigration.
[2] See c. 29, 4, with the notes. [3] *B.G.* i. 31.

the mountain range of central Germany and the Danube, as far east as the Bohemian Forest, passed into German possession. Of all the territory once held by the Celts on the north of the Danube only the mountain-girt quadrilateral of Czechoslovakia still remained in their hands. About 60 B.C. a large body of the Boii retired from Bohemia into Noricum, doubtless under the pressure of their German neighbours, who a century and a half earlier had broken through the rocky gorge of the Elbe at Bodenbach–Tetschen and secured a footing in their land. The remainder of the Boii were driven out about 8 B.C. when the Marcomani and Quadi, the two most important tribes of southern Germany, trekked eastwards from northern Bavaria to escape the danger of subjugation by Rome and established themselves in Bohemia and Moravia. Thenceforward the Danube marked the boundary between southern Germany and Rome, until the establishment of the *Limes* cut off the re-entrant angle which in its upper course it makes with the Rhine.

[The literature on which this section is based is too extensive to cite in detail, but reference may be made to the bibliography appended by J. M. de Navarro to his chapter, 'The Coming of the Celts' in *Camb. Anc. Hist.* vii (1928), pp. 871 ff., especially the contributions of Kossinna, Rademacher, Reinecke, Schumacher, and Stampfuss, and to the following works: K. Schumacher, *Siedelungs- und Kulturgesch. d. Rheinlande*, ii. (1923); Chr. Hawkes and G. C. Dunning, 'The Belgae of Gaul and Britain', *Arch. Journ.* lxxxvii (1930), pp. 150 ff.; H. Amberger, *Mannus*, xxiv (1932), pp. 420 ff.; Baron de Loë, *La Belgique ancienne*, t. ii (1931); H. Hubert, *Les Celtes* (1932, esp. vol. ii, pp. 108 ff.); J. Steinhausen, *Archäolog. Siedlungskunde d. Trierer Landes* (1936). On the Helvetii and the Helvetian Desert, see E. Fabricius, *Besitznahme Badens durch die Römer*, c. i; E. Norden, *Urgesch.* c. iv. ii and pp. 472 ff. (H. Phillip); K. Schumacher, *op. cit.* i. 144 ff., ii. 131 ff.; F. Stähelin, *Die Schweiz in röm. Zeit.*², pp. 23 ff.; U. Kahrstedt in *Nachrichten d. Ges. d.*

Wiss. zu Göttingen, 1933, pp. 261 ff.; E. Norden, *Alt-Germanien*, 1934, Sect. iii–iv.]

SECTION V
SOCIAL AND POLITICAL CONDITIONS
IN GERMANY

THE German tribal state (*civitas, natio, populus*) was based on the family. The strength of the family bond is seen in the arrangement of the host for battle, where the squadron of horsemen and the wedge-shaped phalanx of footmen are grouped by families and clansmen standing shoulder to shoulder (cc. 6–7), in the marriage ceremonies (c. 18), in the punishment of adultery (c. 19), in the blood feud (c. 21), in the rights of succession (c. 20), in the scope of the *patria potestas*,[1] and in the perpetual wardship of women, which Tacitus does not mention, probably because he was unaware of it. The tribe was an aggregate of families and clans, as it continued to be for many centuries after Tacitus wrote. These families were grouped in territorial areas of varying number and of varying size, which the Romans called *pagi*, and the modern Germans call *Gaue*, for lack of more suitable terms. On these *pagi* more will be said below.

Social distinctions were strongly marked. The main body of the people was composed of men of free birth (*ingenui, liberi*), who were landholders, furnished the fighting-men, and formed the tribal Assembly (*concilium*, Ger. *Thing*, Eng. *Folk-moot*). The Assembly made elections, decided great issues, such as those of war and peace, and exercised judicial functions in criminal cases of the more serious kind (cc. 11–12). Above the rank and file of the freemen stood a class of nobles (*nobiles, proceres, primores*) of varying degrees of rank,[2] privileged in fact, though not in law. They existed in all German states, whatever their form of government,[3] and formed a considerable element of the population.[4] Although

---

[1] *Ann.* iv. 72.   [2] c. 13, 2.   [3] c. 25, 3; 44, 3.
[4] c. 14, 2, *plerique nobilium adulescentium.*

their numbers were reduced by war, their ranks were re-
plenished by freemen who rose to nobility through their
own or their fathers' prowess.[1] They exercised a decisive influence on the conduct of public affairs and on the whole
policy of the state: they were the leaders in peace and war,
without whose initiative the people were helpless.[2] In contrast to them the mass of the freemen is designated *plebs,
vulgus, multitudo*.[3] From the nobles were chosen kings and
chieftains, and probably the priests. While the ordinary freemen worked their land themselves with the aid of their wives
and families and mostly lived in village communities, the
nobles held large separate properties, which were worked by
slaves and dependants (c. 25).

At the foot of the social scale came the slaves, who existed
in Germany as everywhere else in the ancient world. Tacitus'
account of them is very incomplete, partly, no doubt, because
in his brevity he limited himself to the points of difference
between German slavery and Roman. Domestic slaves he
ignores altogether where we should have expected him to
speak of them,[4] but they certainly existed, as he mentions
incidentally.[5] Yet from his statement that household tasks
were discharged by wife and children, it may be inferred
that domestic slaves were not numerous, even in the houses
of the nobles. What he evidently regarded as the typical
kind of slavery was a mild form of bondage on the land
(doubtless the land belonging to the nobles), a serfdom
approaching to the medieval villeinage, which contrasted
markedly with the Roman system. While Roman slaves
worked by day at the specific tasks prescribed them and
passed the night in the master's establishment, the German
serf had his own home, where he was master, and his allotted
parcel of land which he was left to cultivate independently,

[1] c. 7; 13.
[2] *Ann.* i. 55, 3, *suasit . . . ut . . . proceres vinciret. nihil ausuram
plebem principibus amotis.*
[3] c. 10; 11; *Ann.* i. 55; ii. 19, &c.
[4] c. 25.   [5] c. 20.

subject only to the yearly payment of a rent in kind. In these respects his position resembled that of the Roman tenant farmer (*colonus*), with whom Tacitus compares him. But while the *colonus* was a free man, working under contract, the German serf was a real slave, over whom his master had such unlimited power that he might kill him without legal penalty. Although in practice the German slave was better treated than the Roman, and was rarely scourged or bound or punished by heavy taskwork, his legal position was the same: he was still a human chattel.

About the manumission of slaves Tacitus gives no information beyond the fact that it conferred but a partial emancipation, which raised the freeman only a little above the slave and afforded him no opportunity of rising to an influential position except in monarchical states.[1] The word 'freedman' at once turns his thoughts to Rome, where freedmen could become powerful personages and 'in evil times usurp political functions';[2] and, having pointed the contrast, he passes on without giving any details about the rights enjoyed by this class. German laws of the period following the invasions show that full emancipation by the tribal Assembly was granted rarely, and not unless there was a shortage of fighting-men, while the private manumission of the slave by his master conferred only the more essential rights of a freeman, such as those of acquiring property and making contracts, leaving him dependent on his patron and bound to the soil.[3]

Society in ancient Germany was thus anything but democratic. The distinction between the classes which Tacitus describes was no less strictly maintained in the eighth century, when the laws of the Saxons forbade the noble, the freeman, the freedman, and the slave to marry outside their rank.

[1] c. 25, 3.   [2] *Hist.* i. 76.
[3] The Latinized name of this class was *Liti*, *Leti*, *Laeti*, on whom see note on c. 25, 1.

German tribes were ruled either by kings or by a number of noble chieftains, whom the Romans called *principes*. Monarchical rule may possibly have been the oldest form of government everywhere. In historical times it prevailed in eastern Germany and in Scandinavia, while among the western tribes divided rule was the more common.[1] The king was chosen, so far as possible, from the family that ranked as the noblest and generally claimed divine descent. When there was a departure from the hereditary principle or when a new dynasty was established, the elected king was placed on a shield and swung to and fro on men's shoulders so that he should be recognized by all: the same ceremony accompanied the choice of a leader in war.[2] The king reigned rather than governed. His power was strictly limited;[3] in important political and judicial matters the decision lay with the tribal Assembly. Normally the king commanded in the field, and, as commander, he had the power of life and death,[4] but the execution of the penalty lay in the hands of the priest.[5] Likewise, in the Assembly coercive power belonged not to the king but to the priest.[6] In both cases the reason was that a breach of discipline was a breach of the sacred peace which was enjoined when the people were gathered under divine protection in assembly or in the field, and was consequently a sin against the gods. Although in general the king had more dignity than power, among the less developed tribes he was more of a monarch; but such royalty as that of the Suebic king Maroboduus, who extended his sovereignty over many tribes, was abnormal and obnoxious to the sentiment of independence.[7]

[1] Kings are attested in the case of the Sugambri (*Res gest. divi Aug.* 32), the Cherusci (*Ann.* xi. 16; Dio, lxvii. 5, 1), the Frisii (*Ann.* xiii. 54), and the Bructeri (under Roman influence, Pliny, *Epp.* ii. 7), while there was a *stirps regia* among the Batavi (*Hist.* iv. 13), though no kings are known. [2] *Hist.* iv. 15.
[3] c. 7; so the kings of the Frisii *regebant in quantum Germani regnantur* (*Ann.* xiii 54).
[4] Caes. *B.G.* vi. 23.   [5] c. 7, 2.   [6] c. 11, 4.
[7] *Ann.* ii. 44, 3.

Among the Suiones kingship developed exceptionally into the overlordship of a number of tribes, which seemed to Tacitus to represent unlimited monarchy;[1] but it was merely a loose suzerainty of a sacral character, based on the king's position as priest in a cult of fertility common to all the tribes. The prevalence of monarchy in the later period of migration and conquest was due to the force of circumstances, which made a strong central rule necessary and ultimately led to a very different type of monarchical rule from that of earlier times.

The only substantial difference between government by *principes* and government by a king was that the king's powers were here shared between members of noble families, so that the *principes* might be called *reguli* in their own spheres. Principate was no more democratic than kingship. The historical record shows that when the former was superseded the result was not a development of democracy but the establishment of monarchy. About the status of the *principes* evidence is scanty and not easy to interpret. The main question at issue is whether they were elected magistrates or simply prominent nobles whose position as rulers rested on their actual influence and not on any formal investiture. The view prevalent among German scholars appears to be that the *princeps* was a *Fürst*, chosen by the tribal Assembly to rule a *pagus*: he led the levy of his district in time of war, directed its local affairs in conjunction with the other leading men, and administered justice with the assistance of a hundred men chosen by the Assembly from among the commoners of the *pagus* to advise him and support his authority (c. 12, 3). On the other hand, the *princeps civitatis*, of whom Tacitus speaks as taking the place of a king in public functions for which a single representative of the tribe was required,[2] was not a supreme magistrate: this interpretation would contradict Caesar's explicit statement

---

[1] c. 44, 2.
[2] c. 10, 4, *rex vel princeps civitatis*; 11, 5, *rex vel princeps*.

that kingless tribes had no single ruler in time of peace,[1] and such a magistrate would not have been distinguishable in any obvious way from a king. We must suppose him to have been either the oldest of the *principes* or the *princeps* of the district in which the public act in question took place: he became *princeps civitatis* for the occasion, just as when a tribe went to war or several tribes joined in a common war, one of the *principes* was chosen as leader for the duration of hostilities.

This view does not seem to be well founded. Suggested by the conditions prevailing in later times, it is supported by an interpretation of c. 12, 3, which would make Tacitus say that the *principes* were chosen by the Assembly as rulers of the *pagi*, with the administration of justice as one of their functions.[2] What in fact he does say is that 'those *principes* who administer justice in the *pagi* are chosen' from the whole body (*eliguntur*), a statement which implies that there were other *principes* who had no such judicial functions. As Tacitus gives no further details, any attempt to reach a solution of the question must start from the fact that neither he nor Caesar, who has much to say about *principes* in Gaul and speaks in four passages about *principes* in Germany,[3] thought it necessary to define what they meant by the term; and as they presuppose no knowledge on the part of their readers about either country, it must be inferred that they used the term in the sense in which their readers would understand it. What that sense was, is not doubtful. *Principes* or *principes civitatis* meant the foremost men in public life, the most prominent of the nobles; the phrase dated from the time of the Republic and continued to be used of leading Roman citizens after *princeps* had become established as the designation of the Roman emperor.[4] That this was the sense in

---

[1] *B.G.* vi. 23, *in pace nullus est communis magistratus.*
[2] See the note on the passage.
[3] *B.G.* iv. 11, 13; vi. 22, 23.
[4] e.g. Sen. *De benef.* ii. 27; Pliny *N.H.* xxviii. 29; Suet. *Tiber.* lv. In *Ann.* xv. 25 we have the variant expression *primores civitatis.*

which Caesar used the word of the Gauls is clear from his narrative.[1] Every state had a number of such chiefs, some of greater, some of lesser, importance, who concerned themselves with public affairs, internal and external, promoted warlike enterprises or sought to prevent them,[2] and acted as envoys. Their power rested on prestige (*auctoritas*), which depended on their ability to protect their followers against injustice and so to secure *gratia inter suos*. The most influential of these chiefs was the *princeps civitatis*, whose position was attained by winning popular support. When two chiefs of the Treveri, Cingetorix and Indutiomarus, were contending for this position, Caesar helped the former to secure it by winning over the other *principes* severally to his cause.[3] It is plain, therefore, that the *principes*, as such, were not magistrates, although some of them might hold a magistracy; indeed, the *principatus civitatis* among the Aedui is expressly dissociated from any office.[4] Their power was based not on election by the people but on the voluntary adherence of those who attached themselves to them as their leaders.

When Caesar goes on to use the same term in speaking of the Germans, it is obvious that he cannot have meant something quite different, the more so as he was well aware of the differences between the two peoples; and in one passage he expressly distinguishes *magistratus* from *principes*.[5]

Tacitus evidently used the term in a similar way. The

---

[1] See especially i. 3 and 17; v. 3-4; vi. 11.

[2] Cp. viii. 22.

[3] v. 3-4.

[4] i. 3, *principatum in civitate obtinebat* (*Dumnorix*) *ac maxime plebi acceptus erat*, compared with i. 17, where the chief magistrate, the *Vergobret*, says: *esse nonnullos quorum auctoritas apud plebem plurimum valeat, qui privatim plus possint quam ipsi magistratus* (the reference being to Dumnorix, c. 18).

[5] vi. 22. On this subject see A. Baumstark, *Urdeutsche Staatsalterlümer*, 1873, pp. 507 ff.; G. Braumann, *Die Principes der Gallier u. Germanen* (Progr. d. Friedrich-Wilhelms-Gymn. zu Berlin, 1883); O. Seeck, *Untergang d. ant. Welt*, i³, pp. 532 ff.; Rice Holmes, *Conquest of Gaul*, p. 533, note 2.

principes of whom he speaks in the present treatise are the most prominent of the nobles, who are the leaders of the people in virtue of the prestige they enjoy; but the indefiniteness of the term is shown by the fact that in one passage (c. 11, 1) it appears to include all nobles (*proceres*).[1] The difference between kingship and principate is pointedly expressed in a passage of the *Agricola*, which also shows what the basis of the power of the *principes* really was: *olim regibus parebant, nunc per principes factionibus et studiis trahuntur*.[2] Their influence in public life rested not on election by the people but on their power to attract the allegiance of supporters,[3] not on any legal right but on popular favour. Their government was of an informal kind, while the king was formally elected. From their number were selected those *principes* who were invested with judicial powers, but these are the only officials whom Tacitus mentions. The *princeps civitatis*, who occupied a position corresponding to that of the king in monarchical states, was probably one of the *principes* whose pre-eminence in actual power and influence made him the informal head of the state. A distinctive mark of all *principes* was the maintenance of a *comitatus*, a retinue of free, mostly noble, warriors enrolled in their personal service and bound to them by the strictest ties.[4] This, says Tacitus, was the source of their influence and power. Caesar says the same of the Gallic chiefs.[5]

The only illustration we have of the working of this form of government and of its relation to kingship is furnished

---

[1] So in *Ann.* i. 55, 3 it is used as a synonym of *proceres*; cf. ii. 15, 2, *nec Arminius aut ceteri Germanorum proceres omittebant suos quisque testari*, &c. The same wider meaning sometimes attaches to the equally indefinite word *primores* (used in *Hist.* and *Ann.*) when contrasted with *plebs* or *vulgus*.

[2] *Agr.* 12, 1. Cp. Caes. vi. 11, *in Gallia non solum in omnibus civitatibus atque in omnibus pagis partibusque, sed paene etiam in singulis domibus factiones sunt*.

[3] Cp. c. 22, 3, *de adsciscendis principibus . . . in conviviis consultant*.

[4] cc. 13–14. Such bands of chosen warriors were also, of course, maintained by kings (c. 13, 3, note).

[5] *B.G.* vi. 15 (notes on c. 13, 2, and 4).

by the account which Tacitus gives of the affairs of the Cherusci.[1] At one time this tribe appears to have been ruled by kings, who had been replaced in the early years of our era by *principes* belonging to two families, one of them (perhaps both) of royal descent: on the one hand the famous Arminius, his brother Flavus, and their uncle Inguiomerus, and on the other Segestes, father-in-law of Arminius, and his brother Segimerus. Arminius was chosen as *dux* for war against the Romans, and he succeeded in destroying the legions of Varus. Some years later, after defeating and driving out the Marcomanic king Maroboduus, he began to aspire to kingship (*regnum adfectans*), but he found himself in conflict with the independent temper of his countrymen, and after fighting with varying fortune he fell by the treachery of his kinsmen (the other *principes*). After his death civil war continued until the higher nobility was wiped out and there was only one survivor of the old royal stock, by name Italicus, who lived at Rome. In A.D. 47 he was called to the throne, but those 'who had prospered through party feuds and had no hope save from civil dissensions' stirred up neighbouring tribes against him. They failed, but the king lapsed into monarchical ways and was deposed, to be restored later by a neighbouring tribe. Here the curtain falls on his fortunes, but towards the end of the century the Cherusci were still ruled by a king.[2]

Normally the sphere of influence of a *princeps*, other than the *princeps civitatis*, would no doubt be limited to a *pagus*, though it might be more extensive.[3] In Italy the word *pagus* had a definite signification: it had come to mean a district of tillage and pasture-land containing villages, farms, and country-houses and forming part of the territory of a town. The term was applied to the subdivisions first of the Gallic

---

[1] *Ann.* i. 55 ff.; ii. 44 ff., 88; xi. 16 f.

[2] Cass. Dio, lxvii. 5, 1.

[3] In *B.G.* vi. 23, Caesar speaks of *principes regionum atque pagorum* among the Germans: here *regiones* is undoubtedly a wider term than *pagi*.

and then of the German tribes. It was not a very appropriate designation, since the Italian *pagus* was much smaller
and had lost both the political importance it had once possessed and all trace of the idea of clan relationship among
its inhabitants, which had led Greeks to use φῦλον for the
Celtic *pagus*.[1] But Roman terminology lacked a more suitable term, *tribus* being excluded by the fact that it had long
ceased to be associated with a definite territorial area. It is
most probable that the *pagi* arose not from the subdivision
of an already-existing tribal unit into smaller sections, but
from the coalescence or the welding together of smaller
related groups into the larger whole of the *civitas*, of which
they became subdivisions. This would explain the large
amount of independence enjoyed by the Celtic *pagi* within
the tribe and the use of the term to denote the tribal group
as well as the district which it inhabited.[2]

Tacitus makes only three allusions to these local subdivisions, but these three have exercised commentators and
historians. Each *pagus*, he says, furnished to the tribal army
a hundred picked warriors, whose agility enabled them to
keep pace with the horsemen in the van and who were called
in their own tongue 'the hundred' (*huntari*), though the
word had lost its numerical significance and had become a
title of honour.[3] The second passage states that judges were
chosen by the Assembly from among the *principes* to dispense justice in the *pagi*, and that each was supported by a
hundred *comites* selected from the free men to give him
advice and support.[4] In the third passage the Semnones are
said to have had a hundred *pagi*,[5] a statement which had
been made to Caesar about the Suebi. All three passages
have caused perplexity. How, it is asked, could all German
tribes ever have fixed the number of select footmen to be

---

[1] Posidonius *ap.* Strabo, iv. 3, 3, p. 193. Mommsen, *Gesamm.
Schriften*, v. 394; *Staatsrecht*, iii. 117.
[2] e.g. Caes. *B.G.* i. 12 (in reference to the Helvetii), 37 (in reference
to the Suebi).
[3] c. 6, 5.   [4] c. 12, 3.   [5] c. 39, 4

furnished by each *pagus* at precisely 100 (or 120, the German 'great hundred'), when, as Caesar's account shows, their number was equal to that of the horsemen, whose number would naturally vary in different tribes? Moreover, Caesar says that each horseman chose his footman from the whole army, *ex omni copia*.[1] It is also thought incredible that these footmen should have monopolized the title of 'the hundred', to the exclusion of the equally skilled cavalry, who always ranked above the infantry. As regards the hundred *comites*, suspicion has been aroused by the number, which is thought unduly large for the purpose; by the implication (it is not a statement) that they were chosen by the Assembly, which is thus made to intervene in affairs that were the concern of the *pagenses*; and by the fact that the procedure described is not in accord with later German practice. Finally, the hundred *pagi* of the Semnones is an incredibly large number.

These difficulties, combined with the fact that Tacitus' source knew the German word which he translates by *centeni*, have led many to believe that his statements are based on a misunderstanding of reports which spoke of the subdivisions of German *civitates* into 'hundreds'. These divisions are attested at a much later date in most, though not all, parts of Germany, and they are well known in Anglo-Saxon England (not before the tenth century) as units within the county or shire forming the basis on which were apportioned the duties of military and judicial service. Believing that this institution had its roots in older practice, some hold the quite untenable view that the *pagus* was really the 'hundred',[2] while others think that the 'hundred', though not as yet a territorial subdivision, already existed in the time of

---

[1] *B.G.* i. 48.

[2] See the criticisms of Müllenhoff, *Deutsch. Altertumskunde*, iv. 176 ff. (his own theory that the *pagus* was the equivalent of ten 'hundreds', a *Tausendschaft*, lacks any historical support: see *Savigny Ztschr.* xxvii, 1906, pp. 234 ff.); A. Dopsch, *Wirtsch. und soziale Grundlagen d. europäischen Kulturentwicklung*, ii. 9 ff. (an English translation is now available); L. Schmidt, *Gesch. d. deutsch. Stämme*, i, ed. 2, 1934, pp. 51 ff.

Caesar and Tacitus as a group of persons for military and judicial purposes. If so, the *centeni* in the case of the élite corps would really have meant the contingent of warriors furnished to the joint host by each 'hundred', the select footmen being picked from the various contingents; the *centeni comites* would in reality have been not people specially chosen to accompany the *princeps* on his rounds, but the free landholders of each 'hundred' (or the men composing each 'hundred'), whom the *princeps*, like the later *Graf*, called out for service as jurors at the local court; and the *centum pagi* of the Suebi and the Semnones would be capable of a reasonable interpretation.

But there is not a shred of evidence that the hundreds existed in any shape or form at this date. They probably did not come into being before the period of the migrations. In the earlier centuries there is no trace of a numerical organization of army or people: both were organized by clans, and the persistence of this system is attested as late as the end of the sixth century.[1] The difficulties that have led to this theory are not serious enough to justify the supposition that Tacitus or his informants completely misunderstood the facts.[2] In the case of the select footmen who accompanied the horsemen there is no reason why the number originally furnished by each *pagus* should not have been a hundred, a *centuria*, which was the original unit for cavalry among the Romans (as in Russia, where *sotnia* is etymologically *centuria*). As they formed only a fraction of the whole levy of the *pagus*,

---

[1] Schmidt quotes the testimony of Maurikios, *Strategicon*, xi. 4 (ed. Scheffer): τάσσονται . . . οὐ μέτρῳ τινὶ ὡρισμένῳ . . . ἀλλὰ κατὰ φυλὰς καὶ τῇ πρὸς ἀλλήλους συγγενείᾳ, a statement referring to the Franks, the Langobardi (who tenaciously maintained their traditional institutions), and other tribes.

[2] A still more radical misconception is supposed by Dopsch (*op. cit.* ii. 19), who suggests that the *centeni comites* were really a committee of councillors which acted as a Senate in co-operation with the *principes* at meetings of the Assembly. For the existence of a Senate among German tribes he cites (after Müllenhoff) Caes. *B.G.* iv. 11 (the Ubii), Claudian, *Bell. Goth.*, 479 ff., and Sidon. Apollinaris, *Carm.* vii. 452.

the latter must have been a comparatively large subdivision of the *civitas*: in the army of Maroboduus the proportion of mounted men to infantry was 4,000 to 70,000.[1] The discrepancy of Caesar's statement about the manner of their selection is not important: Caesar's information was evidently not precise, for the German army was organized by clans and families, and the choice of the horseman must have been limited to men from his own district, whom alone he could know well enough to judge of their skill. If the century was used as a unit for a military purpose, it may also have been used in judicial arrangements. Finally, as regards the *centum pagi*, the explanation may be that the reports followed by Caesar and by Tacitus used 'a hundred' in the sense of a large number, a meaning which it often bears in Latin and still bears in Norse (*hundmargr*) and sometimes in English.

We cannot indeed be sure of the complete accuracy of the statements made by Tacitus, which we have no means of checking. It is certainly not easy to believe that the select footmen were specially designated by the title *centeni*. Despite their skill, they were subsidiary to the horsemen, who always ranked above footmen, and it may be that Tacitus transferred to the latter a title that really belonged to the former, who, according to Caesar, chose their mates for their own protection (*suae salutis causa*). It may be, too, that a misconception underlies the description of the German judicial system, but the fact that it does not accord with German practice at a much later date is not a sound reason for such an assumption. German institutions did not remain static. In Caesar's time justice had been dispensed by the leading men when their assistance was invoked, but they evidently had no power to compel recourse to their tribunal.[2] The appointment of public officials for the administration of

---

[1] Vell. Paterc. ii. 109, 2.

[2] *B.G.* vi. 23: *In pace nullus est communis magistratus, sed principes regionum atque pagorum inter suos ius dicunt controversiasque minuunt* (not *tollunt* or *componunt*).

justice in the time of Tacitus marked a notable advance, and the analogy between the German institution as he describes it and the assize system in Roman provinces is close enough to suggest that the former was modelled on the latter.[1] The subsequent modification of an older practice would be nothing strange: the course of conquest brought about many changes in traditional institutions.

SECTION VI

THE MANUSCRIPTS OF THE *GERMANIA*

THERE are in all twenty-nine manuscripts of the *Germania*, excluding the two earliest printed editions, the *editio princeps* of about 1470 and the Nuremberg edition of about 1473, which appear to have drawn from manuscripts now lost. The archetype of all of them (as of the manuscripts of the *Agricola* and the *Dialogus*) was the Hersfeld MS. written in the ninth or tenth century, of which only a few leaves containing a portion of the *Agricola* survive in the Iesi codex (Aesinas), which was discovered by Cesare Annibaldi in 1902.[2] None of the extant manuscripts were copied directly from the archetype; they all descend from copies of it made in the fifteenth century, which have not survived. The generally accepted view has been that these copies were three in number, which are labelled X, Y, Z. From them were copied the five manuscripts on which all the more recent texts of the *Germania* have been based, two from X, two from Y, and one from Z, all being direct copies, except one of the X class.

To the X class belong:

1. Vaticanus, lat. 1862, Halm's *B*, an excellent manuscript.

2. Leidensis (Perizonianus), Halm's *b*, written in March 1460 by Jovianus Pontanus, a distinguished Renaissance

---

[1] Cp. Seeck, *op. cit.*[3], i. 225 f. with the notes.
[2] The history of the Hersfeld MS. and the contents of the Iesi codex are described in the Introduction to the *Agricola*, pp. xiv ff.

scholar, as we learn from a note written in it, though it is generally believed that the manuscript is not the actual copy made by Pontanus but a transcript of it. A photographic facsimile of it, with a long preface, has been published by G. Wissowa.[1] The manuscript is the work of a scholar, but its value as a reproduction of its exemplar is impaired by the introduction of Humanist emendations.

To the Y class belong:

3. Vaticanus, lat. 1518, Halm's *C*.

4. Neapolitanus (Farnesianus), iv C. 21, Halm's *c*. The latter is much less corrupt than the former.

5. Of the Z class the leading representative is Aesinas, lat. 8, labelled *E*. The portion of the codex containing the *Germania* was written in the fifteenth century but was not copied directly from the Hersfeld codex, as its discoverer maintained. (*T*, a manuscript in the Toledo Chapter Library, 49, 2, dated 1474, is of no value for the establishment of the text, having been directly copied from *E*.)

The current view has thus been that these five manuscripts represent three independent lines of tradition, and that the agreement of two of the groups should normally indicate which of two possible readings represents the text of the archetype. The other manuscripts have been regarded as practically negligible and their readings are rarely mentioned.

But this view of the comparative value and the relationship of the manuscripts has been challenged by Prof. R. P. Robinson in his critical edition.[2] After collating all the manuscripts and making an exhaustive study of their readings in the light of the knowledge that can be gained from the extant portion of the archetype (especially as regards the kinds of error that already existed in it), he propounds a new classification. His conclusion is that all but three of the manuscripts which have been assigned to the three

---

[1] *Codices Graeci et Latini photographice depicti*, Suppl. iv, Leyden, 1907.

[2] *The Germania of Tacitus: a critical edition*, Connecticut, 1935.

families X, Y, Z really descend from one copy of the Hersfeld codex, which he calls Y, but none of them are direct transcripts of it, and those which have been taken as the basis of the text were transcribed from three lost copies of two lost apographs of Y. On the other hand, the three excepted manuscripts represent a line of tradition distinct from all the rest, being derived from another copy of the archetype, which he calls X. They are:

    i. Vindobonensis 711, dated 1466, in the Staatsarchiv at Vienna.

    ii. Monacensis, lat. 5307, in the Staatsbibliothek at Munich.

    iii. Hummelianus, named after its former owner B. F. Hummel. It is now lost, but there are two collations of it, as well as a selection of its readings published by Hummel himself in 1776.

The first of these three is held to be a direct copy of X, while the other two are copies of lost intermediaries. The Vienna manuscript is regarded as the best of the group, and it appears to have kept the genuine tradition in matters of orthography, while the Munich manuscript is much the most corrupt.

It will be seen that this new classification assigns to three manuscripts an importance equal to that of all the others combined. That they have reproduced the archetype with greater fidelity is a reasonable inference from the fact that they are free from certain corruptions that are found in the others, some of which betray a fifteenth-century origin. Whether the classification can be accepted in all details is a question that may be left aside; but the contention that these three manuscripts form an ultimate group with independent value would appear to be successfully established. Their readings are therefore taken into account in the apparatus criticus appended to the text.

All the extant manuscripts are of the fifteenth or the early sixteenth century.

SUMMARY OF CONTENTS

PART I

PART II

THE TEXT

SIGLA

CORNELII TACITI
DE ORIGINE ET SITU
GERMANORUM
LIBER

GERMANIA omnis a Gallis Raetisque et Pannoniis Rheno 1
et Danuvio fluminibus, a Sarmatis Dacisque mutuo metu
aut montibus separatur : cetera Oceanus ambit, latos sinus
et insularum immensa spatia complectens, nuper cognitis
5 quibusdam gentibus ac regibus, quos bellum aperuit.
Rhenus, Raeticarum Alpium inaccesso ac praecipiti vertice 2
ortus, modico flexu in occidentem versus septentrionali
Oceano miscetur. Danuvius molli et clementer edito montis 3
Abnobae iugo effusus plures populos adit, donec in Ponti-
10 cum mare sex meatibus erumpat ; septimum os paludibus
hauritur.

Ipsos Germanos indigenas crediderim minimeque aliarum 2
gentium adventibus et hospitiis mixtos, quia nec terra olim
sed classibus advehebantur qui mutare sedes quaerebant, et
15 immensus ultra utque sic dixerim adversus Oceanus raris ab
orbe nostro navibus aditur. quis porro, praeter periculum 2

TITULUS. Cornelii (C. Cornelii *I*Δ) Taciti de origine et situ
Germanorum *cod. Hersf. teste Niccolò Niccoli, WmVI*Δ : Cornelii
(C. Cornelii *N*) Taciti de origine et situ Germanię *cod. Hersf. teste
Decembrio, N*

1 Raetisque *Cellarius* : raetiisque (ret-, rhaet-, rhet-) *codd.* 2 Da-
nubio *VLNE* (-nn-*E*) 8 Danuvius *WhI* (b *s.l. W*, -nn-*I*) : Danubius
cett. 9 Abnobae *h, Rhen.* : Arnobae *vel* Arbonae *cett.* plurimos
Ed.Wolff 15 aversus *Acidalius*

horridi et ignoti maris, Asia aut Africa aut Italia relicta
Germaniam peteret, informem terris, asperam caelo, tristem
cultu aspectuque nisi si patria sit?

3 Celebrant carminibus antiquis, quod unum apud illos
memoriae et annalium genus est, Tuistonem deum terra 5
editum. ei filium Mannum originem gentis conditoresque
Manno tres filios adsignant, e quorum nominibus proximi
Oceano Ingaevones, medii Herminones, ceteri Istaevones
4 vocentur quidam, ut in licentia vetustatis, plures deo ortos
pluresque gentis appellationes, Marsos Gambrivios Suebos 10
5 Vandilios adfirmant, eaque vera et antiqua nomina. ceterum
Germaniae vocabulum recens et nuper additum, quoniam
qui primi Rhenum transgressi Gallos expulerint ac nunc
Tungri, tunc Germani vocati sint : ita nationis nomen, non
gentis, evaluisse paulatim, ut omnes primum a victore ob 15
metum, mox et a se ipsis invento nomine Germani vocarentur.

3 Fuisse et apud eos Herculem memorant, primumque
omnium virorum fortium ituri in proelia canunt. sunt
illis haec quoque carmina quorum relatu, quem baritum 20
vocant, accendunt animos futuraeque pugnae fortunam ipso
cantu augurantur ; terrent enim trepidantve, prout sonuit
acies, nec tam vocis ille quam virtutis concentus videtur.
2 adfectatur praecipue asperitas soni et fractum murmur,
obiectis ad os scutis, quo plenior et gravior vox repercussu 25
3 intumescat. ceterum et Ulixen quidam opinantur longo
illo et fabuloso errore in hunc Oceanum delatum adisse

3 si] sibi *Wh* : cui *Sturm*   5 Tuistonem *IL²* : Tuisconem *sE* :
Tristonem *VL* : bistonem (*in mg.* tuistonem *W*, tuisconem *h*) *WhN△*
6 ei *VEWms²* : et *LNI△s*   conditoresque *Rhen.* : conditorisque
codd. (*nisi quod* em *supers. W*, conditoremque *hs²*)   8 Herminones
WmhNL² : hermiones *VL△IE*   10 sueuos *codd.*, *et sic ubique*
11 vandalios *L* : vandalos *h*   12 auditum *Lipsius*   13 ac] ut
L in ras.   16 et *Wmh△Is* : etiam *VL* : om. *NE*   18 et apud
eos *W, al.* : apud eos et *plurimi codd.*   20 illius *Hertlein*   baritum
△ et in mg. vel s.l. WNsE : barditum *WmVLNIsE*   23 vocis . . .
videtur *Rhen.* : uoces ille (illae) . . . uidentur *codd.*

GERMANIA

Germaniae terras, Asciburgiumque, quod in ripa Rheni
situm hodieque incolitur, ab illo constitutum nominatumque; aram quin etiam Ulixi consecratam, adiecto
Laertae patris nomine, eodem loco olim repertam, monu-
5 mentaque et tumulos quosdam Graecis litteris inscriptos in
confinio Germaniae Raetiaeque adhuc extare. quae neque 4
confirmare argumentis neque refellere in animo est: ex
ingenio suo quisque demat vel addat fidem.

Ipse eorum opinionibus accedo qui Germaniae populos 4
10 nullis [aliis] aliarum nationum conubiis infectos propriam et
sinceram et tantum sui similem gentem extitisse arbitrantur.
unde habitus quoque corporum, tamquam in tanto homi- 2
num numero, idem omnibus : truces et caerulei oculi, rutilae
comae, magna corpora et tantum ad impetum valida.
15 laboris atque operum non eadem patientia, minimeque sitim 3
aestumque tolerare, frigora atque inediam caelo solove
adsueverunt.

Terra etsi aliquanto specie differt, in universum tamen 5
aut silvis horrida aut paludibus foeda, humidior qua Gallias,
20 ventosior qua Noricum ac Pannoniam aspicit; satis ferax,
frugiferarum arborum impatiens, pecorum fecunda, sed
plerumque improcera. ne armentis quidem suus honor aut 2
gloria frontis : numero gaudent, eaeque solae et gratissimae
opes sunt. argentum et aurum propitiine an irati dii negave- 3
25 rint dubito. nec tamen adfirmaverim nullam Germaniae
venam argentum aurumve gignere : quis enim scrutatus est ?
possessione et usu haud perinde adficiuntur: est videre 4
apud illos argentea vasa, legatis et principibus eorum muneri

1 astiburgiumque L^1, assiburgiumque I 2 hodie NI incola-
tur Wmh : incolitur cett. 2 nominatumque ασκιπυργιον $WVNIE$, alii
ασκ. om. notata lacuna vel sine lac. 9 opinioni Meiser 10 aliis
secl. Lips. 12 tamquam $WmNI$ et V in mg.: quamquam cett. (in
mg. W, s.l. N) 13 caeruli $WhVL$ et E s.l. 17 assuerunt (-int
s.l. V) VL 21 patiens Tross 22 pleraque Lips. 24
propitii $N\Delta I$ 27 perinde (pro V s.l.) VLs et E s.l.: proinde
cett.

CORNELII TACITI

data, non in alia vilitate quam quae humo finguntur. quamquam proximi ob usum commerciorum aurum et argentum in pretio habent formasque quasdam nostrae pecuniae agnoscunt atque eligunt: interiores simplicius et antiquius 5 permutatione mercium utuntur. pecuniam probant veterem 5 et diu notam, serratos bigatosque. argentum quoque magis quam aurum sequuntur, nulla adfectione animi, sed quia numerus argenteorum facilior usui est promisca ac vilia mercantibus.

6 Ne ferrum quidem superest, sicut ex genere telorum 10 colligitur. rari gladiis aut maioribus lanceis utuntur: hastas vel ipsorum vocabulo frameas gerunt angusto et brevi ferro, sed ita acri et ad usum habili, ut eodem telo, prout ratio 2 poscit, vel comminus vel eminus pugnent. et eques quidem scuto frameaque contentus est, pedites et missilia spargunt, 15 pluraque singuli, atque in immensum vibrant, nudi aut sagulo leves. nulla cultus iactatio: scuta tantum lectissimis 3 coloribus distinguunt. paucis loricae, vix uni alterive cassis aut galea. equi non forma, non velocitate conspicui. sed nec variare gyros in morem nostrum docentur: in rectum 20 aut uno flexu dextros agunt, ita coniuncto orbe ut nemo 4 posterior sit. in universum aestimanti plus penes peditem roboris; eoque mixti proeliantur, apta et congruente ad equestrem pugnam velocitate peditum, quos ex omni iuven-5 tute delectos ante aciem locant. definitur et numerus: 25 centeni ex singulis pagis sunt, idque ipsum inter suos vocantur, et quod primo numerus fuit, iam nomen et honor 6 est. acies per cuneos componitur. cedere loco, dummodo rursus instes, consilii quam formidinis arbitrantur. corpora

6 argentumque *H. Schütz*   8 promiscua *codd.*, *cf. c.* 44, 3
19 galea *Rhen.* (*cum duobus codd. dett.*): galeae *cett.*: galea est
Mützell   21 dextros (vel sinistros) *Michaelis*   coniuncto *et in mg.* cuncto *VE*: cuncto *WmhΔL*, concto *I*, cuncto *et s.l.* coniucto *N*   22 existimanti *NΔI*   27 quod] quidem *VL*   primo (*et s.l.* u;) *VL*, primo (*et s.l.* mum) *E*: primum *Whs*: primo *cett.*

suorum etiam in dubiis proeliis referunt. scutum reliquisse
praecipuum flagitium, nec aut sacris adesse aut concilium
inire ignominioso fas, multique superstites bellorum infamiam laqueo finierunt.

5 Reges ex nobilitate, duces ex virtute sumunt. nec regi- 7
bus infinita ac libera potestas, et duces exemplo potius
quam imperio, si prompti, si conspicui, si ante aciem agant,
admiratione praesunt. ceterum neque animadvertere neque 2
vincire, ne verberare quidem nisi sacerdotibus permissum,
10 non quasi in poenam nec ducis iussu, sed velut deo impe-
rante, quem adesse bellantibus credunt. effigiesque et signa 3
quaedam detracta lucis in proelium ferunt; quodque praecipuum fortitudinis incitamentum est, non casus nec fortuita conglobatio turmam aut cuneum facit, sed familiae et
15 propinquitates; et in proximo pignora, unde feminarum
ululatus audiri, unde vagitus infantium. hi cuique sanctis- 4
simi testes, hi maximi laudatores: ad matres, ad coniuges
vulnera ferunt; nec illae numerare et exigere plagas pavent,
cibosque et hortamina pugnantibus gestant.

20 Memoriae proditur quasdam acies inclinatas iam et la- 8
bantes a feminis restitutas constantia precum et obiectu
pectorum et monstrata comminus captivitate, quam longe
impatientius feminarum suarum nomine timent, adeo ut
efficacius obligentur animi civitatum quibus inter obsides
25 puellae quoque nobiles imperantur. inesse quin etiam 2
sanctum aliquid et providum putant, nec aut consilia earum
aspernantur aut responsa neglegunt. vidimus sub divo 3
Vespasiano Veledam diu apud plerosque numinis loco
habitam; sed et olim Auriniam et complures alias venerati
30 sunt, non adulatione nec tamquam facerent deas.

1 etiam] et *I*   6 ac] aut *VLEm*   et] etiam *VL*   9 ne]
neque *WmE*   14 et] aut *VL*¹   16 auditur *Kritz*, est audire *Mähly*, possit *post* infantium *suppl. C. Heraeus*   18 et] aut
VLE   28 Velaedam *Ritter*   29 Auriniam *WmhVLIE*: Albriniam Δ *et in mg. vel s.l. VLNE*: Fluriniam *N*: Albrunam *Wackernagel*

9 Deorum maxime Mercurium colunt, cui certis diebus
humanis quoque hostiis litare fas habent. Herculem ac
2 Martem concessis animalibus placant. pars Sueborum et
Isidi sacrificat: unde causa et origo peregrino sacro parum
comperi nisi quod signum ipsum in modum liburnae figura- 5
3 tum docet advectam religionem. ceterum nec cohibere
parietibus deos neque in ullam humani oris speciem adsimulare ex magnitudine caelestium arbitrantur: lucos ac
nemora consecrant deorumque nominibus appellant secre-
tum illud, quod sola reverentia vident.   10
10 Auspicia sortesque ut qui maxime observant. sortium
consuetudo simplex. virgam frugiferae arbori decisam in
surculos amputant eosque notis quibusdam discretos super
2 candidam vestem temere ac fortuito spargunt. mox, si
publice consultetur, sacerdos civitatis, sin privatim, ipse 15
pater familiae, precatus deos caelumque suspiciens ter
singulos tollit, sublatos secundum impressam ante notam
3 interpretatur. si prohibuerunt, nulla de eadem re in eundem diem consultatio; sin permissum, auspiciorum adhuc
fides exigitur. et illud quidem etiam hic notum, avium 20
voces volatusque interrogare: proprium gentis equorum
4 quoque praesagia ac monitus experiri. publice aluntur
isdem nemoribus ac lucis, candidi et nullo mortali opere
contacti; quos pressos sacro curru sacerdos ac rex vel
princeps civitatis comitantur hinnitusque ac fremitus ob- 25
5 servant. nec ulli auspicio maior fides, non solum apud
plebem, sed apud proceres, apud sacerdotes; se enim
ministros deorum, illos conscios putant. est et alia ob-
servatio auspiciorum, qua gravium bellorum eventus explo-

---

3 Martem c. a. placant et Herculem *VL*   5 liburnicae *Gude-*
man   15 consultetur *Halm*: consuletur *codd.* (consulitur *Walch*,
consulatur *Rhen.*)   23 isdem *s*, hisdem *Wm*, iisdem *cett.*   24
contactis *in mg. W*, contactis *s²*, contractis *m* : *unde* contacti sunt
Robinson   27 sed *I et s.l. E, al. quinque*: *om. cett.*   sed apud
proceres; sacerdotes enim *Perizonius, Wölfflin* : sed *post* proceres
transtulit Thomas   29 explorantur *L* : exploratur *V et s.l. L*

rant. eius gentis cum qua bellum est captivum quoquo 6
modo interceptum cum electo popularium suorum, patriis
quemque armis, committunt : victoria huius vel illius pro
praeiudicio accipitur.

5 De minoribus rebus principes consultant, de maioribus 11
omnes, ita tamen ut ea quoque, quorum penes plebem
arbitrium est, apud principes praetractentur. coeunt, nisi 2
quid fortuitum et subitum incidit, certis diebus, cum aut
incohatur luna aut impletur ; nam agendis rebus hoc auspi-
10 catissimum initium credunt. nec dierum numerum, ut nos,
sed noctium computant. sic constituunt, sic condicunt :
nox ducere diem videtur. illud ex libertate vitium, quod 3
non simul nec ut iussi conveniunt, sed et alter et tertius
dies cunctatione coeuntium absumitur. ut turbae placuit, 4
15 considunt armati. silentium per sacerdotes, quibus tum
et coercendi ius est, imperatur. mox rex vel princeps, 5
prout aetas cuique, prout nobilitas, prout decus bellorum,
prout facundia est, audiuntur auctoritate suadendi magis
quam iubendi potestate. si displicuit sententia, fremitu 6
20 aspernantur ; sin placuit, frameas concutiunt : honoratissi-
mum adsensus genus est armis laudare.

Licet apud concilium accusare quoque et discrimen 12
capitis intendere. distinctio poenarum ex delicto : proditores et transfugas arboribus suspendunt, ignavos et imbelles
25 et corpore infames caeno ac palude, iniecta insuper crate,
mergunt. diversitas supplicii illuc respicit, tamquam scelera 2
ostendi oporteat dum puniuntur, flagitia abscondi. sed et
levioribus delictis pro modo poena : equorum pecorumque
numero convicti multantur. pars multae regi vel civitati,
30 pars ipsi qui vindicatur vel propinquis eius exsolvitur.

7 praetractentur *IVN*Δ *et corr. I* : pertractentur *cett.*   13 iniussi *E*
14 turba *I. F. Gronovius*   15 tum] tamen *mVLE* : cum *I*   16 principes *Perizonius*   25 et crate *h* : et grate. *in mg.* crate *W* :
gratem *m*   28 poenarum *codd.* : poena *Acidalius* ; poena : nam
Robinson   30 uindicauit *VL (sed corr. L s.l.)*

3 eliguntur in isdem conciliis et principes qui iura per pagos
vicosque reddunt; centeni singulis ex plebe comites consilium simul et auctoritas adsunt.

13　Nihil autem neque publicae neque privatae rei nisi armati
agunt. sed arma sumere non ante cuiquam moris quam 5
civitas suffecturum probaverit. tum in ipso concilio vel
principum aliquis vel pater vel propinqui scuto frameaque
iuvenem ornant : haec apud illos toga, hic primus iuventae
honos ; ante hoc domus pars videntur, mox rei publicae.

2 insignis nobilitas aut magna patrum merita principis digna- 10
tionem etiam adulescentulis adsignant: †ceteris robustioribus
ac iam pridem probatis adgregantur, nec rubor inter comites

3 aspici. gradus quin etiam ipse comitatus habet, iudicio
eius quem sectantur; magnaque et comitum aemulatio,
quibus primus apud principem suum locus, et principum, 15

4 cui plurimi et acerrimi comites. haec dignitas, hae vires :
magno semper electorum iuvenum globo circumdari in
pace decus, in bello praesidium. nec solum in sua gente
cuique, sed apud finitimas quoque civitates id nomen, ea
gloria est, si numero ac virtute comitatus emineat; expe- 20
tuntur enim legationibus et muneribus ornantur et ipsa
plerumque fama bella profligant.

14　Cum ventum in aciem, turpe principi virtute vinci, turpe
comitatui virtutem principis non adaequare. iam vero
infame in omnem vitam ac probrosum superstitem principi 25
suo ex acie recessisse : illum defendere, tueri, sua quoque
fortia facta gloriae eius adsignare praecipuum sacramentum
est : principes pro victoria pugnant, comites pro principe.

2 si civitas in qua orti sunt longa pace et otio torpeat, plerique nobilium adulescentium petunt ultro eas nationes, quae 30
tum bellum aliquod gerunt, quia et ingrata genti quies et

---

1 hisdem *WmhI*: iisdem *cett.*　　6 tum] cum *WVL¹E et s.l. N*　　7
propinqui *WVLEs* : propinquus *mhNΔI et W in mg.*　　10 dignitatem
VL　　11 ceteri *Lips.*, certis *Gudeman*　　16 haec vires *WIL*
(*sed* c *del. L*)　　17 et electorum *E, al.*　　31 tum] cum *WI*

facilius inter ancipitia clarescunt magnumque comitatum non nisi vi belloque tueare; exigunt enim principis sui **3** liberalitate illum bellatorem equum, illam cruentam victricemque frameam; nam epulae et quamquam incompti, 5 largi tamen apparatus pro stipendio cedunt. materia munificentiae per bella et raptus. nec arare terram aut expect- **4** are annum tam facile persuaseris quam vocare hostem et vulnera mereri; pigrum quin immo et iners videtur sudore adquirere quod possis sanguine parare.

10 Quotiens bella non ineunt, non multum venatibus, plus **15** per otium transigunt, dediti somno ciboque: fortissimus quisque ac bellicosissimus nihil agens, delegata domus et penatium et agrorum cura feminis senibusque et infirmissimo cuique ex familia, ipsi hebent, mira diversitate naturae, 15 cum idem homines sic ament inertiam et oderint quietem. mos est civitatibus ultro ac viritim conferre principibus vel **2** armentorum vel frugum, quod pro honore acceptum etiam necessitatibus subvenit. gaudent praecipue finitimarum **3** gentium donis, quae non modo a singulis, sed et publice 20 mittuntur, electi equi, magn⟨ific⟩a arma, phalerae torquesque; iam et pecuniam accipere docuimus.

Nullas Germanorum populis urbes habitari satis notum **16** est, ne pati quidem inter se iunctas sedes. colunt discreti ac diversi, ut fons, ut campus, ut nemus placuit. vicos **2** 25 locant non in nostrum morem conexis et cohaerentibus aedificiis: suam quisque domum spatio circumdat, sive adversus casus ignis remedium sive inscitia aedificandi. ne **3** caementorum quidem apud illos aut tegularum usus : materia ad omnia utuntur informi et citra speciem aut delectationem. 30 quaedam loca diligentius inlinunt terra ita pura ac splendente ut picturam ac lineamenta colorum imitetur. solent **4**

2 tuentur *VL*   a *post* enim *add. Acidalius*   10 non *ante* multum *del. Lips.*   14 hebent *VNEs et W s.l.*, ebent *h* : habent *cett.*   15 idem *IVmh* : iidem *VLNΔIs*   20 magnifica *Meiser* : magna *codd. Cf. c.* 34, **2** 25 longant *in mg.* E, *in textu (s.l.* locant) *V*   31 imitentur *NΔE*

et subterraneos specus aperire eosque multo insuper fimo
onerant, suffugium hiemis et receptaculum frugibus, quia
rigorem frigorum eius modi loci molliunt, et si quando
hostis advenit, aperta populatur, abdita autem et defossa
aut ignorantur aut eo ipso fallunt quod quaerenda sunt.   5

17 Tegumen omnibus sagum fibula aut, si desit, spina consertum : cetera intecti totos dies iuxta focum atque ignem
agunt. locupletissimi veste distinguuntur non fluitante,
sicut Sarmatae ac Parthi, sed stricta et singulos artus expri-
2 mente. gerunt et ferarum pelles, proximi ripae neglegenter, 10
ulteriores exquisitius, ut quibus nullus per commercia cultus.
eligunt feras et detracta velamina spargunt maculis pellibusque beluarum, quas exterior Oceanus atque ignotum mare
3 gignit. nec alius feminis quam viris habitus, nisi quod
feminae saepius lineis amictibus velantur eosque purpura 15
variant, partemque vestitus superioris in manicas non extendunt, nudae brachia ac lacertos ; sed et proxima pars
pectoris patet.

18 Quamquam severa illic matrimonia, nec ullam morum
partem magis laudaveris. nam prope soli barbarorum sin- 20
gulis uxoribus contenti sunt, exceptis admodum paucis, qui
non libidine sed ob nobilitatem plurimis nuptiis ambiuntur.
2 dotem non uxor marito, sed uxori maritus offert. intersunt parentes et propinqui ac munera probant, munera non
ad delicias muliebres quaesita nec quibus nova nupta 25
comatur, sed boves et frenatum equum et scutum cum
3 framea gladioque. in haec munera uxor accipitur, atque
in vicem ipsa armorum aliquid viro adfert : hoc maximum
vinculum, haec arcana sacra, hos coniugales deos arbitran-
4 tur. ne se mulier extra virtutum cogitationes extraque 30
bellorum casus putet, ipsis incipientis matrimonii auspiciis

2 hiemis *Reifferscheid* : hiemi *codd.*   3 locis *codd.* : loci *Acida-*
lius, lacus *Bährens*   4 autem *secl. Muretus*   16 superiorem
P. Voss   22 pluribus *Halm*   24 munera *priore loco secl. Lach-*
mann, posteriore Bernhardy

admonetur venire se laborum periculorumque sociam, idem
in pace, idem in proelio passuram ausuramque: hoc iuncti
boves, hoc paratus equus, hoc data arma denuntiant. sic
vivendum, sic pariendum : accipere se quae liberis inviolata
5 ac digna reddat, quae nurus accipiant rursusque ad nepotes
referantur.

Ergo saepta pudicitia agunt, nullis spectaculorum ille- 19
cebris, nullis conviviorum irritationibus corruptae. litterarum secreta viri pariter ac feminae ignorant. paucissima 2
10 in tam numerosa gente adulteria, quorum poena praesens
et maritis permissa : abscisis crinibus nudatam coram propinquis expellit domo maritus ac per omnem vicum verbere
agit ; publicatae enim pudicitiae nulla venia : non forma,
non aetate, non opibus maritum invenerit. nemo enim 3
15 illic vitia ridet, nec corrumpere et corrumpi saeculum
vocatur. melius quidem adhuc eae civitates, in quibus
tantum virgines nubunt et cum spe votoque uxoris semel
transigitur. sic unum accipiunt maritum quo modo unum 4
corpus unamque vitam, ne ulla cogitatio ultra, ne longior
20 cupiditas, ne tamquam maritum sed tamquam matrimonium
ament. numerum liberorum finire aut quemquam ex 5
agnatis necare flagitium habetur, plusque ibi boni mores
valent quam alibi bonae leges.

In omni domo nudi ac sordidi in hos artus, in haec 20
25 corpora, quae miramur, excrescunt. sua quemque mater
uberibus alit, nec ancillis ac nutricibus delegantur. domi- 2
num ac servum nullis educationis deliciis dignoscas : inter
eadem pecora, in eadem humo degunt, donec aetas separet

4 vivendum] nubendum *Bährens*   pariendum *WmhVN*Δ :
pereundum *L, al. quattuor*   inviolata reddat ac digna quae *Acida-*
lius   5 rursus quae *N*Δ*Is*   7 saeptae *Croll*   11 abscisis
WmEs : adcisis *V*: accisis *N*Δ*IL*   13 enim] enimvero *Madvig*:
etiam *Lips.* : enim *secl. Nipperdey*   14 invenit *NI* : leniverit
Kraffert   20 ne tam maritum quam matrimonium *Meiser*: ne
tamquam matrimonium sed tamquam maritum *Grotius*   26 ac]
aut *mVL*Δ

3 ingenuos, virtus agnoscat. sera iuvenum venus, eoque
inexhausta pubertas. nec virgines festinantur; eadem
iuventa, similis proceritas : pares validaeque miscentur, ac
4 robora parentum liberi referunt. sororum filiis idem apud
avunculum qui apud patrem honor. quidam sanctiorem artio- 5
remque hunc nexum sanguinis arbitrantur et in accipiendis
obsidibus magis exigunt, tamquam et animum firmius et
5 domum latius teneant. heredes tamen successoresque sui
cuique liberi, et nullum testamentum. si liberi non sunt,
proximus gradus in possessione fratres, patrui, avunculi. 10
quanto plus propinquorum, quanto maior adfinium numerus,
tanto gratiosior senectus ; nec ulla orbitatis pretia.

21 Suscipere tam inimicitias seu patris seu propinqui quam
amicitias necesse est. nec implacabiles durant : luitur enim
etiam homicidium certo armentorum ac pecorum numero 15
recipitque satisfactionem universa domus, utiliter in publicum, quia periculosiores sunt inimicitiae iuxta libertatem.

2 Convictibus et hospitiis non alia gens effusius indulget.
quemcumque mortalium arcere tecto nefas habetur ; pro
fortuna quisque apparatis epulis excipit. cum defecere, qui 20
modo hospes fuerat, monstrator hospitii et comes ; proximam
3 domum non invitati adeunt. nec interest : pari humanitate
accipiuntur. notum ignotumque quantum ad ius hospitis
nemo discernit. abeunti, si quid poposcerit, concedere
moris ; et poscendi in vicem eadem facilitas. gaudent 25
muneribus, sed nec data imputant nec acceptis obligantur.
[victus inter hospites comis.]

22 Statim e somno, quem plerumque in diem extrahunt,
lavantur, saepius calida, ut apud quos plurimum hiems

5 apud *L, Rhen.*: ad *cett.*   7 et animum *m et s.l. h* : et in
animum *cett.* (in *ex v.* 6 *repetitum*)   11 quanto (*posteriore loco*)
cod Urb. in mg., Halm : quo *L in litura, N²h²* : tanto *cett.*   12
gratior *mhΔ, s.l. VN, in mg.* E   13 seu . . . propinqui *om. I*
18 aliqua *VL*   27 comis *V*: communis *Longolius* : vinclum inter
hospitcs comitas *Lachmann* : victus . . . comis *secl. de la Bleterie*
28 e] enim *VL¹E*

occupat. lauti cibum capiunt : separatae singulis sedes et
sua cuique mensa. tum ad negotia nec minus saepe ad
convivia procedunt armati. diem noctemque continuare 2
potando nulli probrum. crebrae, ut inter vinolentos, rixae
5 raro conviciis, saepius caede et vulneribus transiguntur.
sed et de reconciliandis invicem inimicis et iungendis 3
adfinitatibus et adsciscendis principibus, de pace denique ac
bello plerumque in conviviis consultant, tamquam nullo
magis tempore aut ad simplices cogitationes pateat animus
10 aut ad magnas incalescat. gens non astuta nec callida 4
aperit adhuc secreta pectoris licentia loci ; ergo detecta
et nuda omnium mens. postera die retractatur, et salva
utriusque temporis ratio est : deliberant dum fingere ne-
sciunt, constituunt dum errare non possunt.

15 Potui humor ex hordeo aut frumento, in quandam similitu- 23
dinem vini corruptus ; proximi ripae et vinum mercantur.
cibi simplices, agrestia poma, recens fera aut lac concretum :
sine apparatu, sine blandimentis expellunt famem. adversus
sitim non eadem temperantia. si indulseris ebrietati sugge- 2
20 rendo quantum concupiscunt, haud minus facile vitiis quam
armis vincentur.

Genus spectaculorum unum atque in omni coetu idem : 24
nudi iuvenes, quibus id ludicrum est, inter gladios se atque
infestas frameas saltu iaciunt. exercitatio artem paravit, 2
25 ars decorem, non in quaestum tamen aut mercedem : quamvis audacis lasciviae pretium est voluptas spectantium.
alcam, quod mirere, sobrii inter seria exercent, tanta lucrandi 3
perdendive temeritate, ut, cum omnia defecerunt, extremo
ac novissimo iactu de libertate ac de corpore contendant.
30 victus voluntariam servitutem adit : quamvis iuvenior, 4
quamvis robustior, alligari se ac venire patitur. ea est in re

6 sed et *mhVLE* : et *om. permulti codd.* 11 ad hec *VL* : ad hoc
s (*corr. s²*) loci *Wmhs et s.l. VL* : ioci *cett. et s.l. W* 12 res
retractatur *Meiser* 24 parat *Is, al.* 25 mercede *I* 26
spectantium *LE, al.* : expectantium *cett.*

prava pervicacia; ipsi fidem vocant. servos condicionis huius per commercia tradunt, ut se quoque pudore victoriae exsolvant.

25 Ceteris servis non in nostrum morem descriptis per familiam ministeriis utuntur: suam quisque sedem, suos 5 penates regit. frumenti modum dominus aut pecoris aut vestis ut colono iniungit, et servus hactenus paret; cetera 2 domus officia uxor ac liberi exequuntur. verberare servum ac vinculis et opere coercere rarum: occidere solent, non disciplina et severitate, sed impetu et ira, ut inimicum, nisi 10 3 quod impune est. liberti non multum supra servos sunt, raro aliquod momentum in domo, numquam in civitate, exceptis dumtaxat iis gentibus quae regnantur. ibi enim et super ingenuos et super nobiles ascendunt: apud ceteros impares libertini libertatis argumentum sunt. 15

26 Faenus agitare et in usuras extendere ignotum; ideoque magis servatur quam si vetitum esset. agri pro numero cultorum ab universis in vices occupantur, quos mox inter se secundum dignationem partiuntur; facilitatem partiendi 2 camporum spatia praestant. arva per annos mutant, et super- 20 est ager. nec enim cum ubertate et amplitudine soli labore contendunt, ut pomaria conserant, ut prata separent, ut hortos 3 rigent: sola terrae seges imperatur. unde annum quoque ipsum non in totidem digerunt species: hiems et ver et aestas intellectum ac vocabula habent, autumni perinde 25 nomen ac bona ignorantur.

4 ceterum *Ed. Wolff* descriptis *codd.*: discriptis *Reifferscheid* 7 ut] aut *Wm*Δ et] ut *VL* (*corr. s.l.*) *E* 11 liberti . . . argumentum sunt, *in VL hic omissa, in fine capitis 26 inseruntur: eadem verba* (*omissis per incuriam* et super ingenuos) *L hic etiam in inferiore margine habet, cum adnotatione* in hoc loco potius 13 iis] his *WhE, al.*: is *Robinson* regnant *Wmhs*[2] 18 in vices *VE*: invicem *L*: vices *WmNIs*: vice *hs*[a] *et in mg. W*: secl. *Halm*: vicis *Waitz, cum codice* (*ut traditur*) *Bambergensi, qui nunc latet vel deperditus est*: per vicos *Pichena*: vicinis *Hildebrand* 20 praebent *hN*Δ*L et in mg. vel s.l.* Ws*VE* 21 laborare (*in mg. vel s.l.* labore) *WLE, in mg. V, s.l.* N 22 ut prata *Mützell*: et prata *codd.* et hortos *I, al.* 25 proinde *Wm*

Funerum nulla ambitio: id solum observatur ut corpora **27**
clarorum virorum certis lignis crementur. struem rogi nec **2**
vestibus nec odoribus cumulant: sua cuique arma, quorundam igni et equus adicitur. sepulcrum caespes erigit:
5 monumentorum arduum et operosum honorem ut gravem
defunctis aspernantur. lamenta ac lacrimas cito, dolorem
et tristitiam tarde ponunt. feminis lugere honestum est,
viris meminisse.

Haec in commune de omnium Germanorum origine ac **3**
10 moribus accepimus: nunc singularum gentium instituta
ritusque quatenus differant, quaeque nationes e Germania
in Gallias commigraverint, expediam.

Validiores olim Gallorum res fuisse summus auctorum **28**
divus Iulius tradit; eoque credibile est etiam Gallos in
15 Germaniam transgressos. quantulum enim amnis obstabat
quo minus, ut quaeque gens evaluerat, occuparet permutaretque sedes promiscas adhuc et nulla regnorum potentia
divisas! igitur inter Hercyniam silvam Rhenumque et **2**
Moenum amnes Helvetii, ulteriora Boii, Gallica utraque
20 gens, tenuere. manet adhuc Boihaemi nomen signat-
que loci veterem memoriam quamvis mutatis cultoribus.
sed utrum Aravisci in Pannoniam ab Osis [Germanorum **3**
natione] an Osi ab Araviscis in Germaniam commigraverint, cum eodem adhuc sermone institutis moribus
5 utantur, incertum est, quia pari olim inopia ac libertate
eadem utriusque ripae bona malaque erant. Treveri et **4**
Nervii circa adfectationem Germanicae originis ultro ambi-
tiosi sunt, tamquam per hanc gloriam sanguinis a similitudine et inertia Gallorum separentur. ipsam Rheni ripam

11 quae *codd.*: quaeque *Halm*: quae . . . commigraverint *secl.*
Reifferscheid   18 igitur ⟨quantum⟩ *Wölfflin*   Hercuniam *W*: her-
cinam *I*: hercynam *N*: hircyniam *VL*[1]   20 Boihemi *VL*[2]*IE*: boiihemi
h: bohemi *N*: boiihaemionem *W* (Boiiemionem *V in mg.*)   signat-
que *WmhN*Δ*Ls*[2]: significatque *cett.*   22 ab osis *L in mg., al.*:
a boiis, a bois *cett.*   Germanorum natione *secl. Passow*   27 Neruii
Rhen.: neruli (*s.l.* heruli *L*) *cett.*

haud dubie Germanorum populi colunt, Vangiones, Triboci,
5 Nemetes. ne Ubii quidem, quamquam Romana colonia
esse meruerint ac libentius Agrippinenses conditoris sui
nomine vocentur, origine erubescunt, transgressi olim et
experimento fidei super ipsam Rheni ripam collocati, ut 5
arcerent, non ut custodirentur.

29 Omnium harum gentium virtute praecipui Batavi non
multum ex ripa, sed insulam Rheni amnis colunt, Chattorum quondam populus et seditione domestica in eas sedes
2 transgressus in quibus pars Romani imperii fierent. manet 10
honos et antiquae societatis insigne; nam nec tributis con-
temnuntur nec publicanus atterit; exempti oneribus et
collationibus et tantum in usum proeliorum sepositi, velut
3 tela atque arma, bellis reservantur. est in eodem obsequio
et Mattiacorum gens; protulit enim magnitudo populi 15
Romani ultra Rhenum ultraque veteres terminos imperii
reverentiam. ita sede finibusque in sua ripa, mente animoque nobiscum agunt, cetera similes Batavis, nisi quod ipso
adhuc terrae suae solo et caelo acrius animantur.

4 Non numeraverim inter Germaniae populos, quamquam 20
trans Rhenum Danuviumque consederint, eos qui Decumates
agros exercent: levissimus quisque Gallorum et inopia
audax dubiae possessionis solum occupavere; mox limite
acto promotisque praesidiis sinus imperii et pars provinciae
habentur. 25

30 Ultra hos Chatti initium sedis ab Hercynio saltu incohant,
non ita effusis ac palustribus locis ut ceterae civitates in quas
Germania patescit, durant siquidem colles, paulatim rarescunt, et Chattos suos saltus Hercynius prosequitur simul

2 ne Ubii *Gruter*: nubii *codd.*: Ubii *L in mg.*   7 batavi *L et
corr. Wh*: batavii *VNIE*   8 cattorum *V¹L*, cathorum *E* (*et sic
ubique LE*); *cf. c.* 30   13 collocationibus *WΔ* (*in mg.* collationibus *W*) *et in mg. VE, s.l. N*   18 quod hi ipso *Riese*   21 decu-
mathes *VENhs*: de eumathes *W*   26 catti *WmhsΔIL*   hercynio
(*in mg.* herquinio *W*) *WE*: herquinio *mh*: hircynio *V*: hircinio (e
s.l.) *L*: hercinio *NI*   incohatur *V*   28 durant. siquidem *codd.*

atque deponit. duriora genti corpora, stricti artus, minax 2
vultus et maior animi vigor. multum, ut inter Germanos,
rationis ac sollertiae : praeponere electos, audire praepositos,
nosse ordines, intellegere occasiones, differre impetus, dis-
5 ponere diem, vallare noctem, fortunam inter dubia, virtutem
inter certa numerare, quodque rarissimum nec nisi Romanae
disciplinae concessum, plus reponere in duce quam in
exercitu. omne robur in pedite, quem super arma ferra- 3
mentis quoque et copiis onerant : alios ad proelium ire
10 videas, Chattos ad bellum. rari excursus et fortuita pugna.
equestrium sane virium id proprium, cito parare victoriam,
cito cedere : (peditum) velocitas iuxta formidinem, cunctatio propior constantiae est.

Et aliis Germanorum populis usurpatum raro et privata 31
15 cuiusque audentia apud Chattos in consensum vertit, ut
primum adoleverint, crinem barbamque submittere, nec nisi
hoste caeso exuere votivum obligatumque virtuti oris habitum. super sanguinem et spolia revelant frontem, seque 2
tum demum pretia nascendi rettulisse dignosque patria ac
20 parentibus ferunt ; ignavis et imbellibus manet squalor.
fortissimus quisque ferreum insuper anulum (ignominiosum 3
id genti) velut vinculum gestat, donec se caede hostis
absolvat. plurimis Chattorum hic placet habitus, iamque 4
canent insignes et hostibus simul suisque monstrati.
25 omnium penes hos initia pugnarum ; haec prima semper
acies, visu nova : nam ne in pace quidem vultu mitiore
mansuescunt. nulli domus aut ager aut aliqua cura : prout 5
ad quemque venere, aluntur, prodigi alieni, contemptores

1 atque] ac *VL*   2 animis *Wh*   3 rationis] romanis *I*   6
Romanae] ratione *N*Δ*L*² (rōe *IE*)   10 raro *hN*Δ*I et W s.l.*   12 peditum *suppl. Bährens,* ceteris *Eussner*   13 propior *VL* : propiora
*N*Δ*I* : propriora *Wm* : propior a constantia *Robinson*   14 rara *plerique codd. aut in textu aut in mg. vel s.l.*   19 noscendi *V¹LI, E
s.l., al.*   23 hic] et hic *W   post* habitus *lacunam statuit Robinson* :
plurimisque eorum hic *Weidner*   26 uultu *VLE et h(?)* : cultu
*WmN*Δ*Is*

sui, donec exsanguis senectus tam durae virtuti impares
faciat.

32 Proximi Chattis certum iam alveo Rhenum quique
2 terminus esse sufficiat Usipi ac Tencteri colunt. Tencteri
super solitum bellorum decus equestris disciplinae arte 5
praecellunt ; nec maior apud Chattos peditum laus quam
3 Tencteris equitum. sic instituere maiores, posteri imitantur. hi lusus infantium, haec iuvenum aemulatio : perseve-
4 rant senes. inter familiam et penates et iura successionum
equi traduntur : excipit filius, non ut cetera, maximus natu, 10
sed prout ferox bello et melior.

33 Iuxta Tencteros Bructeri olim occurrebant : nunc Chamavos et Angrivarios immigrasse narratur, pulsis Bructeris
ac penitus excisis vicinarum consensu nationum, seu super-
biae odio seu praedae dulcedine seu favore quodam erga 15
nos deorum ; nam ne spectaculo quidem proelii invidere.
2 super sexaginta milia non armis telisque Romanis, sed,
quod magnificentius est, oblectationi oculisque ceciderunt.
maneat, quaeso, duretque gentibus, si non amor nostri,
at certe odium sui, quando urgentibus imperii fatis nihil 20
iam praestare fortuna maius potest quam hostium dis-
cordiam.

34 Angrivarios et Chamavos a tergo Dulgubnii et Chasuarii
claudunt aliaeque gentes haud perinde memoratae, a fronte
Frisii excipiunt. maioribus minoribusque Frisiis vocabulum 25
est ex modo virium. utraeque nationes usque ad Oceanum
Rheno praetexuntur ambiuntque immensos insuper lacus et
2 Romanis classibus navigatos. ipsum quin etiam Oceanum
illa temptavimus ; et superesse adhuc Herculis columnas

---

4 accolunt *Novák*   13 anguiuarios *I* : angrinarios *L*   20 urgentibus *Rhen.* : in urgentibus *N∆I* : in gentibus *Wmhs*, ingentibus *N s.l.* :
urgentibus iam *VLE* : ingruentibus *Wölfflin*   23 Dulgubnii *Iac.*
Grimm : dulgibini, dulcubuni, dulgicubini, &c. *codd.*   Chasuarii :
nomen varie corruptum habent VLNIE   24 cludunt *codd.* (*praeter s*)
25 frisi . . . frisis *WmhN∆ et L corr.* (frisis *VEs*)

fama vulgavit, sive adiit Hercules, seu quicquid ubique
magnificum est, in claritatem eius referre consensimus. nec 3
defuit audentia Druso Germanico, sed obstitit Oceanus in
se simul atque in Herculem inquiri. mox nemo temptavit,
5 sanctiusque ac reverentius visum de actis deorum credere
quam scire.

Hactenus in occidentem Germaniam novimus; in sep- 35
tentrionem ingenti flexu recedit. ac primo statim Chaucorum
gens, quamquam incipiat a Frisiis ac partem litoris occupet,
10 omnium quas exposui gentium lateribus obtenditur, donec
in Chattos usque sinuetur. tam immensum terrarum 2
spatium non tenent tantum Chauci sed et implent, populus
inter Germanos nobilissimus quique magnitudinem suam
malit iustitia tueri. sine cupiditate, sine impotentia, quieti 3
15 secretique nulla provocant bella, nullis raptibus aut latrociniis populantur. id praecipuum virtutis ac virium argu- 4
mentum est, quod, ut superiores agant, non per iniurias
adsequuntur; prompta tamen omnibus arma ac, si res poscat,
exercitus, plurimum virorum equorumque; et quiescen-
20 tibus eadem fama.

In latere Chaucorum Chattorumque Cherusci nimiam ac 36
marcentem diu pacem inlacessiti nutrierunt; idque iucun-
dius quam tutius fuit, quia inter impotentes et validos falso
quiescas : ubi manu agitur, modestia ac probitas nomina
25 superioris sunt. ita qui olim boni aequique Cherusci, nunc 2
inertes ac stulti vocantur; Chattis victoribus fortuna in
sapientiam cessit. tracti ruina Cheruscorum et Fosi, con- 3
termina gens, adversarum rerum ex aequo socii sunt, cum in
secundis minores fuissent.

2 magnum *VE* (*L*[1] *sed corr.*) 3 Druso et Germanico *Freinsheim* :
Druso, Neroni, Germanico *Gruver* : Drusi Germanico, *R. Borchardt*
8 recedit *C. Heraeus* : redit *codd.* 9 Frisis *codd.* 10 obten-
dere *NΔI* 11 sinuetur] sinatur *NΔI, in mg. WhE* nam *VL*[1]
19 exercitus *secl. Walch* : exercitui *Heraeus* plurimorum *Gude-*
man : plurimum enim *Reifferscheid* 24 nomina *Put.*: nomine
codd.: nomina superiori *Heinsius* 27 tracti *WmhNΔs*[2] : tacti *cett.*

37 Eundem Germaniae sinum proximi Oceano Cimbri tenent, parva nunc civitas, sed gloria ingens. veterisque famae lata vestigia manent, utraque ripa castra ac spatia, quorum ambitu nunc quoque metiaris molem manusque gentis et **2** tam magni exitus fidem. sescentesimum et quadragesimum 5 annum urbs nostra agebat, cum primum Cimbrorum audita sunt arma Caecilio Metello ac Papirio Carbone consulibus. ex quo si ad alterum imperatoris Traiani consulatum computemus, ducenti ferme et decem anni colliguntur : tam diu **3** Germania vincitur. medio tam longi aevi spatio multa in 10 vicem damna. non Samnis, non Poeni, non Hispaniae Galliaeve, ne Parthi quidem saepius admonuere : quippe **4** regno Arsacis acrior est Germanorum libertas. quid enim aliud nobis quam caedem Crassi, amisso et ipse Pacoro, **5** infra Ventidium deiectus Oriens obiecerit? at Germani 15 Carbone et Cassio et Scauro Aurelio et Servilio Caepione Maximoque Mallio fusis vel captis quinque simul consulares exercitus populo Romano, Varum tresque cum eo legiones etiam Caesari abstulerunt; nec impune C. Marius in Italia, divus Iulius in Gallia, Drusus ac Nero et Germanicus in 20 suis eos sedibus perculerunt : mox ingentes C. Caesaris **6** minae in ludibrium versae. inde otium, donec occasione discordiae nostrae et civilium armorum expugnatis legionum hibernis etiam Gallias adfectavere, ac rursus pulsi ; nam proximis temporibus triumphati magis quam victi sunt. 25 **38** Nunc de Suebis dicendum est, quorum non una ut Chattorum Tencterorumve gens ; maiorem enim Germaniae partem obtinent, propriis adhuc nationibus nominibusque **2** discreti, quamquam in commune Suebi vocentur. insigne

1 situm VLE   4 ambitu L, al., s.l. VE : ambitum cett.   7 ac] et VLE   14 et ipse WmhΔ, al. : et ipso et ipse cett.   17 Maximoque F. Frahm (Herm. lxix. 434) : Marcoque vel Marco quoque codd. : Cn. quoque Ernesti : Gnaeoque Halm   Mallio E : Malio m : Manlio (vel Manilio) cett.   18 populo ro. L² : po. ro. IV : populi romani VLNΔIEs   25 nam WmhsNΔ, s.l. V, in mg. E : inde VLIE   26 sueuis codd. et sic deinceps   29 quam VLE, quamvis L²

gentis obliquare crinem nodoque substringere : sic Suebi a
ceteris Germanis, sic Sueborum ingenui a servis separantur.
in aliis gentibus seu cognatione aliqua Sueborum seu, quod 3
saepius accidit, imitatione, rarum et intra iuventae spatium :
5 apud Suebos usque ad canitiem horrentes capilli retorquentur, ac saepe in ipso vertice religantur. principes et 4
ornatiorem habent : ea cura formae, sed innoxia ; neque
enim ut ament amenturve, in altitudinem quandam et terrorem adituri bella compti [ut] hostium oculis ornantur.
10 Vetustissimos nobilissimosque Sueborum Semnones memo- 39
rant ; fides antiquitatis religione firmatur. stato tempore in 2
silvam auguriis patrum et prisca formidine sacram (eiusdem)
nominis eiusdemque sanguinis populi legationibus coeunt
caesoque publice homine celebrant barbari ritus horrenda
15 primordia. est et alia luco reverentia : nemo nisi vinculo 3
ligatus ingreditur, ut minor et potestatem numinis prae se
ferens. si forte prolapsus est, attolli et insurgere haud
licitum : per humum evolvuntur. eoque omnis superstitio 4
respicit, tamquam inde initia gentis, ibi regnator omnium
20 deus, cetera subiecta atque parentia. adicit auctoritatem
fortuna Semnonum : centum pagis habitant, magnoque
corpore efficitur ut se Sueborum caput credant.

4 saepius *Wmh* : saepe *cett.*   5 horrentem capillum *codd., corr.*
Gudeman   (capilli) retorquentur *Much* : retro sequuntur *codd.* :
retorquent *Madvig* : retrorsum agunt *Haupt*   6 ipso *msL* : solo
(ipso *s.l.*) *V*, solo (ipso *in mg.*) *E*, solo *s.l. L* : ipso solo *WhNΔI*
religant *mhs²*. rei ligant *W* : religatur *VLE* : ligant *NΔIs*   7 orna-
torem *Wmhs²N*   innoxia *Muretus* : innoxiae (inopiae *I, al.*) *codd.*
9 adituri bella *ante* in altitudinem *transp. Acidalius*   ut *secl. Halm* :
compti et *N* : comptius *Lachmann*   ornantur *NILs² et s.l. vel in mg.*
WVE : armantur *WmsVEΔ et s.l. NL*   10 vetustissimos *Ns* :
vetustissimos seu *Wmhs²* : vetustissimos se *VLEΔI*   semnones *hs²Δ*
et in mg. vel s.l. WVLNE : semones, senones *cett.*   11 statuto, *in mg.*
stato *E*, statuto *m*   12 eiusdem *post* nominis *add. Robinson, trans-*
posui   13 nominis Δ, *al.* : omnis, *in mg. vel s.l.* nominis, *WhN* : omnis
ms²I : omnes, *s.l. vel in mg.* nominis l' numinis, *VE* : omnes *L*   eius-
demque] eiusdem *NΔILs (corr. s²)*   21 habitant *Ernesti* : habitantur
codd. : pagi iis habitantur *Brotier*   22 corpore] tempore *in mg. vel*
s.l. WVLE, in textu hs²Δ

40 Contra Langobardos paucitas nobilitat: plurimis ac valentissimis nationibus cincti non per obsequium sed proeliis et periclitando tuti sunt. Reudigni deinde et Aviones et Anglii et Varini et Eudoses et Suarines et 2 Nuitones fluminibus aut silvis muniuntur. nec quicquam 5 notabile in singulis, nisi quod in commune Nerthum, id est Terram matrem, colunt eamque intervenire rebus hominum, invehi populis arbitrantur. est in insula Oceani castum nemus, dicatumque in eo vehiculum, veste contectum; 3 attingere uni sacerdoti concessum. is adesse penetrali 10 deam intellegit vectamque bubus feminis multa cum veneratione prosequitur. laeti tunc dies, festa loca, quaecumque 4 adventu hospitioque dignatur. non bella ineunt, non arma sumunt; clausum omne ferrum; pax et quies tunc tantum nota, tunc tantum amata, donec idem sacerdos satiatam 15 5 conversatione mortalium deam templo reddat. mox vehiculum et vestis et, si credere velis, numen ipsum secreto lacu abluitur. servi ministrant, quos statim idem lacus haurit. arcanus hinc terror sanctaque ignorantia, quid sit illud quod tantum perituri vident. 20

41 Et haec quidem pars Sueborum in secretiora Germaniae porrigitur: propior, ut, quo modo paulo ante Rhenum, sic nunc Danuvium sequar, Hermundurorum civitas, fida Romanis; eoque solis Germanorum non in ripa commercium, sed penitus atque in splendidissima Raetiae provinciae 25 2 colonia. passim sine custode transeunt; et cum ceteris gentibus arma modo castraque nostra ostendamus, his

1 Langobardos *s.l. hs*: largobardos (longo-) *cett.* 3 et] ac *mhVLE* Reudigni] Veusdigni *VL* (*in L R s.l.*) 4 Suarines *VLNΔIWE*: suardones *s.l. WL, E in mg., al.*: suarines seu suardones *s* 5 Nuitones *L² et cod. Ariminensis*: Nuithones *VNΔIE*: Nurchones *W*: Vuithones *hs²*: Nurtones *L*: Huitones *septem codd. dett.* 6 Nerthum] Neithum *VL*: Nertum *E* 9 eo *Rhen.*: ea *codd.* 15 nota] inmota *Freudenberg* 17 vestis *Andresen*: vestes *codd.* 21 Sueborum] verborum *codd., corr. ed. Vindob., cod. Urb.* 412 *in mg., Rhen.* 22 proprior *WmhN et s.l. VE* 26 et sine *NI*

domos villasque patefecimus non concupiscentibus. in
Hermunduris Albis oritur, flumen inclutum et notum olim ;
nunc tantum auditur.

Iuxta Hermunduros Naristi ac deinde Marcomani et 42
5 Quadi agunt. praecipua Marcomanorum gloria viresque,
atque ipsa etiam sedes pulsis olim Boiis virtute parta. nec
Naristi Quadive degenerant. eaque Germaniae velut frons
est, quatenus Danuvio praecingitur. Marcomanis Quadis- 2
que usque ad nostram memoriam reges manserunt ex gente
10 ipsorum, nobile Marobodui et Tudri genus (iam et externos
patiuntur), sed vis et potentia regibus ex auctoritate Romana.
raro armis nostris, saepius pecunia iuvantur, nec minus
valent.

Retro Marsigni, Cotini, Osi, Buri terga Marcomanorum 43
15 Quadorumque claudunt. e quibus Marsigni et Buri sermone cultuque Suebos referunt : Cotinos Gallica, Osos
Pannonica lingua coarguit non esse Germanos, et quod
tributa patiuntur. partem tributorum Sarmatae, partem 2
Quadi ut alienigenis imponunt : Cotini, quo magis pudeat,
20 et ferrum effodiunt. omnesque hi populi pauca cam-
pestrium, ceterum saltus et vertices montium [iugumque]
insederunt. dirimit enim scinditque Suebiam continuum 3
montium iugum, ultra quod plurimae gentes agunt, ex
quibus latissime patet Lugiorum nomen in plures civitates
25 diffusum. valentissimas nominasse sufficiet, Harios, Helveconas, Manimos, Helisios, Naharvalos. apud Naharvalos 4

4 Narisci (No- s) *Ems, L in mg.*: Varisti *Müllenhoff*   Marcomanni
L.[1]   5 marcomannorum *LWs*   6 Boiis *Lms* : Bois *cett.*   parata
VL   8 praecingitur *Tagmann* : peragitur *codd.*   14 Gotini *et v.* 16
Gotinos *codd. sed v.* 19 Cotini *mNΔI* : *corr. Müllenhoff*   21 iugumque *secl. Acidalius* : montium iugumque *del. Reifferscheid* : *an* montium
v. 23 *delendum ? Andresen*   24 Lugiorum] legiorum (vegiorum
in mg. W, s.l. N) WN : leugiorum *I* : Le'giorum *VE* : le'giorum *L*
25 Helvaeonas *Müllenhoff*   26 Helisios (El-*L*) *mhsLE* : helysios
WVNΔI (var. lect. haliosnas *Ws*[2], halisiosnas *V*, halisionas *E*)   Naharvalos *priore loco L, V s.l., E in mg.* : nahanarvalos *cett.* ; *posteriore loco*
Nahanarvalos Δ *Turicensis* : naharvalos *cett.*

antiquae religionis lucus ostenditur. praesidet sacerdos muliebri ornatu, sed deos interpretatione Romana Castorem Pollucemque memorant. ea vis numini, nomen Alcis. nulla simulacra, nullum peregrinae superstitionis vestigium ; 5 ut fratres tamen, ut iuvenes venerantur. ceterum Harii 5 super vires, quibus enumeratos paulo ante populos antecedunt, truces insitae feritati arte ac tempore lenocinantur: nigra scuta, tincta corpora ; atras ad proelia noctes legunt ipsaque formidine atque umbra feralis exercitus terrorem inferunt, nullo hostium sustinente novum ac velut infernum 10 aspectum ; nam primi in omnibus proeliis oculi vincuntur.

6 Trans Lugios Gotones regnantur, paulo iam adductius quam ceterae Germanorum gentes, nondum tamen supra libertatem. protinus deinde ab Oceano Rugii et Lemovii; omniumque harum gentium insigne rotunda scuta, breves 15 gladii et erga reges obsequium.

44 Suionum hinc civitates, ipso in Oceano, praeter viros armaque classibus valent. forma navium eo differt quod utrimque prora paratam semper adpulsui frontem agit. nec velis ministrant nec remos in ordinem lateribus adiungunt: 20 solutum, ut in quibusdam fluminum, et mutabile, ut res 2 poscit, hinc vel illinc remigium. est apud illos et opibus honos, eoque unus imperitat, nullis iam exceptionibus, non 3 precario iure parendi. nec arma, ut apud ceteros Germanos, in promisco, sed clausa sub custode, et quidem servo, quia 25 subitos hostium incursus prohibet Oceanus, otiosae porro armatorum manus facile lasciviunt: enimvero neque nobilem neque ingenuum, ne libertinum quidem armis praeponere regia utilitas est.

1 religionis *VLEsh(?)*: regionis *cett.*   5 arii *s et Turicensis in mg.*: alii *cett.*   7 trucis *codd.*, *corr. Beroaldus*   12 Lygios (Li- *mL*) *codd.*   Gothones *codd. fere omnes*   regnantur *N∆*: regnant *cett.* 14 Lemovii *WVL²N∆I*: Lemonii *cett.*   17 ipse (ipsae) *VLE*   20 ministrant *Lips.*: ministrantur *codd.*   23 non] nec *N∆I*   24 parendi] imperandi *Passow*   25 promisco *WmN∆*: promiscuo *cett.* 26 otiosae *Colerus*: ociose *W*, ociosa (otiosa *N*) *cett.*

GERMANIA

Trans Suionas aliud mare, pigrum ac prope immotum, 45
quo cingi claudique terrarum orbem hinc fides, quod extremus cadentis iam solis fulgor in ortus edurat adeo clarus
ut sidera hebetet; sonum insuper emergentis audiri formas-
5 que equorum et radios capitis aspici persuasio adicit.
illuc usque et fama vera tantum natura. ergo iam dextro 2
Suebici maris litore Aestiorum gentes adluuntur, quibus
ritus habitusque Sueborum, lingua Britannicae propior.
matrem deum venerantur. insigne superstitionis formas 3
10 aprorum gestant: id pro armis hominumque tutela securum
deae cultorem etiam inter hostes praestat. rarus ferri,
frequens fustium usus. frumenta ceterosque fructus patien- 4
tius quam pro solita Germanorum inertia laborant. sed et
mare scrutantur, ac soli omnium sucinum, quod ipsi glesum
15 vocant, inter vada atque in ipso litore legunt. nec quae 5
natura quaeve ratio gignat, ut barbaris, quaesitum comper-
tumve; diu quin etiam inter cetera eiectamenta maris
iacebat, donec luxuria nostra dedit nomen. ipsis in nullo
usu: rude legitur, informe perfertur, pretiumque mirantes
20 accipiunt. sucum tamen arborum esse intellegas, quia 6
terrena quaedam atque etiam volucria animalia plerumque
interlucent, quae implicata humore mox durescente materia
clauduntur. fecundiora igitur nemora lucosque, sicut Orientis 7
secretis, ubi tura balsamaque sudantur, ita Occidentis insulis
25 terrisque inesse crediderim, quae vicini solis radiis expressa
atque liquentia in proximum mare labuntur ac vi tempesta-
tum in adversa litora exundant. si naturam sucini admoto 8

1 suionos *W*, suiones *Lm*   2 cludique *WVLE*   3 ortum *VL*
5 equorum *cod. Urbinas in mg.*, *Colerus*: eorum, deorum *cett.*   6
usque tantum natura, et fama vera *Döderlein*   et] si *Grotius*   7
saeuici, *in mg. vel s.l.* sucuici *WVLNE*   8 proprior *mE*   10 hominumque *Urlich*: omnique *W²*, *Turicensis*, *Lips.*: omniumque *cett.*
14 glesum *codd.*: glacsum *Müllenhoff*   19 profertur *LE*   23
cluduntur *codd.*   et sicut *Mähly*   24 sudant *VL*   25 quae]
quâ *Detschew (Woch. kl. Phil. xxxv.* 237): solis quia sucina *Hofmann*:
radiis *WmNΔ*: radius *VLEIs*   27 exsudant *N et s.l. E*: exudant *IE*

igne temptes, in modum taedae accenditur alitque flammam
pinguem et olentem ; mox ut in picem resinamve lentescit.

9 Suionibus Sitonum gentes continuantur. cetera similes
uno differunt, quod femina dominatur : in tantum non modo
a libertate sed etiam a servitute degenerant. 5

46 Hic Suebiae finis. Peucinorum Venethorumque et Fennorum nationes Germanis an Sarmatis adscribam dubito.
quamquam Peucini, quos quidam Bastarnas vocant, sermone
cultu sede ac domiciliis ut Germani agunt. sordes omnium
ac torpor procerum : conubiis mixtis nonnihil in Sarma- 10
2 tarum habitum foedantur. Venethi multum ex moribus
traxerunt ; nam quidquid inter Peucinos Fennosque silvarum
ac montium erigitur latrociniis pererrant. hi tamen inter
Germanos potius referuntur, quia et domos figunt et scuta
gestant et pedum usu et pernicitate gaudent : quae omnia 15
diversa Sarmatis sunt in plaustro equoque viventibus.
3 Fennis mira feritas, foeda paupertas : non arma, non equi,
non penates ; victui herba, vestitui pelles, cubile humus :
solae in sagittis spes, quas inopia ferri ossibus asperant.
idemque venatus viros pariter ac feminas alit ; passim enim 20
4 comitantur partemque praedae petunt. nec aliud infantibus
ferarum imbriumque suffugium quam ut in aliquo ramorum
nexu contegantur ; huc redeunt iuvenes, hoc senum recep-
5 taculum. sed beatius arbitrantur quam ingemere agris,
inlaborare domibus, suas alienasque fortunas spe metuque 25
versare : securi adversus homines, securi adversus deos rem

1 igni *LNE* 3 Suionibus . . . 6 Suebiae finis *post finem c.* 44
ponenda, item Sitonas *c.* 45. 1 *legendum censuerunt ed. Bipontinus,*
Meiser, Müllenhoff, alii Sithonum *L* gens *VL (corr. L²)* continua-
tur *V* 6 finis *Put.* : fines *codd.* Peucurorum *hΔ, in mg. vel s.l.*
WVLN Venethorum *(WhVNs²) vel* Venetorum *codd., item v.* 11 :
Venedorum *Rhen.* 10 ac torpor procerum] ac torpor : ora pro-
cerum *C. Heraeus,* at corpora Peucinorum *Miitzell,* ac torpor : ora
Peucinorum *Halm olim* mixtis Δ *Turicensis* : mixtos *cett.* : mixti
Urbinas in mg. 14 figunt *VL* : fingunt *cett.* 15 pedum
Lips. : pecudum *VL¹* : peditum *cett.* 19 sola *Es Turicensis* opes
Meiser

difficillimam adsecuti sunt, ut illis ne voto quidem opus esset. cetera iam fabulosa: Hellusios et Oxionas ora 6 hominum vultusque, corpora atque artus ferarum gerere: quod ego ut incompertum in medio relinquam.

1 difficilem *VL*   2 oxionas *WhVLNE*: etionas *in mg. WE*, *s.l. VL*, Δ : exionas *Is*   3 et corpora *NΔIE*   4 medio *Halm*: medium *codd*.   Cornelii Taciti de origine et situ (moribus *E*) Germanorum liber explicit *WmVE*

NOTES

TITLE.—On the evidence of the Florentine humanist Niccolò Niccoli and several of the better MSS., 'De origine et situ Germanorum' must be accepted as the title of the work given by the Hersfeld MS., despite the fact that *Germaniae* was read by the papal secretary Decembrio. (On these humanists see Introd. to *Agricola*, p. xvi.) *De situ* was an established phrase for the description of a land and its people, and it was often combined with *origo* or *origines*, as may be seen from the instances collected by Norden, *Germ. Urgesch.*, p. 452. *Origo Germaniae* is in itself a possible expression: cp. Pomp. Trogus, *Prolog.* ii, *Scythiae et Ponti situs originesque Scythiae.*

PART I

GENERAL ACCOUNT OF THE LAND, THE PEOPLE, AND THEIR CUSTOMS AND INSTITUTIONS
(CC. 1–27)

CHAPTER I

THE BOUNDARIES OF GERMANY

§ **1. Germania omnis**, 'Germany as a whole', i.e. free Germany, excluding the territory on the west bank of the Rhine from Strassburg to the sea occupied by German tribes within the Roman provinces of Upper and Lower Germany. These Celticized and Romanized tribes are included among the *Galli*: something is said of them in c. 28 f. Similarly the opening phrase of Caesar's Gallic War, *Gallia omnis*, excludes the province of Gallia Narbonensis as well as Cisalpine Gaul; more precise is Pliny's *Gallia omnis Comata* (*N. H.* 4, 105). The formula was a stock one in ethnographic literature (examples in Norden, p. 324), a fact which rules out the idea that Tacitus' readers would recognize in *Germania omnis* a compliment to Caesar.

Raetisque et Pannoniis: *-que* joins to the Gauls on the Rhine frontier the two Danubian peoples coupled by *et*. The **Raeti**, whose language was perhaps Illyrian (with Celtic and Etruscan elements), occupied the central Alps—the Tirol and the adjoining part of east Switzerland as far as the St. Gotthard pass. Tacitus uses the name for all the inhabitants of the province of Raetia (cp. c. 3, 3 and 41, 1), which included also the predominantly Celtic Vindelicia, the Upper Bavarian plateau between the Alps and the Danube, and the territory held by Rome between the river and the *limes* (see c. 29, 4). The **Pannonii**, the most northerly branch of the Illyrian race (now represented by the Albanians), dwelt between the eastern Alps and the Danube; the Roman province of Pannonia bordered the river from Vienna to Belgrade and included the valleys of the rivers Drave and Save. The (mainly Celtic) province of Noricum (c. 5, 1), which lay between Raetia and Pannonia, is omitted by Tacitus in order to avoid overloading the description of the Danubian group of peoples contrasted with the Gauls.

Rheno et Danuvio . . . separatur. The actual frontier between Rome and Germany did not coincide with the rivers, but Tacitus knew that (c. 29), and here speaks broadly, as in *Ann.* I. 9 *mari Oceano aut amnibus longinquis saeptum imperium.* Cp. Sen. *Nat. Quaest.* 6. 7, 1 *qui medius inter pacata et hostilia fluit Danubius ac Rhenus,* and Appian, *praef.* 4. There is no reason to suppose that he is repeating an antiquated statement from Pliny's *Bella Germaniae,* a voluminous history of all the Roman wars with the Germans (Norden, p. 278), although the close resemblance of his description of the Danube to that of Pliny in *N. H.* 4, 79 indicates that here, as elsewhere, he had Pliny's work before him.

The river-names, Rhine and Danube, are of Celtic origin. *Danuvius* does not occur before Caesar: the name *Ister* or *Hister*, given to the river in its lower course, belongs to the language of the Thracians, from whom the Greeks and the Romans adopted it.

Sarmatis Dacisque. These are the eastern neighbours of the Germans. **Sarmatae** was a generic designation of various tribes of Iranian stock which from the second century B.C. moved steadily westward from central Asia into the steppes of south Russia. Their name supplanted that of the Scythians as a general designation of all the little known tribes (including the Slavonic) beyond the river Vistula (c. 46, 1; Mela iii. 25, 33; Pliny, *N. H.* 4, 80 f.; 8, 38). Before A.D. 50 an advance body, the Sarmatae Iazyges (see c. 43, 2), had established themselves at the expense of the Dacians in the great plain between the Theiss and the Danube (*Ann.* 12, 29; Pliny, *N. H.* 4, 80). *Sarmatae* here includes the inhabitants of both these regions, between which lay the Dacians.

The **Dacians**, a Thracian race closely akin to the Getae and often called by their name (especially in Greek sources), occupied the Transylvanian upland enclosed by the Carpathians and the adjoining country to west and south. They had been a serious menace to the Roman frontier under Domitian, who

made a discreditable peace with them nine years before the
publication of the *Germania*, but they were conquered by
Trajan in A.D. 106.

mutuo metu aut montibus, i.e. partly by the one, partly by
the other (cp. *fluminibus aut silvis*, c. 40, 1). The *montes* are
the Carpathians from the head waters of the Vistula south-
eastwards, which separated the Bastarnian group of tribes
(c. 46, 1) from the Dacians, and the mountains which bound
the Hungarian plain on the north-west between the bend of
the Danube and the head waters of the Theiss. 'Mutual fear'
is the psychological result of the open frontier in the plain of
the Vistula between the Carpathians and the Baltic. Such a
combination of physical and mental ideas, here pointed by
the alliteration, is characteristic of Tacitus: cp. c. 7, 4, and
H. 2. 4 *arduo opere ob ingenium montis et pervicaciam superstitionis*.

cetera, the northern parts.

Oceanus, here the North Sea and the Baltic, called *Suebicum mare* in c. 45, 2, but regarded as part of the Ocean (c. 43,
6; 44, 1).

sinus might mean either gulfs of the sea or projecting
stretches of land (cp. c. 37, 1; *Agr.* 23, 2; and Pliny, *N. H.*
4, 1, where Greece is *tertius Europae sinus*). If the former
are meant, *complectens* must be taken, by zeugma, in the sense
of *efficiens*. But it is probable that projections of land are
intended, particularly the peninsula of Jutland (cc. 35, 37),
possibly also the projections between the mouths of the Elbe,
Weser, and Ems, but the plural may have been used to balance
the following *insularum spatia*.

insularum immensa spatia: here *immensa* only means *per-
magna* (cp. c. 6, 2; *Agr.* 10, 4; 23, 2, etc.). The islands meant
are chiefly the Danish islands and Scandinavia (or more
exactly south Sweden), which was supposed to be an island
not only in antiquity (see on c. 44, 1) but as late as the
eleventh century. For *spatia* cp. c. 26, 1 and 37, 1.

nuper cognitis, etc. The ablative absolute is neither causal
nor temporal but is loosely used to add a new fact, 'where
there have recently become known to us', etc. *Nuper* is an
adverb used with much latitude: *nuper, id est paucis ante
saeculis*, says Cicero, *Nat. deor.* 2, 126. The reference is to the
campaign of Tiberius in A.D. 5, when the army reached the
Elbe, and the fleet explored the west coast of Jutland as far
as the Skagerrak (see *Res Gestae d. Aug.* c. 26 (v. 14–18); Vell. 2,
106–7; Pliny, *N. H.* 2, 167). Pliny speaks of twenty-three
islands west of Jutland as *Romanis armis cognitae*, instancing
Burcana (Borkum) and others (4, 97).

gentibus ac regibus, probably not to be taken as 'kingless tribes and kingdoms' (cp., e.g., Sallust, *Cat.* 51, 4 *reges atque populi*) but rather 'tribes and their kings', i.e 'tribes under kingly rule'. But what tribes are referred to is unknown.

aperuit, 'has opened up, disclosed to view', a metaphor not uncommon with *bellum* (*Agr.* 22, 1, etc.).

§ 2. Rhenus, etc. Tacitus returns to the two rivers which form the boundary towards the Roman empire. The main arm of the Rhine (the Vorderrhein) rises in Mt. St. Gotthard, which Caesar (4, 10) apparently regarded as the source of the river. Strabo makes it rise in Mt. Adûlas (4. 3, 3), which is perhaps best identified with the modern Mt. Adula, 23 miles in an airline farther east, where the other arm of the river (the Hinterrhein) rises. There is no means of determining which mountain Tacitus meant, but the Vorderrhein was much better known to Romans than the Hinterrhein.

vertice, 'crest' (but not to be taken quite literally).

modico flexu ... versus, 'turning with a slight bend westward', may refer to the general direction taken by the river north of Mainz, but more probably to the last bend through Holland. The bend at Basle is excluded by *modicus* (= *parvus*, see *Agr.* 18, 3, note) as well as by *in occidentem*.

§ 3. molli et clementer edito ... iugo, 'the easy and gently rising ridge', in contrast to *inaccesso ac praecipiti vertice*. So *collem clementer et molliter adsurgentem* (Colum. 2. 2, 1) and *colles clementer adsurgentes* (*A.* 13. 38, 5), the sense of *clementer* being derived from the use of the word to express gentle motion in winds or streams.

Abnŏbae, the Black Forest, on the eastern declivity of which the Danube rises. The form of the name (which is Celtic) is confirmed not only by Pliny, *N. H.* 4, 79 (whose description, as given probably in the *Bella Germaniae*, Tacitus appears to have followed) and Ptolemy, but also by inscriptions which record dedications to the goddess of the forest, Abnoba or Diana Abnoba (Dessau, *I. L. S.*, 3914–15, 9269).

plures populos, more than the Rhine, i.e. it has a longer course. Pliny has *per innumeras lapsus gentes*, which has suggested the emendation *plurimos*, but no change is necessary. Sometimes Tacitus uses *plures* in the sense of *complures* (cc. 6, 2; 43, 3), but that sense is not suitable here.

donec, often so used with present subjunctive of simple facts by Tacitus (c. 35, 1; *A.* 2. 6, 5, etc.).

meatibus, 'outlets', an ablative of direction, analogous to *via* (*ire*), which is common in Tacitus, e.g. *finibus Frisiorum* (*A.* 1. 60, 2), *litore Oceani* (*A.* 1. 63, 5).

erumpat, probably no more than a stylistic variation of

miscetur above, which is the verb used of the Danube by Ovid, *Tr.* 3. 10, 28.

septimum. The number of mouths is variously stated by ancient authors and probably varied from time to time. Ovid (*Tr.* 2, 189), Strabo and Mela give seven, Pliny gives six (with their names, 4, 79) and so Ptolemy. At present, only three are generally reckoned, but many more may be counted.

CHAPTER II

THE GERMANS AN INDIGENOUS RACE : TRADITIONS OF THE ORIGIN OF THE PEOPLE AND OF THE GENERIC NAME 'GERMANI'

Chapters II–IV deal with the *origo Germanorum*, a topic of such recognized importance as to figure in the title of the treatise. The literary artistry of the narrative is well set forth by Norden, *op. cit.*, p. 45, who points out its resemblance to Herodotus' description of the origin of the Scythians (4, 5–15) and, further, the correspondence between the topics treated by the two writers in their accounts as a whole, although the order varies. Tacitus was bound by a long-established literary tradition with fixed rules of treatment, which imposed themselves on every writer who set himself to describe a country and its people. *Introd.*, p. xiii.

§ 1. **ipsos** marks the transition from the country to its people, like *ipsi Britanni* in *Agr.* 13, 1.

indigenas = αὐτόχθονας, born in the country and its original inhabitants. This view is argued (1) on the negative grounds of geographical position and climatic conditions (§§ 1–2); (2) on the positive ground of the native legendary traditions. The main positive reasons for the autochthony of the people are stated in c. 4.

Here, as in the case of Britain (*Agr.* c. 11) and of Judaea (*H.* 5. 2), Tacitus follows ancient practice by first raising the question whether the inhabitants are indigenous or immigrants (*advecti*, ἐπήλυδες) or a mixed race (*mixti*, μιγάδες): he sets forth the evidence in the form of a statement of divergent views, adopting that which seems to him the most reasonable.

minimeque . . . adventibus et hospitiis mixtos, a second point, 'free from any (subsequent) admixture of foreign blood by immigration and friendly intercourse': cp. c. 4, 1. *Adventibus* probably means invasion by enemies, for such a possibility could not be excluded; on the other hand, in c. 40, 3, *adventu hospitioque* forms a single idea.

advehebantur. With *terra* the general idea *adveniebant* is easily supplied. *Advecti* are contrasted with *indigenae* in *Agr.*

11, 1, etc. The absence of any allusion to overland migration is due to the fact that in the legendary period (*olim*) only migrations by sea were mentioned, and Tacitus had specially in mind the antiquarian hypothesis, which he rejects, that the wanderings of Greek heroes (like Herakles and Odysseus) brought them from the Mediterranean to Germany.

quaerebant, so used with the infinitive, analogously to *cupio*, in Augustan poets and post-Augustan prose but not elsewhere in Tacitus.

immensus ultra, 'the boundless Ocean beyond' (i.e. beyond the northern coast of Germany). *Immensus* has here its full meaning (see c. 1, 1); and *ultra* denotes what lies beyond a definite boundary-line, just as in *Agr.* 25, 1 *universarum ultra gentium* means the tribes beyond the Forth–Clyde line.

utque sic dixerim. This form of expression, which Tacitus sometimes varies to *ut ita dixerim* (*Agr.* 3, 2, note), is a combination of *ut sic dicam* and *ut dixerim*, both of which are modifications in the silver age of the classical *ut ita dicam*. The expressions are all used to qualify a statement which might seem somewhat bold.

adversus has been generally taken to mean 'diametrically opposite', 'antipodal'. Cicero uses the adjective of the antipodes in *Somn. Scip.* c. 6, *eos qui incolunt terram . . . partim etiam adversos stare vobis,* and Pliny speaks of the south pole as *adversus* (2, 172), and of the flight of birds *ex adverso orbe* (10, 19). Tacitus, indeed, was ignorant of the spherical form of the earth (which he conceived as a disk surrounded by the ocean: see *Agr.* 12, 4, note, and c. 45, 1 below), but he may have adopted the language of better informed people who used the expression in the manner of Posidonius when he said of the Iberians and the Indians that they are 'in a sense the antipodes of each other' (τρόπον δέ τινα καὶ ἀντί-ποδας ἀλλήλοις ἴσμεν, Strabo, 1. 1, 13, p. 8). The alternative interpretation 'hostile' is supported by Tacitus' bold personification of the Ocean as an enemy which resists the investigation of men (c. 34, 3) and over whom victories are won (*Agr.* 25, 1); but it is to be noted that in neither of these cases is an apologetic *ut sic dixerim* added.

The same objection applies to the conjecture *aversus* (supported by Wissowa, *Gött. gel. Anz.* 1916, 673; *Neue Jahrbb.* 1921, 26): 'the northern Ocean turns its back, so to say, on the Mediterranean world.' The expression is not figurative enough to require qualification.

orbe nostro, used of the Roman world in *Agr.* 12, 3, etc.; here especially of the Mediterranean nations: so *nostrum mare* of the Mediterranean Sea.

§ 2. **praeter,** 'not to mention'; so in c. 44, 1.

Asia . . . Africa, used here not in the Roman provincial sense (which would be an anachronism) but of the parts of these continents which bordered on the Mediterranean.

peteret, potential, referring to past time, 'who would have left Asia . . . for Germany?'

informem terris, etc., 'wild in scenery (abl. of respect), inclement in climate, dismal to inhabit and to behold'. *Informis* is mostly used by Tacitus of rough material (c. 16, 3; 45, 5, etc.), here of unlovely landscapes (*terris* being used of different parts of the country). Symmetry suggests that *cultu aspectuque* are ablatives, in which case *tristem cultu* would mean 'dismal to cultivate', but a more suitable sense is given by taking them as supines: the third phrase repeats the preceding two in reverse order. Seneca speaks similarly (*de Prov.* 4, 14) of the *perpetua hiems, triste caelum, sterile solum* of Germany.

nisi si patria sit, 'unless it be one's native land'. The incongruity of this clause with *peteret* and the change of tense to the present show that it should be taken only with *tristem*, etc., as describing the impression made by the country on any one who has not been born in it. With *nisi si* the indicative is generally used (*Agr.* 32, 1, etc.).

§ 3. **Celebrant,** sc. *Germani*: a second proof is drawn from their tradition of descent from an autochthonous god.

quod: the relative is attracted into the number and gender of the predicate, as not infrequently.

memoriae et annalium, 'tradition and history', equivalent to *annalium memoria* (*A.* 4. 43, 1), 'historical tradition'. *Annales* is loosely used: the *carmina antiqua*, songs handed down from generation to generation, were neither written, nor historical, but mythological. For these songs Tacitus is our sole authority, but lays have formed the beginnings of history in most nations, and they were in use among the Germans to record not only past traditions but recent events, such as the exploits of Arminius (*A.* 2. 88, 4).

Tuistonem. MS. authority is decisively in favour of this form: **Tuisconem,** given by some MSS., arose from an easy misreading of *t*, which in the Hersfeld MS. is written τ; in the extant part of this MS. confusion of the two letters occurs in several places (see note on *Agr.* 6, 4, p. 54).

Tuisto (Twisto) is derived, like Eng. 'twist', from the root of 'two', so that the god was conceived as in some sense *geminus*, but in what sense it is useless to speculate (probably not as bisexual, an idea belonging rather to eastern mythology, nor as born of earth and heaven, for in that case the father's name could not have been omitted).

Mannum is plainly 'man', the first thinking human being (Germ. *Mann* and *Mensch*, Indian *Manus*, both from a root meaning 'to think'), conceived as the ancestor of the Germans, for whom there were no men but themselves.

originem, so used of a person in *A.* 4. 9, 3, after the Virgilian *Aeneas, Romanae stirpis origo* (*Aen.* 12, 166).

conditoresque : the three sons of Mannus are the founders of the race. The reading *conditorisque* is a type of error (*i* for *e*) common in the Hersfeld MS. The expression *condere gentem* is found in Verg. *Aen.* 1, 33.

tres filios, etc. A triad in the third generation is a feature of Greek and other mythologies. The names of the eponymous heroes are given in Latinized form in a sixth-century Frankish document as Inguo, Ermenus, and Istio (Müllenhoff, *Deutsch. Altert.* iii. 325; cp. Chadwick, *Origin of Eng. Nation,* p. 208), but they were probably invented from the three group-names, just as the Greeks invented Ion, Dorus, and Aeolus as eponymous ancestors of the Ionians, Dorians, and Aeolians. The first two survived as elements of personal names, *Ing* or *Ingve* among Danes, Swedes, and Anglo-Saxons, *Irmin* ('great, mighty') among the Bavarians.

Ingaevones . . . Herminones . . . Istaevones. The forms Ingvaeones, given by one or two MSS. of Pliny, and Istvaeones are usually considered more correct, but the Tacitean forms are etymologically explicable, *-aevones* being derived from O.H.G. *ēwa,* 'law' (R. Much, *Germ. d. Tac.,* p. 25). These ancient group names designated the tribes (1) of the northwest (*proximi Oceano* is to be compared with *proximi Oceano Cimbri,* c. 37), (2) of the interior (*medii*), (3) of the Rhine (*ceteri*). Their antiquity is indicated by the limitation to three, by the exclusion of the East Germans, and by the vocal alliteration (*h* in Herminones being parasitic, as in Hermunduri, Hercynia, etc.), which betrays their poetical setting. The Ingaevones, whom Pliny calls *gens quae est prima in Germania* and locates in Jutland and Scandinavia (*N. H.* 4, 96), appear to have represented the original nucleus of the Germanic people, which remained in its original home, while the Herminones and Istaevones were new groups resulting from expansion southwards. The three names embraced all German tribes at a date prior to the occupation of East Germany. They were probably designations of cult-associations. *Ing, Ingvi,* was a divine name, borne by the Norse god **Frey** (see **on** c. 40, 2; 44, 2), to whom the Swedish royal family of the *Ynglingar* traced its descent and whose cult was popular among the coastal tribes. *Ingaevones* will thus have meant 'followers of the law of Ing'. *Herminones*, derived from *ermen-* (*ermun-*), a word which survived in (*H*)*er-munduri* and *Irmin* and meant 'the almighty', may have denoted 'the people of Ermin', perhaps the older name of the war-god Ziu or Tiu, who was originally the counterpart of Zeus and Juppiter (see on *Martem*, c. 9, 1). The etymology of *Istaevones* is obscure.

Pliny (4, 99) gives the same three names, his Ingaevones comprising the Cimbri, Teutoni, and Chauci, his Hermiones (*mediterranei*) the Suebi, Hermunduri, Chatti, and Cherusci, and his Istaevones the tribes *proximi Rheno* (the names being lost, with the exception of perhaps the Sugambri); but his enumeration of tribes is not wholly trustworthy (e.g. the Cherusci, hereditary foes of the Suebi, and the Chatti, bitter enemies of the Hermunduri, can hardly have been true Herminones). To these three groups he adds two, (1) the Vandili (see below) and (2) the Peucini and Bastarnae. These do not belong to the same category as the first three and were evidently added at a later date in order to include the German peoples of the East and South-East.

In the sequel Tacitus takes no account of these old groups, and manifestly never considered how the tribes mentioned in the second part of the *Germania* fit into the threefold division. The names were probably not in ordinary use at the time when they were first noted down.

§ 4. quidam, not German informants but Roman (or Greek and Roman) antiquaries who desired to find an explanation of names which did not appear to them to be included under the above three, and yet belonged to groups rather than to single peoples. This is plain, not only from the fact that the names given below are not homogeneous like those before mentioned, and are clearly not drawn from ancient minstrelsy, but also from the fact that the view of the *quidam* extends to the end of the chapter and deals with matters that could not have been argued by native Germans. Their view was probably based on information derived from the Gauls. Tacitus in all probability found it reported by Pliny (in his *Bella Germaniae*), who may have derived his information from Livy, bk. civ. Similarly in Herodotus' account of the origin of the Scythians the native tradition is followed by a foreign version. See *Introd.*, p. xxx.

ut in licentia vetustatis, 'as is natural in view of the scope allowed by antiquity to conjecture'. For this use of *ut*, cp. c. 22, 1; 39, 3; 45, 5.

plures deo ortos, 'that the god (Tuisto) had more descendants'.

pluresque gentis appellationes, etc., 'and there were more (than three) designations of the people', i.e. designations of tribal groups to be found among the people as a whole (*gens*, as in § 5, etc.). The four mentioned are given only as instances, not as a full enumeration. Tacitus makes no further reference to any of them except the Suebi, to whom he gives an abnormally wide extension (see c. 38). Of the others the Marsi are not known to have been a group of tribes, but they were an important tribe and their sanctuary of the goddess Tamfana was a religious centre for the surrounding tribes (*A.* 1. 51). The Gambrivii, mentioned only by Strabo with other central tribes (7. 1, 3, p. 291), may have been the parent stem of the Sugambri (settled between the R. Lippe and the Westerwald before their transference in 8 B.C. to the west bank of the Rhine), who bore what is etymologically the same name, derived from O.H.G. *gambar* (= *strenuus*) with the added prefix *su* (= *bene*). **Vandilii,** normally spelt *Vandali* (the Vandals of later history), is used by Pliny (see above) as a collective designation of the east German tribes (comprising the Gutones, Goths, who did not count themselves as Vandals, the Burgondiones, Burgundians, and the Varinnae and Charini). The name Vandili corresponds to that of Lugii in Tacitus (c. 43). Only two individual tribes are directly attested as Vandals, neither of them before the second century, the Hasdingi (Dio 71, 12) and the Silingi (Ptol. 2. 11, 10), who have left their name to Silesia: see *infra*, c. 43.

eaque, etc., sc. *esse,* 'and that these are genuine and ancient names', as opposed to the generic name *Germani,* which is an artificial appellation of relatively modern date. The statement of the *quidam* plainly extends to *vocarentur,* and this sentence is part of it. To supply *sunt,* and to take it as a remark interposed by Tacitus, is arbitrary.

§ 5. **ceterum Germaniae vocabulum,** etc. This is one of the most disputed sentences in Latin literature. Norden has written a bulky volume (*Urgesch.*) round it. The view which it reports is not quite logically expressed, but the meaning is tolerably clear. 'On the other hand, "Germany" is a modern name which has been recently given (to the country), since those who first crossed the Rhine and drove out the Gauls, and are now called Tungri, were then called *Germani*: thus what had been the name of a tribe, not of the whole race, gradually prevailed, so that all (i.e. the whole people) were called *Germani,* first by the conquerors (i.e. the Tungri) from fear (or "to inspire fear") and subsequently by themselves as well, adopting the name which

had been devised for them.' That is to say, the name *Germani*
was originally a tribal name borne by the first invaders of
Gaul, who, feeling insecure amid the surrounding Gauls, represented the tribes beyond the Rhine as being *Germani* like
themselves (and therefore ready to support them); and this
designation was in course of time adopted by the latter as a
national name. The argument is illogically stated in so far
as the proof of *recens et nuper additum* is only partially given
by the *quoniam* clause.

The main thought here expressed, that the generic name
Germani was an extension of a tribal name, is no doubt
correct, for it is in this way that national names have usually
arisen. *Hellenes*, the name of a Thessalian tribe, became (in
Asia) the generic name of all Greek-speaking peoples. The
Hellenes were called *Graeci* by the Romans after a small tribe
in Epirus, the *Grai*, and they were called *Javan* by the
Phoenicians and other eastern peoples after the Ionians. The
Italians owe their name to the Itali (a tribe settled in the toe
of the peninsula), the French to the Franks, the English to
the Angles. The French still call the Germans *Allemands*
after the Alamanni, while the ancient German name for the
Celts, still surviving as *Welsche* in German and *Welsh* in English, was derived from the Volcae, once their nearest neighbours (in Thuringia, see *Introd.* p. xliv). Examples might be
multiplied. But in detail, as will be shown, the view reproduced by Tacitus is erroneous.

Germaniae vocabulum : the name of the country is substituted for that of the people in order to avoid confusion
between the generic and the tribal signification of *Germani*.
recens et nuper additum, contrasted with *vera et antiqua
nomina*. *Nuper* is elastically used (as in c. 1, 1); *additum*,
not in the sense of 'added' (for one cannot speak of the name
'Germany' being added either to the *gens* as a whole or to the
antiqua nomina of tribal groups), but with the meaning of
inditum, as in *H.* 1. 62 *nomine Germanici Vitellio statim
addito*; Ovid, *Met.* 9, 356 *hoc . . . illi addiderat nomen*; Varro,
Ling. Lat. 7, 82 *nomen additum Andromachae* (a variant of
Ennius' *Andromachae nomen indidit*). The generic name
Germani originated among the Gauls after the Germanic
invasion referred to in the next clause, which probably
took place some time after *c.* 250 B.C., and from them it passed
to the Romans. See *Introd.*, p. xliii. The conjecture *auditum*
is not only unnecessary but is unsuitable : it would naturally
mean *auditum a Romanis* (as in c. 37, 2 ; 41, 2), a meaning
excluded by the context.

qui primi Rhenum transgressi, etc. The invaders were not

the Tungri alone (as Tacitus states) but the group of tribes
settled in north-eastern Gaul, between the Treveri on the
south and the Menapii on the north, which Caesar describes
as bearing the collective name of *Germani* (*B.G.* 2, 3–4; 6, 2;
32; see *Introd.* p. xliii). Of this group he names five tribes,
among them the Eburones, but there were others he does not
mention, having had no dealings with them, such as the
Tungri, Texuandri, Baetasii, etc. After the Eburones had
been practically, though not completely, annihilated by him,
the central portion of their territory (the region of Liège and
Maastricht) was inherited by the Tungri, who in the Imperial
age were the most important member of the group. That is
apparently the reason why their name is used by Tacitus to
represent the whole group.

The Tungri furnished the Roman army with auxiliary
regiments of horse and foot (*alae* and *cohortes*), and they have
left their name to Tongres or Tongern, which represents
Aduatuca, a town of the Eburones, subsequently called
Adua⟨tu⟩ca Tungrorum by the Antonine Itinerary, Tungri
simply by Ammianus (15. 11, 7).

Primi implies later German invasions. Tacitus had probably in mind the Cimbri and Teutoni, the Germans under
Ariovistus, the Vangiones, Nemetes, and Triboci (c. 28), and
the Usipetes and Tencteri. The whole clause seems to be a
silent correction, probably taken over from Livy, of the
statement made to Caesar by the Remi that most of the
Belgae were of German origin (*plerosque Belgas esse ortos ab
Germanis, Rhenumque antiquitus traductos . . . ibi consedisse
Gallosque . . . expulisse*, *B.G.* 2, 4; Norden, pp. 353 ff.), which
was an exaggeration of the fact that they had a very strong
admixture of German blood. The Germani Cisrhenani, whom
Tacitus identifies with the Tungri, were not in fact the first
German invaders of Gaul: see *Introd.*, p. xl ff.

nunc Tungri, sc. *vocentur* from *vocati sint*; so in c. 36, 2
vocati sunt is supplied from *vocantur*, and in c. 41, 1 *secutus
sum* from *sequar*.

Germani vocati sint, i.e. bore the name at the time of their
invasion, not 'got the name' (from the Gauls) at or after their
invasion, an interpretation excluded by the tenor of the sentence as a whole, and especially by the antithesis *nunc—tunc*.
The sentence is not concerned with the origin or meaning of
the name *Germani*, but only with the origin of its generic
use. The perfect tense is related to the present (*vocentur*) as
past to present ('were then called—are now called'), and the
time reference is the same as that of *expulerint*. That *Germani*
was the name of a single tribe, which became extended to the

whole people, was known to the Byzantine historian Procopius (Norden, p. 412), who probably derived his information from Pliny (Much, *Germ.*, p. 41).

In point of fact, when a tribal name has become a national name, it is always the native name of the tribe that has been so extended. Consequently all attempts to derive *Germani* from Celtic—whether from *gair*, 'neighbour', or from *garm*, 'clamor', with the meaning 'of the loud battle-cry', βοὴν ἀγαθοί—are wholly wrong in principle as well as philologically unsatisfactory (R. Much, 'Der Name Germanen' in *Sitzb. Akad. Wien* 195 (1920), pp. 61 ff.). Latin and Greek popular etymology inevitably, but quite wrongly, associated *Germanus* with the Latin *germanus*, 'brother'.

ita nationis nomen, non gentis sums up the preceding *quoniam* clause. *Ita*, 'in these circumstances', 'consequently', is equivalent to *itaque*, which Tacitus does not use except in the *Dialogus*. *Natio* here, as often, denotes a particular tribe (so in cc. 33, 1; 40, 1; 46, 1), while *gens* means the race as a whole (cp. cc. 4, 10, 14, 19, 21, 22); but in other places *gens* is used not only of tribal groups (c. 34, 1; 39, 4; 43, 3) but also of separate tribes (c. 27, 3; 29, 1 and 3; 30, 2; 36, 3, etc.), while in c. 4, 1 *natio* is used in the wider sense of *gens*. Norden's view (p. 316) that *non gentis* is a silent correction made by Livy of Caesar, who calls the *Cisrhenani Germani* a *gens* (6, 32), seems far-fetched.

evaluisse corresponds to ἐκνικᾶν in Thucydides (1, 3) and ἐπικρατεῖν in Polybius (2. 38, 1) and Strabo (4. 1, 12). Norden, pp. 318 ff.

victore, a technical term for the occupying power (here the Tungri), as Norden has shown (pp. 328 ff.). The preposition can only mean 'by', not 'after' (like ἀπό), for although Tacitus sometimes uses a preposition in two senses in the same sentence, and other authors, especially the elder Pliny, use *a* in both its meanings in a single sentence, the studied parallelism between the two parts of the present clause, *primum a victore* and *mox et a se ipsis*, and the use of *et* (= *etiam*) show beyond a doubt that the first *a* has the same sense as the second. 'After the conqueror' is what *should* have been said, for the development of a tribal into a national name has always been due not to the tribe which bore the name but to its alien neighbours (here the Gauls).

ob metum is usually interpreted 'to inspire fear': elsewhere in Tacitus it always means 'from fear'. While Tacitus may possibly in this one instance have used the preposition in the final sense which he sometimes gives to it (in *A*. 1. 3 both meanings occur in a single sentence, *magis ob amissum* . . .

exercitum quam . . . dignum ob praemium), there is no need to suppose that he did so, because in either case the sense is substantially the same: the invaders were afraid of being unable to maintain their ground against the Gauls.

a se ipsis (taken only with *vocarentur*) is another error. The Germans beyond the Rhine never called themselves collectively *Germani*. Individual Germans called themselves by this name only when they were in the service of Rome and spoke in the Roman way (e.g. Dess., *I. L. S.*, 4640, 4760). The Germans had no national name till the eleventh century, when the adjective *diutisc*, 'popular', now *deutsch*, which had been used three centuries earlier to designate the ordinary language in contrast to the Latin of the church, came into vogue as a generic designation of the people.

invento nomine emphasizes the artificiality of the name: the phrase corresponds to *additum* at the beginning of the sentence, as *Germani vocarentur* does to *Germaniae vocabulum*, and the correspondence indicates that it should be taken as meaning that they called themselves 'by the name that had been invented for them' rather than 'by the name which they had come by'. *Nomen invenire* may mean 'to invent a name' (as in *A*. 13. 51, 2) or 'to give a name' without emphasis on its invention (so *inde nomine invento* in Plin. *N. H.* 26, 22; 33, 68) or, with the person or thing named as subject, 'to come by, get, a name', a common idiom in Cicero (e.g. *Tusc.* 4, 49 *Torquatum illum qui hoc cognomen invenit*) and Pliny (e.g. *N. H.* 37, 131 *asteria . . . regerit . . . radios in modum stellae, unde nomen invenit*).

CHAPTER III

ALLEGED FOREIGN CONTACTS: HERCULES AND ULIXES IN GERMANY

Germany was no exception to the rule that ancient writers could not describe a country without connecting it somehow or other with Greek heroes, especially Herakles and Odysseus. Even Scotland was ultimately found to have been visited by the latter: *Ulixem Calidoniae adpulsum manifestat ara graecis literis scripta*, says Solinus in the third century (ed. Mommsen, p. 100, 3). While Tacitus does not believe that Hercules and Ulixes reached Germany, the fact that he lays the supposed evidence before his readers and leaves the decision to them perhaps betrays a certain inability to shake himself quite free from the influence of legend.

§ 1. **Fuisse et apud eos**, etc., 'it is said that Hercules visited

them as well as others, and in fact they sing the foremost
of all heroes when they are about to go into battle'. The
subject of *memorant* is either indefinite, 'people say' (as in
c. 39, 1; 43, 4; Liv. 1. 7, 4 *Herculem . . . boves abegisse memorant*),
or, less probably, the *quidam* of the previous chapter (cp. § 3
below); it cannot be *Germani*, not so much because of *eos*
for *se*, which is found elsewhere in Tacitus, but because the
Germans could not possibly have made the statement. The
change of subject with *canunt* is saved from awkwardness by
ituri.

et = *etiam*. Most MSS. place it before *Herculem*, 'Hercules
among others' (of whom Ulixes is mentioned in § 3), but this
gives a less natural statement. For this use of *et* (which is the
same in either case), cp. c. 12, 3 *eliguntur et principes* (where
no other elections are mentioned); *A.* 11. 4 *rogatus sententiam
et Scipio*; *H.* 1. 31 *missus et Celsus Marius* (in both cases no
others being mentioned).

Herculem: here the Roman hero (as *fuisse* and *vir fortis*
show), in c. 9, 1 the Roman identification of a German god;
in the case of Hercules, Romans did not sharply distinguish
the heroic and the divine. Tacitus means that the belief that
Hercules visited Germany is based on the fact that the battle-
songs (ἐμβατήρια μέλη) of the Germans celebrate a native
hero whom Romans have identified with Hercules. The
sentence thus involves no inconsistency with the denial of
intercourse between Germans and foreign peoples. The
German 'Hercules' was no doubt of the type of Siegfried,
the hero of the *Nibelungenlied*, perhaps even his ancestor, as
Norden suggests (p. 179); but his further suggestion that he
was identical with the Hercules of two Batavian cults (for
which see c. 9, 1) is unacceptable, since Hercules there was a
god, not a hero.

sunt illis haec quoque, etc. This sentence and the next
(to *intumescat*) appear to be a digression in the manner of
Herodotus (cp. Norden, p. 181), describing another kind of
battle-*carmen*, which is to be distinguished from those just mentioned: a modern writer would have made them a footnote.
Objection has been taken to the use of *haec* with forward
reference to a new fact stated by a relative clause. But *haec*
may (as in c. 20, 1 *haec corpora quae miramur*) be taken as
denoting what is presupposed as known, 'those chants which
we have heard about' (from the reports of Romans who had
fought with Germans).

An ingenious interpretation (Sternkopf, *Hermes*, 59, 232)
would give *haec* its normal retrospective meaning and avoid
the necessity of taking the passage as a digression: the

carmina are identical with those to Hercules, '[for] they have
such songs also (i.e. as well as songs to Tuisto, c. 2, 3), by the
recital of which', etc. *Carmina* would thus take up *canunt*,
and the omission of a connecting word is paralleled by c. 5, 4
adficiuntur. est videre. . . . But here the absence of some
such word as *nam, quippe, scilicet* is sensibly felt, and it is
more than doubtful whether the *carmina* had any words at
least articulate enough to suggest a connexion with Hercules.
Moreover, the following description (*terrent enim*) shows that
the Germans chanted them, not *ituri in proelia*, but in the
actual presence of the enemy.

   carmina. These are apparently referred to in *H. 2. 22
cantu truci*, and 4. 18 *ut virorum cantu, feminarum ululatu
sonuit acies*, where the *cantus* in each case takes place just
as battle is joined. The description here shows that if the
chants began with words, they speedily became inarticulate
cries. *Carmen*, indeed, is often a 'song without words', any
rhythmical and not necessarily melodious utterance, such as
the funereal notes of the owl, the song of the swan, the sound
of a trumpet or of waves (Verg. *Aen.* 4, 462; Ovid *Met.* 5,
387; Enn. *Ann.* 508; Claudian 17, 319).

   relatu, 'rendering, recital', hardly mere 'utterance'. The
word seems to indicate that Tacitus thought that the *carmina*
were not mere cries. It is a very rare substantive, used with
virtutum in *H.* 1. 30.

   baritum. The variant. **barditum** has better manuscript
authority, but no satisfactory explanation of the word is to
be found (see R. Much, *Germ.*, p. 49). It has no connexion
with the Gallic *bardus*. Grimm explained it to mean 'shield-
song', deriving it from old Norse *bardi*, 'shield', but *bardi*
is a late word which occurs only once. *Barditus* is probably an
incorrect form. A comparison of Tacitus' description with
Ammianus 16. 12, 43 leaves small room for doubt that the
word he used was *baritus* or *barritus*. Ammianus describes
the *barritus* as a *clamor* raised just as battle is joined, which
begins as a low whisper and gradually swells into a roar like
that of waves dashing against rocks (*fractum murmur*, as
Tacitus says). Vegetius also calls it a *clamor* which should not
be raised until the combat begins (3, 18). The absence of verbal
content seems clear from Amm. 31. 7, 11, where the Germans
in the Roman army raise the *barritus*, while the Goths
maiorum laudes clamoribus stridebant inconditis. The
word meant the roar of an elephant, which was called *barrus*
from the sound of its voice (Isidor. *Etym.* 12. 2, 14; Festus,
s.v. *barrire*). The same onomatopoeic word was evidently
coined by the Germans for the roar of their *cantus*. The

form *barditus* may have been due to a fifteenth-century Humanist who associated the word with *bardus*.

ipso cantu augurantur. That the Germans divined the issue of the coming battle from the character of the sound, is a Roman interpretation. The object of the battle-cry was to fire their own courage (Ammianus 31. 7, 11) and to frighten the foe (*Id.* 16. 12, 43). So Livy says of the Galatian Celts in 189 B.C. *cantus ineuntium proelium et ululatus . . ., omnia de industria composita ad terrorem*, 38. 17, 4. The author of the mantic interpretation was probably Livy, who, speaking not of Germans or Celts but of Volscians and Romans, draws precisely the same inference: *clamor indicium primum fuit quo res inclinatura esset, excitatior . . . ab hoste sublatus; ab Romanis dissonus, impar, segnius saepe iteratus prodidit pavorem animorum* (4. 37, 9). Cp. W. Capelle, *Philol.* 84, 1929, p. 207.

sonuit acies, so in *H.* 4. 18, 5 (quoted above).

vocis . . . videtur, a thoroughly Tacitean phrase, 'they regard it (viz. the sound of the battle-line) as a unison not so much of voice as of valour': cp. *voce Martia concinentes . . . quam . . . appellant barritum*, Ammianus 31. 7, 11.

Nec stands for *non enim*, as elsewhere in Tacitus, the clause giving the reason of their confidence or fear; *ille* for *illud* (sc. *quod sonat acies*), attracted to *concentus* (cp. c. 18, 3; 31, 3; 32, 3, etc.).

A similar meaning would be clumsily given by the MSS. reading *voces illae . . . videntur*, 'the sound seems to them not so much (mere) voices as a unison of valour'. But it is hard to believe (despite the defence of Valmaggi, *Boll. di fil. class.* xxvii. 14) that this is what Tacitus wrote: *concentus* must be common to both nouns, and the emendation of Rhenanus is supported by the variant *ille* for *illae*.

§ **2. fractum,** a 'broken', i.e. intermittent, roar, like that of waves breaking on rocks, with which Ammianus compares it (note on *baritus*). So used by Virgil of trumpet blasts in *G.* 4, 72 and of *voces*, probably 'voices' heard amid the tumult of the sea in *Aen.* 3, 556, where some give it what seems to be the impossible meaning of 'crashing'.

obiectis ad os, etc., 'and therefore they put their shields before their mouths in order that, through the reverberation, the voice may swell to a fuller and deeper note'. The fact is not mentioned by Ammianus, and it is to be noted that the German shield was not half-cylindrical.

§ **3. ceterum,** resuming after the digression and going back to *Herculem memorant.*

Ulixen quidam opinantur, etc. *Ulixes*, later corrupted into

Ulysses, was the Latin equivalent of the Greek Odysseus. *Opinantur*, elsewhere used by Tacitus only in the *Dialogus*. This legend of Ulixes, as Norden has shown (pp. 186 f.), cannot have taken shape until the region of the lower Rhine had been opened up by Rome: the Greek hero wandered thither with the Roman soldiers. The entrance to the underworld, where Odysseus conversed with the souls of dead heroes (*Od.*, bk. xi), was localized at Boulogne (Gesoriacum-Bononia), as appears from Claudian, *In Rufinum*, 1, 123 ff.; and thence he was made to sail to the mouth of the Rhine and up the river to Asciburgium. The authorities, *quidam*, who narrated the legend were probably Livy and certainly Pliny, who had served as an officer in both Upper and Lower Germany and whose *Bella Germaniae* was the most recent work on everything German; to him was plainly due the information about the inscriptions in Greek letters.

fabuloso, probably 'storied', as in *fabulosus Hydaspes* (Hor. *Carm.* 1. 22, 8), rather than 'legendary', as in c. 46, 6.

hunc Oceanum, i.e. the German Ocean, already mentioned in cc. 1 and 2 and brought close to the reader by the description; so *hic* (in Germany) *notum*, c. 10, 3.

Asciburgium, mentioned in *H.* 4. 33 and in the Peutinger Table as a Roman fort between Novaesium (Neuss) and Vetera (Fürstenberg near Xanten), lay a little to the south of the village of Asberg near Mörs, opposite the mouth of the Ruhr. The site is now over a mile from the Rhine, which has changed its course. The name (which was also the designation of the Gesenke mountains bounding Moravia on the north, Ptol. 2. 11, 5) is German, but its etymology is disputed: the first element is probably *Esche*, 'ash', and *-burgium* is the Latinized form of Ger. *Berg*, which would give the meaning 'Ash Hill'. This explanation is supported by the fact that *Gesenke* (a Slavonic name) means 'Ash Mountains'.

hodieque, post-Augustan for *hodie quoque*, 'to this day', as in *Dial.* 34 *fin.*; Vell. 1. 4, 2–3, etc.

constitutum nominatumque, 'was founded and named by him'. The words can only mean that Ulixes gave his town the name of Asciburgium: they cannot be read (with Norden, p. 199) to mean that another unmentioned Greek name given by its founder was afterwards displaced by a barbaric one. The form of expression is exactly paralleled by such passages as *Taras . . . a quo Tarentum civitas et condita et appellata est* and *Olisipona* (Lisbon) *ab Ulixe est condita et nuncupata* (Isidorus, *Origines*, 15. 1, 62 and 70). The name Ἀσκιπύργιον, which the MSS. have after *nominatumque*, cannot have been written by Tacitus, who avoids Greek words, translating them when necessary (cp. *A*. 3. 65, 3; 15. 71, 3, etc.), but had its origin in a gloss inserted by an ancient scribe or scholar, who understood the meaning quite rightly. The author of the legend regarded *Asciburgium* as the Latinized form of a Greek name and saw in it an allusion to the bag (ἀσκός) given by Aeolus to Odysseus with the unfavourable winds tied up in it, the opening of which (by his comrades) was the cause of all his wanderings; and from that silly etymology (to which ancient literature supplies many parallels) he deduced the presence of the hero on the Rhine. This old explanation, recently defended by Lillge (*Sokrates*, 4, 1916, pp. 287 ff.) and Wissowa (*Gött. gel. Anz.* 178, 1916, p. 666; *Neue Jahrbb.* 47–8, 1921, p. 29), seems the most probable.

quin etiam, always thus used postpositively by Tacitus.

Ulixi consecratam, etc. *Ulixi* is dative of the agent. As Strabo explains (3. 5, 6, p. 171), it was a common custom in antiquity for travellers and conquerors to mark the limit of their travels or conquests by setting up altars or towers or pillars in a conspicuous place; and so it was quite natural that Ulixes should dedicate an altar (to the river-god) to mark the north-western limit of his wanderings. It has been thought that there may have existed an altar (no longer extant) with a Celtic inscription in the Greek alphabet (cp. *CIL*. xii, p. 966; Rhŷs, *Proc. Brit. Acad.*, 1905–6, 285 ff.) which had a sequence of letters bearing some resemblance to the names Ulixes and Laertes. The addition of the father's name (which was, of course, regular) is mentioned as a proof that the Ulixes of the altar was really the Odysseus of Homer. But the inscription, like the Scottish one, is no doubt a legend; in what was in Caesar's time one of the most backward regions of Gaul it is highly improbable that inscribed stone monuments existed *olim*, much less monuments with Greek letters.

monumentaque et tumulos, 'barrows with monuments'. It has been supposed that the inscriptions in Greek letters were really inscriptions in North-Etruscan script (based on the Greek alphabet), of which a considerable number have been found in southern Raetian and Norican districts (Mommsen 'Die nordetruskischen Alphabete' in *Mitt. d. Antiquar. Gesell. in Zürich*, vii, 1853, p. 197; C. Pauli, *Altital. Forsch.* i, 1885; Whatmough, *Prae-Italic Dial. of Italy*, ii, p. 65 ff.); there is also a helmet of *c*. 300 B.C., found at Negau (Steiermark), bearing an apparently Germanic name in Etruscan letters (*Studi Etruschi*, vi, 523). The difficulties are that such inscriptions have not been found anywhere near the boundary between Germany and Raetia, and that if (as is probable) Tacitus' authority was Pliny, he would hardly have confused Etruscan with Greek script.

It might be supposed that the inscriptions were Celtic inscriptions in Greek lettering set up by the Helvetii of north Switzerland. The Greek alphabet would reach them by way of the trade route from Massilia (Marseilles) along the valleys of the Rhone and Aare; in later time it was used by the Helvetii on their coins and for records (Caes. *B.G.* 1, 29). But such an explanation is untenable if *tumulus* bears its full original sense, for on Swiss soil burial under barrows had been replaced by burial in flat graves in the earliest La Tène period (beginning *c.* 450 B.C.),[1] and even if the Helvetii were already in north Switzerland at that time (which is far from certain), they cannot have adopted the Greek alphabet so early, since its use by the much more civilized Celts of southern France did not antedate the end of the third century (Jacobsthal, *Jahrb. d. Inst.*, 1930, *Anz.* p. 236). The chronological difficulty would disappear if *tumulus* could be used for the low mound that doubtless covered the flat graves; but although the word may mean 'tomb' (e.g. *Dial.* 13, 6; *A.* 14, 9, 3), it implies some sort of superstructure, and it seems doubtful if Tacitus would have used it of an ordinary grave-mound, *congesta humus* (*A., l. c.*). Norden's attribution of the *tumuli* to the pre-Helvetic inhabitants of north Switzerland in the middle La Tène period (pp. 202 ff., 503 f.) is untenable.

in confinio, etc. The boundary between Germania Superior and Raetia ran from the eastern limit of the *Decumates agri* (c. 29, 4) along the west side of the Lake of Constance and then southwards by the station Ad Fines, now Pfin. The boundary between Raetia and free Germany is defined in c. 1, 1 note. *Confinium* (also in *H.* 4. 72) is originally a technical term of the land-surveyors (*agrimensores*) for the strip of ground dividing two pieces of land.

adhuc extare, in contrast to the Ulixes altar.

§ 4. While himself rejecting the Ulysses tradition, Tacitus will not force his opinion on his readers: cp. *volgatis traditisque demere fidem non ausim, H.* 2. 50.

neque confirmare, etc., coincides almost verbally with Liv. *Praef.* 6, *ea* (sc. traditions already described as *decora fabulis*) *nec adfirmare nec refellere in animo est.* The phrase may have been repeated by Livy in his account of the Germans in bk. 104.

ex ingenio suo, etc., 'every one may believe or disbelieve them according to his temperament'. A formula of the type

[1] D. Viollier, *Les Sépultures du second âge du fer sur le plateau suisse,* 1916.

which had been used by Greek writers since Herodotus' time in expressing or reserving judgement: Herod. 2, 146; 5, 45; Thuc. 6. 2, 1; Dionys. Hal. 1. 48, 4; and Lucian, *Hist. conscr.*, c. 60 μῦθος εἴ τις παρεμπέσοι, λεκτέος μέν, οὐ μὴν πιστωτέος πάντως, ἀλλ' ἐν μέσῳ θετέος τοῖς ὅπως ἂν ἐθέλωσιν εἰκάσουσι περὶ αὐτοῦ. Cp. Liv. 37. 48, 7 *neque affirmata res mea opinione sit nec pro vana praetermissa*. (On this section, cp. Latte, *Philol.* 87 (1932), pp. 265 f.)

CHAPTER IV

THE PURITY OF THE RACE SHOWN BY THE UNIFORMITY OF PHYSICAL TYPE

§ 1. **Ipse**, in contrast to *quisque*. Tacitus here carries further what he has said in c. 2, 1, and holds the Germans not only to be autochthonous, and a single race, but also to have remained always unmixed, as is shown by the uniformity of type. He thus implies disbelief in these tales of foreign visitors, but he goes much too far in conceiving that the Germans had kept themselves free from any admixture of foreign blood. The skulls found in ancient graves—short, long, and intermediate—prove a prehistoric intermingling of races; see further *infra*.

opinionibus, often corrected to *opinioni*, because there was only one opinion, no matter how many people expressed it nor whether they based it on somewhat different grounds. Nevertheless *opiniones* may be taken as an opinion expressed by various authorities, just as Pliny says *contra priscorum opiniones*, where only one opinion is in question (*N. H.* 7, 39), and Seneca says *in magnis erroribus sunt qui credunt* . . . (*Ben.* 6, 43).

aliis is rightly bracketed by most editors, as a variant which arose by assimilation to *nullis* and found its way into the text. It cannot mean 'foreign', for no one could say 'by no foreign intermarriages with other peoples'. Similarly in *Dial.* 10, 4 *ceteris aliarum* (*artium studiis*) for *ceterarum* arose from '*al. arum*' written above *ceteris* (Andresen, *Woch. kl. Phil.* 1916, col. 1133). That Tacitus imitated or reproduced a Greek idiom (like ἄλλαισιν ἄλλων ψυχαῖς, Plat. *Phaedr.* 278 b) is hardly credible.

nationum. We should have expected *gentium* as in c. 2, 1 (see note on c. 2, 5). *Aliae nationes* are thus contrasted with *Germani* in *A*. 4. 72, 3.

infectos, probably to be taken as the equivalent of *mixtos* in c. 2, 1 rather than in the bad sense of 'tainted'; cp. *corruptus* in c. 23, 1. As regards the statement, *mixta conubia are* admitted by Tacitus himself in the case of the Peucini, c. 46, 1, and Caesar mentions that Ariovistus married a Norican woman (*B.G.* 1, 53).

propriam et sinceram, 'peculiar (distinct) and pure'.

tantum sui similem. Tacitus was plainly unconscious of the close resemblance of his description to that given of the Gauls by Romans (see below). The physical features he names as distinctive of Germans were in fact originally common to the whole Indo-Germanic race. The phrase *tantum sui similis*, which seems so genuinely Tacitean, is really an inheritance from the Ionian Greeks. First coined in all probability by Hecataeus for the Egyptians, it was adopted by Parmenides (ἐωυτῷ πάντοσε τωυτόν, τῷ δ' ἑτέρῳ μὴ τωυτόν, 8, 57), applied to the Scythians by the author of the treatise περὶ ἀέρων κτλ. in the Hippocratic corpus (ἔοικεν αὐτὸ ἑωυτῷ ὥσπερ τὸ Αἰγύπτιον, c. 19), and probably taken over from him by Posidonius, from whom Tacitus inherited it, whether through Livy or directly (Norden, pp. 54, 67 ff., with Capelle, *Philol.* 84, p. 354 n.). On the supposed implication of this borrowing, see *Introd.*, p. xxix ff.

§ **2.** This description reflects Posidonius' exposition (reproduced by Vitruvius, 6. 1) of the racial characteristics of northern peoples as contrasted with southern, which was based on his knowledge of Celts and Scythians, but this fact does not impair the truth of Tacitus' statements: there is no question of a mechanical transference of Celtic characteristics to the Germans. See *Introd.*, p. xxxiv. Tacitus' description is fully confirmed not only by other writers but also by the representation of Germans on the column of Trajan and the metopes of the Tropaeum of Adamklissi in the Dobrudja, by bronze figurines of the first century and a realistic terracotta in the Bonn Museum, as well as by the bodies found in the moors of north-west Germany, Denmark, and Holland.

habitus corporum, 'the physical type', so used of the Britons in *Agr.* 11, 1.

tamquam in tanto . . . numero, 'so far as can be said (or 'ascertained') in the case of a population so vast'. *Tamquam* is similarly used with limiting force in *H.* 1. 8 *tamquam in tanta multitudine* (such was the unfavourable attitude to Galba in Rome), 'so far as one may speak for so great a multitude'. The variant *quamquam* would be pleonastic with *in*, which by itself has a concessive meaning, as in c. 19, 2 *in tam numerosa gente*; *A.* 3. 44 *in tanto rerum motu*; 15. 57 *in tanta necessitate*. On this variant, cp. *Class. Rev.* li (1937), p. 185.

idem omnibus: here, as elsewhere in the first part of the *Germania*, Tacitus has in view the western tribes, and it should be remembered that to the ordinary observer a foreign race always seems more uniform than it really is.

truces ac caerulei oculi, etc. These and the following characteristics are mentioned by other Roman writers: thus *caerulea pubes,* Hor. *Epod.* 16, 7; *caerula lumina,* Juv. 13, 164. The truculent look of their eyes (*acies oculorum,* Caes. 1. 39, 1) is plain in the reliefs of the Trajan column and the Tropaeum of Adamklissi. But Posidonius noted the blue eyes of the Celts (*oculis caesis,* Vitruv. 6. 1, 3) and Ammianus speaks of their *luminum torvitas* (15. 12, 1). See *Introd.,* p. xxxiv.

rutilae, ruddy or blond. The colour is called *rufus* by Seneca (*de Ira* 3. 26, 3), *flavus* by others (e.g. Juv., *l.c.*). But the Gallic hair is similarly described: Strabo, 4. 5, 2, p. 200; Diod. 5. 28, 1 (Posidonius); Livy, 38. 17, 3; Amm. 15. 12, 1. Yet in *Agr.* 11, 2, Tacitus regards *rutilae comae* as a proof of the Germanic origin of the Caledonians. Germans and Gauls could produce this colour artificially or deepen it with a kind of soap (Pliny, *N.H.* 28, 191; cp. *rutilatum crinem, H.* 4. 61), which was procured for the purpose by Roman ladies (Ov. *A.A.* 3, 163; Mart. 8. 33, 20).

magna corpora: cp. c. 20, 1 and *Agr., l.c.*; Caes., *l.c.*, and 4, 1; *H.* 5. 18. Measurements of skeletons give an average height of 5 ft. 9-11 in., and often a greater stature; Sidonius speaks of Burgundians 7 ft. tall. The average height of the Roman legionary was 5 ft. 7 in. The northern Germans, especially those belonging to Mecklenburg and East Friesland, are still among the world's biggest men. But the Gauls also had *magna corpora* (Caes. 2. 30, 3; Livy, 5, 44; 38, 17; Strabo, 4. 4, 2; Diod. 5, 28; Ammianus, *l.c.*).

impetum, 'a violent effort'. So *A.* 2. 14, 5, etc. Roman writers often note the same quality in Gauls (see Livy, 10. 28, 3; 38. 17, 7, etc.).

§ 3. **laboris atque operum,** 'toil and work', *labor* being the wider term, defined more closely by *opera,* which refers to military work other than fighting (as in *A.* 1. 35, 1; 11. 18, 2). The combination is common, but usually with the second noun in the singular.

non eadem patientia, sc. *est,* 'no corresponding ability to endure', i.e. corresponding to the *magnitudo corporum.* The same was true of the Gauls; see Livy, 10. 28, 3; 27. 48, 16; 34. 47, 5.

minimeque sitim, etc. Cp. c. 23, 2. The inability to bear heat is illustrated by the rapidity with which the soldiers of Vitellius, who were mostly Germans, became demoralized in Italy (*H.* 2. 93, cp. 32). The same is noted of Gauls (Livy, *ll. cc.,* 38. 17, 7, etc.).

tolerare, sc. *adsueverunt,* with which *tolerare* is in turn supplied below.

caelo solove, causal ablatives, referring respectively to *frigora* and *inediam.* For *-ve* cp. *A.* 3. 36 *liberti ac servi patrono vel domino.*

CHAPTER V

THE COUNTRY AND ITS PRODUCTS

The sparseness of the information which Tacitus gives about the land and its products is due to the fact that he was not concerned to do more than picture the rough environment which produced the simplicity of the German style of life as compared with the luxurious civilization of the rich land of Italy.

§ **1. Terra,** etc. The transition is suggested by *caelo solove.*

etsi, etc., 'though somewhat varying in appearance'. *Specie* **is** abl. of respect, *aliquanto* of measure. Some interpret *specie* as 'in parts', as contrasted with *in universum;* but the word is only once so used by Tacitus in contrast to *genere* (*Dial.* 25).

in universum, 'generally': cp. c. 6, 4.

aut silvis, etc., 'is wild with forests or hideous with swamps'. Such was the general impression made on southerners by the primeval forests of Germany and the marshes of the northwest and even of the Rhine valley (though it was then drier on the whole than it now is), which were so troublesome to Roman armies (cp., e.g., *A.* 1. 63–8). The statement is exaggerated, but does not mean that western Germany (of which Tacitus was thinking) was nothing but forest and morass, as is shown by the qualifications here made, *differt, satis ferax,* etc., and by his later detailed description. Germany was, of course, more extensively wooded than it is to-day, but the Italian is still struck by the sylvan richness of the country. The most notable forest was the Hercynian (c. 28), extending from the middle Rhine to beyond the sources of the Vistula and serving for centuries as a barrier against German penetration southwards (*Introd.,* Section iv); among others named were Bacenis (perhaps the Rhön in Hessen), Caesia and Teutoburgiensis (both in Westphalia), and Abnoba (Black Forest). Even in the eleventh century *omnis tractus Germaniae profundis horret saltibus* (Adam of Bremen, 4, 1); but archaeological remains show that most of the open cultivable land was thickly studded with human settlements, often of astonishing size.

ventosior, contrasted with *humidior,* as implying that the winds make it drier. The West of Germany is in fact rainier and foggier than the East, and in the valley of the middle

Danube strong winds are frequent as the result of variations
of temperature, and the rainfall is lower.

satis, 'in crops of grain' (in contrast to *arborum*). The
ablative of respect with *ferax* is used by Virgil (*G.* 2, 222),
but elsewhere Tacitus uses the genitive. Pliny (18, 149)
mentions oats as the chief German cereal; but barley, wheat
(cp. c. 23, 1), and millet were cultivated from the later Stone
Age. According to Tacitus, they grew no other crop but corn
of some kind (c. 26, 2).

frugiferarum arborum, i.e. such fruit trees as southern
climates have. This is consistent with the mention of *agrestia
poma* in c. 23, 1; and the *frugifera arbor* of c. 10, 1 has a
different meaning (but the use of the adjective in two different senses is a literary lapse). The statement is borne out
by the fact that, with the exception of the apple (which was
cultivated in middle and northern Europe from the later
Stone Age), the German names for fruits, such as cherries,
plums, pears, peaches, olives, and grapes, are all derived from
Latin. Some, however, think that Tacitus had in mind only
the vine and olive, which constituted the wealth of Italy.

impatiens, so *solum . . . patiens frugum* (*Agr.* 12, 5), etc.
pecorum is distinguished from *armenta* in c. 21, 1, *A.* 13.
55, 3 and by other writers and from *equi* (c. 12, 2), and the
word may here be understood of sheep, goats, and swine, but
is much better taken in the wide sense of flocks and herds
generally, as in Lucr. 1, 163, Cic. *Phil.* 3, 31 (*armentorum
reliquique pecoris*); we thus get the usual three aspects of
husbandry—*sata, frug. arbores*, and *pecora* (as in Verg. *Georg.*
1–3).

plerumque improcera, sc. *sunt*, 'are mostly undersized'.
Plerumque varies in meaning in Tacitus between 'often',
'very often' and 'mostly', 'usually'. The change of subject
is awkward, but it is impossible to call the land itself *improcera*. The word seems elsewhere used only by Gellius of
stunted human bodies (4. 19, 1).

§ 2. armentis, 'cattle'. In *A.* 4. 72, 3 the *modica domi armenta*
of Germans are contrasted with the huge buffaloes (chiefly
known by exaggerated report) of their forests. Caesar speaks
of their *iumenta* (perhaps draught cattle) as *prava atque de-
formia*, but trained to hard work (4. 2, 2).

suus honor, 'their natural beauty', such as Virgil describes
in well-bred cattle (*G.* 3, 51).

aut is often used by Tacitus in negative clauses, especially
to connect two synonymous or nearly synonymous ideas
(cp. c. 24, 2; 35, 3). It is also used frequently by other writers
(Löfstedt, *Syntactica*, 1928, p. 273 n.).

gloria frontis, 'pride of brow': they had **not** the fine branching horns of Italian oxen, and native German cattle do not have them to-day. The expression is poetical and suggested by Virgil's *gloria ruris* (*G.* 1, 168), etc.

numero gaudent, 'the number (not the quality) of their herd is their pride; these are their sole and greatly cherished wealth'. *Gaudent,* as in c. 15, 3; 21, 3; 46, 2. *Solae,* for their land was hardly held as private property (c. 26, 2), and their household goods were few. Caesar similarly speaks of them as *pecoris . . . cupidissimi* (6. 35, 6). The old German words represented by mod. Germ. *Vieh,* Eng. *fee,* signified both cattle and wealth (cp. *pecunia and pecus*), the latter meaning having already become the only one in Gothic, Old Norse, and Anglo-Saxon; and cattle are an established medium of exchange (c. 12, 2; 18, 2; 21, 1, etc.), as with the Homeric Greeks.

§ 3. **propitiine an irati,** 'whether it be in mercy or in wrath that the gods have denied them'. *Propitii* expresses the common sentiment: *effodiuntur opes, irritamenta malorum* (Ov. *Met.* 1, 140); *aurum inrepertum et sic melius situm cum terra celat* (Hor. *Carm.* 3. 3, 49); but *irati* admits the value of silver and gold.

nec . . . adfirmaverim nullam, stronger than *negaverim ullam.* When writing the *Annals,* Tacitus knew of silver mines in the Taunus district (11. 20, 4); this information, probably derived from Pliny, he had overlooked or forgotten when he wrote the *Germania.* The Rhine gold (cp. the Nibelungen saga), carried down by the two rivers Emme, tributaries of the Aare, and extracted by washing, is not heard of till the fifth century, and mining was not practised till the tenth. It is shown below that the precious metals were at this time known to Germans, and their names, which are the same as in the Baltic and Slavonic languages and have no connexion with Latin, would show that they were not originally procured through Roman intercourse.

§ 4. **haud perinde,** 'not as much as might be expected', 'not particularly' (so in c. 34, 1). The expression is so used with an implied comparison in *Agr.* 10, 6; *A.* 2. 88, 4, etc. (*Perinde* and *proinde* are often confused in MSS. of Tacitus owing to the similarity of the abbreviations of *per* and *pro*.) The context shows that Tacitus is here saying that the possession and use of precious metals as such was little valued, which is not inconsistent with the fact that they were valued by some as a medium of exchange. But the archaeological evidence shows that the Germans were by no means indifferent to the precious metals: see *Introd.,* p. xxxvii.

est videre, ἔστιν ἰδεῖν, 'one may see', a 'Graecism' common in poets, but very rare in prose till after Livy's time. Livy has it in 42. 41, 2, and Tacitus again in *A*. 16. 34, 2 (*coniectare erat*). The fact is taken from the account of an eyewitness, pretty certainly Pliny in his *Bella Germaniae*.

legatis et principibus, 'to their envoys abroad and chiefs at home'. On the term *principes*, see *Introd.*, pp. liii ff. They were the leading men of the tribe, the most prominent of the nobles, some of whom were *de facto* rulers in virtue of their prestige and influence; but the word *principes* does not connote the tenure of an official position, although some of the *principes* were appointed judicial magistrates (c. 12, 3). They all maintained a retinue of chosen warriors (c. 13 f.), and the gifts were a tribute to the reputation which they and their fighting men enjoyed beyond the borders of their tribe.

non in alia vilitate, 'held no less cheap', for *in eadem . . . atque*: cp. *neque alia . . . pietate*, *A*. 3. 16, 5. But the silver-mounted drinking-horns described in *B.G*. 6, 28, the silver treasure of Hildesheim (Hanover), and rich grave finds of the first century in Saxony, Silesia, Pomerania and elsewhere show that *non in alia vilitate* is an overstatement.

quamquam, 'and yet', 'however', so used in a main clause to qualify a statement in c. 18, 1; *Dial*. 28, 3; 33, 5; *A*. 12. 65, and elsewhere.

proximi, 'those nearest to us', on the Rhine and Danube frontier.

usum commerciorum, 'trade intercourse'. On Roman traders in Germany, see *A*. 2. 62, 4, etc.: they brought cloth stuffs, metal and glass vessels, pottery of a finer kind, ornaments, and wine. The Germans exported slaves (c. 24, 4), amber (c. 45, 4), hides, furs, wild animals for the Roman arena, goose feathers, honey, and blond ladies' hair.

in pretio habent, a variation of the commonplace *magni habent*.

agnoscunt atque eligunt, 'know well ("recognize" as known before) and prefer'. The practice of the Germans had its parallel among the Caledonians beyond the Roman frontier, who used Roman coins as a native currency for at least three hundred years (Sir. G. Macdonald, *Proc. Soc. Ant. Scot*. lii, 1917–18, p. 234; lviii. 327; lxviii. 36).

simplicius et antiquius, 'in a more natural and old-fashioned manner'.

§ 5. probant, 'they like', cp. Hor. *Carm. Saec*. 15.

serratos bigatosque, sc. *denarios*, 'with notched (not "milled") edges and stamped with the two-horse chariot'. The chariot contained a figure of Victory or of Diana. These two types of coin were old Republican denarii, issued during the century (or a little more) preceding 55 B.C. The purpose of the serration is uncertain, but probably it was to show at a glance the purity of the metal; yet the fact that some *serrati* are plated coins shows that the device was not proof against counterfeiting. See fig. 1.

The German preference for these old coins was due to their long familiarity with them (*diu notam*). In such matters primitive peoples are notoriously conservative: the Austrians continued to mint the Maria Theresa dollar for the Levantine and East African trade long after it had passed out of use elsewhere. But it was not only the Germans who liked the old denarii. After Nero had reduced the silver content of the denarius, they continued to circulate (owing apparently to the superior quality of the metal, despite Gresham's law) within the Roman Empire as well as beyond its frontiers until they were demonetized by Trajan in A.D. 107 (Dio, 68. 15, 3[1]). The statement of Tacitus is amply confirmed by scattered coins and hoards found in western Germany. Hoards of pre-Neronian coins consist of *bigati*, *serrati* and other Republican denarii with a few of Augustus and Tiberius: one found at Liebeshausen in northern Bohemia contains about 200 Republican denarii, mostly serrate. Hoards of later coins show that the old denarii were still in circulation, though in small numbers, and the Liebeshausen find seems to have been buried about the end of the first century. Consequently Norden's view (pp. 280 ff.) that Tacitus was reproducing from a pre-Neronian source a statement which was not true of his own time is untenable. (The numismatic material has been most fully studied by S. Bolin, who gives a summary of his results in *Röm.-Germ. Komm. Bericht*, xix. 86–145.)

quoque, i.e. besides preferring old silver to new, they prefer silver generally to gold. Roman gold coins are in fact rare in Germany, but three hoards (found at Düsseldorf, near Hanover, and in Bohemia) contain *aurei* of Augustus or Augustus and Tiberius, and one in Schleswig-Holstein consists of six *aurei* of Tiberius, Claudius, and Nero. Bolin, *op. cit.*, p. 108.

nulla adfectione, causal ablative, 'not from any predilection', varied to *quia*, etc.

promisca, articles in general use (cp. c. 44, 3), not costly luxuries for the few.

CHAPTER VI

ARMS AND MILITARY TACTICS

§ 1. **Ne ferrum,** etc. The mention of metals leads on to weapons, and thus introduces the section on manners and customs lasting down to c. 27 and dealing first with public life (cc. 6–15).

superest, 'is abundant', as probably in c. 26, 2, and in *Agr.* 44, 2; 45, 6, etc.

ex genere telorum, 'from the character of their weapons'. The inference, which—as *colligitur* (instead of *colligi potest*) shows—is that of Tacitus' source, probably Pliny, is not reconcilable with the archaeological evidence; but the amount of iron produced was no doubt small in comparison with the output of the eastern Alps, the Jura, and Lorraine, and it was of inferior quality. Bog iron is common in North Germany, and iron was obtained from ironstone and other ores in the Taunus, Westerwald, Sauerland (Westphalia), and other places. Tacitus himself mentions the iron mines worked by the Cotini (c. 43). No bronze weapons have been found in graves after the late Hallstatt period.

rari, 'only a few': cp. *raris . . . navibus* (c. 2, 1).

gladiis. This statement was true only of the large cutting sword, which was rare in the first century A.D. In the time of Tacitus, however, short swords were used by the Germans —in the west, two-edged thrusting swords of the Roman type (which replaced the long sword soon after the beginning of our era), in central and eastern Germany one-edged swords, which were originally East-German (particularly Burgundian) weapons but gradually spread westwards beyond the Elbe (M. Jahn, *Bewaffnung d. Germ.*, Mannusbibl. 16, 125 ff., 145 ff.). *Gladii* are mentioned in c. 18, 2 (a passage which does not tally with the statement made here); 24, 1; 43, 6. (See figs. 2–4.)

maioribus lanceis, like the Gallic lances (*gaesa*) with their long and broad leaf-shaped heads and long shafts. The *enormes* or *ingentes hastae* of Germans are mentioned several times (*A.* 1.64, 3; 2. 14, 3; 21, 1; *H.* 5. 18, 1; Lucan, 6, 259) as very formidable except at close quarters, but archaeological evidence shows that they were not common in the time of Tacitus. In *A.* 2. 14, 4 Germanicus is made to say that only the front rank had *hastae*, the rest *praeusta aut brevia tela*, but that is the exaggeration of a general seeking to encourage his troops (cp. note on *scuto*, § 2).

frameas. These spears with narrow and short iron heads (here called *hastae*, in contrast to the *maiores lanceae*) seem to be the *brevia tela* contrasted with *hastae* in *A., l. c.* Many

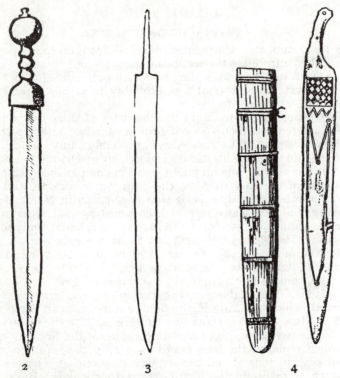

FIG. 2. Roman sword. After Jahn.
FIG. 3. German sword-blade of the early Imperial period. After Jahn.
FIG. 4. One-edged German sword and scabbard (3rd cent. A.D.). National Museum, Copenhagen.

heads of *frameae* have been found (see fig. 5) and they prove the accuracy of Tacitus' description. The German word (derived by Müllenhoff from *fram*, 'forwards', as denoting its mode of use) is used by Tacitus only in the *Germania*. It is used without reference to Germans in Juv. 13, 79, and given in a list of weapons in Gell. 10, 25, and Ulpian, *Dig.* 43. 16. 3, 2.

ad usum habili applied to the spear-head alone (instead of the head and shaft together) is the result of stylistic condensation.

§ 2. scuto frameaque, in contrast to the Roman horsemen, who always appear on tombstones of the first century armed with shield, lance, and sword. The statement is confirmed by dis-

a

b

FIG. 1

a. A *bigatus* of c. 160 B.C. (in the British Museum).
Obv. Head of Bellona. Rev. Diana in *biga* drivig
b. A *serratus* of (probably) 118 B.C. (in the British Museum).
Obv. Head of Bellona. Rev. Gaul in chariot fighting.

FIG. 8. Roman auxiliary horseman riding over a fallen German, naked save for light mantle.

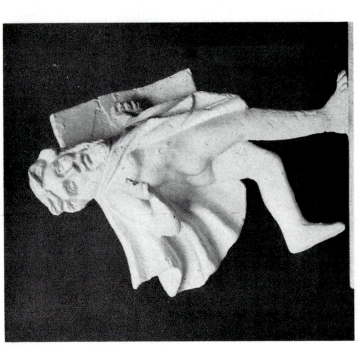

FIG. 7. Bronze figure from Dalmatia: bearded German running, clad only in mantle, holding long hexagonal shield (sword missing from right hand).

FIG. 9. Tombstone from Procolitia of a *signifer* (probably of cohors I Batavorum) holding a standard surmounted by the figure of a bull.

coveries for the Rhenish tribes (though leaders sometimes had swords) and for the horsemen of the Danubian Suebi by the column of Marcus (Petersen, Bild 8, 24, 28, etc.), although there also a few have swords. Elsewhere graves of horsemen belonging to the early imperial period usually have swords (Jahn, *op. cit.*, p. 217).

The German shields are described by Germanicus (*A., l. c.*) as very large, but of wicker or thin coloured boards, not strengthened by iron or leather. The description is only par-
tially confirmed by grave-finds, which show that they were sometimes covered with leather (cp. Caes. *B.G.* 2, 33) and that they mostly had an iron boss and were surprisingly small. The shape varied. Monuments of the first century show footmen with rectangular or hexagonal, and occasion-
ally oval, shields. Round shields are noted as exceptional in c. 43, 6, but the monuments show that they were

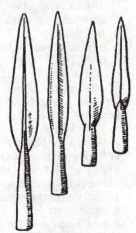

FIG. 5. Frameae. After Schumacher. $\frac{1}{6}$.

used by German horsemen (as well as larger or smaller oval shields, the former like those of the Roman cavalryman), and on the Antonine column the prevalent form is round or oval. See fig. 6.

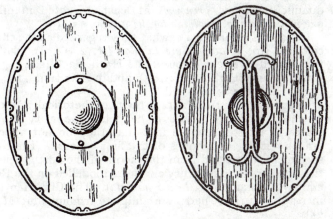

FIG. 6. German oval shield. Restored by Schumacher and Kossinna. About $\frac{1}{12}$.

missilia, hardly the *saxa glandesque* of *H.* 5. 17 (in which case *pluraque singuli* would be otiose), but probably small lances, *lanceolae,* such as those mentioned as used by the Goths in *Hist. Aug.,* vit. Claud. 8, 5.

spargunt, so used of missiles in poetry (Verg. *Aen.* 7, 687; 8, 695; 12, 51) and later in prose.

in immensum vibrant, 'hurl to a vast distance'.

nudi, etc., explaining *in immensum,* 'naked or lightly clad in a short cloak'. On the *sagum,* see c. 17, 1; *levis* is used of one lightly armed in Verg. *Aen.* 9, 548. The contrast *sagulo leves* suggests that *nudi* is to be taken literally (not in the sense of 'scantily clad', as in Verg. *G.* 1, 299; Pliny, *N.H.* 18, 20), and in fact Germans often fought completely naked, as is shown by Polybius' account of the Gaesatae, German mercenaries of the Gauls in Etruria, discarding not merely their *saga* but all their clothing (2, 28), and by first-century tombstones of Roman cavalry soldiers on the Rhine, which portray fallen Germans wearing no clothes at all or at most a light mantle; battles were, of course, fought in summer. Sometimes however, though seldom, they are shown in trousers (*bracae*) with the upper part of the body bare, and *nudi* would be applicable to such a partial garb: this *may* be what is meant by *nudis corporibus* in *H.* 2. 22. See figs. 7, 8.

cultus. The next clause shows that the word is to be taken of the adornment of arms and horses, and perhaps also military decorations, such as were fashionable among Romans (*H.* 1. 88; *A.* 1. 24, 4, etc.) or Gauls (Livy, 7. 10, 7; Verg. *Aen.* 8, 660, etc.). The statement would seem to require some qualification: the *principes* at least delighted in gifts of *magn⟨ific⟩a arma, phalerae torquesque* (c. 15, 3).

lectissimis coloribus, i.e. what they regarded as the choicest colours. Cp. *fucatas colore tabulas* (*A.* 2. 14, 4). Different tribes used different colours: the Harii black (c. 43, 5), the Cimbri white (Plut. *Marius,* 25), and in later times, the Frisii brown, and the Saxons red.

§ 3. **paucis loricae.** In *A.* 2. 14, 4 they are rhetorically described as wholly without cuirasses or helmets. The rarity of breastplates is attested by the fact that they do not appear in graves nor on tombstones of the first century. The earliest specimens, recovered from the moors of the north, belong to the third or fourth century and were modelled on the Roman cuirass of chain-mail (*lorica hamata*). The Cimbrian horsemen appear to have had more complete armour (Plut. *Marius,* 25).

vix uni alterive, 'hardly one or two', i.e. very few. Cp. *Dial.* 21, 1; *Agr.* 15, 5, etc.

cassis aut galea. Where these terms are distinguished, the former denotes a helmet of metal, the latter one of hide (κυνέη): Isidorus, *Etym.* 18, 14, 1. The German warrior fought bareheaded, as he is always represented on Rhenish tombstones. A few helmets have been found on German soil, mostly near the Roman frontier, but they are late and they were not worn by the rank and file. On the Antonine column a leather cap (*pileus*) is shown in a few cases.

equi, etc. Caesar rehorsed his German auxiliaries, because their horses were *minus idonei* (7. 65, 5); but he speaks of the skill of the Suebi and of the Usipetes and Tencteri in dismounting and fighting (4. 2, 3; 12, 2). The Tencteri are exceptionally noted in c. 32, 2 as good horsemen, but the Batavi were no less skilful (Dio, 55. 24, 7; Plut. *Otho*, 12). The Germans despised saddles (Caes. 4. 2, 4).

sed nec, 'but also they are not taught'.

variare gyros, equivalent to *varios gyros peragere* or *flectere*, to wheel in various directions, now to right, now to left, in executing complicated movements, like the description of the figure 8 or the evolutions of the *Troiae lusus* (*Aen.* 5, 584; Suet. *Caes.* 39; *Aug.* 43). Cp. *in gyros ire coactus equus* (Ov. *A. A.* 3, 384), etc.

in rectum, etc., 'they ride them straight forward or, with but one turn, to the right, keeping line so closely as they wheel that no one drops behind'. The horsemen form the radius of a circle, and the line wheels rightwards from the centre with an even front. Conciseness of expression has produced an inexactitude: each rider describes an arc, longer in proportion to his distance from the centre, but it is not the *orbis* that is *coniunctus*, but the even line which the riders keep during the movement. It is not to be supposed that the Germans could not make the left turn: the right wheel was preferred in order to avoid exposing to the enemy the side unprotected by the shield. Tacitus' information about the cavalry manœuvres was probably derived from Pliny, who in his youth wrote *de iaculatione equestri* (*N.H.* 8, 162).

§ 4. in universum aestimanti, dative of the person judging, 'on a broad view', as in *Agr.* 11, 3.

plus penes peditem, etc. This is specially noted of the Chatti (c. 30, 3), as of the Britons in *Agr.* 12, 1.

eoque = *ideoque*. So frequently in Tacitus (c. 20, 3; 28, 1; 41, 1; 44, 2, etc.), as in Sallust and Livy.

mixti proeliantur. The subject is general. The Germans practised a mixed mode of fighting, which is more clearly described by Caesar (1, 48). The horsemen in advance of the line were supported by an equal number of picked footmen, who could keep up with them by holding on to the horses' manes and protected them if they fell wounded. The same tactics were practised by the Bastarnae (Plut. *Aem. Paul.* 12), by the Gauls (Livy, 44, 26, 3; cp. Pausan. 10. 19, 6), and by others, and they were occasionally adopted by Caesar himself (7, 65; *B. C.* 3, 75 and 84). The German motive was hardly, as Tacitus says, to utilize their greater strength in infantry, but rather to strengthen their cavalry. When their cavalry increased in number, this method of fighting fell into disuse: it is not heard of after A.D. 357 (Ammianus 16. 12, 21–2).

5. definitur et numerus, sc. *peditum delectorum.* It seems plain that Tacitus is speaking only of the picked footmen and contrasting them with the mass of infantry which forms the main line, *acies.* The number of the horsemen is not mentioned, because it was obviously equal to that of the footmen (as indeed Caesar's description shows that it was).

centeni ex singulis pagis. *Pagus* was the term used by Romans for the subdivisions of Gallic and German *civitates*; in both countries the *pagi* varied in number and in size according to the size of the tribe and its territory. See *Introd.*, p. lvii. *Centeni*: the select corps of *pedites* was called by a German name meaning 'the hundred men' (*huntari*), but the word had lost its numerical significance (the number 100 being usually exceeded?) and had become a title and a distinction. Similarly the Roman court of *Centumviri* numbered 180 in Trajan's time (Pliny, *Epp.* 6. 33, 3), while it was only originally that the Roman military *centuria* numbered exactly 100. According to Caesar, each horseman chose his footman from the whole force (*ex omni copia*), a statement which is not easy to reconcile with the clan organization of German armies (c. 7, 3). The century was also used in judicial arrangements (c. 12, 3). For the theory that Tacitus in both passages radically misunderstood the facts, see *Introd.*, p. lviii ff.

idque ipsum, viz. *centeni.*

nomen et honor, 'a title and a distinction'.

per cuneos, 'in wedge-like formations', like a Greek Δ, fenced all round with shields (*H.* 4. 20). The formation was likened to a boar's head and was called by later Romans *caput porcinum* (Veg. *de re mil.* 3. 19, 6). The composition of each separate *cuneus* is described in c. 7, 3; and these again could be combined into one of the whole people. Such *cunei* of distinct tribes are mentioned in *H.* 4. 16; 5. 18, etc. German auxiliaries in the Roman army retained their native formation (Dessau, *I. L. S.*, 2635, 4761).

§ 6. loco, 'from your position'; to a Roman this was disgraceful. This German tactic is mentioned in *A.* 1. 56, 6, and with rhetorical contempt by Germanicus in *A*. 2. 14, 5. The strict military discipline of the Chatti was exceptional (c. 30, 2).

dummodo, equivalent to *dum*, which Tacitus always uses in this sense except here and in *Dial*. 25, 2.

instes, 'you press forward'. The subject is general, as with *tueare* in c. 14, 2.

consilii quam formidinis, 'a mark of prudence rather than of cowardice', qualitative genitive. The omission of *magis* or *potius* in comparative sentences is very common in Tacitus' later works, e.g. *pacem quam bellum* (*A*. 1. 58, 2), but does not occur elsewhere in his earlier.

dubiis, 'which they are in danger of losing', rather than 'indecisive'. *Corpora* includes the wounded. It would be only in utter defeat that the dead were left on the field.

praecipuum, 'the greatest'. The adjective has often in silver Latin, and always in Tacitus, the force of a superlative (c. 7, 3; 14, 1; etc.).

concilium, the Assembly, described in c. 11–12.

ignominioso, 'the disgraced' (ἀτίμῳ), explained by the context. The penalty is thus loss of civil rights. Similarly in Gaul, prohibition of attendance at sacrifice made a man legally and socially an outcast (Caes. *B. G.* 6, 13).

multique . . . laqueo, 'and so many', etc., as in c. 7, 3 and frequently. The shame is expiated by a shameful mode of death. For confirmed cowardice sentence of death by a special mode of drowning was passed by the Assembly (c. 12, 1).

superstites bellorum. So with genitive in *Agr*. 3, 2, etc., with dative in c. 14, 1, etc.

CHAPTER VII

THE LIMITATIONS OF LEADERSHIP IN PEACE AND WAR, AND THE SPRINGS OF GERMAN VALOUR

What is said about *reges* and *duces* is meant, not to supplement the description of the government of German states given in cc. 11–12, but to show that German valour is not the result of *obsequium* and *disciplina* (like the Roman) but depends on religious and social forces. Kingship was hereditary in so far as the people, when possible, chose a successor from the ruling family, but election was always necessary. If the old royal family became extinct, or if for other reasons a new dynasty were established, the new ruler was uplifted on a shield to be displayed to the people gathered in Assembly, and the same ceremony followed the election of a *dux* (see *H.* 4. 15). Tacitus makes no mention here of *principes*, who were also men of

68 NOTES

noble birth, perhaps because they were not elected like kings
and *duces*. See *Introd.*, pp. liii ff.

The word *king* (Anglo-Saxon *cyning*, Ger. *könig*, old Norse
konungr) was borrowed by the West Germans from Scandinavia,
and is now held to be derived from *kona*, 'woman' or 'wife',
and to mean consort of the goddess of fertility (see on c. 44, 2).
Cp. *Camb. Anc. Hist.* xi. 75.

§ 1. **Reges**, etc., 'they choose kings by noble birth, generals by
prowess'. *Ex*, 'in accordance with', as in c. 3, 4; 9, 3, etc.

duces. The king would normally be leader in war, unless in-
capacitated by age or other causes, but a *dux*, *Herzog* (O.H.G.
herizogo), would have to be chosen when rule was divided
or when several tribes united to wage a war. Instances of
such elected leaders are Ariovistus, Arminius (A.D. 9), Civilis
and Brinno (in A.D. 69, *H.* 4. 13 ff.). Cp. Caes. 6, 23 *cum bellum
civitas aut illatum defendit aut infert, magistratus qui ei bello
praesint . . . deliguntur*.

infinita ac libera, 'unlimited and arbitrary'. The two
adjectives are practically synonymous. So the kings of
the Frisians are said to rule *in quantum Germani regnantur*
(*A*. 13. 54, 2); cp. c. 43, 6. The contrast which Tacitus had in
mind was primarily Eastern monarchies (cp. c. 37, 3).

For *ac* several MSS. read *aut*, which is equally possible (note
on c. 5, 2), but *ac* has much better authority; cp. *nec quicquam
grave ac serium* (*A*. 3. 50, 5), *nihil tam instabile ac fluxum*
(*A*. 13. 19, 1), etc.

exemplo, etc., 'lead by example rather than by authority,
owing to the admiration they win if they show themselves
energetic', etc. The words *si prompti . . . agant* go with
admiratione (causal ablative) and explain *exemplo*. Cp. *suadendi magis quam iubendi potestate* (c. 11, 5). Illustrations
are furnished by Florus, *Epit.* 1. 38, 18, where the Cimbrian
king Boiorix falls fighting *in prima acie*; *H.* 3, 21, where the
Suebic kings Sido and Italicus *primori in acie versabantur*;
and Amm. 16. 12, 24, who describes how at the battle of
Strassburg in A.D. 357 Chnodomar, king of the Alamanni,
*anteibat cornu sinistrum . . . armorum nitore conspicuus ante
alios*.

§ 2. **ceterum**, restrictive, as in c. 9, 3, etc., introducing a limitation of the *imperium* of the *dux*, which is in strong contrast to
Roman custom.

animadvertere, 'to put to death', usually with *in aliquem*.
The penalties are enumerated in descending order, pointed by
the alliteration, and contrast with Roman custom, although
vincire is not attested as a Roman military punishment.

ne verberare quidem, as every Roman centurion could do.

sacerdotibus permissum. Caesar states that the power of
life and death lay in the hands of the leader chosen to conduct a war (6. 23, 4). The apparent discrepancy is to be explained by distinguishing the execution of the sentence from
its pronouncement, as the words *nec (quasi) ducis iussu*
suggest. Other explanations, both unacceptable, are that
Caesar's information may have applied only to tribes among
which a state of constant warfare led to an increase of the
general's power, or that in the century and a half intervening
between Caesar and Tacitus the powers of the *dux* had been
curtailed. The exercise of penal powers independently of the
supreme command is not conceivable; see further next note.
Of German priests Caesar says nothing: he merely contrasts
the Germans with the Gauls as having no Druids to superin-
tend divine worship, i.e. no priestly caste, which does not
exclude the existence of priests. A priest of the Chatti,
named Libes, is mentioned by Strabo among the captives
led in triumph by Germanicus in A.D. 17 (7. 1, 4, p. 292). See
further on *sacerdos civitatis*, c. 10, 2; and on the whole subject, Dopsch, *Grundlagen d. europ. Kulturentwicklung*, ii, 29 ff.

non quasi in poenam, etc., 'and that not as if by way of
punishment or at the general's order, but as if by command
of the tutelary god'. The force of *quasi* extends to *ducis
iussu*. *In*, 'with a view to', as often. The *deus* was primarily
Tiu (Mars), but Wodan may be included: on them see c. 9, 1.
Breaches of discipline were regarded as sins against the god,
and their punishment was an expiatory sacrifice to him,
carried out by the priest as his minister. In a similar spirit
some or even all of the vanquished in battle were offered as
victims to the gods of the victors (*A.* 1. 61, 5; 13. 57, 3). If
Tacitus' interpretation was his own, as is usually the case, it
is at least in accord with primitive belief. The Romans also
regarded 'the execution of the criminal condemned to death
as an expiatory sacrifice offered to the outraged deity, just as
much as the slaying of an enemy in righteous war' (Mommsen, *R.H.* i. 221, E. Tr.). The penal power of the priest in the
Assembly (c. 11, 4) was likewise based on religion.

§ 3. effigiesque, etc., 'and so (because of the god's presence in
battle) they carry with them into battle certain images and
emblems', etc. These were their standards. The subject of
ferunt, as of *credunt*, is the Germans. According to Müllenhoff's generally accepted explanation, the *effigies* were images
of animals sacred to the gods (such as the snake and wolf of
Wodan, the ram of Tiu, the bear and goat of Donar, the boar
of Frey), while the *signa* were attributes of the gods (such as
the spear of Wodan, the sword of Tiu, the hammer of Donar).

The explanation of *effigies* is borne out by *H.* 4. 22 *depromptae silvis lucisque ferarum imagines.* The Cimbri carried with them a bronze figure of a bull (Plut. *Marius,* 23), and Roman monuments occasionally depict *signiferi* of auxilary units holding standards consisting of a pole surmounted by figures of animals (fig. 9).

quodque, etc., appositional relative clause, referring to the following *non casus . . . facit.* For *praecipuum,* see on c. 6, 6.

turmam aut cuneum, 'squadron or division': on the *cuneus,* see c. 6, 5.

familiae et propinquitates, i.e. families and clans fought together. The same tactical arrangement is recommended to Agamemnon in *Il.* 2, 362 κρῖν' ἄνδρας κατὰ φῦλα, κατὰ φρήτρας, Ἀγάμεμνον, | ὡς φρήτρη φρήτρηφιν ἀρήγηι, φῦλα δὲ φύλοις. Among the Slavs of Herzegovina members of the *bratstvo,* 'brotherhood', still fight together. Caesar states that the allotments of land (see c. 26, 1) followed a similar principle: *gentibus cognationibusque hominum, qui una coierunt, quantum et quo loco visum est agri attribuunt* (6. 22, 2).

et in proximo, etc. The women and children were thus brought into the field by Civilis (*H.* 4. 18) and by Ariovistus (*B.G.* 1. 51, 3), also by Thracians (*A.* 4. 51, 2) and Britons (*A.* 14. 34, 4). The wives of the Teutons are represented as even slaying their own warriors in their flight (Plut. *Marius,* 19). But it was not, as Tacitus represents, the general practice to bring women and children into the field, which would have fatally hampered military movements and increased the difficulty of food-supply: cp. Caes. *B. G.* 4, 19, where the Suebi ordered their wives, children, and belongings to be placed for safety in forests.

pignora, 'their dearest', often so used for *pignora amoris* (*Agr.* 38, 1; *A.* 12. 2, 1, etc.) in poetry, Livy, and later prose.

unde . . . audiri. Although the historical infinitive is used by Tacitus in dependent clauses, e.g. with *cum, ubi, donec,* there is no precedent for its use to express what is customary (see Dräger, *Synt. und Stil des Tacitus,* §§ 28 d, 172); nor is Virgil's *hinc exaudiri gemitus* (*Aen.* 6, 557; 7, 15) really parallel, though there may be a reminiscence of it in this poetical and rhetorical passage. The use of *praeponere,* etc., in c. 30, 2 is quite different.

§ 4. **hi,** the wives and mothers, supplied from the sense. The gender is attracted to that of *testes* and *laudatores.*

ferunt, 'take', for treatment, not merely in the sense of 'go and show them'. Such knowledge as existed of the art of healing was in the hands of the women: their practice of the art is mentioned in German epics.

exigere, 'to examine', comparing them with others, in respect of their honourableness. The verb is so used by Livy, Seneca, and Quintilian. The sense 'require' or 'demand' does not suit *pavent*; and *exigere* can hardly mean 'to examine medically' (*inspicere*).

cibosque, etc., a zeugma for *cibos apportant et ad virtutem hortantur.* Tacitus often thus joins material and mental ideas, as e.g. *metu aut montibus* in c. 1, 1. *Hortamen* (for *hortamentum*) is a rare poetic form. The frequentative *gestant* expresses regular practice. Another function of the women in war was to bind and guard the prisoners.

CHAPTER VIII

REVERENCE FOR WOMEN

§ 1. Memoriae proditur, 'it is recorded', the reference being to some literary source, perhaps Pliny or Livy, going back possibly to Posidonius, whose graphic descriptions of the women's intervention in a rout are reproduced by Plutarch, *Marius*, 19 and 27. The present tense (also in *A.* 3. 65, 3) has been thought to imply a still living oral tradition, but *prodere* is not so used by Tacitus.

inclinatas et labantes, 'wavering and giving way'. *Inclinare* is also used intransitively in the same sense both by Tacitus and by Livy.

obiectu pectorum, a gesture imploring the men to kill them rather than let them become slaves, or preferably to rescue from such a fate the mothers of their children or of themselves: cp. Hecabe's entreaty (*Il.* 22, 81) 'Have regard unto this bosom and pity me, if ever I gave thee consolation of this breast'.

monstrata comminus captivitate, 'pointing (by word and gesture) to the imminence of captivity'. For the sense of *comminus* (= *prope*), cp. *viso comminus . . . agmine* (*H.* 1. 41). The adjectival use of this and other adverbs is common in Tacitus, e.g. c. 37, 3, *Agr.* 10, 2 (*nullis contra terris*), etc. Caesar, *B. G.* 1. 51, 3, gives an example of the women's entreaties: *mulieres in proelium proficiscentes passis manibus flentes implorabant ne se in servitutem Romanis traderent.*

longe impatientius, etc., 'of which they have a far more intolerable dread on their women's account' (than on their own). *Impatienter,* 'unendurably', for the classical *intoleranter. Nomine,* 'on account of', a common phrase borrowed from the headings of business accounts.

puellae quoque nobiles. *Quoque,* as well as male hostages. Only the highborn of either sex would be of value as hostages (cp. *H*. 4. 28). Female hostages are mentioned in *H*. 4. 79 (the wife and sister of Civilis). They were sometimes required by Augustus (*a quibusdam novum genus obsidum feminas exigere temptaverit, quod neglegere marum pignera sentiebat*, Suet. *Aug.* 21), and they appear in ancient Roman history, as in the story of Cloelia (Livy, 2. 13, 6).

§ 2. inesse (sc. *feminis*), etc., a stronger illustration of the respect felt for women. Besides their faith in prophetesses, Müllenhoff notes the respect paid to the feminine ideal in the conception of the female *idisi* or semi-deities, as a link between earth and heaven.

  providum, 'a prophetic gift': cp. *fatidicas* (*H*. 4. 61, 3). Caesar speaks of German *matres familiae* as declaring by lots and prophecies whether or not it was expedient to give battle (*B.G.* 1. 50, 4).

  nec, 'and so they do not', as often.

§ 3. vidimus, in a general sense, 'we Romans'.

  Veledam. This prophetess, one of the Bructeri, played an important part in inspiring the rising of Civilis: see *H*. 4. 61, etc. From Stat. *Silv*. 1. 4, 90 *captivaeque preces Veledae*, we learn that she was captured by Rutilius Gallicus. His campaign against the Bructeri took place in A.D. 77–8 (Dessau, 9052). It does not, however, necessarily follow from the words of Statius that she was taken as a prisoner to Rome. *Velaeda* is the form of the name given several times in the *Histories*, and Dio has Οὐελήδα (67. 5, 3), while Statius makes the second *e* short.

  apud plerosque, 'by many'.

  sed et = *sed etiam*, without a preceding *non solum*, as in c. 17, 3. The use of *et* and the antithesis *tamquam facerent deas* show that *venerati sunt* is synonymous with *numinis loco habuerunt*.

  olim : the time is unknown, but may have been that of the wars of Drusus and Tiberius.

  Auriniam is not a German name, but it may be Celtic (Schönfeld, *Wörterbuch d. altgerm. Personen- und Völkernamen*, p. 38), and there is nothing impossible in the occurrence of Celtic names among West Germans who were in close relations with the Celts: even the Cimbrian king Boiorix had a Celtic name. There is therefore no need to correct to *Albrunam*, a conjecture based on the reading *Albriniam* given in the margin or above the line by several MSS., and yielding the meaning 'gifted with the magical power of the elves' (O.H.G. *alb*, 'elf', *runa*, 'secret').

  complures alias. The prophetesses of the Cimbri are mentioned by Strabo (7. 2, 3, p. 294); Vitellius had one belonging

to the Chatti, *cui velut oraculo acquiescebat* (Suet. *Vit.* 14);
one named Ganna, a successor of Veleda, visited Domitian
(Dio, *l. c.*); and an Egyptian *ostrakon* of the second century
A.D. mentions a 'Sibyl' named Walburg (Βαλουβουργ), belonging to the Semnones, in the service of the governor (*Arch.
f. Religionswiss.* xix, 196).

non adulatione nec tamquam, etc., 'not out of servility nor
as if they were making goddesses': their belief in the divinity
of their prophetesses is genuine (*plerasque feminarum fatidicas
. . . arbitrantur deas, H.* 4. 61)—a palpable hit at the Roman
practice of deifying women, such as Drusilla, sister of Gaius
(Suet. *Cal.* 24), Claudia, the infant daughter of Nero (*A.* 15.
23), Poppaea, wife of Nero (*A.* 16. 21, 2), and others. Tacitus
is very fond, especially in the *Germania*, of closing a chapter
or a description with an epigrammatic sentence or clause.
Here the closing sentence forms a skilful transition to the
next chapter.

CHAPTER IX

THE CHIEF GODS OF THE GERMANS

In this chapter, as in the first part of the *Germania* generally,
Tacitus had in view the western tribes, with which the Romans
came into contact from the line of the Rhine and which he
distinguishes from the Suebic tribes. The three chief gods are
those generally worshipped in the west; neither the first
mentioned nor the second were pan-Germanic deities. The view
put forward by Zangemeister on the basis of the votive inscriptions of the *Equites Singulares* (*CIL.* vi. p. 3069), Dessau, 4634,
and a Marburg relief, that Mercurius, Hercules, and Mars
formed a fixed triad of Germanic divinities, is hardly tenable
(*Neue Heidelb. Jahrbücher*, v (1895), p. 46 ff.: see the criticisms
of Haug, *Germania*, ii. 102, and Drexel, *Röm.-Germ. Komm.
Bericht*, xiv, 1922, p. 16).

Tacitus' account has nothing in common with that of Caesar
(*B. G.* 6. 21, 1), whose statement that the Germans knew no
gods but those whom they see—the Sun, Moon, and Fire—
was based on superficial information. Superstitions and usages
based on a primitive nature-worship no doubt still existed:
thus in *A.* 13. 55, 6 an Ampsivarian king *solem suspiciens et
cetera sidera vocans quasi coram interrogabat*, etc., and the influence of the moon on mundane affairs is illustrated by c. 11, 2
below and Caes. *B. G.* 1. 50, 5. But the Germans had long passed
the most primitive stage of religious development.

§ 1. Deorum maxime Mercurium colunt. The same phrase is
used by Caesar of the Gauls, *deum maxime Mercurium colunt,*

and had been used by Herodotus of the Thracian kings (σέβονται Ἑρμέην μάλιστα θεῶν, 5, 17); but no inference is to be
drawn from these coincidences except perhaps that the
formula had become a stock one in ethnographic literature.

Mercurium. Greeks and Romans alike took it for granted
that the gods of foreign peoples did not essentially differ in
character from their own, and so they called each by what
seemed to be the equivalent name in their own tongue, judging from some aspect of divine power which they recognized
as common to both. This procedure is what Tacitus calls
interpretatio Romana (c. 43, 4), on which cp. Wissowa, *Arch.
f. Religionswiss.* xix. 1–49. The identity of Mercurius and of
Mars (see below) is clear from the German translation, dating
from about the third century A.D., of the Roman planetary
names for the days of the week. The fourth day, *dies Mer-
curii* (Fr. *Mercredi*, Ital. *Mercoledi*), became *Wodanstag*,
which survives in Eng. *Wednesday*. Consequently Mercurius
represents Wodan, Norse Othin, and this identification is expressly made in the eighth century by Paulus Diaconus (1, 9).

The ground of the identification was no doubt the same as
that given by Caesar (6, 17) in the case of the Gallic 'Mercury', that he was regarded as the protector of trade and the
promoter of business activities: in both lands Roman trade
preceded the flag. The hat and wand of the god, resembling
the *petasus* and *caduceus* of Mercury, if they already figured as
attributes, would contribute to the identification. Originally
conceived as the master of magic (O.H.G. *wuot*, 'possessed'),
Wodan was the god of wind and storm, who led through air
and forest the raging host of the spirits of the dead. Later he
became a god of war and victory (his wand transformed into
a spear), in this role ultimately eclipsing the war-god (see
below); and under Gallic and Gallo-Roman influences he took
on the attributes of a culture god, promoting and protecting
the avocations of peaceful life.

certis diebus, 'on definite (festival) days' (cp. c. 11, 2), at
the opening of spring, at the end of the harvest, and perhaps
at the summer and winter solstices. For other instances of
human sacrifice (common among primitive peoples and formerly very prevalent in Gaul), see c. 39, 2; 40, 5, and note on
c. 7, 2. *Quoque* means that other sacrifices were also offered.
The limitation of human sacrifice to Mercurius is an indication of the god's primacy.

Herculem ac Martem. Hercules[1] can only represent Donar,

[1] *Herculem* has been suspected of being an interpolation, because
two of the five MSS. taken as the basis of the text have *et Herculem*
at the end of the sentence. The first two words were in fact dropped

Norse Thor, who could not fail to be mentioned among the great gods and who was the only German god comparable to him. Features common to both were superhuman physical strength and constant journeyings to do battle with giants and monsters and generally to protect mankind from evil (ἀλεξίκακοι): the hammer which Donar wielded would also suggest the club of Hercules. The Roman identification is illustrated by *A*. 2. 12, 1, where mention is made of a forest beyond the Weser consecrated to Hercules, by the name *Castra Herculis* given to a station on the road from Noviomagus to Lugdunum Batavorum, and by two Batavian cults, that of Hercules Magusanus, who was worshipped by soldiers and civilians of the Lower Rhine (Dessau, 2188 with *add.*, 4628 ff.), and that of Hercules Deusoniensis who figures along with him on coins of the emperor Postumus. Later, when divine names were given to the days of the week, Donar was equated with Juppiter: the fifth day (*dies Iovis*, Fr. *Jeudi*, Ital. *Giovedì*) was named *Donnerstag*, Norse *Thorstag*, Eng. *Thursday*. Hercules had no day named after him, and Donar was bound to find a place among the gods of the week.

Mars is undoubtedly Zīu or Tīu, usually believed to have been originally the sky-god (Sanskrit *Dyaus*, Gk. Ζεύς, Lat. *Iuppiter*), but soon developing into a god of war among most German tribes, except perhaps the conservative Semnones (see c. 39, 4). The equation with the sky-god is, however, very dubious (see Shetelig-Falk, *Scandin. Archaeology*, p. 417). His identity with Mars is clear from the fact that the third day of the week *dies Martis* (Fr. *Mardi*, Ital. *Martedì*) became Tīu's day, Eng. *Tuesday*, Scandinavian *Tysdagr*, while the German *Dienstag*, older *Dingstag*, is derived from Mars Thingsus (Dessau, 4760), i.e. Tīu as the god of the *Thing*, the assembly of warriors (cc. 11–12). In A.D. 58 Wodan shared with him the sacrifice of their Chattan prisoners offered by the Hermunduri (*A*. 13. 57); when the Tencteri in A.D. 70 called Tīu *praecipuus deorum* they had war in their minds (*H*. 4. 64).

concessis, best taken to mean such as were 'permissible' by general civilized opinion, in contrast to human sacrifices, which were revolting. Cp. the contrast between *concessa* and *incesta* in *H*. 5. 4, and the use of *concessae voluptates* of those regarded as venial (*A*. 13. 2, 2; 14. 21, 5). Others take it to mean such as are 'permissible' as being clean, eatable by men (only such were in fact sacrificed), or as being allowed for the particular god, which would make a weak remark.

by mistake and afterwards added at the end. No other MS. has the transposition.

Animals sacred to particular deities were not offered in sacrifice. When Caesar says of the Germans *neque sacrificiis student* (6. 21, 1), he means that as compared with the Gauls (6, 16) they did not lay special stress on sacrifices. He uses the same words of their agriculture (6. 22, 1), without meaning that they had no agriculture at all.

§ 2. **pars Sueborum.** On the Suebi see c. 38. As the northern 'Suebic' tribes were votaries of the goddess Nerthus (c. 40), it is often supposed that those here meant were the southern tribes bordering on the Danube, but they were not accessible by sea (*advectam*). Tacitus himself may not have known what tribes were meant.

Isidi. According to Tacitus, Isis is not an *interpretatio Romana* but the Egyptian goddess. Although he sees in the ship-symbol only a proof that the cult was an importation, it was no doubt the ground of the identification. The authority he followed must have known the ship as an emblem of the Egyptian goddess, who in the Graeco-Roman period added the protection of shipping to her manifold functions. In her honour was performed on March 5 the ceremony of the *navigium Isidis* (Dessau, 8745) described by Apuleius (*Met.* 11, 16), in which a ship was dedicated to the goddess and launched to celebrate the re-opening of navigation in the spring. It is possible that the Egyptian cult reached the Germans both from the Danubian provinces, where it was widespread (Drexler, *Kultus d. ägypt. Gottheiten in d. Donauländern*), and from Gaul; but it is also possible that the goddess in question was a German deity whose symbol had the shape of a galley. It is suggested that the *signum* was not really a ship but a ceramic fire-dog, a symbol used in connexion with the cult of the hearth from the Stone Age down to Roman times, which often looks just like a boat. Such symbols have been found in southern Germany, Switzerland, etc., and their occurrence in Noricum might explain the designation of the goddess Noreia as Noreia Isis or Isis Noreia (Dessau, 1467, 4864); see K. Schumacher, *Röm.-Germ. Komm. Bericht*, x. 60 f., and Drexel, *ibid.*, xiv. 5.

The view that *pars Sueborum* refers to a section of the Suebi settled by Augustus in Gaul, supposedly in Flanders, and that Isis represents Nehalennia, a local goddess of Walcheren at the mouth of the Schelde, who resembled Isis in form and symbols, is plainly impossible. On these Suebi, see note on *Agr.* 28, 4, Schönfeld in Pauly-Wissowa, *R. E.*, s.v. *Suebi*, col. 566; and on Nehalennia, Drexel, *l. c.* p. 41.

unde, sc. *sit.* The omission of the subjunctive of *esse* is frequent in Tacitus (cp. c. 13, 3; 19, 3, etc.).

causa et origo, a stereotyped phrase, first used by Cicero. *Peregrino*, in contrast to the true German gods above mentioned. Tacitus' source did not explain how the cult had come to be adopted.

nisi quod, 'except that': cp. *Agr.* 6, 1, etc.

signum ipsum, 'the symbol in itself': *signum* is ambiguous and might denote either a symbolical representation of the goddess or her attribute, emblem (cp. c. 7, 3).

liburnae, a chiefly poetical word for *liburnica* (the only form used elsewhere by Tacitus and perhaps to be read here), which properly denoted a light ship of war with two banks of oars and a central sail, but came to have sometimes a wider meaning.

advectam, 'imported', by sea: cp. *Agr.* 11, 1, etc.

§ 3. ceterum, marking a contrast to Roman custom, the practice of sacrifice being a feature common to both. In this passage, as in others, the facts stated are to be distinguished from the explanation given of them, which is an imaginary interpretation of what was merely a result of primitive conditions.

nec cohibere parietibus, etc., a periphrasis for 'to build temples and make images', in keeping with the elevated philosophical tone of the passage. The primitive Romans likewise had no images of their gods: *dicit Varro etiam antiquos Romanos plus annos centum et septuaginta deos sine simulacro coluisse; 'quod si adhuc', inquit, ' mansisset, castius di observarentur'* (August. *Civ. dei*, 4, 31). The absence of temples and images of gods among primitive peoples was a commonplace of ancient ethnography: cp., e.g., Herod. 1, 131 (of the Persians), and Cic. *De. rep.* 3, 14, where Xerxes is said to have ordered the Athenian temples to be burnt, *quod deos, quorum domus esset omnis hic mundus, inclusos parietibus contineri nefas esse duceret.*

On the apparent inconsistency of Tacitus' statement with the mention of a *templum* in c. 40, 4 and *A.* 1. 51, 2, see the note on the former passage and *Introd.*, p. xxxvi. Romanized Germans learnt to build temples, such as that of Mars Leucetius and Nemetona, the common sanctuary of the Vangiones and Nemetes near Kleinwinternheim (*Altert. heidn. Vorzeit*, v. 108). But in Germany proper temple-building was not common, even in the south, in the fifth century and did not begin in the north till the end of the seventh.

The statement about the absence of images in human form, which is repeated in the case of an East-German tribe in c. 43, 4, is not inconsistent with *numen ipsum* in c. 40, 5 (see the note there). Some primitive wooden and bronze images, supposed (not always with probability) to be representations of deities, have been found in Denmark and one has been found near Berlin (G. Wilke, *Archäol. Erläuterungen z. Germania,* pp. 75 ff.). They appear to be prehistoric, but at most they indicate that here and there rude images of deities were sometimes made.

adsimulare, 'to liken': cp. *Agr.* 10, 3.

ex, 'in accordance with', as in c. 3, 4; 7, 1, etc.

lucos ac nemora, often thus coupled as synonyms or nearly so: cp. c. 10, 4; 45, 7; *Dial.* 12, 1, etc. Such sacred groves are often mentioned: c. 7, 3; 39, 2; 40, 2; 43, 4; *A.* 2. 12, 1; 4. 73, 7, etc.; *H.* 4. 14, 3.

deorumque nominibus, etc., 'and give the names of deities to that mysterious presence which they see by devotion alone'. Cp. *H.* 5. 5, 6 *Iudaei mente sola unumque numen intellegunt: profanos, qui deum imagines mortalibus materiis in species hominum effingant;* 2. 78 *nec simulacrum deo aut templum* (on Mt. Carmel), *ara tantum et reverentia.* Tacitus' interpretation would be readily understood by Romans, who were sensitive to the effect of the solitude and mysterious stillness of deep woods in inspiring a feeling of religious awe: cp. cc. 39–40; Seneca (*Ep.* 41, 3) *secretum loci et admiratio umbrae... fidem tibi numinis faciet;* Tac. *Dial.* 12; Pliny, *N.H.* 12, 3; Quint. 10. 1, 88. But it is not to be supposed that the German religion at that date was as spiritual as Tacitus makes it.

CHAPTER X

ASCERTAINMENT OF THE DIVINE WILL BY LOT AND AUGURY

§ 1. **Auspicia sortesque.** The lot is here described as preliminary to divination (§ 3).

ut qui maxime (sc. *observant*), 'they pay attention, as those do who pay most', i.e. pay as much attention as any people. The ellipse is common, but does not occur elsewhere in Tacitus. Cp. *te sic colam . . . ut quem diligentissime* (Cic. *ad Fam.* 13, 62); *grata ea res ut quae maxime* (Livy, 5. 25, 9).

sortium consuetudo simplex, 'the customary procedure in casting lots is uniform', one and the same everywhere, whereas the Romans had several methods.

frugiferae, not from the Roman point of view and so not inconsistent with c. 5, 1: such trees as oak, beech, and hazel are meant. The branch must be cut from a fruit-bearing tree, because such trees were lucky and by sympathetic magic the luck passes to the act performed with part of them. So with the Romans fruit-bearing trees, with the exception of those that produced black fruit or berries (Macrob. *Sat.* 3. 20, 3) and were consequently sacred to the gods of the underworld, were *arbores felices* (Pliny, *N. H.* 16, 108); on the other hand, *arbores infelices* brought destruction.

arbori decisam: the German word *Los*, Eng. *lot*, originally meant a piece of wood broken off (from a tree), like Gk. κλάδος (from κλᾶν, with which κλῆρος is connected). This was the oldest form of lot: cp. Kern in Pauly-Wissowa, s.v. *Baumkultus*, col. 165.

in surculos amputant, 'cut up into slips', an unusual meaning of *amputare*.

notis, 'marks' of some sort which had a recognized meaning and could not be arbitrarily interpreted. They are not likely to have been runes, for which there is no evidence before about A.D. 200; see Shetelig and Falk, *Scandinavian Archaeology*, 1937, ch. xiii.

super candidam vestem, 'on a white cloth' (so *vestis* in c. 40, 2, 5). White, a symbol of purity, was the colour used in religious ritual: so in § 4 the horses must be white, as in Persia (Herod. 1, 189; 7, 40). Cp. Cic. *De leg.* 2. 18, 45 (quoting Plato) *color albus praecipue decorus deo est cum in cetero tum maxime in textili.*

temere ac fortuito, 'at random (in no deliberate order) and as they chance to fall'. The first word has more a subjective, the latter more an objective meaning, but they are practically synonyms and often conjoined. Cicero, speaking of the lot-oracles of Praeneste, says *temeritas et casus, non ratio nec consilium valet* (*Div.* 2, 85). In popular superstition chance plays an important part in bringing luck: a horseshoe or a four-leaved stalk of clover is of no avail if deliberately looked for.

§ 2. publice, 'for the community', in contrast to *privatim*, 'for individuals'.

consultetur (subjunctive of repeated action), 'if counsel be taken on behalf of the community', is the best correction of the MSS. *consuletur*, corresponding to *consultatio* in the next sentence. The normal meaning of *consultare* in Tacitus is 'to take counsel, deliberate', as in cc. 11, 22; occasionally it means 'consult' in the sense of 'ask advice of', with an accusative of the person consulted, but this meaning is excluded here by the impersonal passive. The alternative correction *consulitur* (indicative for iterative subjunctive is not unparalleled) is equally easy palaeographically, but while it *may* bear the sense given above to *consultetur* (as is shown by *A.* 15. 25, 2 *consuluit inter primores civitatis Nero*), this meaning is extremely rare in Tacitus; and the impersonal passive is against taking the verb in the other sense of 'consult' (to seek counsel from).

sacerdos civitatis, a phrase parallel to *princeps civitatis* in § 4, denotes the priest who acted on behalf of the whole tribe, as opposed to the priests of local sanctuaries. It was he who executed penal justice in time of war (c. 7, 2) and in the public Assembly (c. 11, 4). How he was chosen and for how long is unknown. In the fourth century the Burgundians had a permanent chief priest (*sacerdos maximus et perpetuus*), entitled *sinistus*, 'the eldest' (Amm. 28. 5, 14). Priestly and kingly functions were occasionally combined (as in Scandinavia, c. 44, 2), but there is no evidence that this had once been the case among German tribes generally and that the separate priesthood was a later development which had taken place in the interval between Caesar and Tacitus (cp. on c. 7, 2).

ter singulos tollit, 'takes up three, one at a time'. Among the Germans, as among many other peoples, the number three had a mystic significance. When Caesar's interpreter Procillus was arrested by Ariovistus, the lots were consulted three times to see whether he should be burnt to death at once (*B. G.* 1. 53, 7).

interpretatur, 'reads their meaning', a technical term in divination.

§ 3. **prohibuerunt,** used of the *sortes* as of evil omens in Roman augury.

nulla . . . consultatio, 'no consultation' in the sense of 'deliberation'. The Roman practice was to repeat the observation of auspices until the desired answer was obtained. To supply *sortium* with *consultatio* is in itself possible (cp. *A*. 16. 14, 2 *consultationes non frustra ratus*), but see note above.

in eundem diem, 'for the same day'.

auspiciorum, etc., 'confirmation by auspices is yet further required'. *Adhuc = praeterea,* 'further', as in c. 38, 1; *Agr.* 29, 4, etc. So with comparatives as the equivalent of *etiam,* c. 19, 3, perhaps c. 29, 3.

etiam hic notum, i.e. in Germany, *hic* being used like *hunc* in c. 3, 3; on the other hand, in c. 19 we have *illis* and *ibi.* In c. 3, 3 *illum* may have been avoided because *illo* immediately precedes, but that reason is not applicable here, where *ibi* might have been written. *Hic* is often interpreted as 'in Rome', which would give a sharper antithesis to *proprium,* but Tacitus would hardly state so obvious a fact and an antithesis still remains: 'divination from birds is known among them also (as at Rome), but peculiar to them is divination from horses.'

avium voces volatusque, 'the notes and the flight of birds'.

Alliteration is common in Tacitus and in Latin generally. The Germans divined, not (like the Romans) from the direction of the flight of birds, but from the mere appearance of certain species: the eagle and the raven portended good, the owl, the crow, and the cuckoo evil. (Among the Romans also the mere appearance of some birds, such as the horned owl, *bubo*, foreboded ill, Pliny, *N. H.* 10, 34.) German peasants still regard the coming of some birds as a good omen, that of others as inauspicious, and the notes of many as of good augury, the cries of others as ill-omened.

proprium gentis, etc., 'but their distinctive practice is to make trial of the presentiments and warnings of horses'. The Persians, however, also drew an augury from the neighing of horses (Herod. 3. 84, 86), but apparently from the mere fact of their neighing or not.

§ 4. isdem, those mentioned above, c. 9, 3. The ablative is local as in *isdem castris* (*Agr.* 25, 1), *isdem hibernis* (*H.* 1. 55, 3), and many other analogous expressions, mainly derived from poets.

candidi, see on *candida vestis*, § 1.

et nullo, rather stronger than *neque ullo*: cp. c. 20, 5; 28, 1, etc.

mortali, 'human': cp. c. 21, 2; *Agr.* 11, 1, etc.

contacti, 'defiled'; so *nullis contacta vitiis pectora* (*Dial.* 12, 2).

pressos, 'yoked', a poetic word, often used (with *iugo*, etc.) by Ovid (*Met.* 1, 124; 12, 77, etc.).

princeps civitatis, 'chief of the state', i.e. one of the *principes* in kingless states who in virtue of his pre-eminence in actual power and influence held the *principatus civitatis*, like Arminius among the Cherusci. The expression, like *sacerdos civitatis* in § 2, and the use of *vel*, show that Tacitus did not mean 'a chief' (*principum aliquis*, c. 13, 1) but some one person whose position corresponded to that of the king in monarchical states; so *rex vel princeps* in c. 11, 5. It is not at all probable that he was merely one of the *principes* who was chosen to represent the whole tribe when a single representative was needed, as being the *princeps* in whose district the public act in question took place. See *Introd.*, p. lvi.

hinnitusque ac fremitus, 'neighings and snortings', a common combination: *quorum* is easily supplied from *quos*.

§ 5. proceres . . . sacerdotes, in contrast to the disbelief in augury and divination prevalent at Rome among the upper classes. Cp. Cic. *Div.* 2, 51 *mirari se aiebat* (Cato) *quod non rideret haruspex, haruspicem cum vidisset.*

se enim ministros, etc., 'for they (i.e. the nobles, represented at the ceremony by *rex vel princeps*, and the priests) regard themselves as but servants of the gods, the horses as cognisant of their counsels'. It may be that the procession did not really take place (as Tacitus seems to imply) at any time when an oracle was desired, but only at regular yearly festivals when the omens would be specially important and a great throng would be assembled (Müllenhoff, *D. A.* iv. 231). This would explain the particularly devout faith of the whole people which Tacitus emphasizes.

The text of the sentence is uncertain. Most MSS. omit *sed*, which however is necessary, for though Tacitus often omits either *sed* or *etiam* after *non solum* or *non modo* he never omits both (except in *A*. 16. 26, 2, where the place of *etiam* is taken by *superesse*). In other authors the omission of both is rare and, where it occurs, is not sensibly felt (e.g. Cic. *ad Q. Fr.* 1. 3, 6; Plaut. *Bacch.* 973 f., cited by Persson, *Krit. Bemerk.*, p. 95 f.). The correction *sed apud proceres; sacerdotes enim*, etc., is supported by the feeling that, as *plebs* and *proceres* describe the whole people, the mention of priests as a third element is out of place, and that as Tacitus is concerned with the beliefs and customs of the people as a whole we should expect them to be the subject of *putant*, as of *explorant* and *committunt* in the following sentences. These objections are met by excising the third *apud*, as an erroneous repetition, and *se*, as having arisen from the last letter of *sacerdotes* and the first of *enim*. This gives a good sense, but the changes are rather violent. Others transpose *sed* to follow *proceres*, in which case *sacerdotes* is the subject of *putant*; but the priests are not the sole participants in the ceremony.

est et alia. The same formula of transition in c. 39, 3.

§ 6. **gentis,** here 'tribe', as in c. 1, 1; 30, 2, etc., not as in c. 2, 5.

quemque for *utrumque*, as elsewhere in Tacitus.

committunt cum, 'pit against', an expression from the gladiatorial arena, especially frequent in Suetonius.

praeiudicio, 'an anticipatory decision', by the gods who were conceived as presiding both over the duel and the coming battle (cp. c. 7, 2). No parallel to this is elsewhere recorded. Contests between selected champions occur among the early Greeks and Romans and among the later Germans, but they were decisive of the main issue, not a presage of it. Victory might hearten the tribe that staged the duel, but what would result from defeat? There may be some misconception here.

CHAPTER XI

METHOD OF GOVERNMENT: THE COUNCIL OF CHIEFS AND THE
PUBLIC ASSEMBLY

The description of modes of augury leads on to the subject of
the popular Assembly: to a Roman the two were inseparably
associated, and in Germany every public meeting began with
sacrifice and observation of the auspices.

§ 1. De minoribus rebus: what these lesser matters were
cannot be said, but they were unimportant enough for the
decision of the chiefs (*consultant* implies decision, as the
following words show) to be accepted without demur.

principes: see on c. 5, 4; 10, 4-5. Here the contrast with
omnes, all the freemen of the tribe, the *plebs*, parallel to the
contrast of *plebs* and *proceres* in the preceding chapter, appears
to show that *principes* is used in its wider sense to include all
nobiles (*Introd.*, p. lvi), for none of the latter could be classed
with the *plebs*. The chiefs act as a senate or βουλή, before which
measures to be submitted to the popular vote are previously
discussed. Their president would presumably be the *princeps
civitatis* in kingless states, the king in monarchical, but Tacitus
eschews details.

ea quoque, etc., i.e. the *res maiores*.

plebem, as in c. 10, 5; 12, 3, the mass of freemen, *ingenui*
(c. 25, 3; 44, 3), who compose the *concilium* (cp. c. 12, 1),
answering to the ἀγορή, ἐκκλησία, or *comitia*. The old
German term for the Assembly is *Thing* or *Ding*, and the
Anglo-Saxon *Mōt* (Engl. 'moot', 'meeting').

praetractentur, 'are discussed beforehand'. The verb is
not found elsewhere before Tertullian and extremely seldom
after him; but Tacitus coined compounds with *prae* (Draeger,
Synt. u. Stil, § 249). In this sense Suetonius uses *ante tractare*
(*Aug.* 35, 3). *Pertractentur*, 'are thoroughly discussed', has
much better MSS. authority: the verb occurs in *Dial.* c. 1 but
not elsewhere in Tacitus. Emphasis on the thoroughness of
the discussion, however, seems out of place here, whereas
praetractentur gives just the meaning required. The abbreviations of *prae* and *per* (p̄ and ꝑ) could easily be confused: cp.
c. 42, 1.

§ 2. nisi quid fortuitum, etc.: in the case of a sudden emergency
a special meeting was summoned. An emergency meeting
was in later times called *gebotenes Ding* in contrast to the
regular, unsummoned meetings.

certis diebus, 'on definite days' (as in c. 9, 1), at a time of new or full moon. It is not meant that meetings were held every fourteen days but that, when they were held, they took place at such times. The number of meetings varied in later time from one to three a year as a rule. They were held in consecrated places, sometimes at least in sacred groves (*A*. 2. 12; *H*. 4. 14), and originally in connexion with religious festivals (such as those held in spring and autumn).

cum aut incohatur luna, etc., the natural result of their method of reckoning time by the moon (see below).

auspicatissimum initium. The influence of the moon on human fortunes was an article of belief in most parts of the ancient world: the period of its waxing was auspicious, that of its waning the reverse. When Caesar asked why Ariovistus declined to fight a decisive battle, he learnt that Heaven forbade that the Germans should win if they fought before the new moon (*B. G.* 1. 50, 5). So in the first Persian war the Spartans refused to fight till the circle of the moon should be full (Herod. 6, 106). Pliny, *N. H.* 18, 322, gives a list of things which should be done *luna nova, plena,* and *decrescente.* The old belief is still widespread in Germany: between new and full moon is the time to contract marriages, to begin the building of a house or to occupy a new one, to expect recovery from illness, and to do many other things.

agendis rebus, 'for the transaction of business' in general. The gerundive dative of purpose dependent on adjectives occurs only here in Tacitus' minor works, that dependent on verbs twice (*Agr.* 23, 1; 31, 3): both usages are very common in the *Annals* and *Histories.*

nec dierum, etc., 'they do not count by days ("reckon the number of days", from one point of time to another), as we do, but by nights'. This was the result of reckoning time by the phases of the moon, a method much easier and consequently older than reckoning by the sun, which was used also by the Gauls (*B. G.* 6. 18, 2), the Indians, the Persians and others, and is still used in Mohammedan and Jewish ritual. We have its survival in *fortnight, se(ve)nnight, Twelfth Night, ·Hallowe'en,* in the German *Sonnabend* (Saturday), *Weihnachten* (Christmas), etc., as well as in *acht Tage* for a week, where, as in the French *quinze jours* for a fortnight, the reckoning began with the first night and included the day following the last night.

sic constituunt, sic condicunt, 'in this manner they fix and settle their appointments', not merely times for the Assembly, for this is part of a general statement about the mode of reckoning time. With the verbs sc. *diem. Condicere* means either 'to declare', 'give notice of' (*dicendo denuntiare,*

Festus), whence its legal use, to bring an action by giving notice to the defendant to appear on a definite day before the praetor, or 'to agree about' (*in commune dicere = convenire de aliqua re*). Cp. Plaut. *Curc.* 5 *si status condictus cum hoste intercedit dies* (similarly Cincius *ap.* Gell. 16. 4, 4 *status condictusve dies cum hoste*).

nox ducere diem videtur, 'night is regarded as ushering in day'. Caesar, speaking of the Gauls, says more prosaically *noctem dies subsequitur* (6. 18, 2). In Norse mythology Day is conceived as the child of Night, and so in the mythologies of other countries, including Greece, where the day likewise began at sunset (Hesiod, *Theog.* 124; Soph. *Trach.* 94).

§ 3. ex libertate vitium, sc. *est*. The German spirit of independence is remarked by Caesar in the case of the Suebi (*B. G.* 4, 1), and in *H.* 4. 76 Tutor is made to say *Germanos . . . non iuberi, non regi, sed cuncta ex libidine agere.*

ut iussi, 'as if commanded to attend'. To the regular (*ungebotene*) *concilia* no summons was issued, at least in later time; but it was the duty of every free man to attend.

cunctatione coeuntium. In Gaul dilatoriness in assembling for an *armatum concilium*, summoned when war was afoot, was punishable by death (*B. G.* 5, 56); later German laws imposed severe penalties on unpunctuality in arriving for the Assembly.

§ 4. ut turbae placuit, 'when the crowd thinks fit', a further *vitium ex libertate*. The meetings afforded an opportunity of doing business of all sorts and of meeting friends, and time was spent over that. The old Norse saga literature shows that for such purposes people arrived before the appointed time. Gronovius' emendation *ut turba placuit*, 'when the crowd is deemed sufficient' (by the *principes*? or by itself?), is unnecessary and unconvincing. Such parallels as *vis et arma satis placebant* (sc. *Augusto*) (*H.* 4. 23), *cum primum ei vires suae satis placuissent* (Livy, 33. 31, 6), *ubi satis placuere vires* (*id.* 39. 30, 8), suggest that *satis* would have been added; and it is far from probable that Tacitus would have used *turba* in the sense of *numerus* (cp. *placebat barbaris numerus suus*, Vell. 2, 112), an extremely rare use, of which the only real instance cited is Quint. *Inst. Or.* 1. 2, 15. The *turba* is the unorganized mass, which does not become a *concilium* till it sits down. We may suppose that after a time a certain number took their seats and the rest followed suit.

considunt, in contrast to Roman custom. armati, a feature of primitive civilizations: see on c. 13, 1. Armed assemblies are mentioned also in Gaul (Livy, 21. 20, 1; cp. *B. G.* 5, 56), and they survived in some cantons of Switzerland up to recent times.

silentium per sacerdotes, etc. In Greece and Rome silence was enjoined by a herald. The German assemblies met in hallowed places (see above), a sacred peace (*Thingfrieden*) was proclaimed by the priests, and any breach of it was punished by them as being a sin against the god, Mars Thingsus (see on c. 9, 1), under whose protection the meeting was held.

tum, implying that they had not such power at all times. For their penal powers in war, see c. 7, 2.

§ 5. **rex vel princeps,** 'the king or chief of the state', see on c. 10, 4. The plural *audiuntur* is paralleled by *Dial.* 37 *P. Quintius . . . aut L. Archias faciunt,* and several similar examples in the *Annals,* as well as in various authors from Cicero onwards (*De off.* 1, 148). For *cuique* used of two persons, cp. c. 10, 6.

Others interpret *princeps* as 'a chief' or read *principes* on the ground that all the *principes* must have had the right to speak, as in the Homeric Assembly: the limitation to one would not have been in accord with German *libertas*. This interpretation is ruled out by the following *iubendi potestate,* which could only apply to persons representing the state as a whole. It is not a question of the right to speak, but of the submission of proposals by the president of the meeting.

prout aetas, etc., according to the normal usage of Tacitus, should go with the following *audiuntur*: 'they are listened to in accordance with their years,' etc., i.e. the hearing they obtain depends on their age and personal qualities, which give *auctoritas* to their counsel.

Those who understand *princeps* to mean 'a chief' or who read *principes* mostly regard the *prout* clause as describing the qualities which gave *principes* a claim to address the meeting, as the king's claim to be heard could not depend on his age or nobility; while some (including Furneaux) who take *princeps* as 'the chief' would supply *ceteri* 'from the sense' before *prout,* but if Tacitus had meant this, he would have expressed himself in somewhat the same manner as in *H.* 1. 51 *Sequanis Aeduisque ac deinde, prout opulentia civitatibus erat, infensi.* What Tacitus says is that the reception given to the president's proposal depended, not on his *potestas,* but on the *auctoritas* resulting from age, nobility, etc. A king need not always be of the highest nobility.

decus bellorum, 'distinction in war', as in c. 32, 2.

auctoritate . . . potestate, modal ablatives, contrasted with *coercendi ius* above, 'on the basis of the prestige attaching to their counsel rather than of their power to command'.

§ 6. sententia, 'the proposal'.

concutiunt, 'they clash' their spears. But as the clashing of spears would make no great noise, we should understand that the spears were struck against the shields: *arma* would have been more precise, as in *H.* 5. 17 *sono armorum,* and in Caes. *B. G.* 7, 21, where *armis concrepare* is noted as a Gallic custom. Another, sometimes at least concurrent, form of applause was the *tripudium,* a rhythmical stamping of the feet (*H. l. c.*)

CHAPTER XII
JUDICIAL POWERS OF THE ASSEMBLY

§ 1. Licet . . . accusare quoque, i.e. besides deliberative functions, the *concilium* has also judicial functions in criminal cases involving the death penalty.

discrimen capitis intendere, 'to bring a capital charge', a more precise definition of *accusare. Intendere,* 'to threaten with', is common in legal phrases (*litem, actionem, periculum,* etc., *intendere*).

distinctio, etc., 'the modes of (capital) punishment vary according to the crime'. Tacitus does not give a full list of crimes: he does not, for instance, mention murder; his examples are mostly crimes against the community as a whole.

proditores et transfugas, 'traitors and deserters', those who betrayed them to the enemy or went over to him.

arboribus. Leafless, withered trees were chosen for the purpose, as being *infelices,* and the execution was an expiatory sacrifice to the god (Wodan). So an old Roman law against treason ordained: *infelici arbore reste suspendito* (Livy, 1.26,6). On *arbores infelices,* see c. 10, 1.

ignavos et imbelles, 'cowards and cravens'. The words are so coupled in c. 31, 2 (also *Agr.* 15, 3; Livy, 26. 2, 11, etc.) and are nearly synonymous, the former being opposed to *fortes* or *strenuos* (*Agr.* 30, 2; *H.* 2. 46, 4), and the latter being also used of cowards (*H.* 4. 80, etc.), though often merely of non-combatants (*A.* 4. 49, 3; 13. 54, 2; 56, 6). It is obvious that all cowardice was not thus punished (cp. c. 6, 6; 14, 1, etc.); the meaning is that when the extreme penalty was inflicted (perhaps especially in the case of defaulters from military service, which is often taken as the meaning of *imbelles* here), it took this form. *Corpore infames,* as in *A.* 1. 73, of those addicted to unnatural vices.

caeno ac palude, etc., 'in mire and swamp, with a hurdle put over them'. *Insuper* in the literal sense, 'overhead', as in c. 16, 4; elsewhere in Tacitus it means 'besides', 'moreover'.

This custom survived through the Middle Ages. In the moors of the north-west, from Hanover to Holland and Denmark, 55 bodies have been found sunk in swamps, one of them bound with wickerwork, many of them in unnatural postures with limbs tied and pierced and with traces of wounds; most of these *Moorleichen*, as they are called, were victims of the *poena* described by Tacitus. But as this penalty could be inflicted only in regions where moors and bogs existed, Tacitus has plainly generalized a fact which was true only of the low-lying parts of the country. The same mode of punishment is mentioned as being used by the early Romans (Livy, 1. 51, 9; 4. 50, 4) and by the Carthaginians (Plaut. *Poen.* 5. 2, 65). Gudeman quotes Matthew Arnold's lines in *Balder Dead*, 2, inspired by the present passage:

Behind flock'd wrangling up a piteous crew,
Greeted of none, disfeatured and forlorn—
Cowards, who were in sloughs interr'd alive;
And round them still the wattled hurdles hung,
Wherewith they stamp'd them down, and trod them deep,
To hide their shameful memory from men.

(On the *Moorleichen*, Mestorf, *Bericht* xlii and xliv of the Schleswig-Holstein Museum in Kiel.)

§ 2. **illuc respicit, tamquam**, lit. 'looks to this, namely as though', i.e. 'is based on the view that'. So in c. 39, 4. *Tamquam* is frequently used to express the ground assigned for an action by the agents or attributed to them (c. 20, 4; 22, 3, etc.). The interpretation is that of Tacitus himself, though it may have represented the instinctive feeling of the Germans. The purpose of the hurdle was, no doubt, to prevent the body from rising to the surface, not (as has been suggested) to prevent the ghost from returning to do harm.

scelera . . . flagitia. *Scelera* are crimes against the *patria*, viz. treason and desertion; *flagitia* shameful and immoral actions, viz. cowardice and self outrage (cp. *A*. 15. 37, 8; 16. 19, 5, etc.). But the words are not always so distinguished.

sed et = *sed etiam*, as in c. 15, 3; 35, 2, &c.

levioribus delictis. These include homicide (c. 21, 1), assault, larceny, etc., which could all be expiated by the payment of a fine, *Wergeld*. The State intervened only when its intervention was demanded by the injured person: he was at liberty to secure satisfaction for himself (c. 21). It seems unlikely, however, that such lighter offences were tried in the Assembly; more probably they came before the local tribunals mentioned in § 3, *sed et levioribus . . . exsolvitur* being an anticipatory parenthesis, suggested by the penalties for *delicta maiora*.

pro modo, sc. *delicti,* 'proportional'. *Poena* has here the force of *multa*; old German laws show an elaborate system of compositions for such offences.

equorum pecorumque: on these as a medium of exchange, see note on c. 5, 2.

regi vel civitati, to the king as representing the state or, where there was no king, to the state (not, it will be noted, *principi civitatis*). This payment was in recognition of the breach of the peace, and was used towards the expense of sacrificial feasts at the great festivals.

vel propinquis, when the injured person had been killed (c. 21, 1).

§ 3. **eliguntur . . . reddunt,** 'in the same assemblies are chosen, among others, the chiefs who dispense justice in the districts and villages'. *Eliguntur* means 'are chosen' out of a number, viz. the whole body of *principes*. *Et,* by its position (cp. c. 3, 1), implies that there were other elections which are not mentioned. The relative clause *qui . . . reddunt* defines the functions of these chiefs and distinguishes them from others who had no judicial functions. *Iura reddere* or *ius dicere,* 'to give judicial decisions', is a technical phrase for the administration of justice by the Roman praetor and other magistrates. *Pagi vicique* is a description of tribal districts and the villages in them, as in *A.* 1. 56, 5.

Not a few believe that this sentence relates to the election of the ruling *principes,* whom they regard as formally appointed chiefs of the *pagi (Gaufürsten).* As it cannot be maintained that the one function defined by the relative clause was the only function of these *principes,* it is supposed that it alone is specified because of the context in which their election is mentioned. This is an artificial interpretation, which neglects the manifest distinction between the judicial and other *principes* and would attribute to Tacitus the clumsiness of stating at this late stage of his narrative, and in an almost parenthetical manner, that the *principes* (who have been repeatedly spoken of) were in fact formally elected magistrates. On this matter, see *Introd.,* p. liv ff.

centeni singulis, etc., 'each chief is assisted by a hundred men chosen from the people to accompany him as advisers and sponsors'. These men were apparently selected by the tribal assembly from the mass of the freemen (*plebs* being used as in c. 11, 1, where the word is equated with *omnes*), not from the freemen of each *pagus.* The selection of both judges and assessors by the whole tribe should indicate that their sphere of action was not limited to a single *pagus.*

consilium simul et auctoritas = *et consiliarii et auctores.*

Cp. *A.* 12. 49, 2 *regium insigne sumere cohortatur, sumentique adest auctor.* *Auctoritas* is often combined with *consilium* in the sense of authority, weight, influence (*Dial.* 36; Cic. *Cat.* 1. 1, 3, etc.). For *simul et,* c. 30, 1; 31, 4. The jurisdiction of these *principes* was limited to civil cases (as *iura reddunt* strictly implies), but in Germany civil cases included such offences as homicide (c. 21, 1). Many explain *auctoritas* as legal authorization or sanction, believing that the judicial *princeps,* like the later Frankish *Graf,* was only president of the court, being bound by the decision of his *comites* and pronouncing judgement in accordance with it, as the Roman praetor was bound by the decision of the *iudices.* But it is false method to interpret Tacitus in the light of much later German practice. The phrase *consilium . . . adsunt* shows that in his view the *comites* were not *iudices* but assessors, whose counsel was not binding on Roman judicial officials (Mommsen, *Staatsr.* I³. 307 ff.). The system here described resembled the assize system in Roman provinces, and marked an advance since Caesar's time, when *principes regionum atque pagorum inter suos ius dicunt controversiasque minuunt* (6, 23), these chiefs being informal judges with no power to compel disputants to appear before them or accept their judgement.

For the theory that here, as elsewhere, Tacitus or his informants misunderstood some account of an already existing institution of 'hundreds', see *Introd.,* p. lix ff.

CHAPTER XIII

ADMISSION OF YOUTHS TO CITIZENSHIP AND THEIR ENROLMENT IN THE RETINUE ('COMITATUS') OF A CHIEF

§ 1. **Nihil autem,** etc. The conjunction is not adversative, but connects the thought with the *considunt armati* of c. 11, 4, and the remark here leads naturally to the following subject. The use of arms in daily life is recorded also among the Celts (Posidonius in Athen. 4. 40, p. 154; Nicolaus Damasc. *F.H.G.* iii. 457), and among the early Greeks (Thuc. 1. 6, 1; Arist. *Pol.* 2, 8). It still exists in parts of Europe where individual security is not ensured by public authority.

arma sumere, on the analogy of *togam virilem sumere.*

moris, sc. *est,* so in c. 21, 3, and often elsewhere for *mos est:* cp. note on *Agr.* 33, 1.

civitas, 'the community', as in c. 8, 1; 10, 4.

suffecturum probaverit, 'has approved him as likely to be competent' (to use them, sc. *armis*). *Probare* would suggest to Roman readers the scrutiny of recruits for the army (cp.

Pliny, *Epp.* 10. 30, 2). The verb is repeated in § 2, where it bears the same meaning as here.

in ipso concilio emphasizes the public character of the act as compared with the assumption of the *toga virilis* by young Romans, which was more of a private ceremony, though accompanied by *deductio in forum*.

vel principum aliquis, etc. Ordinarily the youth was admitted to bear arms by his father, or, in case of his death, by one of his nearest relations, but sometimes, as a special distinction, he was admitted by a *princeps*, no doubt a friend of the father (who may have served in his *comitatus*, § 2). The plural *propinqui* is a substitute for the singular with the indefinite article, as often (cp. e.g. *deducebatur a patre vel a propinquis, Dial.* 34).

haec . . . toga, sc. *virilis*, the plain white *toga* of manhood, assumed usually about the age of 16. The comparison emphasizes the military character of the German investiture.

honos, 'public distinction'.

ante hoc, etc., 'up till then they are regarded as only members of a household, thereafter as members of the State'. The investiture does not appear to have carried with it emancipation from the *patria potestas* of the father, any more than the assumption of the *toga virilis* at Rome: emancipation was secured by the establishment of a separate home or by entry into a *comitatus*.

§ 2. Tacitus is interested not in the rank and file of the *iuvenes probati* but only in those who are to become leaders, and he proceeds to describe how they are trained for leadership by service in the *comitatus* of a *princeps*, the retinue of chosen warriors whom he maintained as a sort of private military force, bound to him by the strictest ties of loyalty and service (Anglo-Saxon 'Gesiths'). The detailed description, the use of every kind of rhetorical device, and the poetic phrasing show how much he was impressed by this institution. A similar institution existed among the Celts both in Cisalpine Gaul (Polyb. 2, 17) and in Gaul itself, where the *comites* were called ambacti or soldurii (Caes. *B. G.* 6, 15; 3, 22); but nothing is said about the Celtic *entourage* sharing the house and home of their chief. The *comitatus* played an important part in the development of medieval feudalism, particularly in respect of the ideas and the spirit by which it was inspired.

insignis nobilitas, etc. The reading and interpretation of this passage have been, and still are, much disputed. *Dignatio* in Tacitus is practically synonymous with *dignitas* and always denotes a person's rank or position, or the distinction

attaching to it, or the consideration in which he is held (cp.
c. 26, 1; *dignatio Caesaris, imperatoris, H.* 1. 19; 52, etc.).
The meaning would thus be 'distinguished rank or great services of parents award even to striplings the rank of a prince'.
The difficulty of connecting the sentence thus interpreted
with the following words (see note below), added to that of
supposing that *adulescentuli* could become *principes* in any
such sense as that of *principum aliquis* in § 1, has led many to
take *principis dignationem* to mean 'the esteem, or approval,
of a prince', i.e. a prince sometimes selects even striplings,
whom he himself invests with arms (§ 1), and whom he at
once enrols among his *comites*. This active sense of *dignatio*,
though otherwise foreign to Tacitus, is found in writers like
Seneca, the elder and younger Pliny, and Suetonius (Sen.
Epp. 21, 6 *ingeniorum crescit dignatio*; 64, 10; Pliny, *N. H.*
35, 55; Pliny, *Paneg.* 47, 1; Suet. *Cal.* 24), though not to the
exclusion of the passive sense, and it certainly yields a good
meaning here, although *adsignare* is hardly a natural word for
'procure' or 'secure'. But it is difficult to believe that Tacitus,
who uses the word frequently, used it here alone in this sense,
and this interpretation does not remove the difficulty of the
next clause. By 'rank' is not meant the position of a *princeps*:
these youngsters were *principes* in the same anticipatory
sense as a child of the house is *dominus* (c. 20,2), or the youthful Agricola a *senator* (*Agr.* 3), or the youthful Caesar and
Augustus *principes liberi* (*Dial.* 28); in due course they might
become actual *principes* through service in a *comitatus*.

insignis implies the existence of grades of nobility (cp.
c. 11, 5).

patrum merita: the fathers might be *nobiles* of lower rank
or commoners.

adulescentulis: the word denotes a very young *iuvenis* who
has just emerged from boyhood (*Dial.* 35). Though it is not
always used in this strict sense, here it plainly implies an
age lower than that of the *iuvenes probati* in § 1.

adsignant, 'bestow, confer, award', as in *H.* 1. 30 (with
imperium as object) or 1. 52 (with *militiae ordines*).

ceteris robustioribus, etc., 'they join (*or* are attached to)
the rest of the older men who have been long since invested
with arms'. These older men are—most awkwardly—not
defined till the next clause as the *comites* of a *princeps*: it is
most unusual to supply a word from a following clause, and
no mention has hitherto been made of the association of
comites with *principes*. If *dignationem* be taken as 'rank',
the clause will mean that the *adulescentuli* serve in a *comitatus* as a training for actual leadership, which is ultimately

attained in the manner described in c. 14. With the other interpretation of *dignationem*, the clause will mean that the privileged youths are attached by the *princeps* to his retinue of older warriors—a distinction in so far as they are admitted at a very early age.

But with either interpretation 'the rest of' (or 'the rest, namely') makes no sense. *Ceteris* can only be used of the rest of a class of which one or more individuals have already been specified. What is required is 'they join a retinue of older warriors' or 'they are attached to his retinue', etc. The only noun that could be supplied with *ceteris* from what precedes is *principibus*, 'they join the older chiefs', but *robustioribus* etc. would be a ridiculous description of men in the position of *principes*, and the clause would mean that they become actual *principes*, which would be impossible for striplings and inconsistent with enrolment in a *comitatus*. It would appear, therefore, that *ceteris* cannot be right. The difficulty would be removed by Lipsius' conjecture *ceteri*, but this is open to the objections (1) that it would imply that all the other *iuvenes probati* found a place in a *comitatus* (which is incredible), for we can hardly understand *ceteri* as *ceteri nobiles* who have not *insignis nobilitas*, (2) that the following remark *nec rubor . . . aspici* most naturally refers to men of high birth, and (3) that the reader would be left to suppose that the privileged youths immediately become actual *principes*. Possibly *ceterum* is what Tacitus wrote: cp. *ceterae coloniae* for *ceterum coloniae* in *A.* 13. 31, 2. Gudeman's *certis*, 'they are assigned to certain older retainers' for purposes of training, is unsuitable: the adjective is really superfluous, and Tacitus would have joined it with a substantive, not with other adjectives.

robustioribus, more mature in age and physique, often used in contrast to *pueri*.

probatis, sometimes translated 'long tried', but not to be dissociated from *probaverit* in § 1.

adgregantur: the verb means 'to attach to', and is used by Tacitus almost invariably in the passive (with middle sense) or with *se*, 'to attach oneself to', 'to join'.

nec rubor (poetical for *dedecus*) for *nec rubori*: so in Ovid, *A.A.* 3, 167; Tibull. ii. 1, 30. The nominative was often preferred by poets from Ennius onwards as choicer and more emphatic than the dative, but was also used by prose writers (Livy, Seneca, etc., once even by Cicero). A bold use of it is *regia utilitas* in c. 44 for *regibus utilitati* (Löfstedt, *Syntactica*, pp. 161 ff.). A comma after *adgregantur* is preferable to a full stop, since *comites* supplies the needed definition of *robustioribus . . . probatis.* If *ceteri* be read, there would be here no special reference to the *adulescentuli*, but a general remark, with an implied contrast to the position of a client at Rome, so often described as humiliating; it may be noted that elsewhere Tacitus uses *clientes* for *comites* (*A*. 1. 57, 4; 2. 45, 2; 12. 30, 3), like Caesar in *B. G.* 7, 40, who, however, also uses *comites* (6, 30).

§ 3. **gradus,** etc., 'there are ranks within the train of followers, assigned by the judgement of its leader'.

    magnaque, ' and so there is great '.

    quibus, sc. *sit.* So *sint* is supplied with *cui* in the next clause, and in other places in indirect questions (*A*. 1. 11, 2; 16, 5, etc.).

    plurimi. The number of his followers was the measure of his power; it would vary greatly according to his wealth: the 200 *comites* of king Chnodomar (see below) in A.D. 357 represented a very large following.

§ 4. **haec . . . hae,** referring to what precedes, as in § 1. The usual punctuation, with a comma after *vires* and another after *circumdari*, makes the pronouns refer, in an unusual manner, to what follows. *Dignitas*, 'position'. Caesar uses similar language of the Gallic chiefs: the more noble and wealthy they are, the greater the number of their *ambacti* (liegemen) and clients; this is the one form of influence and power, *gratia potentiaque*, known to them (6, 15).

    magno . . . electorum . . . globo. Some MSS. (*E* and its congeners) read *magno et*, which in itself is attractive, the conjunction emphasizing the number and the quality of the members, *plurimi et acerrimi* above, *numero ac virtute* below. Cp. *Dial.* 10 *privatas et nostri saeculi controversias.* But it is unlikely that this group of MSS. alone preserved the genuine tradition. An explanation of the appearance of *et* in their text is suggested by Robinson, *Germ.*, p. 205.

    decus . . . praesidium, answering to *dignitas* and *vires* above.

    cuique, sc. *principi* (not taken with *sua*).

    id . . . ea, explained by the *si* clause. **nomen . . . gloria,** ' name and fame '; *nomen* in the sense of *clarum nomen, fama* is common in Tacitus. The same combination, *gloriam nomenque*, recurs in *H*. 2. 37.

    comitatus, best taken as genitive, as the *princeps* is the subject of the whole description in this section. The subject of *expetuntur*, 'are courted' (by other tribes), is easily supplied from *cuique*.

    plerumque, 'often', see c. 5, 1 note.

    profligant, 'virtually bring to an end', the invariable meaning of the verb in Tacitus when joined with *bella* or *proelia*

(*H*. 2. 4; 3. 50; 4. 73; *A*. 14. 36, 3). So in Cic. *ad Fam.* 12.
30, 2; Livy, 21. 40, 11, who distinguishes three stages—*bellum
committere, profligare, conficere* (but in other places uses *profligare* for *conficere*); and with *opera* in *Res Gest. d. Aug.* 20.
Tacitus' meaning can hardly be, as some explain, 'settle,
ward off, threatening wars'.

CHAPTER XIV
THE RETINUE IN WAR

§ 1. iam vero, 'furthermore', introducing a new and stronger
statement.

infame . . . probrosum, 'it is lifelong infamy and oppro-
brium'.

superstitem, etc. Ammianus records that the 200 *comites* of
Chnodomar, king of the Alamanni, on his surrender to Julian
in A.D. 357, gave themselves up to be bound, *flagitium arbitrati
post regem vivere vel pro rege non mori* (16. 12, 60). Instances
of a similar fellowship are found among the Gauls (Caes. 3,
22; 7, 40) and the Celtiberi (Val. Max. 2. 6, 11). The obligations described by Tacitus in this section are emphasized in
later German epics.

defendere, defend against actual attack; tueri, protect from
a possible danger. So *tueri et defendere, Dial.* 7; Cic. *ad Fam.*
13. 64, 1; *de Or.* 1, 172.

gloriae eius adsignare (= *imputare*). The German principle
of conduct is the same as that imposed by the Roman military
oath taken to the *imperator*, to whom belonged the credit of
victory. The *comes*, like the young Agricola, *ad auctorem ac
ducem . . . fortunam referebat* (*Agr.* 8).

praecipuum sacramentum, 'the essence of their plighted
allegiance'. For the superlative force of *praecipuum*, see
note on c. 6, 6. The Roman term for the military oath is
introduced by way of comparison, like *haec apud illos toga*
above: Tacitus was not thinking of an oath actually taken
by the *comites*. Cp. the Celtic and Celtiberian *devoti* mentioned by Caesar (*l. c.*) and Valerius Maximus (*l. c.*).

§ 2. plerique, 'many'. From what follows it is fairly clear that
these noble youths were already *comites* (who, if unaccom-
panied by their chiefs, obtained leave of absence from them).
Some at least of them were prospective *principes* who desired
to win a name and the necessary *materia munificentiae*.

ultro, 'on their own account', their own tribe not being
involved in hostilities.

nationes, other German tribes.

ancipitia, 'perils', so used four times in Tacitus' historical
works.

clarescunt, sc. *adulescentes,* 'become renowned'; leaders of a retinue were already *clari.*

tueare, with indefinite subject ('one cannot maintain'), like *persuaseris* and *possis* in § 5 and *instes* (c. 6, 6).

§ **3. exigunt,** sc. *comites,* implied in *comitatus:* 'they demand of their leader's bounty' their warlike equipment as a condition of taking service. The preposition *a* is often inserted after *enim,* but seems unnecessary; *exigere a* is in fact extremely rare except with an abl. of a person, and there is good MSS. authority for the use of the simple ablative with verbs of asking or demanding (*impetrare, petere,* etc.), where editors usually insert *a.* Baehrens (*Philol.,* Suppl. xii. 1912, p. 363) cites Val. Max. 5. 3, 2 f.; 8. 10, 2; Petr. *Sat.* 65; Quint. *Decl.* 267, p. 89, 7; Tac. *A.* 14. 21, 4 *efflagitanti certamina magistratibus,* where however *a* could easily have fallen out. To take *liberalitate* as abl. of cause, 'on the ground of', is hardly natural.

Principis liberalitas was a phrase familiar to Romans in connexion with imperial bounties (Pliny, *Epp.* 7. 31, 4, *Paneg.* 27, 3; Dessau, 6620, etc.). Giving figured so prominently among the obligations of the *princeps comitatus* that in Anglo-Saxon poetry his throne is 'gift-chair' (*gifstôl*) and his palace 'gift-hall' (*gifheal*). In later times the horse and arms of the vassal are not a gift but a loan, returned to the lord on death.

illum, 'that glorious', 'much-prized' (rather than 'the well known', 'usual', since Romans were probably not familiar with the details here given).

bellatorem equum, first used by Virgil in imitation of Theocritus' ἵππος πολεμιστής (*Id.* 15, 51) and subsequently common in poetry, but not in prose, although the adjectival use of other substantives is frequent in Livy and Tacitus (e.g. *imperator populus, A.* 3. 6, 2).

cruentam victricemque, applied by anticipation to the spear, is also the language of poetry. The *framea* is named as the chief weapon, but as it was not very costly, the gifts probably included armour generally (especially shield and sword) and the horse's caparison. These and other gifts were normal in later time (Müllenhoff, *op. cit.* 269).

nam epulae, etc., 'for meals and feasts, with their plentiful though homely fare (in contrast to the luxury of Roman banquets), count as pay'; or *et . . . apparatus* may be taken as a closer definition of *epulae,* cp. c. 21, 2 *pro fortuna apparatis epulis.* The force of *nam* seems to be: 'meals are not regarded as a charge on the leader's *liberalitas,* for they are reckoned as pay.' For the rare phrase *cedere pro,* cp. Cato, *De agricult.* 150, 2; Columella, 2. 13, 1, etc.

materia, in the unusual sense of 'the means'.

munificentia, a stronger word than *liberalitas,* includes the meals as well as the gifts. Wealth and power were inseparable ideas: 'rich' (Ger. *reich*) is derived from the same root as Lat. *rex.*

raptus: so Caesar says *latrocinia nullam habent infamiam, quae extra fines cuiusque civitatis fiunt* (*B. G.* 6, 23). Tacitus records that the Suebic king Vannius, dethroned in A.D. 50, had enriched his realm by thirty years of plundering and levying of dues (*A.* 12. 29). The prevalence of the same practice in Thrace is noted by Herodotus: τὸ ζῆν ἀπὸ πολέμου καὶ λῃστύος κάλλιστον (5, 6).

§ 4. **nec arare terram.** They have *agri,* but the tillage of them is left to the women (c. 15, 1). This practice, contrasting strongly with the *labor improbus* of the Roman farmer, is a German *vitium,* but it is a *vitium* that emphasizes the restless and bellicose character of the people. This sentence forms a transition to the next chapter.

annum = *annonam,* 'the yearly produce'; so in *Agr.* 31, 2 (*ager atque annus*), and often in post-Augustan epic poets.

persuaseris (cp. *tueare* above), rarely followed by the infinitive.

vocare = *provocare,* as in Verg. *G.* 4, 76 *vocant . . . hostem,* and often in later epic poetry.

vulnera mereri, 'to earn wounds', as the reward of valour, in piquant contrast to the common *stipendia mereri.*

quin immo, stronger than *quin etiam* (c. 3, 3, etc.); elsewhere used by Tacitus only in the *Dialogus.*

sudore . . . sanguine: the contrast between the two words, which are often combined, is strengthened by the alliteration. The epigrammatic sentence rounds off, in Tacitus' favourite manner (see c. 8, 3), a chapter which is notable for its poetic colouring.

CHAPTER XV

THE RETINUE IN PEACE

§ 1. **non ineunt.** The subject is still the *comites* and *principes*; the daily life of the common people is not described till c. 22.

non multum, sc. *temporis* (as with *plurimum* in c. 22, 1), i.e. relatively little time, as compared with that passed in idleness. The statement contradicts what Caesar says about the Suebi, *multum sunt in venationibus* (4, 1), and about the Germans in general, *vita omnis in venationibus atque in studiis rei militaris consistit* (6, 21); and the negative form of expression suggests, according to Norden, that the contradiction

is intentional (pp. 316 ff.), which is improbable. The genuine-
ness of *non* is questioned. The discrepancy with Caesar
(which is no argument), the weakness of *plus* (for which we
should expect 'most' or 'almost all' of their time), and the
abundant evidence furnished by later sources—heroic poetry,
historical notices, and laws—about the place of hunting in
the life of the Germans have led many editors to excise *non*
as an erroneous repetition from the preceding clause. But
the negative is supported by the fact that the description
works up to *sic ament inertiam*: Tacitus emphasizes the indolence by representing hunting as only a brief, and perhaps
occasional, interruption of the *otium* of the *comites* and their
leaders (cp. Strache, *Woch. klass. Phil.*, 1919, 70; Wissowa,
Gött. gel. Anz., vol. 178, p. 661).

  dediti, etc., recalls Sall. *Cat.* 2, 8 *dediti ventri atque somno.*

  fortissimus quisque, etc. The whole passage is somewhat
disjointed, and variously punctuated by editors. It seems
best to make *fortissimus quisque*, repeated in *ipsi*, the subject
of *hebent*, which strengthens *nihil agens. Quisque* with a superlative is not infrequently followed by a plural. Others take
fortissimus quisque in apposition to *dediti* and place a colon
after *familia.*

  delegata . . . cura, ablative absolute.

  domus et penatium, 'house and home'.

  agrorum cura feminis, as usually among primitive peoples.
The fact is recorded by Strabo in the case of Gauls, Iberians,
Thracians, and Scythians (3. 4, 17, p. 165), and by Justin
(Trogus) of the Parthians (44. 3, 7). In north Friesland
the women are said still to do the field work, while the men
go to sea, and in Turkey agriculture is largely left to the
women.

  familia, of members of the family proper (c. 7, 3); not, as
in c. 25, 1, of the whole household establishment, including
slaves. By the weakest members of the family are meant
children and others incapable, for some reason other than
age, of bearing arms.

  hebent, 'they lounge'; cp. *torpeat* (c. 14, 2), *torpor* (c. 46, 1),
and *sanguis hebet* (Verg. *Aen.* 5, 396).

  mira diversitate, 'by a strange inconsistency of temperament'. A reaction from severe exertion (in war) to idleness
(in peace) is common to many or most rude races. But it is
obvious that the description given in this section is greatly
exaggerated. Such a purely animal existence would have been
incompatible with the military efficiency of the *comites*,
which is abundantly attested, and the *principes* had duties
to perform in time of peace.

inertiam, 'indolence', in contrast to *quietem*, 'peace' (with others).

§ 2. ultro ac viritim, 'voluntarily and by individual contribution', each man contributing what he chose. *Viritim* corresponds to *a singulis* in the next sentence, as opposed to *publice*. Such gifts continued to be free offerings until after the Carolingian period, when they passed into a compulsory tribute.

armentorum . . . frugum. The use of a partitive genitive without some such word as *aliquid* (c. 18, 2) is paralleled by *A*. 15. 53, 3 *ut quisque audentiae habuisset*, and is occasionally found in other writers both of prose and verse. Here it is somewhat softened by the following *quod*, but the genitive does not depend on the relative as it does in *H*. 2. 44 *superesse . . . militum quod trans Padum fuerit*.

pro honore, 'as a gift of honour'.

necessitatibus, 'their needs', i.e. necessary expenses in connexion with the maintenance of a *comitatus*.

§ 3. gaudent praecipue, 'they take special delight in', partly at any rate because the gifts sent included *equi* and *arma*, and with these their followers had to be equipped (c. 14, 3). The gifts presented by neighbouring tribes were an insurance against plundering raids.

sed et = *sed etiam*, as in c. 12, 2; 35, 2.

publice, 'by states as such'.

electi equi, 'choice steeds': German horses were usually *non forma conspicui* (c. 6, 3).

magnifica arma. The MSS. reading *magna* would mean 'large', i.e. of a larger size than the ordinary, like the *maiores lanceae* of c. 6, 1; it cannot mean *magnifica* or *conspicua* (*II*. 1. 88), which is the meaning we should expect. *Magna arma* might be taken to mean long spears, heavy swords, massive cuirasses and shields; but extra size and weight would not be attractive features (*ingentibus telis* in *H*. 2. 88 means only huge in conformity with the *magna corpora* of Germans), and the idea of special adornment can hardly be excluded. The correction *magnifica* seems therefore necessary, and is supported by the fact that in c. 34, 2 some of the best MSS. have *magnum* for *magnificum*. The character of the gifts emphasizes the warlike preoccupation of the people.

phalerae . . . torques. The former were embossed metal disks or plates resembling those granted to Roman soldiers as military decorations. *Torques* (also one of the *dona militaria* given to Roman soldiers) were collars or necklaces of gold, silver, or bronze, like those worn by the Gauls, which were used as military decorations. These ornaments rarely occur among finds made in Germany, perhaps just because they were often made of precious metal, but they occasionally figure in works of art (Schumacher, *Mainzer Ztschr.* iv. 7).

iam et . . . docuimus, 'we have now taught them to accept money also'—a sign of the impairment of the *mos patrius*: on this view, see the note on c. 5, 4. Tacitus is here speaking not of trade, as in c. 5, 5, but of bribes to princes in Roman interest, such as are spoken of in c. 42, 2 and *A*. 11. 16, 3 (cp. *pecuniam et dona, quis solis corrumpantur*, sc. *Germani, H.* 4. 76). In A.D. 83 or 89 Domitian gave money but no military aid to the Cheruscan king Chariomerus who had been expelled from his kingdom by the Chatti on account of his friendship with the Romans (Dio 67. 5, 1); but there is no allusion here to the money which he gave, with promise of future subsidies, to the Dacian king Decebalus on the conclusion of peace in A.D. 89: the Dacians were not Germans.

CHAPTER XVI
VILLAGES AND DWELLINGS

Chapters 16–27 deal with the customs and institutions of private life.

§ **1. populis,** dat. of agent, as in c. 31, 1.

urbes, in the Roman sense, of compact towns built in an orderly fashion, with regular streets lined by blocks or rows of houses presenting an even front and sometimes surrounded by walls. The Germans had no such cities. *Oppida* are indeed frequently mentioned by ancient writers. Occasionally they were permanent settlements, like Mattium the capital of the Chatti (Altenburg near Metze, south-west of Cassel), described in *A*. 1. 56 as *genti caput*, or the *oppidum Batavorum* (*H*. 5. 19) or the *castellum* adjoining the palace of Maroboduus (*A*. 2. 62), where traders and sutlers had settled. These were, however, merely large fortified villages. Their character has been revealed by the excavation of the first-named site, where at a central point inside the multiple defences of earthworks and stone walls lay numbers of round and rectangular huts in irregular groups or regular rows. Most of the *oppida*, however, were strongholds (*Ringwälle*) either on hills or in the plain—in woods, marshes, and between rivers—serving as places of refuge from hostile inroads, like the *oppida* of the Britons which Caesar describes (*B. G.* 5, 21). Strongholds of this type, dating to the late La Tène period (100 B.C.–A.D. 100), abound in the region of the Taunus and the Odenwald, on the Rhine and elsewhere. Walled cities were an abomination to the Germans, who called them 'bulwarks of slavery'

(*H.* 4. 64) or 'tombs encircled by nets', *circumdata retiis busta* (Ammianus 16. 2, 12).

ne pati quidem . . . iunctas, 'they do not even like dwellings joined together' (in the urban manner). *Inter se iunctas* is amplified in § 2. *Pati* is used in a weakened sense which occurs elsewhere (e.g. *Dial.* 10, 5; 40, 4) and here amounts to no more than a statement of the fact that they do not have their dwellings attached to each other, as the suggested reason *inscitia aedificandi* shows. *Sedes* is used also in the sense of 'settlements', territory (e.g. c. 28, 1; 29, 3; 30, 1), and Schumacher would so take the word here, seeing in it an allusion to the German custom of (sometimes) separating tribal territories by an uninhabited zone, when there were no natural barriers (Caes. *B. G.* 4, 3; 6, 23). But that meaning is quite alien to the context.

colunt discreti, etc., 'they dwell separated and scattered, according as they have been attracted by spring, plain, or wood'. *Diversi*, 'in various places', as in *H.* 3. 46 *si . . . diversi inrupissent.* German place-names frequently end in *-brunn* or *-brunnen* (fons), in *-wald, -loh,* or *-rode* (nemus), and less often in *-feld* (campus).

The mode of settlement described is the antithesis of urban concentration, but the exact meaning is not perfectly clear. To Greeks and Romans the antithesis to dwelling in towns was dwelling in villages, which was the normal form of settlement in early times in all Indo-European countries (Herod. 1, 96; Thuc. 1, 10; 3, 94; Strabo 3. 2, 15; 14. 1, 37, etc.) and which Tacitus evidently regarded as the normal form in Germany (c. 12, 3; 19, 2; *A.* 1. 50, 6). The reference would thus be to scattered villages which consisted of separate homesteads grouped in higgledy-piggledy fashion. But there also existed in Germany from the later Stone Age onwards isolated farmsteads, which Caesar distinguishes from *vici* as *aedificia* (*B. G.* 4. 4, 2; 4. 19, 1) and which seem to be implied in c. 21, 2 (n. on *proximam domum*) and 25, 1; and some think that these alone are referred to here, and that they are mentioned before the *vici* as being either the preponderating form of settlement (which is untrue) or the one most widely divergent from the urban system. The description would cover both modes of settlement, but it may be doubted whether Tacitus realized the existence of such isolated properties (cp. on c. 26, end of § 2).

§ 2. vicos locant, etc., 'their villages they do not lay out in the Roman fashion with the buildings contiguous and connected: every one keeps an open space round his house'. The open space, including the farmyard, was surrounded by a wooden

fence. The description is confirmed by excavation at Laden-
burg (Lopodunum), near Heidelberg, which has disclosed
round German huts of the late La Tène period surrounded
by a space enclosed by a palisade fence.

remedium, in explanatory apposition to the preceding
clause. **inscitia,** causal ablative, 'from lack of skill in building'.[1]
The reasons given are imaginary: the real reason was the
spirit of isolation, bred of the love of independence, which
English people have inherited.

§ 3. **caementorum . . . tegularum.** The former are small un-
dressed quarry stones used with mortar to make concrete
walls. *Tegulae* means not roofing-tiles but wall-tiles, bricks
(*lateres cocti*), used to face the concrete work. Cp. *Dial.* 20,
7 *rudi caemento et informibus tegulis.* Tacitus' statement is
fully confirmed by linguistic and archaeological evidence.
The German words for all materials used in stone building
(cement, tiles, bricks, mortar, etc.) are of Latin origin. The
art of building in stone was subsequently learnt from the
Romans: in A.D. 357 the emperor Julian found German houses
in the country between the Main and the Neckar built in the
Roman style (Ammianus 17. 1, 7).

materia ad omnia, etc., 'for all purposes they use timber
which is unshaped and without beauty or attractiveness'.
Materia is frequently used in this specific sense (so in *A.* 1.
35, 1, etc.). As wood was not in fact the only material used
(see below), Schumacher would take *materia* in the wider
sense of building materials (which would simplify the explanation of the next sentence); but this is not favoured by
the antithesis between it and *caementa,* and *informi* would
then mean 'ugly-looking', so that *citra speciem,* etc., would be
pure tautology, whereas it aptly describes roughly trimmed
and even crooked timber, which seemed ugly to a Roman
accustomed to the straight lines of his houses. *Citra* for *sine*
is common in silver Latin, but is not used by Tacitus in his
historical works (see n. on *Agr.* 1, 3).

Log-cabins built of wooden uprights and horizontally laid
logs, with the interstices filled with clay or sand, dated back
to the Bronze Age, as excavation has established (A. Kieke-

---

[1] In his note on the contents of the Hersfeld codex, Decembrio
said with reference to the *Germania*: 'utitur autem Cornelius hoc
vocabulo inscientia, non inscitia'. *Inscientia* means 'ignorance', but
what the present passage requires is 'unskilfulness': Tacitus has not
yet spoken of German ignorance of stone-building. Decembrio
evidently erred in connecting his remark with the *Germania* instead
of the *Dialogus,* where alone the word is used by Tacitus. Cp.
Robinson, *Germ.*, p. 12.

FIG. 12. German huts, from the Column of Marcus.

FIG. 10. Cinerary urn of the Bronze Age modelled in the shape of a hut ('house-urn') from Scandinavia.

FIG. 13. Rectangular house of wood and plaster. Photograph of a model in the Röm.-german. Zentral-Museum, Mainz.

FIG. 15. German horseman clad in tunic, trousers, mantle, and shoes (pointed oval shield, sword missing from r. hand).

FIG. 14. German with tunic, trousers, and woollen shoes.

FIG. 16. German with tunic, trousers (both held by a girdle), and shoes.

busch, *Praehist. Ztschr.* 2, 371 ff.), and houses of this type were common in the third century A.D., as may be seen from the description of Herodian (7. 2, 4), who attributes the use of timber to the scarcity of stone or bricks (πλίνθοι ὀπτοί = *tegulae*). But excavation has shown that in the first century the normal dwelling, at least in the middle west and south-west of Germany, was a wattle-and - daub structure, either round or of rectangular (or four-angled) form. The round hut of the poorer man was of beehive shape, made of poles inserted in plastered wattle-work and thatched with straw or reeds, with a hole at the top to serve as flue and window: it resembled the Belgic huts described by Strabo as dome-shaped dwellings of planks and wickerwork, heavily thatched (4. 4, 3, p. 197). The rectangular huts were barn-like build-

FIG. 11. 'House-urn' from Königsaue bei Aschersleben.

ings with high-pitched roof, made of posts set at a short distance from each other or of timber framework, with the intervening spaces filled with wattlework coated with clay; sometimes there was a socle of dry masonry. Portions of the clay plaster bearing imprints of the posts or balks and the wicker rods have been found on several sites. These represent the primitive form of the half-timbered house. Reliefs of the column of Marcus (which may not be trustworthy for details) show round or sometimes rectangular huts (of the Marcomani, Quadi, etc.) with a socle of beams or of dry stonework and vertical logs bound together at intervals by what looks like plaited wicker bands. See figs. 10–13.

quaedam loca, etc., 'some parts they plaster carefully with earth of such purity and brilliance as to resemble painting and coloured designs'. *Lineamenta colorum* for *lineam. colorata.* The 'parts' in question were on the outside, not the inside, of the house: for not only does Tacitus say nothing here of the interior, but inside decoration would soon be blackened by the smoke of the fire. The statement is very difficult to explain. Excavation has yielded clay slabs with a thin, smooth, white-coloured layer covering the upper surface, and it is thought that such a coating of lustrous white clay may be the decoration to which Tacitus refers. But if by *materia* in the preceding sentence only wood is meant, a smearing of white clay would hardly produce the effect of *lineamenta colorum*, even against the dark colour which age would give to the timber, and clay would scarcely adhere to wood. The effect would hardly be produced even in the case of houses of timber and clay-coated wattlework. If this be so, we should have to understand *terra* to mean some mineral colour like ochre (or more than one colour, *terra* being collective singular) used as a wash. Any coloured ornamentation, however, needs a flat surface, which would not be furnished by rough timbers, and it may be that Tacitus has fused accounts of the two types of house.

[On this subject, see Schumacher, *op. cit.*, p. 7 f.; *Sied. u. Kulturg. d. Rheinlande*, i. 158; and appendix to Reeb's edition, pp. 115 ff.; G. Wolff, *Neue Jahrbb.* xlii, ii, 181 ff.]

§ 4. **solent et**, i.e. besides building *domus*, they also make pit-dwellings.

subterraneos specus. These were of two kinds, underground chambers for use in winter (*suffugium hiemis*) and pits for storing produce (*receptaculum frugibus*). Some think that Tacitus confused the two, but he plainly had in mind only the former: there was room in them to store some provisions. Underground *specus* were used by many other peoples, e.g. by Scythians and Armenians as dwellings (Verg. *G.* 3, 376, cf. Mela, 2. 1, 10; Xen. *Anab.* 4. 5, 25), by Cappadocians and Thracians for storage (Varro, *R. R.* 1, 57). In Germany numbers of them have been found, many of them of great antiquity. Remains of weaving implements found in them substantiate Pliny's statement that they were used by women as weaving places (*N. H.* 19, 9); and this use of them is attested through the Middle Ages, one reason being that in these damp rooms the threads did not dry so quickly. Even to-day weaving is carried on in cellars in some parts of Germany, and in many parts the word 'cellar' attaches to weaving-rooms above-ground (*Webekeller*).

The supposition of a confusion in this passage between dwelling-rooms and dung-covered storage pits has led to the identification of the former with the cellars that have been found under the floor of many houses, chiefly in south-west Germany (Wolff, *l. c.*, p. 185). These are shaped like a truncated cone or a kettle, widening downwards from a narrow circular opening to a maximum depth of about 6½ ft. But this view is ruled out by the analogies quoted below.

insuper, 'on the top', as in c. 12, 1.

fimo: the old German word for the underground *specus* was *tunc*, the same word as Eng. *dung*, and in parts of Bavaria a weaving-room is still called *dunk*. We should picture the pits as roofed over with sticks covered with a thick padding of straw, earth, and dung, like the pit-dwellings that still exist in Hungary and Rumania, whose inhabitants use the roofs as rubbish-heaps (see *Antiquity*, x, 1936, 25 ff.). An interesting parallel has been discovered at Skara Brae in Orkney, where a group of huts connected by passages (both built of flagstone slabs) are covered by a great midden which forms an integral part of the structure (*Anc. Mon. Comm. Scot.*, 1938, no. 683).

suffugium hiemis, 'a refuge from the winter'. The genitive expresses that from which one flees, as in c. 46, 4; *A*. 4. 66, 3. The manuscript reading *hiemi* would balance *frugibus*, but can hardly be equivalent to *hibernum*; *hieme* is a possible correction but is stylistically inferior.

loci, 'places', in the sense of chambers, rooms, as in *H*. 3. 84 *tacentes loci* (*Palatii*); *A*. 14. 5, 2 *ruere tectum loci*.

advenit, perfect tense (otherwise *adveniat*, subj. of repeated action, would be expected).

abdita . . . defossa, so combined in *H*. 3. 33.

aut ignorantur, etc., a weak rhetorical antithesis, to round off the chapter. The meaning is that such places are either not known to exist or, if they are, they escape detection (*fallunt*, sc. *hostem*) by the very fact that they have to be searched for (and the enemy has no time to search). The remark can hardly have been true of the pit-dwellings, which would not be difficult to find, but it would apply to storage pits covered with a row of sticks overlaid with straw and earth (*Antiquity, l. c.*). Cp. Curt. 7, 4, 24 *barbari scrobes ita sollerter abscondunt ut, nisi qui defoderunt, invenire non possint*. Here, therefore, there seems to be a confusion between pit-dwellings and storage pits.

CHAPTER XVII

CLOTHING OF MEN AND WOMEN

Tacitus' account of German dress—the only connected account which we have—though brief and incomplete and taking no account of times and seasons, was based on trustworthy sources (in the main probably Pliny's lost work on the German wars) and is, in general, confirmed by the monuments. Here, as elsewhere in the first part of the treatise, he has in view the western Germans.

§ 1. sagum or *sagulum* (c. 6, 2), a thick woollen cloak, longer or shorter according to the season, clasped over the right

shoulder and leaving the arms free. It was worn by many
other peoples, Celts, Ligurians, Spaniards, etc., as well as by
Roman soldiers, workmen, and country-folk, and was sometimes of various colours (*H.* 2. 20, 1; 5. 23, 1; Verg. *Aen.* 8,
660). The Scottish plaid and Spanish cloak are its survivals.

fibula: such clasps or brooches, made of various metals
and in various forms, have been found in great numbers in
German tombs, and at a later date they were often of costly
workmanship. The expression *tegumen spina consertum* is
borrowed from Verg. *Aen.* 3, 594 (whence Ovid, *Met.* 14, 166
spinis conserto tegmine nullis).

cetera intecti, 'otherwise unclad' (accusative of respect, as
in cc. 29, 3; 45, 9). Tacitus is here speaking of the dress worn
indoors round the fire in cold weather. In c. 6, 2, *nudi aut
sagulo leves*, he is speaking of warriors in the field in summer.
It is at least meant (whether rightly or not) that indoors they
had no other clothing, but it is not to be supposed that such
light clothing was worn out of doors, especially in winter.

totos dies, accusative of time. agunt, sc. *vitam*, 'live'.
Passing whole days round the fire is contrasted with the out-
of-door life of the Italians.

locupletissimi, etc., 'the richest are distinguished by clothing which is not loose, like that of the Sarmatians and Parthians, but close-fitting and showing the shape of each limb'.
Locupletissimi is contrasted with *omnibus*, and the sentence
implies that the *vestis* is confined to the rich: it cannot mean
that they were distinguished by the material and the quality
of the *vestis*, which all had. Yet it is undoubted that the *vestis*
was not confined to the rich, as the evidence of the monuments and the description of women's dress in § 3 show, so
that we have here an inaccuracy of language or a misconc-
ception. *Vestis* means body-garments as opposed to *sagum*.
Tacitus does not define it, but the monuments show that it
included tunic or shirt, mostly long-sleeved, and trousers
(*bracae*, 'breeches'). This was the normal attire in time of
peace, but in battle the tunic at least was usually discarded
(see on c. 6, 2), as shown on the Augustan gem at Vienna, the
Paris cameo of Tiberius, the monument at Adamklissi in
the Dobrudja, bronze figurines, etc. (see figs. 14–16). So at
the beginning of the second century *bracae* and mantle form
the dress of the leader of a German embassy who confers with
Trajan (fig. 23).

Tight-fitting garments may have been normal at least
among the West Germans, although the Celticized Vangiones
in the Palatinate wore loose trousers (Lucan, *Phars.* 1, 430):
probably they were originally adopted as a protection against

the cold, while the hot climate of the East led to the adoption of loose caftan and trousers.

§ 2. gerunt, sc. *Germani.* et = *etiam,* i.e. besides the *sagum.* Caesar had spoken of skins as the sole clothing of the Germans (*B. G.* 6, 21, cp. 4. 1, 10 of the Suebi).

ripae, sc. *Romanae.* Where the word is used absolutely, as here and in c. 23, 1, without qualification by the context, it is best interpreted as meaning the bank of the Rhine and the Danube: as these rivers are for Tacitus the boundary between the Empire and Free Germany (c. 1, 1), *ripa* is the equivalent of 'the frontier' (Wissowa, *Gött. gel. Anz.,* 1916, p. 667). In the fourth century the frontier troops are called *ripenses* or *riparienses* (Grosse, *Röm. Militargesch.,* p. 66). Nevertheless it is probable that, as elsewhere in the first part of the treatise, Tacitus had primarily in view the Rhine frontier.

neglegenter . . . exquisitius, 'without discrimination . . . with more careful choice'. The explanation of the latter adverb by *eligunt,* etc., shows that both refer not to the manner of wearing the skins but to the preparation of them for wear—an idea involved in *gerunt.*

ut quibus, etc., 'since trade brings them no finery': sc. *est,* instead of the more usual subjunctive, as in c. 22, 1. For *cultus,* cp. c. 6, 2.

eligunt, sc. *ulteriores.*

detracta, sc. *feris*: the word *velamina* is used with a proleptic reference to the clothing made from them.

spargunt, etc., 'they variegate with patches of the (differently coloured) skins of animals produced by the outer ocean and its unknown waters'. *Maculis pellibusque* is a hendiadys to avoid a double genitive. Only one sea is meant, as the singular *gignit* shows, and that was the Oceanus of cc. 2, 1 and 44, 1, in which the land of the Suiones was an island. The allusion is probably not only to marine animals, such as seals, but to those of the islands and the mainland beyond: the skin and fur trade with Scandinavia was of great importance throughout the Middle Ages (cp. note on c. 44, 1).

§ 3. nec alius feminis, etc., 'the women have the same dress as the men, except that they generally drape themselves with linen over-garments which they embroider with purple, and that they do not lengthen the upper part of their clothing into sleeves, thus leaving their fore-arms and upper arms bare; (and not only that) but the adjoining part of the breast is also exposed'.

saepius, 'rather frequently' (cp. c. 22, 1; 38, 3; and note on *Agr.* c. 9, 3).

amictibus, distinguished from *vestitus,* as the *sagum* from the *vestis* in the case of men. The garments in question were (1) a kerchief of varying size forming a large veil or a mantilla, which was secured to the head by a fillet and fell over the shoulders, and (2) a mantle or cloak corresponding to the *sagum*, which appears on monuments of the second and later centuries. Linen was considered by German women the most beautiful dress-material: *vela texunt . . . et transrhenani hostes, nec pulchriorem aliam vestem eorum feminae novere* (Pliny, *N. H.* 19, 8; note on *specus*, c. 16, 4).

purpura, not true purple, but a vegetable dye resembling it in colour. Probably strips of linen were dyed and sewn on to the white garment as a border or as stripes.

superioris for *superiorem*, by a transference not uncommon in poetry and even in prose (cp. c. 27, 2).

in manicas, etc., implies a sleeved garment in the case of men, which is subsumed in *veste* (§ 1). This was a striking contrast to Roman custom; Roman women never had the arms bare, men always.

brachia ac lacertos, fore-arms and arms (from elbow to shoulder).

proxima . . . patet: the alliteration is striking.

The description of women's dress is extremely concise, and the opening statement is too wide, for *bracae* were not a characteristic garment of German women and their tunic or gown was a long garment falling to the feet. That in some parts of Germany the dress of men and women was substantially the same is held by some scholars to be confirmed by a relief of the Flavian age from the Roman fortress at Mainz, depicting what appears to be a captive German woman clad in tight long-sleeved tunic and trousers, both with a diamond-shaped pattern, and a long veil (*lineus amictus*) which falls from her head over her back and is gathered together over her lap (fig. 17).[1] A similar type of

FIG. 19. Coin of M. Aurelius (mourning German woman in sleeveless tunic and loose *bracae*).

---

[1] This interpretation is rejected by Kossinna and others, who think

costume, with what seem to be less close-fitting *bracae*,
is depicted on coins of M. Aurelius bearing the legend *Germania subacta* (fig. 19). It seems probable, therefore, that
male attire was sometimes adopted (in the cold climate
of north Germany ?); but Roman works of art (such as the
Augustan gem, the column of Marcus, coins, etc.), while bearing out Tacitus' statement about the bare arms and upper
part of the breast, show a long gown falling in folds to the
feet and girt round the waist or above it (figs. 12, 18, 20); and
these representations, while perhaps not realistic in every
detail (since the artists worked under the influence of an established tradition), were no doubt substantially true to life.

The whole subject of German dress is fully treated by
G. Girke in *Mannusbibliothek*, vol. 23–4 (1922).

CHAPTER XVIII
MARRIAGE CUSTOMS

§ 1. **Quamquam,** 'and yet' (note on c. 5, 4), in spite of the bare
arms and breast (which would have been immodest in Rome)
their chastity is remarkable. This forms a skilful transition
to a new subject. In this chapter Tacitus limits himself to
one aspect of the ceremonial of marriage which he regarded
as specially significant, and the elevated rhetorical and expository style of this and the next chapter reflect his admiration of the German conception of marriage (as he understood
it) and his desire to win the sympathy of his readers and
stimulate them to reflection.

prope soli barbarorum. Polygamy was not legally forbidden, though only exceptionally practised by people of
wealth and standing. Concubinage was an old and common
practice. Monogamy was the rule also among Gauls and
Iberians.

exceptis, etc. A historical instance is Ariovistus, who had
two wives (Caes. 1. 53, 4).

libidine, causal ablative, answering to *ob nobilitatem,* but
a harsh zeugma is involved in its combination with *ambiuntur,*
from which must be supplied *plures uxores ducunt;* for the
gratification of the lust of a *nobilis* could not be a motive
for the promotion of matrimonial alliances by the relatives
of the bride.

ob nobilitatem, i.e. for the advantages to be expected by

that the figure is a personification of *Germania* in the dress of a
male warrior, a Roman mode of representing a conquered people
for which parallels can be cited (*Deut. Vorgesch.*², pp. 112 ff.); but
the veil is against this view, and so are the remains of the foot of a
male German seated opposite the female figure.

the parents or guardians from alliances with powerful and wealthy nobles.

plurimis nuptiis ambiuntur, 'are courted with numerous offers of marriage', perhaps a reminiscence of Virgil's *neu conubiis ambire Latinum Aeneadae possint* (*Aen.* 7, 333). *Plurimi* in Tacitus means not 'several' but 'very many' or 'most'; but there is no reason to emend (with Halm) to *pluribus*, on the ground that the opposite of *singuli* is not *plurimi* but *plures* (*H.* 4. 30; *A.* 14. 44, 3). Tacitus does not say that they have very many wives.

§ 2. dotem, etc. Tacitus' source was misled by the apparent contrast to Roman custom. The nature of the actual gifts goes to show (what is fully confirmed by later evidence) that they were not a dowry to the wife but a gift (like the Homeric ἕδνα) to her parents, by which the *patria potestas* over her ('munt', in medieval Latin *mundium*) was purchased. The Gallic women had *dos*, and a kind of settlement in marriage (Caes. 6. 19, 1).

intersunt parentes, etc. The family assembled to examine and approve the gifts. The repetition of the word *munera* —a favourite poetic device of stressing an idea, naturally infrequent in prose—serves to emphasize the contrast with Roman practice. A precisely similar repetition of *munera* is found in Propert. 1. 3, 25 f.

non ad delicias, etc., 'not sought out to please a woman's taste', like the jewelry, gems, pearls and articles of the toilet which a Roman lady demanded.

boves, etc. See notes on cc. 5, 2; 12, 2.

gladioque: this fact is at variance with the statement in c. 6, 1 *rari gladiis utuntur* (see the note there).

§ 3. in haec munera, 'in consideration of these gifts', 'under condition of' them. The use of *in* with the meaning 'with a view to', 'in view of', is not uncommon in Tacitus. The same force of the preposition is found in several passages of Livy, e.g. 34. 35, 1 *condiciones in quas ... pax fieret*; 23. 34, 1 *in has ferme leges ... ictum foedus*, etc.

ipsa ... adfert. This again is a misconception. Later records of marriage customs show that a sword (*armorum aliquid*) was given to the bridegroom, not by the bride, but by her father or guardian, evidently as a symbol of the transference to him of the power of life and death over the woman.

hoc maximum vinculum, etc. This explanation and those which follow are due to Tacitus himself. *Hoc* means the interchange of gifts. The frequent use of anaphora in this chapter (*hoc—haec—hos, extra—extraque, idem—idem*, etc.) expresses warmth of feeling.

FIG. 17. Relief from Mainz.

FIG. 18. Part of a sarcophagus found in Rome (early 3rd cent. A.D.):
captive German family (husband sitting on r. with trousers and mantle,
wife opposite in short-sleeved gown, girt above waist, and large mantle.

FIG. 20. *Gemma Augustea* (lower part): on left German with trousers and shoes, and German woman with sleeveless gown.

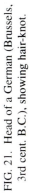

FIG. 22. Head of a German with a hair knot over left temple, from the tombstone of a Roman horseman at Mainz (*CIL*. xiii.7033).

FIG. 21. Head of a German (Brussels, 3rd cent. B.C.), showing hair-knot.

FIG. 23. German (probably Bastarnian) embassy conferring with Trajan (from the Column of Trajan): leader in mantle and trousers with hair-knot.

arcana sacra, 'their mystic rites', an allusion to the Roman patrician ceremony—nearly obsolete in A.D. 23 (*A*. 4. 16, 2)—of *confarreatio*, which began with the offering of a cake of spelt to Juppiter.

coniugales deos, such as Juppiter, Juno pronuba, Hymenaeus, etc. Among the Germans the simple interchange of gifts took the place of all this.

§ 4. extra virtutum, etc., 'excluded from aspiring to manly deeds and exempt from the casualties of war'.

ipsis incipientis . . . auspiciis, a pleonastic phrase, 'by the very opening ceremonies with which her wedding begins'. Cp. *initium incohant*, c. 30, 1.

idem . . . ausuramque, 'destined to suffer and to dare alike with him in peace and war'. *Proelio* instead of *bello* for the sake of the alliteration; on the presence of women in war, see c. 7, 3. The order *passuram ausuramque*, emphasizing adversity, recurs in *H.* 2. 46 *extrema passuros ausurosque*.

hoc . . . denuntiant, 'this is the intimation given by'. The gifts, as has been seen, had no such meaning.

sic vivendum, sc. *esse*, i.e. in such conviction of indissoluble partnership. The preceding clause is parenthetical.

pariendum, 'be a mother'. This reading is supported by what follows. *Pereundum*, which has very poor authority, would mean: this conviction she must cherish till her dying day.

accipere se quae. If the relative refers to the gifts (which is the natural interpretation of the Latin), it is really applicable only to the *arma*, which alone could be transmitted to posterity. A better meaning would be obtained by making it refer not to the gifts themselves but to the idea conveyed by them; but, if this is what Tacitus meant, he has not expressed himself clearly.

digna, not to be connected with the following *quae* but to be taken absolutely: ' she receives what she is to hand down to her children (i.e. her sons, in conformity with § 2; so also in c. 20, 5), intact and worthy to be prized, what her daughters-in-law are to receive, and what is to be again transmitted to her grandsons.' From the accusative *quae* a nominative has to be supplied as subject of *referantur*.

CHAPTER XIX

MARRIED LIFE

§ 1. Ergo, 'consequently', because of the conception of wedlock as an indissoluble partnership.

saepta, 'fenced in', i.e. 'well-protected'; the chastity of

the German woman was, like that of Agrippina, *impenetrabilis* (*A*. 4. 12, 4). The conjecture *saeptae* may be supported by Livy, 3. 44, 4 *omnia pudore saepta*, but it was the lofty conception of wedlock that furnished the protection, not the *pudicitia* which was the result of it.

agunt, sc. *vitam* (c. 17, 1).

nullis, etc., 'with no shows to corrupt them by their allurements, no banquets by their incentives'. The corrupting influence of shows upon Roman women is often noted: see Prop. 2. 19, 9; Ov. *A*. *A*. 1, 97–100; Juv. 11, 201; and many other passages collected in Friedländer, *Sittengeschichte*, ed. 10, i. 288 ff. The Roman banquets and their accompaniments are also often spoken of as demoralizing: cp. Ov. *A*. *A*. 1, 229 ff.; Quint. 1. 2, 8; and other references in Friedländer, p. 291 f.

litterarum secreta, 'clandestine correspondence'. The allusion is plainly to the clandestine love-letters of Roman ladies (Juv. 6, 277). The art of writing was altogether unknown to Germans for many centuries after Tacitus wrote. Theodoric, the Ostrogothic king of Italy (died 526), was unable to sign his name, and Charlemagne (died 814) in his mature age strove with indifferent success to acquire the practice of writing (Gibbon, cc. xxxix, xlix). Letters of German princes to the emperor or senate are spoken of in *A*. 2. 63, 1; 88, 1; but these were written for them in Latin, no doubt by Roman traders or captives in their country.

§ 2. **in tam numerosa,** 'though the race is so numerous'. For this concessive force of *in* ('despite'), see note on c. 4, 2 *in tanto numero.*

praesens, 'immediate'; so with *supplicium* in *A*. 1. 38, 1.

maritis permissa: so in earlier Roman law, but the *lex Iulia de adulteriis coercendis*, enacted by Augustus in B.C. 17, withdrew from the husband the right of killing his wife taken in adultery, and substituted the right of prosecution, with civil penalties for the convicted woman (loss of half her dowry and one-third of her separate property, and banishment to an island).

abscisis crinibus. Long hair, a mark of free birth, was characteristic of Germans generally (see c. 38, 2), and was the special pride of the women. Later German laws attest all these penalties, and others more severe, that of death, even by burning, being permissible. Unchastity among unmarried women could be similarly punished by the parent or guardian. The variant reading *accisis*, supported by Wissowa (*Herm.* 51, 318) would mean 'cut short', περικείρειν, but this sense of the verb is not attested till late Latin.

coram propinquis. The relatives act as his assessors in the

trial. A similar family tribunal to try the wife was sometimes
allowed at Rome even under the Empire, as is shown by the
cases described in *A*. 2. 50; 13. 32 (cp. Suet. *Tib*. 35).

per omnem vicum: on the village as the normal form of
settlement, see note to c. 16, 1.

verbere, 'with a lash', not collective singular for 'blows',
a usage alien to Tacitus.

publicatae enim, etc. As the subsequent sentences still
relate to married life, it is most natural to suppose that
Tacitus is here also speaking of the adulteress: 'for prosti-
tuted chastity finds no pardon: neither beauty nor youth nor
wealth would procure the culprit a (second) husband' (as
they easily might at Rome). *Publicata* is a rather strong word
to use of a single lapse from virtue, and *maritum* is somewhat
loosely used for *alterum maritum*, but the following *melius
quidem adhuc*, etc., shows that Tacitus had second marriages
in mind. The alternative is to suppose that Tacitus means
here to speak, as it were parenthetically, of the unmarried
(there were no *meretrices* in Germany). Those who so take it
either omit or bracket *enim*, or alter it to *etiam*, or *enimvero*,
or give it an elliptical meaning: i.e. 'no wonder that the
penalty for adultery is so severe, for unchastity generally
(even among the unmarried) finds no pardon'. This is a
forced interpretation. As regards *enimvero*, which Tacitus
often uses to mark a transition, it is to be noted that he always
places the word at the beginning of a sentence.

aetate, 'youth': the ablatives are causal.

opibus. Tacitus speaks from the Roman point of view:
the German wife had no separate property save the presents
given her by her parents and the members of her family.

invenerit. The subject is supplied from *publicatae pudicitiae*. At Rome an adulteress or a woman of easy virtue had
no great difficulty in securing a husband, if she were beautiful, young, or rich.

§ 3. **corrumpere et corrumpi**, so coupled in *A*. 14. 20, 5.

saeculum, 'the spirit of the age', with bitter sarcasm.
Saeculum in a depreciative sense (arising from the often
recurring idea that the contemporary generation is worse
than its predecessors) is as old as Terence, but usually has an
explanatory attribute (*hoc saeculum, huius saeculi mores*, etc.).
Cp. Löfstedt, *Syntactica*, p. 472.

melius adhuc, sc. *agunt*, 'better still is the practice'. Verbs
of motion or action, as well as of speaking, are often omitted
by Tacitus. *Adhuc* adds force to the comparative (= *etiam*),
as perhaps in c. 29, 3, and has often the sense of 'further':
see note on c. 10, 3.

in quibus tantum virgines, etc. Some German tribes, which are not specified, forbade remarriages. In north Friesland the remarriage of widows is said to be still banned. The ban, however, was not exclusively German: it appears to have existed in early Greece (Pausan. 2. 21, 7), and a more primitive custom, similar to the Hindu suttee, by which the widow immolated herself beside her husband's tomb, prevailed not only among the Germanic Heruli (Procop. *Bell. Goth.* 2, 14) but also among various non-Germanic tribes, such as Thracians, Scythians, and Slavs. In saga literature Nanna follows Balder and Brunhild Siegfried to death.

cum spe votoque . . . transigitur, 'the hope and aspiration of the wife (i.e. a woman's hope and desire of wedlock) are done with once for all'. *Spe votoque* is explained by *ne ulla cogitatio,* etc.; the same phrase recurs in *Agr.* 3, 1 and *A.* 4. 39, 2. *Transigitur* is a legal and business expression: cp. *transigite cum expeditionibus, Agr.* 34, 4.

§ 4. **sic,** answering to *quomodo* ('so . . . as'), as in *Agr.* 34, 2; *Dial.* 36, 8, etc. This idealizing interpretation of motive is, of course, due to Tacitus himself.

ne, sc. *sit*: cp. c. 13, 3, etc.

ultra = *ulterior,* beyond one marriage. *Longior* bears the same sense.

ne tamquam, etc., 'that her love may be, as it were, not for the husband, but for wedlock'—by which she is elevated to the permanent dignity of a mother of children. *Tamquam,* 'so to say', apologizes for an unusual expression, as in *Dial.* 37, *A.* 6. 24, 4; but the elder Seneca uses a similar phrase without a qualifying particle, *videat an nuptias suas amet an nil pluris faciat marito* (*Controv.* 1. 6, 6, quoted by Ed. Wolff). The double *tamquam* has been a cause of offence, and some would read (with Meiser) *tam maritum quam matrimonium* or *maritum tam quam matrimonium.* Grotius' transposition of *maritum* and *matrimonium* would give the meaning that the wife should love not the married state as such but her husband; Tacitus would be speaking of her attitude both after marriage and after her husband's death, but the transposition would make the second *tamquam* quite intolerable.

§ 5. **numerum . . . finire** (= *definire*), 'to limit the number'.

agnatis = ἐπιγόνοις, children born after there was already an heir. A similar prohibition among the Jews is mentioned in *H.* 5. 5 (cp. Joseph. *c. Apionem,* 2, [24], 202). *Agnati* was a Roman technical term for sons born or adopted after the father had made his will; *agnatio* had the effect of making the will invalid (Cic. *de Or.* 1, 241; *pro Caec.* 25, 72), and hence recourse was had to procuring abortion (Juv. 6, 595). As the Germans made no wills (c. 20, 5), *agnati* must mean late-born sons, whose death might be desired to prevent a diminution of the amount of the inheritance falling to the older sons. Tacitus' statement would, however, appear to be an exaggeration. In later times at any rate, as the evidence of German sources attests, infants were exposed in case of deformity or illegitimacy or in time of famine, and Tacitus himself narrates that the Frisians under severe stress sold their wives and children into slavery (*A*. 4. 72).

mores . . . leges, an antithesis which was a commonplace in idealizing and moralizing descriptions (Sallust, *Cat.* 9, 1; Hor. *Carm.* 3. 24, 35, etc.). The German sanctity of custom is contrasted with the futility of such laws as the *lex Papia Poppaea* at Rome (see *A*. 3. 26, 1 ff.). No written German laws are certainly traceable earlier than the still extant Salic of the sixth century.

CHAPTER XX

THE UPBRINGING OF CHILDREN AND THE RULE OF SUCCESSION

§ 1. The last sentence of the preceding chapter leads naturally to the subject of the present one.

in omni domo, even those of the richer class.

nudi, to be taken literally (cp. c. 6, 2; 17, 1; 24, 1); cp. Mela, 3. 3, 26 *nudi agunt antequam puberes sunt . . . viri sagis velantur.* Observations of this kind were made by Romans in summer time.

sordidi, 'dirty', not inconsistent with c. 22, 1 *lavantur*, which refers to adults.

hos . . . haec, those well known to us, explained by *quae miramur*. They were often seen, whether as slaves or soldiers, at Rome: cp. *magna corpora* (c. 4, 2), *procera membra* (*A*. 1. 64, 3), and other such expressions in *H*. 5. 18, 1; Caes. *B. G.* 1. 39, 1, etc.

excrescunt, 'they grow up', here alone in Tacitus and rarely followed by *in*.

nec ancillis, etc., in strong contrast to the habits of fashionable ladies at Rome, who had abandoned the old Roman practice of personal nurture and supervision of children (see *Dial.* 28, 4; 29, 1; *Agr.* 4, 2).

delegantur, sc. *infantes* (change of subject as in c. 18, 4). The same expression is used in *Dial.* 29 *at nunc natus infans delegatur Graeculae alicui ancillae.*

§ 2. dominum, in the sense of *infantem dominum* (*Dial. l. c.*); for the anticipatory use, cp. notes on *dignatio*, c. 13, 2, and *Agr.* 4, 4 *senatori.*

servum. It is here admitted that there were slaves in the house: see c. 25, 1, and note.

educationis deliciis, 'by any pampering in upbringing': cp. *infantiam deliciis solvimus* (Quint. 1. 2, 6). This community of child life mitigated the condition of slavery.

pecora . . . humo. The cattle were under the same roof in the homestead, which had only a mud floor.

aetas, that at which they receive arms (c. 13, 1).

virtus agnoscat, 'valour recognizes, acknowledges, them as her own', as a father acknowledges his offspring as legitimate. *Virtus* is a personification of the martial spirit.

§ 3. **sera . . . venus.** The stress laid by Germans on youthful purity of life is attested by Caesar, *B. G.* 6. 21, 4 *qui diutissime impuberes permanserunt, maximam inter suos ferunt laudem* and Mela, 3. 3, 26 *longissima apud eos pueritia est.* According to Caesar, *l. c.*, youths did not marry before 20; at Rome the minimum age was 14, but among the middle and lower classes marriages of men under 18 or 19 seem to have been exceptional, in the senatorial class the age was higher (Agricola married about 22, *App.* i to *Agr.*, p. 166, and Tacitus himself about the same age). Cp. Friedländer, *Sittengesch.*, ed. 10, i. 274.

inexhausta, 'unimpaired', or possibly 'inexhaustible' as in *H.* 5. 7 and perhaps in Verg. *Aen.* 10, 174, who first used the word.

festinantur, 'hurried into marriage'. The verb is often used passively (as *A.* 6. 50, 6), or in the active transitively (as *A.* 1. 6, 4) by Tacitus, as well as by poets and Sallust. Here it is a bold expression for *festinanter collocantur.* At Rome girls were marriageable at 12 (note on *Agr.* 9, 7), though the average age was probably 14 (Friedländer, *op. cit.*, p. 273, and *Anhang*, xi, by M. Bang). In Germany the age for marriage at this time was about 20, as this passage combined with Caesar's evidence shows. Later, marriage at 15 and subsequently at 12 became general.

iuventa, 'youthful vigour'.

pares validaeque miscentur = *pares aetate ac pariter validae miscentur,* 'they are matched in age and strength when they mate'. The adjectives plainly repeat the facts expressed by *eadem iuventa, similis proceritas.*

referunt, 'reproduce'. Cp. c. 43, 1, and Verg. *G.* 3, 128 *invalidique patrum referant ieiunia nati.*

§ 4. **sororum filiis,** etc. An illustration of this special relationship between the nephew and the maternal uncle is perhaps furnished by two facts recorded by Tacitus, that Civilis placed two sons of his sister (or sisters) in high commands

(*H*. 4, 33; 5, 20), and that when the Suebic king Vannius was deposed in A.D. 50, his kingdom was divided between two of his sister's sons (*A*. 12. 29-30). The explanation of the relationship is obscure. It is found in the primitive state of society called matriarchal, in which marriage was frequently polyandrous and relationships and succession were reckoned through the mother: the sister needed the support of her brother to ensure that her children were properly cared for. But there is no clear trace of the matriarchal system in German society. The same relationship is attested among polygamous peoples, where it is a safeguard against the neglect or maltreatment of the offspring of one or more of the wives; but there is no reason to believe that polygamy was ever general in Germany (cp. c. 18, 1). A similar situation might, however, arise when a man married again after the death of his first wife; the maternal uncle would then become the natural protector of the children of the first marriage. It is worthy of note that a similar relationship seems to have been originally implied by the Latin *avunculus* (= *avus minor*) and by the use of *nepos* in the sense of nephew. The German words correspond: the first syllable of *Oheim*, uncle, represents the stem of *avus*, and *Neffe*, nephew, is the same word as *nepos*.

quidam, certain German tribes.

magis, sc. *quam filios*.

exigunt, 'insist on this blood-tie', viz. *sororum filios*, or rather *liberos*, since *puellae* were also sometimes demanded as hostages (c. 8, 1, with the note).

tamquam, etc., 'in the conviction that they thus secure a firmer hold on the feelings and a wider hold on the family' (of the contracting party), wider because the relatives on the father's as well as on the mother's side are thereby involved. For *tamquam*, see on c. 12, 2. Others take the subject of *teneant* to be *huiusmodi obsides*.

latius, as embracing more relationships.

§ 5. heredes tamen, i.e. despite the close tie between maternal uncle and nephew, inheritance is not affected by it.

liberi: sons only are meant (as in c. 18, 5), for daughters took no share of the immovable property nor (until a much later date) of the movables, the reason being that the property belonged to the family and could not pass from it, as a woman's portion would do when she married. Here Tacitus mentions only the general rule of succession: further details, including a custom of primogeniture, are recorded in connexion with the Tencteri in c. 32, 4, but it is doubtful whether they applied to all German tribes.

nullum testamentum, because there was an established rule of succession, based on blood relationship. The absence of testation is in accordance with primitive usage, but in strong contrast to Roman law. It was from the Romans that the Germans ultimately learned the practice of testation, which at first took the form of an oral declaration.

proximus gradus, etc., 'the next in order of succession are'. *Proximus gradus* is equivalent to *qui proximum gradum obtinent,* and *in possessione* means 'in the matter of taking possession' (from *possido,* as in *Agr.* 18, 4, etc.). *Avunculi,* if correctly added (which is doubted), could only come into account when there were no relatives on the father's side.

propinquorum . . . adfinium, 'relatives by blood and by marriage'. *Plus propinquorum* for *plures propinqui* is a most uncommon usage.

gratiosior, 'more esteemed'; not elsewhere in Tacitus, but frequent in Cicero and other writers.

nec ulla orbitatis pretia, a great contrast to Rome, where the servility of legacy-hunters gave a great social power to those who were wealthy and childless. References to legacy-hunting abound in Roman literature from Horace (*Sat.* 2, 5) onwards: Friedländer, *Sittengesch.,* ed. 10, i. 248 ff. *Pretia* (cp. c. 24, 2), for the more usual *orbitatis praemia* (Pliny, *Epp.* 4. 15, 3).

CHAPTER XXI
BLOOD-FEUDS AND HOSPITALITY

The subject of inheritance leads to that of feuds and friendships, which were also inherited, and from this the transition is easy to a contrasted trait of the German character, the hospitable treatment of strangers.

§ 1. **inimicitias,** 'feuds' (Ger. *Fehden*). The duty of exacting blood vengeance (*Blutrache, Vendetta*) for homicide devolved on the whole sept, and especially on the nearest of kin. It is found very generally in ancient institutions, is recognized in the Mosaic code, and received various restrictions and modifications from law-givers, gradually passing into legal redress. Even now it is not altogether extinct among European peoples (Albanians, Montenegrins, and Corsicans).

propinqui, 'a blood-relation' generally (c. 20, 5).

amicitias: of these nothing more is said, probably because there was little of interest to say.

necesse est, 'is a duty', imposed by German opinion and moral sentiment, expressed in long-established custom.

nec . . . durant, 'but they (the feuds) do not continue irreconcilable': *nec* for *nec tamen.*

luitur . . . homicidium, 'even homicide is expiated', not only lesser injuries (cp. c. 12, 2). The compensation, *satisfactio*, the ποινή of the Homeric poems, in German called *Wergeld* ('man-money'), was in later time payable in money and assessed by a regular code according to the rank of the person slain, the damages for a noble being normally twice those for an ordinary freeman. The acceptance of compensation, however, was not compulsory upon the relatives.

certo armentorum, etc., 'a fixed number of cattle and sheep': in c. 5, 1 and 12, 2 *pecora* is used more generally. For the payment of fines in cattle, cp. c. 12, 2.

universa domus, 'the whole family', all relatives on the father's and mother's side, as in c. 20, 4.

utiliter in publicum, 'to the advantage of the community': *in publicum* is used in several places by Tacitus, with the force of *publice* (e.g. *A.* 2. 48, 1; 11. 17, 4; 12. 8, 3): cp. note on *in universum*, c. 5, 1.

iuxta libertatem, 'side by side with liberty', i.e. where liberty reigns and there is no strong State control. Cp. *illud ex libertate vitium* (c. 11, 3). For a different use of *iuxta*, in the sense of 'near to', see c. 30, 3 and *A.* 6. 13, 1; 6. 42, 3 (*iuxta libertatem*).

§ 2. convictibus et hospitiis, 'feasting (among themselves) and hospitality (to strangers)'. The hospitality of the Germans is noted in similar terms by Caesar (*B. G.* 6. 23, 9): *hospitem violare fas non putant; qui quacumque de causa ad eos venerint, ab iniuria prohibent, sanctos habent, hisque omnium domus patent victusque communicatur*. Similar praise is accorded to the Celtiberians by Posidonius (Diod. 5, 34). The hospitable reception of strangers is, in fact, usual in undeveloped countries. See below on *nec interest*.

effusius indulget, 'indulges more freely in' : cp. *indulge hospitio*, 'give rein to' (Verg. *Aen.* 4, 51).

nefas, because the stranger is *sanctus*, under divine protection.

pro fortuna, 'according to his means' (so in *A.* 14. 21, 2), taken closely with *apparatis*, 'well-furnished' (cp. *apparatis accipere epulis*, Livy, 23. 4, 3, and the substantive *apparatus* in c. 14, 3; 23, 1).

cum defecere, sc. *epulae*, 'when they have come to an end': cp. *cum omnia defecerunt*, c. 24, 3. On this passage, cp. *Introd.*, p. xxxiii. In later times two or three nights were the limit for which the right of hospitality could be claimed. Similarly the Greeks regarded a guest who prolonged his visit beyond three days as outstaying his welcome (Plaut. *Mil. Glor.* 742 f.).

hospes, 'the host'.

monstrator, etc., 'guides and escorts him to further hospitality', not merely to show him the way but to shield him from injury. What follows shows that the host now becomes in turn a guest. *Monstrator* is a Virgilian word.

proximam domum: the next house on the stranger's route would be at some distance from his previous lodging. The use of the word *domus*, without mention of a village, suggests that the reference is to an isolated farmstead on the way (see on c. 16, 1 and 19, 2), but such an inference is by no means certain.

§ 3. **nec interest,** 'it makes no difference': no distinction is made between invited and uninvited, as the next sentence repeats. This indiscriminateness of hospitality is characteristic of ancient civilization, and grows out of its circumstances: without it, travelling would have been impossible. It can be illustrated abundantly from the Homeric poems, and from many other sources, and has its counterpart now in scantily peopled countries, though in strong contrast to modern society generally, or to the Rome of Tacitus.

humanitate reproduces φιλανθρωπία in Hellenistic Greek.

quantum ad, 'so far as concerns' (=*quantum attinet ad*), as in *Agr.* 44, 3 and elsewhere. Hence the French *quant à*.

abeunti. Gifts to the guest on departure, and the asking for them, are illustrated in the Nibelungenlied. Such ξεινήια are constantly mentioned in the Homeric poems.

moris, sc. *est* (cp. c. 13, 1).

facilitas, 'freedom from constraint'. *Facilis* is used in the sense of 'frank' in *Agr.* 40, 4; *A.* 3. 8, 4, etc.

gaudent, emphatic, as in c. 15, 3.

data ... obligantur. The verbs all belong to the language of book-keeping, *data (expensa)—accepta, imputare—obligari.* With *imputant* sc. *ei cui dederunt.* They neither reckon the gifts they make as a debt to be repaid nor incur any obligation for those they receive: the giver does not regard himself as a creditor, nor the recipient as a debtor.

[victus inter hospites comis.] This remark, 'social intercourse between host and guest is courteous' (*victus* is not used in this sense by Tacitus), is so patently weak and out of place that it has generally been regarded as a marginal summary of the paragraph, which found its way into the text (according to Andresen, a fusion of two notes, *victus inter hospites*, a summary, and *comes*, a repetition from § 2). Norden, pp. 135, 454 ff., takes it as the sigh, evoked by the words *ius hospitis*, of a reader or scribe of the *Germania* in the fifth century who had suffered from the German invaders billeted on him and thought of the good old times (or, alternatively, had had unusually pleasant experiences). Attempted emendations are either insipid or violent and inapposite. Plainly the chapter ended with the antithetical sentence which precedes.

The Greek colouring of Tacitus' account of German hospitality is so strong that the passage can be translated directly into the typical language of Greek ethnography, as Norden has shown by doing it (p. 138). It is to be traced, as he points out, to Posidonius' descriptions of the Celts and the Rhine Germans, whom he regarded as similar in habits and modes of life (Diod. 5, 28; Athenaeus, 4, 151 e; Strabo, 7. 1, 2, p. 290). These descriptions were in turn influenced by older comparisons of the customs of the Homeric Greeks with those of other primitive non-Hellenic peoples. Hence Norden suspects that Tacitus' picture is not so true to actual fact as that of Caesar (quoted above). But while he could not escape the influence of an established ethnographic style, there is no reason to believe that he incorporated in his picture facts not recorded about the Germans. On this subject, see *Introd.*, Sect. III.

CHAPTER XXII

DAILY LIFE

§ 1. quem plerumque, etc., in contrast to the Romans who usually rose before daybreak: warm climates naturally lead to early rising. *Plerumque*, 'very often': see note on c. 5, 1.

lavantur, saepius calida, 'wash, mostly with warm water'. *Saepius*, sc. *quam frigida. Lavantur* is not 'bathe': the use of warm baths was learnt by northerners from the Romans. For their enervating effect on the Cimbri in Italy, Dio, 27, frag. 94, 2. Boudicca derided them as an effeminacy (*id.* 62. 6, 4). The German's bath was the river and his fondness for swimming is abundantly attested (Caes. *B. G.* 4. 1, 10; 6. 21, 5; *A.* 2. 8, 3; Herodian 7. 2, 6).

ut apud quos plurimum, sc. *temporis* (c. 15, 1), a very large part of the year. For *ut*, see on c. 17, 2.

cibum capiunt: a second meal, which was the principal one, was taken in the afternoon towards sundown.

separatae, etc. This also is contrary to the Roman custom of reclining on the *triclinium* round a common table. The German seat was a stool, and the tables were small and low. The Celts sat on bundles of straw and used low wooden tables (Posidonius *apud* Athen. 4, 151 e), while the Gauls, although they were Celts, are said by the same authority to have sat on skins laid on the ground (Diod. 5. 28, 4). The fact that the German word for 'table', *Tisch*, like Eng. *dish*, is derived from Lat. *discus* and in old High German denoted also 'dish', indicates that originally the tables served the purpose of dishes. Separate tables as well as separate seats were also used by Greeks in early times (*Od.* 17, 333; 22, 74, etc.).

convivia: besides public feasts at festivals there were family feasts to celebrate births, investiture of youths with arms, marriages, etc. But *nec minus saepe* is an obvious exaggeration.

armati, in emphatic position; see c. 11, 4; 13, 1.

§ 2. **diem noctemque continuare potando,** 'to drink through the day and night': *potando*, ablative of manner. So *A.* 16. 5, 2 *diem noctemque sedilibus continuant*, 'sit through the day and night'. This German failing is noted again in *H.* 4. 79 and *A.* 11. 16, 4, but such intemperance was doubtless limited to special occasions. Many other races were accused of excessive drinking, Celts, Iberians, Thracians, Persians, etc.; among Romans it was uncommon, as it generally is in wine-producing countries, where the climate is warmer.

ut, 'as is usual' (or 'natural'): cp. c. 2, 4. **vinolentos,** in a general sense for 'intoxicated'.

caede. The frequency of this is attested by a Salic law holding the surviving members of the feast responsible in such cases.

transiguntur, 'are settled'.

§ 3. **invicem** = *inter se*, as often.

adfinitatibus, 'marriage alliances'.

adsciscendis principibus, 'adopting chiefs', choosing the *principes* to whom they are to attach themselves. Cp. *H.* 1. 16 *ab aestimantibus adsciti* (Galba speaking of himself); *A.* 12. 10, 4 *rex ... adscisceretur*. Tacitus is plainly thinking, not of the ordinary free men, but of those whose circumstances gave them a voice in affairs, who were leaders of *factiones* (*Agr.* 12, 1), and whose feuds (*inimicitiae*) and marriage alliances (*adfinitates*) were matters of some importance. Cp. *Introd.*, p. lvi. Those who believe that the ruling *principes* were formally elected by the Assembly understand the words to refer to the choice of candidates. Others take the allusion to be to the judicial *principes* (c. 12, 3), or to the courting of princes of neighbouring tribes (c. 13, 4), but matters of peace and war are not mentioned till the next clause. (The view taken above follows that of Baumstark and Müllenhoff.)

de ... bello. The rising of Civilis (*H.* 4. 14) and that against Varus (*A.* 1. 55, 3) were thus projected at feasts, and a similar ancient Greek custom is seen in Hom. *Il.* 9, 89 ff., etc.

tamquam, assigning the supposed reason, as in c. 12, 2, etc., 'their idea being that'. But the explanation is that of Tacitus himself.

simplices, ἁπλοῦς, 'ingenuous', 'frank', as often.

§ 4. non astuta nec callida, 'without cunning, natural or acquired'.

aperit adhuc, etc., 'furthermore, discloses its innermost thoughts', in contrast to the Romans, who had learnt reticence even in their cups owing to the ubiquity of informers (cp. *Agr.* 2, 3). *Adhuc* is perhaps best taken in the sense of *praeterea, insuper,* πρὸς τούτοις (cp. note on c. 10, 3). Many interpret it as = *etiam nunc,* 'still continues to disclose', in contrast to the Romans, but this would involve the implication that they were likely sooner or later to drop the habit, and it is difficult to believe that Tacitus meant this. Others connect it with *secreta,* which would make it redundant.

licentia loci, 'in the freedom of the occasion', the unconstraint that rules at feasts: cp. c. 2, 4. Most MSS. read *ioci,* 'in the freedom of jesting', but this is not suitable to the description in § 3, and *iocus* is not 'merriment', 'festivity'.

retractatur, used impersonally, 'the matter is reconsidered'. A similar practice among the ancient Persians is described by Herodotus (1. 133) and is mentioned by a Scholiast on Hom. *Il.* 9, 70 Πέρσαι μεθύοντες συμβουλεύονται, νήφοντες δ' ἐπικρίνουσιν (*retractant*). The same custom prevailed also among the Scythians according to Eustathius on Hom. *Od.* 3, 138. On this subject, cp. Norden, pp. 127 ff., 502, and *Introd.,* pp. xxxii, xxxv.

et salva . . . ratio, 'and so due regard is paid to both times', 'both times get their due'; *salva = integra,* as often.

deliberant, etc., 'they deliberate when they are unable to feign, and decide when they cannot go wrong' (under the influence of drink)—a mere rhetorical epigram to close the description in Tacitus' favourite manner, with an obvious exaggeration to make the contrast as pointed as possible.

CHAPTER XXIII

DRINK AND DIET

§ 1. Potui, sc. *est,* a predicative dative, expressing the purpose served: cp. *victui, vestitui* (c. 46, 3).

humor . . . frumento, 'a liquid made from barley or wheat', i.e. beer. *Frumentum* is here used for the specific term *triticum,* one species of which at least (*triticum vulgare*) was grown throughout Germany from the Stone Age onwards: cp.

Netolitzky in *R.-G. Komm., Bericht,* xx. 34 f. Intoxicating drink made from grain was known to many nations and had many names, *zythum* (ζῦθος) in Egypt, *caelia* and *cerea* in Spain, *cervesia* in Gaul, etc. (Pliny, *N. H.* 22, 164). An epigram on the Gallic beer written by the emperor Julian is preserved in *Anth. Pal.* ix. 368; it ends:

ἤ ῥά σε Κελτοὶ
τῇ πενίῃ βοτρύων τεῦξαν ἀπ' ἀσταχύων.
Τῷ σε χρὴ καλέειν Δημήτριον, οὐ Διόνυσον,
πυρογένη μᾶλλον καὶ βρόμον, οὐ Βρόμιον.

Another German beverage, not mentioned by Tacitus, was mead made from honey, a drink known to all Aryan-speaking peoples.

in quandam . . . . corruptus, 'fermented into something resembling wine'. *Corruptus* expresses no more than an alteration of the natural taste by artificial means: cp. Sen. *Epp.* 95, 15 *cibo per artem voluptatemque corrupto*; Petron. 141 *neque enim ulla. caro per se placet, sed arte quadam corrumpitur.*

proximi ripae, see on c. 17, 2.

et vinum mercantur. The importation of wine was forbidden in Caesar's time by the Suebi (4. 2, 6), as also by the Gallic Nervii (2. 15, 4), not only perhaps because of its enervating effect, as he states, but because slaves were received by the Italian traders in exchange (Diod. 5, 26). That the trade in wine, probably as early as the time of Tacitus, was much greater than his statement suggests is shown by the number of wine-ladles (*trullae*) found in Germany far beyond the river frontier. The German words for wine and all connected with wine-making are borrowed from Latin.

cibi, etc. Tacitus' account is far from complete: he mentions only some German articles of food which were strikingly different from Roman.

agrestia poma, 'wild fruit', including crab-apples, wild pears, berries, and hazel nuts. Nothing is said of vegetables, though several species were grown—peas, beans, leeks, carrots, gourds, etc.—nor of corn, although it is referred to in the preceding sentence and in cc. 5, 1; 25, 1. And oatmeal porridge was one of the chief articles of German food (Pliny, *N. H.* 18, 149).

recens fera, 'fresh game', not hung (as at Rome) to become tender and even high. The statement would imply that hunting was common (see c. 15, 1), but the staple flesh foods were beef, mutton, and pork. These were all lightly roasted, at least in the time of Posidonius (Athen. 4, 153 e): boiled meat was unknown to the Cimbri until their arrival in Italy (Florus, 1. 38, 13 from Livy, who followed Posidonius). Mela states that the Germans ate raw meat, both fresh and dried on the skin (3. 3, 28): the second part of the statement may be correct (smoked meat being meant), but the first is a misconception or a false generalization. Dio makes the same mistake about the Cimbri, though his ultimate source was Posidonius (27, fr. 94, 2: cp. Norden, p. 74).

lac concretum, 'curdled milk', so Verg. *G.* 3, 463. Caesar mentions cheese, as well as milk and meat, among the staple foods of the Germans in general (6. 22, 1). On the other hand, Pliny states that it was unknown to *barbarae gentes* (*N. H.* 11, 239), and the English word like the German, *Käse*, is derived from Lat. *caseus*; but Pliny probably meant the finer kinds of cheese, the Latin word being adopted when these became known to the Germans.

apparatu, 'without elaborate preparation' (cp. c. 14, 4), further explained by *blandimentis*, 'appetizing condiments', the *irritamenta gulae* of Sall. *Jug.* 89, 7, or the *qualia lassum pervellunt stomachum* of Hor. *Sat.* 2. 8, 8. These were not used because they were unknown. That salt was valued as a condiment is shown by battles fought for the possession of salt springs (e.g. *A.* 13. 57, 1).

adversus, 'in relation to', as in 46, 5, and often elsewhere in Tacitus. This German failing is noted in c. 4, 3. Their propensity to drunkenness (on which see c. 22, 2) was taken advantage of in war (*A.* 1. 50, 6; *H.* 4. 79, 3), and this fact suggested the epigram with which the chapter ends.

§ 2. si indulseris, etc., 'if you indulge their intemperance by supplying as much as they crave, they will be conquered as easily by their vices as by arms'. A rhetorical embellishment of a commonplace sentiment: cp. Pompeius Trogus (Justin.) 1. 8, 7 *priusque Scythae ebrietate quam bello vincuntur (a Cyro)*; Sen. *Epp.* 83, 22 *ebrietas invictos acie mero domuit.* It is not meant that it would ever be easy to subdue them by arms (past experience had disproved that, *tam diu Germania vincitur*, c. 37, 2), but that Roman hopes for the future rested as much on the encouragement of German failings as on arms. So *delenimenta vitiorum* had facilitated the conquest of the Britons (*Agr.* 21). Cp. *Introd.*, p. xix.

The sentence has been condemned as un-Tacitean and bracketed as a marginal observation which has intruded into the text (Gudeman, in *Philologus*, 58, 34-8, and Eng. ed. 1927, p. 388); but it is a favourite device of Tacitus to end a description with an epigram, and the stylistic objections may be met. *Indulgere* has a similar meaning in *A.* 1. 54, 3 *indulserat ei ludicro Augustus. Ebrietas* is somewhat boldly used in the sense of the rare word *ebriositas*, but Tacitus delights in unusual expressions, and Eng. 'drunkenness' may be used for the habit ('inebriety'). *Vitiis* here refers only to drunkenness, the plural being used to balance *armis*; another German failing which Tacitus, like Tiberius, regarded as favourable to Rome was *discordia* (c. 33, 2). *Haud minus facile* cannot be taken as an understatement for *facilius*, but Tacitus is alluding to the future, not to the past.

CHAPTER XXIV

AMUSEMENTS: SPEAR-DANCE AND DICE-PLAYING

§ 1. **Genus**, etc., 'they have but one (in contrast to the variety at Rome) and in all festal gatherings the same public game'. This is the most ancient account of what (by disuse of the *framea*) was afterwards known as the sword dance, kept up in some parts of Germany to the present day. *In omni coctu* links on the present chapter to the preceding description of *convivia*.

nudi, in the literal sense: see below. In later times a shirt or tunic was worn.

quibus id ludicrum est, 'who practise this sport'; or possibly 'to whom it is a pastime', which, however, would anticipate *non in quaestum* (below).

infestas, 'threatening', levelled threateningly against them; cp. *infestis pilis* (*H.* 1. 31) and note on *Agr.* 25, 1. *Se saltu iaciunt* is a poetic variation of *saltant* (Verg. *Aen.* 8, 257, etc.).

§ 2. **artem ... decorem**, 'skill ... gracefulness'.

non in quaestum, 'not with a view to profit' (*exercent* is supplied from *exercitatio*). For the use of *aut* in a negative clause, see on c. 5, 2. Gifts were later, perhaps always, given, but it was not a trade, like that of Roman jugglers, or practised for wages (*mercedem*), like the gladiator's calling.

quamvis audacis, etc., 'for the sport, daring as it is, the only recompense. . . .' *Lascivia* in a good sense, as in *H.* 2. 68; *A.* 11. 31 (elsewhere in Tacitus in a bad sense). *Pretium* = *praemium*, originally a poetical use, common in Tacitus. It was, no doubt, in origin, a religious act in honour of the war god (Tiu, c. 9, 1), and joined with the feasts: cp. *noctem sollemnibus epulis ludicram* (*A.* 1. 50, 4). This would account for the nudity of the performers, which was based on the primitive idea that the gods, who were conceived as unclothed, could only be approached by worshippers who wholly or partially uncovered their bodies (G. Girke, *Mannusbibliothek*, 24, 15). But this sort of dance was not peculiar to

Germany: the pyrrhic dance was of the same class, and a similar Thracian dance is described by Xen. *Anab.* 6. 1, 5.

§ 3. **aleam**, etc. At Rome dicing was forbidden by law (*vetita legibus alea*, Hor. *Carm.* 3. 24, 58), though tolerated in hours of revelry or during the Saturnalia; but it was a common after-dinner amusement, and many of the early emperors were very fond of the game.

inter seria, 'as one of their serious occupations'.

temeritate, 'recklessness'. For *ludendi* words expressing the result are substituted.

extremo ac novissimo, 'the last, decisive throw'. The adjectives are really synonymous: cp. *extremus et ultimus* (Cic., etc.), and c. 7, 1.

de libertate . . . contendant, 'they stake their freedom and their very persons', perhaps merely a redundancy of expression for emphasis, for *libertate* needs no closer definition. Others take *corpore* to mean 'life', since the German master could kill his slave (c. 25, 2), but such slaves were got rid of, as Tacitus goes on to say.

§ 4. **voluntariam**, opposed to *necessariam* (Cic. *Phil.* 1, 15), there being no legal compulsion to redeem a debt of honour.

iuvenior, denoting youthful vigour. This comparative form is post-Augustan and rare in the first century.

alligari. The verb was so commonly used for the simple *ligari* in the Imperial period that Plutarch, a contemporary of Tacitus, says τὸ δὲ δῆσαι Λατῖνοι πάλαι μὲν λιγᾶρε, νῦν δὲ ἀλλιγᾶρε καλοῦσιν (*Romulus*, 26).

ipsi fidem vocant. Tacitus would not use the term 'honour' of adherence to a bargain so disgraceful to both parties. He would rather call it 'obstinacy', *pervicacia*.

servos condicionis huius, 'slaves of this class': *condicio* means 'status', as in *condicione fugitivus, H.* 2. 72.

per commercia tradunt (sc. *aliis victores*), 'dispose of by traffic'. Cp. *Agr.* 28, 5; 39, 2.

se quoque, themselves as well as the slave. The motive is no doubt an imaginary one: while it is likely enough that the retention of the slave would have involved both parties in a sense of shame, the main reason probably was to avoid the troubles that were sure to arise with the kinsmen of the enslaved man. The clause is clumsily expressed, for *victoriae* is applicable only to the winner.

pudore . . . exsolvant, a phrase repeated in *H.* 3. 61; *A.* 6. 44, 7.

CHAPTER XXV

SLAVES AND FREEDMEN

§ 1. **Ceteris servis,** in contrast to those just described, whom they did not keep. *Ceterum* (Ed. Wolff) is an easy emendation, but nothing seems to be gained by the change, and the transition to the subject of the new chapter is made more formal than with *ceteris.* Slavery was most frequently the result of capture in war or raids (cp. *A.* 12. 27, 4; 13. 56, 6; *Agr.* 28, 5; Sen. *Epp.* 47, 10); others became slaves by inability to pay debts, or by sale by husbands or parents to escape starvation (*A.* 4. 72, 4), or by descent from servile parents. Tacitus here describes only one form of bondage, a kind of serfdom approaching to the colonate of the later Roman empire and the medieval villeinage, and ignores, or rather expressly denies, the existence of slaves in the house, though such are clearly alluded to in c. 20, 2, and undoubtedly existed, possibly even in the simple homes of ordinary free men, certainly in the houses of nobles, to whom alone Tacitus' description is applicable. Cp. Sen., *l. c., fortuna alium ex illis* (captured Romans) *pastorem, alium custodem casae fecit.* Cp. *Introd.,* p. l.

descriptis . . . ministeriis, 'with duties exactly defined throughout the establishment', for the whole body of slaves. At Rome the various duties that had to be performed, both by the *familia urbana* and by the *familia rustica* (with which alone this passage is concerned), were divided among the slaves, who had each his special function. The size which these servile establishments might reach is shown by *A.* 14. 42 ff., where the prefect of Rome had 400 in his service.

Describere is equivalent to *definire,* as in Cic. *Acad.* 2, 114 *ut . . . mores fingas, . . . officia describas, quam vitam ingrediar definias;* Q. Cic. *de pet. cons.* 20 *ut descriptum ac dispositum suum cuique munus sit.* The verb is sometimes confused in MSS. with *discribere,* which is probably the right reading wherever the idea of division into parts or allotment to different persons is required, but correction is not needed here.

suam quisque sedem, etc., 'each is master of his own domicile, his own home'. On *sedes,* see c. 16, 1: the context shows that the slave had not only a separate dwelling but also a piece of land tenable at the pleasure of his master. The description also shows plainly that the slaves here spoken of belonged to the nobles, who did not till their lands (or not all their lands) themselves. There was thus already in existence a condition of things from which the manor of later times ultimately developed.

frumenti modum, etc. *Frumentum,* corn generally; *pecoris* in the wider sense (see on c. 5, 1; 12, 2); *vestis,* 'cloth', chiefly no doubt of wool, which they had to spin and weave. *Aut . . . aut* has the force of *modo . . . modo* or *partim . . . partim* (as often): sometimes one form of rent, sometimes another was imposed, but not all three in each case. Such rents in kind are abundantly attested by medieval evidence. It may be that the whole estate was parcelled out on these terms among the slaves, but if a portion was retained in hand by the lord we should suppose that they had an additional obligation to labour on it.

ut colono: the master exacts a rent in kind from his slave, as a Roman landlord does from his tenant (*colonus*). In Italy the tenant-farmer usually paid a money rent, but not always: during the agricultural depression which prevailed in the time of Tacitus the younger Pliny was forced to substitute a proportion of the produce (*medendi una ratio, si non nummo sed partibus locem, Epp.* 9, 37), and such rents in kind were very likely commoner than we know; in Africa they were normal. The analogy is limited to this one point, for the Roman *colonus* was a free man who made a contract and was not in the earlier Empire bound to the soil, like the German *servus.* It may be that slaves thus settled on the land were usually given a partial freedom and so corresponded to the class of half-free serfs called *liti* or *leti* in later German laws, whose position answered to Tacitus' description. When the Roman emperors, from the time of Marcus Aurelius, settled Germans within the Empire, they put them under this system of tenure: in Gaul they were called by the German name of *laeti* (Ammianus 16. 11, 4; 20. 8, 13, etc.), elsewhere *inquilini.* See Kornemann in Pauly-Wissowa, *R. E.* iv, col. 494 f., and Schönfeld, *ib., s.v. Laeti.*

hactenus paret, 'this is the limit of his obedience': cp. *hactenus iussum* (*Agr.* 10, 6), and several other passages. The subjection is much understated: the serf was bound to the soil and passed, like buildings, etc., with the estate; also the power to scourge and kill existed, as the next sentence shows. Probably slaves furnished the human sacrifices described in c. 9, 1; 39, 1; certainly in c. 40, 5.

cetera domus officia, 'the rest, the household duties' (of the master's house). For this use of *cetera,* cp. *ceterum vulgus,* opposed to officers, in *H.* 3. 12; 4. 56, 2; *alius* is similarly used and the Greek ἄλλος very frequently. For the fact here stated, cp. c. 15, 1.

§ 2. **verberare**: in a Roman household scourgings were constant.

opere coercere, 'to punish (cp. c. 11, 5) by taskwork', as Roman masters did when they sent refractory slaves to an *ergastulum* or *pistrinum* or a quarry.

disciplina et severitate, 'to maintain strict discipline', hendiadys for *disciplinae severitate* (*Dial.* 29, 4; *H.* 1. 51), an extreme case of which was the Roman practice of executing the whole household when a master was murdered by any one of his slaves (cp. *A.* 14. 42–5).

impetu et ira, 'in a fit of rage', another hendiadys.

ut inimicum, 'as they would kill an enemy'.

impune, i.e. if the slave were his own. He who killed the slave of another had to pay his value as a chattel.

§ 3. **liberti** were not much above slaves (i.e. slaves of the class here described), because private emancipation did not confer full freedom: the freedman remained dependent on his former master, and he needed his protection, as he had no family to defend his interests. Full emancipation was an act of the Assembly, and in later times it is attested only among Franks, Lombards, and Scandinavians.

momentum, sc. *sunt*, 'have any influence'. *Momentum* is 'a weight in the scale', cp. *H.* 1. 59 and 76.

numquam in civitate, a contrast to Rome, especially under Claudius, whose chief freedmen, Pallas and Narcissus, were the most influential men in the State.

dumtaxat, 'only', not used by Tacitus elsewhere.

quae regnantur, as in eastern Germany and Scandinavia (cc. 43–45). The personal passive of *regnare* is poetical (first used by Virgil).

ibi enim, etc. Freedmen rose to prominence in the personal service of the king, as being wholly dependent on him and more amenable than free men, who moreover would not readily have accepted such menial services as those from which, in later times, the high offices of seneschal and marshal developed. So at Rome, under the earlier Empire, it was imperial freedmen who dealt with the secretarial and accounting work of the Emperor's household: the posts filled by the *ab epistulis, a libellis* and *a rationibus* were beneath the dignity of persons of higher status, but they soon developed into important State offices, which gradually passed into the hands of men of higher birth. Whether such a general statement as Tacitus here makes was justified by the knowledge then available about monarchical states may well be doubted.

apud ceteros: the transition from the preceding *gentibus* to the masculine is not difficult and is paralleled by such passages as *Agr.* 12, 2 *civitatibus* . . . *singuli*, or *A.* 3. 63, 3 *civitates* . . . *ceteros*. The emendation *ceteras* is unnecessary.

impares (sc. *ingenuis*) **libertini**, equivalent to an abstract noun with genitive as subject to the verb, 'the inferiority of freedmen'. The construction is more common with participles (Draeger, *Synt. und Stil*, § 210). *Libertinus* denotes the freedman in relation to his class, *libertus* in relation to his former master. The distinction is uniformly observed by Tacitus.

libertatis argumentum, 'is a proof of (political) freedom', just as the ascendancy of freedmen is a sign of political servitude. Thus the sense of freedom in the Britons is said to have made them disdain Nero's freedman Polyclitus when sent to them (*A.* 14. 39, 3).

CHAPTER XXVI

AGRICULTURE

The usual skilful transition to a new subject is missing here, but the description links on to the account of the condition of slaves on the land in c. 25, 1.

§ 1. Faenus . . . ignotum, 'to exploit capital and increase it by interest'.

faenus, here interest-earning capital, as in *H.* 1. 20; *A.* 6. 17, 2; 14. 53, 6; 55, 5.

agitare = *exercere*, 'to make a business of', 'manage', as in *A.* 6. 16, 3 (where both verbs are used with *faenus*) and *A.* 4. 6, 4.

in usuras extendere, a closer definition of *faenus agitare*, is a novel phrase, to be compared with *in manicas non extendunt* (c. 17, 3): 'to stretch out capital into interest', as a garment is lengthened into sleeves, means no more than *pecunias faenore auctitare* in *A.* 6. 16, 1. The phrase could not mean 'increase by compound interest', by charging interest on arrears of interest.

It seems superfluous to say that people who mostly had no money and dealt by barter (c. 5, 4) did not put capital out at interest, but to a Roman the exploitation of capital and the exploitation of land were intimately connected: every large fortune consisted partly of land, partly of money lent or invested in business (cp. Caesar's law *de modo credendi possidendique*, *A.* 6. 16, 1), and the younger Pliny's remark *sum quidem prope totus in praediis, aliquid tamen fenero, Epp.* 3. 19, 8). As usual, Tacitus is making a comparison with Roman practice, and has in mind the evils arising from it (described in *A.* 6. 16–17).

ideoque . . . vetitum esset, 'and consequently it is better guarded against than if it had been forbidden', a rather absurd remark, repeating a thought already better expressed in c. 19, 5 *plusque ibi boni mores valent quam alibi bonae leges.* **servatur** is used in the sense of *cavetur* (J. Golling, *Wien. Stud.* 30, p. 342), but it is a bold use, because, although *servare* (in Cicero *observare*) can bear the sense of *cavere*, 'to take care' to prevent something happening or to secure its happening, in the present context a *ne*-clause, such as *ne fiat*, is strictly needed to give the required meaning, as in Livy, 39. 14, 10 *ut . . . servarent ne qui nocturni coetus fierent.* It is not possible to supply in thought *faenus non agitare* as the subject of *servatur* (though the preceding clause is really a negative) and translate 'the principle (of not lending money) is better observed', for apart from the stylistic harshness the positive *faenus agitare* is required with *vetitum esset.*

agri pro numero, etc. The interpretation of this passage has been more disputed than that of any other in the *Germania* owing to the obscurity produced by the extreme conciseness of the description, by the phrase *in vices* (or *vices*), and by the difficulty of harmonizing the description with that given by Caesar a century and a half earlier. What Tacitus is concerned with is the way in which the land was cultivated, but his description implies a particular form of land tenure, and on this matter there is a conflict of opinion, some denying and others affirming that private property in land existed among the Germans at this time.

The first sentence may be translated: 'lands proportionate in extent to the number of cultivators are taken for tillage in turn (i.e. now one set of lands, now another) by the whole body of them, and these they then divide among themselves according to rank (social standing); partition is rendered easy by the wide expanse of open ground'. The meaning will be that agricultural land is not, like the Roman, permanently held in private possession and permanently worked, but that each community sets apart for tillage from time to time a portion of the cultivable land within its domain sufficient to meet its needs. After a time another tract is taken into cultivation instead, the previously worked portion being allowed to run back to grass. The land allocated for tillage is not worked in common, but is divided among the cultivators according to their standing, some getting more, some less.

The period of cultivation of any one tract is probably defined by the following words *arva per annos mutant* (see below). The method of cultivation described is the 'field-grass system of tillage' (*Feldgraswirtschaft*, as Germans call it), an alternation of cropping and fallowing practised by primitive peoples who do not know that exhaustion of the soil can be prevented by rotating crops and by manuring. The procedure described in this section is intelligible if it be borne in mind that among the Germans agriculture was for many centuries wholly subsidiary to pastoral husbandry (see below): their chief means of subsistence was stock-raising, and only a portion of the available land was devoted to tillage, the rest being used as pasture land, which was common to all.

agri means not the whole territory but (as the contrast with *faenus* by itself shows) the cultivable lands, as opposed to *pascua* and *silvae* (Cato, *De agri cult.* 6, etc.). As continuity of settlements in Germany is proved by archaeological evidence back to prehistoric times, the *agri* were no doubt lands which had been under cultivation at various times.

cultorum, 'cultivators', as the context requires, not 'inhabitants', as in c. 28, 2 (cp. note on *occupantur*).

universis, sc. *cultoribus*, opposed to *singulis* Being an adjective, it must be related to a noun, expressed or supplied by the context: it cannot be taken substantively in the sense of 'the community'. Who the *universi cultores* were is not defined, but they can hardly have been other than those of the village communities of which the *pagi* were composed and which Tacitus plainly regarded as the normal form of settlement (see note c. 16, 1), as also did Caesar (6. 22, 2, see below). *Universi cultores* would strictly include the serfs of the richer landlords mentioned in c. 25, but they would naturally have no voice in the matter: *cultores* really means householders and their families, including nobles so far as they lived in the villages, but the outlying lands tilled by their serfs, which had probably been reclaimed by their forbears, were no doubt held in absolute ownership. It is doubtful if Tacitus realized the existence of such isolated properties.

in vices occupantur. The prevailing meaning of *occupare* in Tacitus is 'to take possession of', and here in all probability it means to appropriate, take out of the village land, for cultivation. In agricultural contexts the verb often means 'to put to use', 'to cultivate', as opposed to leaving land waste or fallow (e.g. Colum. 1. 3, 12 *fines* . . . *quos proculcandos pecudibus et vastandos ac populandos feris relinquunt aut occupatos nexu civium et ergastulis tenent*; Cod. Theod. 9. 42, 7 *quot mancipia in praediis occupatis* . . . *teneantur*). But here the cultivation does not begin until the land has been allotted. *Occupantur* cannot refer, as some believe, to the original conquest of the tribal territory, because, whether or not *in vices* is correct, the present tense indicates that the *occupatio* is repeated from time to time, and the number of *cultores* could not be constant, and because the tribe took possession of the whole territory at the time of conquest, not of a part proportionate to its numbers; moreover, Tacitus is describing here, as elsewhere, the customs of tribes which had long been living under settled conditions and within definite boundaries.

in vices is the reading of two good MSS., while one has *invicem* (an obvious correction). Others have *vices* (sometimes with the variant *vice*), which is meaningless but points to the dropping of *in* before *ui*. *In vices* is open to suspicion because it is nowhere else used by Tacitus, while *in vicem* occurs often, mostly in the reciprocal sense; but it is not infrequent in poetry and the plural may have been used here because frequent exchanges are referred to. The use of the phrase is similar to that of *in vicem* in Celsus 3, 2 *bibenda aqua, postero die etiam vinum, deinde in vicem alternis diebus modo aqua modo vinum*. More commonly *in vices*, or *in vicem*, is used of two or more persons or groups of persons taking turns in performing an act (or two different acts), but this use is inapplicable here. No less inapplicable is the reciprocal use (= *inter se*): *in vicem occupantur* cannot mean 'are taken possession of for each other's benefit', as is maintained by Dopsch (*Grundlagen d. europ. Kulturentwickl.* i², p. 69, and in Reeb's ed., p. 153). The emendation *vicis* is unacceptable; the corruption would not be impossible but *vicanis* would be required: *vicis* is not compatible either with *secundum dignationem* or with *inter se partiuntur*. *Vicinis* is too indeterminate a term to express a sharply defined unit.

secundum dignationem: for the meaning of *dignatio*, 'rank', 'social position', see on c. 13, 2. The *princeps* or *nobilis* would get more than the simple freeman; but even among the freemen who were not *nobiles* there would be differences of standing based on greater wealth and the possession of larger establishments. The distribution would be carried out under the supervision of the local notables.

camporum spatia. *Campi* means tracts of unwooded and unplanted or uncultivated land; the meaning is that the large tracts of such land available make it easy to satisfy the claims of every one, whereas in Italy there were no such vast unutilized spaces.

§ 2. arva per annos, etc., 'they change their plough-lands every year, and yet there is (cultivable but uncultivated) land in abundance. For they do not by dint of labour vie with the fertility and extent of the soil by planting orchards, separating off meadows, and making well-watered gardens'.

Arva . . . mutant is best taken as defining the period of cultivation of any one set of lands: the change takes place every year. This interpretation brings the statement into line with Caesar's (6, 22, see below). By the yearly change of fields might be meant that the individuals till in any one year only part of their allotments, ploughing another piece next year and letting the previously cropped land go back to grass, this change being distinct from the periodical change of the arable area, *in vices occupantur* (Hoops, *Waldbäume u. Kulturpflanzen*, pp. 520 ff.). But this would leave the latter change without any time definition; it reads much into the Latin; and it would make a complicated procedure without any advantage being gained.

arva, fields under tillage, strictly fields ploughed in readiness for sowing, as opposed to *ager*. Varro defines the word as meaning *quod aratum necdum satum est* (*R. R.* 1. 29, 1).

per annos, 'annually', as in *A.* 1. 8, 5, elsewhere *per singulos* (or *omnes*) *annos*.

superest, as in c. 6, 1, 'is abundant', which is better than 'there is land over and above'.

nec enim, etc., i.e. for they do not work enough to make the soil produce all that its quality and extent make it capable of producing: they do not practise intensive cultivation (*agri culturae non student*, Caes. 6. 22, 1; 29, 1; *ne illa quidem (quae possident) enixe colunt*, Mela 3. 3, 27).

ut (= *ita ut*) **pomaria conserant**, as in Italy. Varro (*R. R.* 1. 2, 6) asks, *Non arboribus consita Italia ut tota pomarium videatur?*

prata separent, i.e. separate off meadows from the rough pasture for the production of hay for winter fodder and of finer pasture for stock-raising. In Germany part of the pasture land must have been reserved for hay, which was needed for winter feeding.

hortos rigent = *hortos riguos faciant*. By *horti* are meant not pleasure-gardens but fruit and vegetable gardens. Pliny describes the Roman method of watering them (*N. H.* 19, 60). Nevertheless the Germans did grow vegetables (see c. 23, 1, n.).

Tacitus' description shows that private property in land, apart from dwelling-house and homestead, did not exist at this period among the ordinary freemen; and obviously it could not develop so long as the same piece of land was cultivated only for a year (or, on any interpretation, for a few years). Each householder had a right to the use of as much land as he needed, but proprietorship was in the hands of the community. This is confirmed by the definite statement of Caesar that neither the Suebi nor the Germans in general held land in private possession (4, 1 ; 6, 22), and in other essential points his account agrees with that of Tacitus. He states that the magistrates and chiefs annually assigned to the communities of clansmen as much land and in such place as seemed good to them, and compelled them a year later to pass on elsewhere (*magistratus ac principes in annos singulos gentibus cognationibusque hominum, qui una coierunt, quantum et quo loco visum est agri attribuunt atque anno post alio transire cogunt*). The last statement, which means that every year they changed their dwellings as well as their fields (as is shown by the reasons he proceeds to give and by the definite statement in 4, 1), was a misconception. A yearly change of dwellings would be intelligible in the case of tribes in movement and engaged in constant warfare, but it is incompatible with the continuity of settlements in Germany from the Bronze and even the Stone Age onwards, and it was not regarded even by the Suebi as normal (*B. G.* 1, 36 *intra annos* XIV *tectum non subissent*, their dwellings had not been real houses). But apart from this, his account agrees with that of Tacitus in regard to the annual assignment of land, the assignment of no more than was necessary, and the units concerned in the distribution, which he plainly, and Tacitus in all probability, regarded as village communities. The only important divergence is the assignment by *magistratus ac principes*, but even this divergence is lessened by the probability that the distribution in Tacitus' time was made under the supervision of the local leading men.

A system similar to that described in this chapter persisted to the end of the eighteenth century in the North Frisian island of Föhr, off the Schleswig coast, where side by side with lands which were periodically cultivated and then left fallow there existed arable land long held in private possession (Haff, *Savigny Ztschr., germ. Abt.*, 47 (1927), 675 ff.; Ch. Jensen, *Die nordfries. Inseln*[2], 214 ff.); and analogies are to be found elsewhere, e.g. in West Bulgaria up to 1868 (Peisker, *Ztschr. f. Soz. u. Wirtschaftsg.* 7, 28). In Germany private property in land gradually developed in the centuries after Tacitus wrote as a result of the decline of stock-farming in favour of a more intensive cultivation of the land, but even in the sixth century the transformation was not complete (cp. Kulischer, *Allgem. Wirtschaftsg.* i, 1928, 18 ff.).

sola . . . imperatur, 'the corn crop is the only one exacted from the soil'. *Terrae* is dative, as in c. 8, 1 *quibus puellae imperantur*, not genitive (which would make the word super-

fluous, while the dative is required). For the metaphor, cp.
Verg. *G.* 1, 99 *imperat arvis*; Cic. *De sen.* 51 *terra numquam
recusat imperium*; Sen. *De tranq. an.* 17, 5; etc.

§ 3. unde, 'hence', because they have no autumn fruits.

totidem, sc. *atque nos*: they do not divide the year into as
many seasons as we Romans do.

hiems et ver et aestas. The order of enumeration follows
the Roman year, which began on Jan. 1. The Greeks also in
early times had names only for these three seasons. The
original division of the year, attested by Aryan languages
generally (and still used by Thucydides), was into summer
and winter, spring being a later addition. The German word
for autumn, *Herbst*, is old and probably Pan-Germanic, but
it originally meant, like its English equivalent, 'harvest':
it is to be noted that our names for the seasons are all English
with the exception of 'autumn', which is Latin.

intellectum ac vocabula, 'a meaning and names', viz.
Winter, Lenz (cognate with 'Lent', now more usually *Frühling*)
and *Sommer*.

bona, wine and fruits.

CHAPTER XXVII
THE BURIAL OF THE DEAD

This forms a fitting epilogue to the description of German
customs.

§ 1. Funerum nulla ambitio, 'there is no pomp'; in contrast
to Romans, whose funerals, especially by the addition of
gladiatorial shows, had risen to enormous cost. The Gauls
had become extravagant in this respect (Caes. 6. 19, 4). Tacitus'
statement about the simplicity of cremation burials is confirmed by excavations for the region of the Lower Rhine, but
in other parts of Germany inhumation graves (see next note)
have abundant furnishings, which include Roman wares
imported during the first century.

certis lignis, oak, beech, pine, and juniper, according to the
evidence of Lower Rhenish graves. Cremation superseded
inhumation in the later half of the Bronze Age and remained
the general practice (although inhumation burials began to
reappear, probably under Celtic influence, in the first century
A.D.) until the adoption of Christianity with its doctrine
of the resurrection of the body. Charles the Great prohibited
it among the Saxons under pain of death.

§ 2. struem, defined by the genitive *rogi*.

vestibus ... odoribus, 'garments ... spices', as at Rome:
prodiga flammis dona ... maestoque ardentia funera luxu,

Stat. *Silv.* 2. 1, 157. Cp. θυμιαμάτων καὶ ἱματίων πολυτελῶν συγκατακαέντων, Plut. *Cat. Min.* 11; Suet. *Caes.* 84; *A.* 3. 2, 2 (*vestem odores cremabant* in honour of Germanicus); Pliny, *N. H.* 12, 83.

sua cuique arma . . . adicitur, to serve their needs in Valhalla. *Quorundam,* some notables. Weapons have been found in many German graves; remains of horses are very rare in tombs of the first century, but occur more frequently in later times. The horse of the Gothic king Alaric thus shared his funeral; there is also evidence that favourite hounds, and sometimes slaves, and even wives (see on c. 19, 3) were sacrificed. Similar customs prevailed at Gaulish funerals (Caes. *l. c.*) and among the early Greeks (Hom. *Il.* 23, 171–5).

sepulcrum caespes erigit, 'a mound of turf forms the tomb'. The same poetic personification is used by Sen. *Epp.* 8, 5 *hanc (domum) utrum caespes erexerit an lapis . . . nihil interest.* Cp. also *H.* 5. 6. Tacitus' statement applies to the region of the Rhine and suits best the lower Rhine, where the tumuli are higher (16–20 ft.) than those farther up the river; elsewhere flat graves were the rule in the Roman period. See A. Kiekebusch, *Einfluss d. röm. Kultur auf d. germanische,* p. 34; Schumacher, *Mainz. Ztschr.* iv, p. 10.

monumentorum, such as those at Rome, the mausoleum of Augustus, pyramid of Cestius, and other great family tombs, the *magnae moles sepulcrorum* of Sen. *De brev. vit.* 20, 5.

arduum . . . honorem, for *arduorum,* etc., to avoid the dissonance of several plural genitives.

ut gravem, etc., is of course Tacitus' own explanation of the absence of elaborate monuments in Germany. The idea is the Graeco-Roman one frequently expressed in epitaphs, *sit tibi terra levis.*

lamenta ac lacrimas, 'wailing and weeping'. The double alliteration in this sentence (*l—l, t—t*) gives rhetorical point. In medieval times the period of mourning lasted thirty days and closed with a memorial feast in honour of the dead.

ponunt for *deponunt* is frequent. Cp. *ad ponendum dolorem,* Cic. *Tusc.* 3. 28, 66.

lugere . . . meminisse, an effective ending to the first part of the treatise, recalling Seneca's words *meminisse perseveret, lugere desinat* (*Epp.* 99, 24).

§ 3. **in commune,** equivalent to *in universum* (c. 5, 1; 6, 4), 'in general'. So in c. 38, 1 and 40, 2.

origine (cc. 2–4) **ac moribus** (cc. 6–27).

accepimus, used frequently by Tacitus (and others) of knowledge acquired from literary or oral tradition; here the former is primarily meant, but the latter is not excluded, although it played a greater part in the account of the East Germans.

gentium . . . nationes, here used for variation, without such distinction of meaning as in c. 2, 5.

instituta ritusque, perhaps '(political and social) customs and religious usages', the prevailing meaning of *ritus* in Tacitus; but the words may be practically synonymous, 'customs and usages' (cp. c. 45, 2).

quatenus, usually interpreted 'in so far as' (so in c. 42, 1), but the balance of the two clauses seems to require the meaning 'how far': cp. Caes. *B. G.* 6. 11, 1 *de Galliae Germaniaeque moribus et quo differant hae nationes inter sese proponere*. Elsewhere Tacitus uses the word only with the force of *quoniam*. The description of the differences between lands and peoples was a common topic in ethnographic literature (cp. Norden, p. 100).

expediam = *exponam*, 'I will set forth'; so used several times in Tacitus, and in poets, also in Sall. *Jug.* 5, 3.

PART II

THE INDIVIDUAL TRIBES (cc. 28-46)

I. WESTERN AND NORTH-WESTERN TRIBES (CC. 28-37)

CHAPTER XXVIII

INTRODUCTION. NON-GERMAN TRIBES IN GERMANY: GERMANS IN GAUL

§ 1. Validiores, sc. *quam Germanorum.*

res, 'power'.

summus auctorum, 'the highest authority', in respect of his knowledge of Gaul.

tradit. The reference is to *B. G.* 6. 24, 1 *ac fuit antea tempus, cum Germanos Galli virtute superarent, ultro bella inferrent, propter hominum multitudinem agrique inopiam trans Rhenum colonias mitterent*. The same reference is made in *Agr.* 11, 5 *Gallos quoque in bellis floruisse accepimus*. Among the Gallic immigrants Caesar mentions the Volcae Tectosages, who had occupied the most fertile tract bordering on the Hercynian forest, and were still living there. On them and the other Celts beyond the Rhine, see *Introd.*, Sect. IV.

etiam, closely with *Gallos*, and referring back to *quae nationes e Germania in Gallias commigraverint* (c. 27, 3).

in Germaniam transgressos. For Tacitus, as for Caesar, the Rhine had always been the boundary between the Celts and the Germans, and Germany as they knew it had always been inhabited by Germans. In actual fact (as historical, linguistic, and archaeological evidence abundantly proves) Lower Germany west of the river Ems and Middle and South Germany up to (and partly beyond) the great wooded mountain belt which runs across central Germany—the 'Hercynian Forest'—had long been Celtic territory before it became German; and the Celtic elements found there by the Romans were remnants which had been left behind when the mass of the population retired before the slow but steady advance of the Germans. See *Introd.*, Sect. IV.

quantulum, etc., 'what a small obstacle was a river'.

ut, 'whenever', as in *H*. 1. 29 *ut quisque obvius fuerat*, etc.

gens = *natio*, any individual tribe.

occuparet permutaretque, etc., 'seize and change settlements still open to all and partitioned among no powerful kingdoms (able to resist invasion)'. *Permutaret*, 'again exchange for others', as in *H*. 4. 11 *domos hortosque permutans*, 'kept changing houses and gardens'. *Promiscas*, 'unappropriated', common property. For *et nulla*, see on c. 10, 4. *Regnorum*, apparently conceived to be the only possible form of government for a compact state with definite boundaries and power to maintain them.

§ 2. igitur, taking up the narrative after the parenthetical passage, as often.

inter, 'the country between', an extremely harsh abbreviation (if the text be sound) of the usual expression *quantum inter* (*A*. 1. 60, 5; *H*. 2.14). Tacitus' source for the important historical data given in this section was no doubt Pliny (Norden, p. 265).

Hercyniam silvam, a general (Celtic) designation of the chain of forest-clad mountains, extending from the Rhine to the Carpathians and enclosing Bohemia, which cuts off the north German plain from southern Germany. It was known by report to Aristotle as τὰ Ἀρκύνια ὄρη, to Eratosthenes and other Greek geographers as ὁ Ὀρκύνιος δρυμός, later as Ἑρκύνιος δρ. Caesar describes the mountain tract as beginning with the Black Forest (so also Strabo, 4. 6, 9; 7. 1, 3 and 5) and extending along the Danube to the Carpathians (*B. G.* 6, 24 f.); this reproduces the account of Posidonius written in the early first century B.C. The portion here referred to by Tacitus is distinct from that spoken of in c. 30, 1, and may be the Swabian and Franconian Jura, or the Fichtelgebirge and the Bohemian Forest (Böhmerwald), as the Boii are regarded as adjoining the Helvetii on the east.

Moenum, the Main, also a Celtic name, like *Hercynia silva*

and *Rhenus*. The district meant is that represented by Baden, Württemberg (north of the Danube), and part of Bavaria. This region had been occupied by the Helvetii from about 400 B.c. till the end of the second century, when under the pressure of invading Germans they retired southwards across the Rhine into Switzerland, of which they already possessed the northern part at the time of the Cimbric invasion, viz. the district of the river Aare and its gold-bearing tributaries, the two rivers Emme (Athen. 6, 233 d; Norden, pp. 230 ff.). See *Introd., l. c.*

ulteriora, the country beyond the Helvetii, not only Bohemia, but also the adjacent country south of the Danube as far as north-western Hungary (Pannonia, see Strabo, 4. 6, 8; 5. 1, 6; 7. 3, 11; Pliny, *N. H.* 3, 146) and possibly the eastern part of northern Bavaria (if *Hercynia silva* here means the Swabian Jura).

Boii, a Celtic tribe (which is what is meant by *Gallica gens*) with a chequered history. About 60 B.c. a large body of them (not all) left Bohemia to attack Noricum: of these 32,000 went to Gaul with the Helvetii and finally found a home in the land of the Aedui (Caes. 1, 5; 28; 29), while the rest fought along with the Norican Taurisci against the Dacian king Boirebistas and were annihilated by him, leaving their Pannonian territory a desert (ἡ Βοίων ἐρημία) which their neighbours used as a grazing land (Strabo, 5. 1, 6; 7. 1, 5; 3, 11; 5, 2). The portion of the tribe that remained in Bohemia was driven out by the Marcomani about 8 B.c., see c. 42, 1 with the note.

Boihaemi, Bohemia, 'home of the Boii' (the last part of the name being the German *haim*, later *heim*). The name is given by Velleius (2. 109, 3) to the tract occupied by Maroboduus (see. c. 42, 2), by Strabo (7. 1, 5) to his headquarters (βασίλειον).

signat, etc., 'attests the old tradition about the land'. This is the meaning required, and it is not given by *significat*, the reading of most of the MSS.: the name Boihaemum might be said to 'indicate' the ancient inhabitants, but not the ancient tradition about the country. For the use of *signare*, cp. Vell. 2. 115, 1 (quoted by Robinson) *quali adiutore . . . usus sit, ipsius . . . praedicatione testatum est et amplissimorum donorum . . . signat memoria.*

§ 3. Aravisci, spelt *Eravisci* in Pliny, *N. H.* 3, 148, and in some inscriptions (though two have *Araviscus, CIL*. iii. 3325, 13389). They were an Illyrian tribe, settled in the north-eastern corner of Pannonia from the bend of the Danube southwards to the Platten See (Pelso lacus). One of their chief centres was

Aquincum, Buda(-pest): cp. *CIL*. iii. 10418. Coins which they struck in imitation of Roman denarii down to the time of Augustus bear the names *Ravisci* or *Iravisci*, *Rausci* or *Irausci*, etc. That they were deeply affected by Celtic civilization has long been clear from personal and place-names, and excavations now being conducted in the oldest quarter of Budapest have shown that their material culture was of a predominantly Celtic character at the time when they were incorporated by Augustus in the province of Pannonia (A.D. 9). See A. Alföldi, 'Les Anciens Habitants du Tabán', *Nouv. Rev. de Hongrie*, 1937.

Osis, settled on the opposite bank of the Danube in the region of the river Eipel, which joins the Danube just before it bends sharply southwards. As it is distinctly stated (in c. 43, 1) that their Pannonian language showed them not to be Germans, the words *Germanorum natione* appear to be an interpolation or else *Germanorum* is corrupt, since the phrase should bear the same sense as *Germanorum populi* in § 4 and can hardly be taken to mean 'a tribe living among the Germans' or 'a subject tribe of the Germans'; nor is Tacitus likely to have said twice in one sentence that they were domiciled in Germany.

The argument is that the Aravisci and the Osi were so completely alike (and apparently differentiated from the Pannonians generally) that they must have originally dwelt together, but whether on the north or the south side of the river is uncertain. The occurrence of the place-name Osones (mod. Öskü) in Pannonia, about five miles north of the Platten See, may well indicate the earlier home of the Osi, who may have been separated from their kinsfolk during the troublous period of the Boian emigration (see above). This seems more probable than the alternative view that they were an isolated remnant of the Illyrian population which in prehistoric times extended far to the north of the Danube into the plain of east Germany (see on c. 46, 1).

At the end of the second century A.D. the tribe was, at least for a time, under Roman authority, being governed by a *praepositus gentis Onsorum*, who was at the same time military tribune of legio II Adiutrix stationed at Aquincum (*Année épigr*. 1914, 248; Ritterling, *Germania*, i, 1917, p. 132). The form *Onsi* shows a parasitic *n*, like *formonsus*, *thensaurus*, etc.

adhuc, despite their separation.

pari olim . . . libertate, ablat. absol., 'as there was in old times the same poverty and the same freedom'. Because the economic and political conditions were the same on both banks, there was no more motive for migration one way than the other. *Inopia* and *libertas* were features characteristic of Germany.

§ 4. **Treveri, etc.** After the digression (§§ 1-3) Tacitus reverts to the theme of migrations from Germany into Gaul (c. 27, 3). The Treveri lived in the valley of the Moselle: they have left their name to their capital, Trèves or Trier, which received from Claudius the title of a Roman colony, *colonia Augusta Treverorum*.

Nervii. This people, whose chief towns were Bavai and Cambrai (Bagacum and Camaracum), were the most warlike of the Belgic Gauls (Caes. 2. 4, 8; 15, 5, etc.) and offered determined opposition to Caesar.

circa adfectationem . . . sunt, 'actually make a display of, take ostentatious pride in, claiming German descent'. *Circa,* 'in regard to', frequently used in silver Latin for *de*. *Ultro,* 'even', 'go so far as to'; cp. *Agr.* 19, 4, etc.

tamquam, expressing their view, 'in the belief that', 'as though'. Tacitus' contempt for the Gauls of his day (cp. c. 29, 4; *Agr.* 11, 5, etc.) was shared by the Romans of that time generally (*A.* 3. 46, 2, etc.); yet from the three provinces of Gallia Comata came more than a quarter of the Roman auxiliary infantry in the pre-Flavian period and nearly half the cavalry (Cheesman, *Auxilia,* p. 64).

similitudine et inertia, hendiadys for *similitudine inertiae,* 'resemblance to the listless (unwarlike) Gauls': *inertia* in a different sense from that in which it is used of the Germans. The sarcastic tone of this sentence and the following *haud dubie* show that Tacitus did not believe in the claim of German origin. Yet it had some foundation, for the archaeological evidence leaves little room for doubt that the Treveri had some admixture of German blood and the Nervii a very strong admixture (*Introd.,* Sect. IV). This is the truth underlying the exaggerated statement made by the Remi to Caesar, that most of the Belgae were descended from Germans who had crossed the Rhine in ancient times (*B. G.* 2. 4, 1), and the statement of Strabo that the Nervii were a German tribe (4. 3, 4, taken perhaps from Timagenes, on whom see *Introd.,* p. xxiv, note, as Norden believes, p. 371). The *feritas* for which both Nervii and Treveri were noted in Caesar's time (2, 4 and 15; 8, 25) was a German characteristic (Strabo, 7. 1, 2).

haud dubie, taken closely with *Germanorum,* 'unquestionably German'.

Vangiones, Triboci, Nemetes: settled in Upper Germany along the Rhine, the Vangiones round Worms (Borbetomagus), the Nemetes round Speyer (Noviomagus), the Triboci round Brumat (Breucomagus), near Hagenau, and Strassburg (Argentorate). In his enumeration Tacitus does not observe the geographical order, nor does Pliny (*N. H.* 4, 106), whose description in the *Bella Germaniae* Tacitus probably had before him. These three tribes formed part of the German flood which about 100 B.C. poured across the Rhine at Mainz; they fought under Ariovistus and shared his defeat by Caesar, but were allowed to settle in the Rhine valley as a bulwark against further German invasion. There they speedily became Celticized: even the names *Nemetes* and *Triboci* are Celtic. *Introd.*, p. xlv ff. The eastern provenance of the Vangiones (Elbe region) is confirmed by the fact that, unlike the western Germans, they wore loose *bracae* (see on c. 17, 1).

§ 5. **Ubii.** In Caesar's time they lived beyond the Rhine, opposite to the Treveri, in the district extending from Wiesbaden to the river Wied (*Praehist. Ztschr.* vi. 277 f.), but the pressure of the Suebi drove them to seek Roman protection (*B. G.* 1, 54; 4, 16). In 38 B.C. they were taken across the river by M. Agrippa, with their own consent (Strabo, 4. 3, 4; *A.* 12. 27, 2).

quamquam, with the subjunctive, as most frequently in Tacitus (c. 29, 4; 35, 1; 38, 1), more rarely with the indicative as in c. 46, 1.

Romana colonia. Their *oppidum* (*A.* 1. 36, 1, etc.) became *colonia Claudia Ara Agrippinensis* (or -*ium*) or more shortly *colonia Agrippinensis* (or -*ium*), now Cologne or Köln, under Claudius in A.D. 50, taking its name from his wife Agrippina, who procured the settlement of a colony of veterans in the town (*A.* 12. 27, 1). Henceforward the people drop their German name, and are called *Agrippinenses* (*H.* 4. 28, 2).

meruerint, 'earned' by their fidelity: used with the infinitive in two other passages, and frequently by Ovid.

libentius, not 'they prefer to be called' but 'they like to call themselves': for the comparative, cp. *H.* 1. 22 *cupidine ingenii humani libentius obscura credendi*, and note on *saepius*, c. 17, 3.

conditoris sui, sc. *Agrippinae.* The feminine form *conditrix* belongs to later Latin, and such feminine nouns are very sparingly used by Tacitus. Cp. c. 7, 4 *hi (feminae) maximi laudatores.*

erubescunt, with simple ablative, as in *Agr.* 42, 3, Livy, etc.

experimento, causal ablative, equivalent to *propter expertam fidem,* 'by reason of their tried loyalty', because they had given proof of their loyalty.

arcerent, sc. *transrhenanos hostes.*

CHAPTER XXIX

OTHER TRIBES UNDER THE ROMAN 'IMPERIUM': THE BATAVI AND
MATTIACI. THE 'DECUMATES AGRI'

§ 1. harum gentium, viz. the German tribes in Gaul (of which
several have not been mentioned, e.g. Tungri, Cugerni, etc.;
but Tacitus did not aim at completeness).

Batavi (with long second *a*, except in Lucan, 1, 431),
described also in similar language in *H*. 4. 12, where mention
is made of their horsemanship and skill in swimming (cp.
Agr. 18, 5 *nandi usus, quo simul seque et arma et equos regunt*).
Before Caesar's time (4. 10, 1) they had occupied the island
formed by the bifurcation of the old or true Rhine, which
passes Utrecht and Leiden, and the Waal (Vahalis, *A*. 2. 6, 5),
where their name survives in the Dutch district of Betuwe
between the Waal and the Lek. No mention is here made of
the Cannenefates, who adjoined them on the north in the district called Kennemerland.

non multum, etc., 'not much of the river-frontier', *extrema Gallicae orae* in *H*. 4. 12, viz. a strip of land on the
southern bank of the Waal. With *ripa*, sc. *nostra*; *multum ex*
is post-classical for the partitive genitive.

Chattorum . . . populus, *pars Chattorum* in *H*. 4. 12. The
statement, which is repeated in the *Histories*, has been
questioned, without good reason. Tacitus drew his information from Pliny: here he is following the *Bella Germaniae*,
while his narrative in the *Histories* of the great rebellion on
the Rhine in A.D. 69-70, headed by the Batavian Civilis, was
based on Pliny's account in his historical work, *A fine Aufidii
Bassi* (Münzer, *Bonner Jahrbb*. civ. 67 ff.; Norden, p. 265 ff.).
Cp. Holwerda, *Mnemosyne*, 1913, p. 1 ff.

in quibus . . . fierent, 'in which they were destined to
become'. For the subjunctive, cp. *in quibus . . . victoriam
ederetis, Agr*. 34, 3.

pars Romani imperii. The Batavians first appear on the
side of the Romans in 12 B.C., when Augustus' offensive
against Germany was launched by Drusus. Their land was
needed as a base of operations for an attack from the north,
and an alliance (*societas*) was evidently negotiated which
allowed the canalizing of the river Vecht, *fossa Drusiana*, to
provide a safe waterway to the North Sea, and the appropria-
tion of a strip of land as a glacis to protect the canal. A
tribal levy is mentioned as assisting Germanicus in A.D. 16
(*A*. 2. 8; 11). After the abandonment of the attempt to con-
quer Germany the Batavians remained a client state within

the Empire (*pars imperii*) under the exceptional conditions mentioned in § 2. By the middle of the first century tribal levies were replaced by regularly organized auxiliary regiments commanded by native chiefs (*A*. 14. 38; *H*. 1. 59; 4. 12). The tribe also furnished most of the recruits for the imperial bodyguard of *Germani* until this corps was disbanded by Galba in 68 A.D. (Suet. *Galb.* 12).

§ **2.** **honos,** explained by the more specific words following: 'they still retain a distinction which is the token of an ancient alliance'. The expression shows that, after their rising with Civilis in A.D. 69–70, they had submitted on honourable terms. Archaeological evidence shows that the strip of territory which they occupied south of the Waal was annexed and became part of the fortified Rhine frontier, secured by a legionary fortress at Nymwegen (Noviomagus), while their territory north of the Waal remained a client state with Roman garrisons stationed at certain important points, Fectio (Vechten near Utrecht) and Praetorium Agrippinae (Arentsburg near Voorburg on the coast). See Holwerda in Reports IV and XV of the *R.-G. Komm.* (pp. 80 ff., pp. 1 ff.); and on the position of the Batavi generally, J. Klose, *Roms Klientel-Randstaaten,* 1934, pp. 17 ff.

nam nec tributis, etc., 'for they are neither insulted by tribute, nor ground down by the tax-farmer' (collecting *vectigalia*). Similar phraseology is used in *H.* 4. 12 *nec opibus (rarum in societate validiorum) attritis,* etc. They are represented as themselves making a similar boast (*II.* 5. 25).

oneribus (dative with *exempti*), regular burdens of taxation, requisitions of corn, etc.

collationibus, contributions on special occasions, such as horses for service, money, etc., nominally voluntary (*A.* 1. 71, 3), but really burdensome (2. 5, 3). Hence Trajan is praised for having remitted *collationes* (Pliny, *Paneg.* 41).

tela atque arma, weapons and armour. In the period before the rebellion of A.D. 69–70 they furnished nine regiments of foot and one of horse, making in all 10,000 men. Of these all but the ninth cohort mutinied and were disbanded. After A.D. 70 three or four new cohorts and one *ala* were created (so far as is known), making with the surviving ninth cohort about 5,500 men in all. The new regiments were no longer commanded by native officers, and they were removed to distant provinces.

§ **3.** **obsequio,** 'allegiance': cp. *ad obsequium redegit,* Suet. *Aug* 21, 1, etc.

Mattiacorum, a strongly Celticized tribe living in the district between Mt. Taunus, Rhine, and Main: their hot springs

(Pliny, *N. H.* 31, 20), *Aquae Mattiacae*, being those of Wiesbaden. They were a subdivision of the Chatti, as is proved
by their name, the stem of which is the same as that of Mattium, the chief *oppidum* of the Chatti, while -*āci* is a common
Celtic suffix. The Chatti had been allowed by Agrippa to
occupy the land left vacant by the transportation of the Ubii
in 38 B.C. (c. 28, 5; Dio, 54. 36, 3), but the main body retired
before the advance of Drusus in 11 B.C. The Mattiaci, however, stayed behind and passed under the suzerainty of the
Romans, to whom they remained consistently loyal except
during the rising under Civilis (*H.* 4. 37), when they joined the
Chatti and Usipi in attacking the fortress of Moguntiacum
(Mainz). In A.D. 83 their territory was annexed by Domitian
and enclosed within the new frontier (*limes*) which he then
established against the Chatti and later extended southwards
(§ 4).

magnitudo populi R. is usually taken as a circumlocution
for Domitian, to avoid the mention of his hated name; for
at the time when Tacitus wrote the country of the Mattiaci
had been incorporated in the Empire as part of the province
of Upper Germany (see below). But it is impossible to
interpret the phrase as referring exclusively to the work
of Domitian, because *imperii reverentia* had been extended
beyond the Rhine in this region long before his reign and
had even been assured by military measures. The fort of
Kastel opposite Mainz (*castellum Mattiacorum*) had probably
been continuously held; Drusus had planted a fort *in monte
Tauno* (*A.* 1. 56), usually identified with Höchst on the Main,
which Germanicus restored in A.D. 15; and archaeological
evidence shows that in A.D. 39–40 forts were established at
Hofheim and Wiesbaden, both of which were destroyed by
the Chatti, the former in A.D. 50 (*A.* 12. 27–8), the latter in
the rising of A.D. 69–70 (cp. *H.* 4. 37). (On these forts see
Fabricius in Pauly-Wissowa, xiii. 584; Balsdon, *The Emperor
Gaius*, p. 194.) Indeed, it is probable that in this chapter
and the next, as R. Syme suggests, Tacitus followed closely
an authority who described the situation as it had been in
the Julio-Claudian period, without bringing that description
up to date. Cp. notes on *agunt* (below) and *ultra hos*, c. 30, 1.

imperii, objective genitive with *reverentiam*, as in *H.* 1. 55.

sede finibusque, ablative of respect: the words are virtually
synonymous, as are also *mente animoque*, 'in mind and spirit',
a frequent combination.

agunt, in the sense of 'dwell' with *in sua ripa* (as in c. 17,
1, etc.), in the sense of *se gerunt* ('are with us') with *mente
animoque* (as in c. 35, 4, etc.). The language used by Tacitus

might imply that the Mattiaci, although now part of the
empire, were not yet subjected to provincial administration
(Klose, *Klientel-Randstaaten*, p. 57); but see note above on
magnitudo p. R.

nisi quod ipso adhuc, etc. The meaning of *adhuc* is very
doubtful. It is perhaps best taken as equivalent to *insuper*
(as in c. 10, 3; 38, 1, etc.), 'besides', 'in addition', practically
the same as *etiam*: 'except that, among other factors, the
very soil and climate of their land gives them a more spirited
temperament'. The bracing highland country of the Mattiaci is contrasted with the dead level of the low-lying and
humid Batavian 'island': the livelier temperament of the
Rhinelanders as compared with the more stolid Dutch is still
noticeable. Cp. Martial 6, 82 *cuius nequitias iocosque novit* |
aurem qui modo non habet Batavam! The influence of
climate on national character was familiar to the ancients
from the days of the old Ionian ethnographers (*Introd.*, p. xiv;
Norden, pp. 53, 105 ff., etc.). Others take *adhuc* with *suae*,
'the land which is still their own', which they have not
changed, like the Batavians, for another; but the sense is
poor and neither the order of the words nor the use of *caelo* is
in favour of this interpretation. The position of *adhuc* shows
that it belongs to *ipso . . . caelo* and cannot be taken either
with *acrius*, 'still more spirited', or with *animantur* in the
sense of 'to this day' (which indeed would make the word
redundant, as Tacitus is describing the Mattiaci as they are).

§ 4. **numeraverim**, 'I should not count', the usual tense where
a writer speaks for himself (cp. *dixerim, crediderim*, etc.).

Decumates agros. Tacitus perhaps had no precise conception of the limits of this district; but his description seems
to make it coextensive with the territory between the Main,
Rhine, and Danube annexed by Rome up to A.D. 98, corresponding to Hessen-Starkenburg, Baden, and part of Württemberg, which had once been occupied by the Helvetii (see
on c. 28, 2). The term *Decumates agri*, which occurs nowhere
else, evidently applied to the period preceding the Roman
occupation. Its meaning is disputed, but it is most probable
that *decumates* is a Romano-Celtic word formed from the
Celtic ordinal for 'ten' (Old Irish *dechmad*) with the Celtic
suffix *-tes* to express a collective idea, a group of ten cantons
or districts: analogous designations are *Decempagi*, the centre
of a community of ten *pagi*, in the land of the Mediomatrici
(Tab. Peut., Itin. Ant. 240, Ammianus 16. 2, 9), *Novem
populi* in Aquitania (Dessau, 6961), *Quinquegentanei* in Mauretania (Dessau 645, 1194). The traditional explanation 'tithe
lands' (*decumas* being formed from *decumus*, like *supernas*

from *supernus*, or on the analogy of *ager Interamnas, Arpinas,*
etc.) is untenable. Not only is the term pre-Roman, but
'tithe lands' were called by Romans *agri decumani*, there is
no evidence of the institution of tithes under the Empire, and
Romans never called any region by a name derived from the
manner in which it was taxed. Although part of the *Decumates agri*, viz. the district round Rottenburg (Sumelocenna),
near Tübingen, went through the stage of an Imperial *saltus*
cultivated by *coloni* of the Emperor, most of it was organized
like any other provincial district and passed through a similar
development, conditioned by the sparseness of the population.
See E. Hesselmeyer, *Klio*, xix. 253 ff., xx. 344 ff., xxiv. 1 ff.;
Norden, *Alt-Germanien*, ch. iii.

exercent, 'cultivate'; so in *Agr.* 31, 3, etc., and not infrequently in post-Augustan prose.

levissimus quisque, 'all the wastrels of Gaul'. For the
change to the positive in *audax* there are several parallels
in Tacitus (e.g. *A.* 1. 48, 3; *H.* 1. 88). Gauls economically
ruined and driven to emigrate found a home in a region which
(apart from the Rhine plain) was thinly inhabited, chiefly by
remnants of the old Celtic population (*Introd.*, p. xlv ff). The
influx took place in the period following Caesar's campaigns,
which aggravated economic conditions in Gaul: Caesar himself frequently speaks of *egentes ac perditi, magna multitudo
perditorum hominum latronumque*, etc. The distress continued under the early Empire (*A.* 3. 40-2).

dubiae possessionis solum, 'a land which was precariously
held', because inhabited by no compact tribes which were
strong enough to defend their territory against invaders.
Cp. *de possessione dubitatum, Agr.* 41, 2. The establishment of
the *limes* and the incorporation of the land in the Roman
Empire made it *certae possessionis solum*.

mox limite acto, etc., 'subsequently a frontier-road was
driven, the garrisons were moved forward, and these lands
are now reckoned an outlying recess of the Empire and part
of the province (of Upper Germany)'. *Mox* marks the last
phase of the history of the district, the Roman occupation,
while the preceding clause describes the previous phases.
Limes, originally denoting the path between the lands owned
by different persons, which also served as a boundary between
them, came to be used of a road made for military purposes,
and then of a road, guarded by forts and signal stations, which
formed the boundary where no natural frontier existed.
Limitem agere is one of the technical expressions for driving
such a road (whence *latumque per agmen . . . limitem agit
ferro*, Verg. *Aen.* 10, 514): other verbs used are *aperire* and

scindere (or *secare*), the latter when the road had to be driven through a forest (*A.* I. 50, 2).

The *limes* here spoken of is the southern section of the Upper German frontier-line, which was laid out by Domitian in and after A.D. 89 to protect the territory beyond the Rhine annexed by himself and by Vespasian, who in A.D. 73–4 had incorporated the Black Forest region. This frontier-line consisted of a chain of forts, connected by a road, extending from Hanau on the Main southwards to the valley of the Neckar and then along the course of that river. The establishment of this line was followed by the transformation of Germania Superior from a military command into a regular province (Dessau, 1015, 1998), but the military defence took years to complete. It was not finished when Tacitus wrote in A.D. 98 (note on *habentur*): Trajan was then busy completing Domitian's work and developing the annexed region by building roads and founding towns. On the whole subject of the Upper German *limes*, see (apart from the detailed description in *Der obergerm.-rät. Limes,* now complete) Fabricius in Pauly-Wissowa, *R. E.* xiii. 582 ff., and Syme in *Camb. Anc. Hist.* xi. 159 ff.

praesidiis, here (as often) equivalent to *castella* (note on *Agr.* 16, 1).

sinus, 'a recess' bending inwards to Germany, equivalent to *flexus* in c. 35, 1. See note on c. 1, 1.

provinciae, Upper Germany.

habentur, 'are reckoned': the expression implies that the military defence and the organization of the annexed territory were still incomplete. The grammatical subject is *ii qui Decumates agros exercent,* the logical the lands themselves.

CHAPTER XXX

THE CHATTI

The description of the Chatti is exceptionally detailed, and shows a warm appreciation of their martial qualities which is reflected in the stylistic elaboration of the narrative. Tacitus was evidently specially interested in this tribe, which was Rome's most formidable enemy in west Germany in his time. It is no less plain that he had before him the account of an eye-witness who was an acute observer and had an eye for military details. This witness was in all probability the elder Pliny, who served as an officer in both Lower and Upper Germany and may well have taken part in the campaign of Pomponius Secundus against the Chatti in A.D. 50 (*A.* 12. 27 f.). See

Norden, p. 265 ff., who convincingly develops a suggestion made by Schumacher in *Mainzer Ztschr.* iv, 1909, p. 13. It is less likely that the eye-witness was an officer who fought in Domitian's campaigns.

§ 1. **ultra hos.** The reference is to the Mattiaci, as well as the inhabitants of the *Decumates agri*, or more probably to the former alone, the mention of the latter being parenthetical. If the latter alone were referred to, the description would be very loose, unless we accept Kahrstedt's view, insecurely based on Vell. 2, 109 and hardly consistent with the present passage, that the Chatti had advanced south of the Main to the region of Ansbach and bordered the Hermunduri over a long front (*Gött. Nachricht.*, 1933, p. 267). R. Syme makes the attractive suggestion that the *Decumates agri* were not mentioned by the authority whom Tacitus was following, and that, after adding the paragraph about them, he inadvertently repeated *ultra hos* (sc. *Mattiacos*) from his source.

Chatti. They occupied the highland tract drained by the upper arms of the Weser (the Werra and Fulda) and its tributary the Diemel, where their name survives in the modern Hessen. They are not mentioned by Caesar, in whose time they may have been dependent on the Suebi (*Introd.*, p. xlv), but, except during the short supremacy of Arminius (see c. 36, 1), they were the most constant and most powerful enemies of Rome in western Germany, though their action was hampered by feuds with their own neighbours the Cherusci (c. 36, 2, *A*. 12. 28, 2) and Hermunduri (*A*. 13. 57, 1). They had been lately the object of Domitian's attack (see on c. 29, 3), and are last heard of towards the end of the fourth century, but in the eighth century they reappear in the same district under the name of Hassi or Hessi.

initium . . . incohant, a pleonasm found in Livy, 3. 54, 9; 39. 23, 5. Similar pleonasms are found in c. 18, 4; *H*. 1. 39 (*initio orto*); *A*. 13. 10, 2 (*principium inciperet*), etc.

Hercynio saltu: see on c. 28, 2. The part of the forest here meant is the Spessart, Vogelsberg, Rhön, and the hills to the north in the direction of Kassel.

non ita effusis . . . locis, 'where the country is not so open and marshy'. The ablative is local, depending on the idea of *sedent* implied in the preceding clause. *Effusis = longe patentibus*, 'spread out': similarly used by Lucan (6, 270) of a wide plain, and by Vell. (2. 43, 1) of the broad expanse of the Adriatic.

durant, etc. The punctuation and meaning of this passage are much disputed. It seems best, with Rhenanus, to make *colles* the subject of both verbs, so that *durant* answers to *prosequitur* and *rarescunt* to *deponit.* The meaning will be, 'since the hills last (continue, extend) through their territory, only gradually open out, and the Hercynian forest escorts its own Chatti to its limits and sets them down' (i.e. they end where the hills end). *Durant colles* is a personification, paralleled by Mela 3, 78 *non perdurat (Euphrates) in pelagus, verum . . . tenuis rivus despectus emoritur,* and stressed by the anastrophe of *siquidem,* which in post-Augustan Latin is almost always used in the causal sense: the anastrophe also occurs in Pliny (*N. H.* 2, 173; 11, 2, etc.), and Tacitus is fond of placing *quippe, quin etiam, quin immo* in this position. Others punctuate *incohant; non ita . . . patescit durant, siquidem colles . . . rarescunt,* thus making *Chatti* the subject of *durant* and *colles* that of *rarescunt,* 'they extend continuously over country that is not so level . . . , since the hills only gradually open out'. But this makes a clumsy and unbalanced sentence; *Chatti durant locis* is a strange expression; and if *Chatti* be the subject of both *incohant* and *durant,* a conjunction is needed to connect the two contrasted verbs, while the following *et Chattos suos* seems to imply a different subject for *durant.*

rarescunt, grow thin and so make gaps: similarly Verg. *Aen.* 3, 411 *angusti rarescent claustra Pelori,* the headlands, which at a distance seem to form a barrier, become *rara* (show an interval between them), and Sil. Ital. 17, 422 *rarescit miles* of the thinning of the ranks.

prosequitur . . . deponit, a picturesque personification: the *saltus* is a mother who escorts her children, carrying them on her shoulders and setting down the last of them at the edge of the high ground where it sinks to the plain. For such personifications, cp. *bellum aperuit* (c. 1, 1), *caespes erigit* (c. 27, 2), etc.

simul atque, often used for the threadbare *et . . . et* (cp. c. 12, 3; 31, 4).

§ 2. duriora, 'hardier' (than other Germans).

stricti, 'close-knit', sinewy: cp. *stricta veste,* c. 17, 1.

et, adding a mental quality to the physical traits denoted by the asyndeta.

animi vigor, 'activity of mind'.

ut inter Germanos, qualifying *multum* and expressing the standard by which the judgement is formed: 'as the standard is among Germans', 'for Germans', who in general are a *gens non astuta nec callida* (c. 22, 4). Arminius and Civilis are mentioned as exceptions (Vell. 2. 118, 2; *H.* 4. 13). In c. 2, 4; 22, 2, the meaning of *ut* is different.

rationis, 'judgement'. The historical infinitives which follow are explanatory nominatives in apposition to *multum* . . . *sollertiae*.

praeponere electos. The stress is on *electos*: they choose (military) leaders carefully, and obey them (*audire*). Germans in general did not obey the command of their leaders, but followed their example (c. 7, 1). The Treveran leader, Julius Tutor, said of the Germans: *non iuberi, non regi, sed cuncta ex libidine agere* (*H*. 4. 76). On the other hand, the Cherusci and the Suebi had learnt from the Romans *sequi signa, subsidiis firmari, dicta imperatorum accipere* (*A*. 2. 45, 3), a passage based on Pliny (Norden, pp. 213, 268).

nosse ordines, 'know how to keep rank', like a Roman soldier. Cp. Livy, 23. 35, 6 *ut tirones adsuescerent signa sequi et in acie agnoscere ordines suos*. The Germans had an order of battle (c. 6, 6), but did not observe strict discipline.

intellegere occasiones, 'to note (not overlook) opportunities' (cp. *terga occasioni patefecit, Agr*. 14, 4). The meaning is indicated by the next phrase.

differre impetus, 'reserve their attacks' (for the right moment).

disponere diem, 'to map out the day' (have regular hours for various duties). The phrase is common (Sen. *Cons. ad Pol.* 6, 4; Pliny, *Epp.* 9. 36, 1; Suet. *Tib.* 11, 2, etc.).

vallare noctem, to make night safe by defences, 'entrench for the night', a strained variation of *noctu castra vallare* for the sake of a concise antithesis to *disponere diem*.

fortunam, etc., 'to count luck doubtful but valour sure', a commonplace sentiment.

Rom. disciplinae concessum, 'granted to Roman discipline', said with not unjustifiable national pride, like Caesar's *docuit quid populi Romani disciplina atque opes possent* (*B. G.* 6. 1, 4). For the phrase, cp. *rarissimam laudem et nulli adhuc principum concessam* (Sen. *De clem.* 1. 1, 5). The Chatti had learnt from the Romans, like the Cherusci and the Suebi. Some adopt the reading of certain MSS. *ratione disciplinae* ('by a system of discipline'), but a dative is required with *concessum* (c. 40, 2; *A*. 13. 46, 2), and instead of *concessum* a participle meaning 'attained' would be needed; moreover, *ratio disciplinae* (*militaris*) should mean 'the theory, doctrines, of the art of war'. *Ratione* is due to the misreading of *ro^e*, an abbreviation for *Roman(a)e* (in c. 33, 2 one MS. (*I*) has *ro^is* for *Romanis*), as *rõe*, i.e. *ratione*: a few lines above the same MS. expanded *rõis* into *Romanis* instead of *rationis*.

plus reponere, more fully *plus spei reponere* (Livy, 2. 39, 1).

§ 3. **omne robur,** stronger than what is said of the Germans generally in c. 6, 4: cp. c. 32, 2.

super, 'besides', a sense frequent in and after Livy; cp.
c. 32, 2; 43, 5.

ferramentis, 'tools' for entrenching (spades, axes, mattocks, etc.).

copiis, 'provisions' (*H*. 2. 32, etc.).

proelium . . . bellum: 'a battle'—'a campaign', a common
antithesis (*A*. 2. 88, 3; *H*. 2, 40, etc.).

excursus, 'sudden dashes', the opposite of *nosse ordines*
above, explained by *fortuita pugna* (sc. *rara est*), 'casual
fighting'. The ordinary German practice is described in
A. 2. 45, 3 *vagis incursibus aut disiectas per catervas*.

equestrium sane, etc., i.e. of course, if they had had an
army of horsemen, their practice would have been different.
'It is, of course, characteristic of a cavalry force to secure a
victory quickly and quickly retire: but, in the case of infantry, fleetness approaches timidity, deliberateness is near
to steadiness'. *Iuxta*, 'next door to' (note on c. 21, 1), is
answered by *propior* (absolute comparative, 'rather near')
in *A*. 6. 42, 3. *Cunctatio* used here of the movements of foot
soldiers, in *H*. 3. 20 of the deliberate action of generals. The
insertion of *peditum* seems necessary to make clear what
must in any case be the sense. These general reflections are
not much to the point: the Chattan preference for infantry
would be better explained by the hilly character of their
country; their deliberate tactics were learnt from the
Romans.

parare: *parere* (*victoriam*) is more common, but should not
be read here. Cp. c. 14, 4; 24, 2; *Dial*. 36, 4, etc.

CHAPTER XXXI
PECULIAR CUSTOMS OF THE CHATTI

§ 1. Et aliis, etc., 'a custom practised also by other German
tribes, though rarely and as a result of the personal bravery
of individuals, has become general among the Chatti'. *Et =
etiam*; *populis*, dative, as in c. 16, 1, etc.

usurpatum, in apposition to the infinitive subject, *submittere nec exuere*; this use of a past participle in place of a
relative clause is frequent in Tacitus (*Agr*. 1, 1 *usitatum*;
H. 1. 18 *observatum id*, etc.).

audentia, causal ablative. The word is used in c. 34, 3;
A. 15. 53, 3, and a few other places in silver Latin, in a good
sense only. *Audacia temeritatis est, audentia fortitudinis*
(Nonius, 442).

in consensum vertit, here only for *in consuetudinem vertere*
or *verti*.

submittere, 'to let grow wild', for the more classical *crinem promittere* (so also in Seneca, Pliny's *Letters* and Suetonius). Germans usually wore their hair long, but not wholly unshorn, and kept it in some order (cp. c. 38, 2), as contrasted with the *squalor* here (§ 2). Long hair properly dressed was a mark of high nobility.

votivum, etc., 'a facial garb which they had vowed and pledged to valour' (i.e. and by which they had pledged themselves to valour). *Habitus* may mean 'facial aspect', the word being often used of general appearance or physical form (*Agr.* 11, 1; 44, 2, etc.); but here it is better taken to mean 'facial garb', the wild hair and beard being regarded as a covering which is afterwards taken off (*revelant frontem*). The phrase combines a religious term (*votivum*) with a legal one (*obligatum*): they were under a contractual obligation to *virtus*, which is half-personified in the Roman fashion. Instances of this practice pending the attainment of a specific purpose are recorded in the case of Civilis (*H.* 4. 61) and among the Saxons in later time (Paul. Diaconus, 3, 7). It is also attested among the Jews (*Numbers* vi. 5; *Acts* xviii. 18). At Rome such *squalor* was a token of mourning: when Julius Caesar made a vow to let his hair and beard grow long until he had avenged the disaster at Atuatuca (Suet. *Jul.* 67), he wished to make an impression on the Germanic Eburones.

§ 2. super sanguinem et spolia, rhetorical (with alliteration), 'as they stand over the bleeding and despoiled foe'.

tum demum, etc., 'then, and not till then, have they repaid (to country and parents) the price of their birth', i.e. the debt they owe for their existence. Cp. the Greek phrase θρέπτρα (or τροφεῖα) ἀποδοῦναι, 'to pay the recompense of nurture'.

dignosque (sc. *esse*), 'and so are worthy'.

ignavis et imbellibus, see note on c. 12, 1 Here *imbellibus* means 'unwarlike'.

§ 3. fortissimus quisque, etc., 'the bravest of them also wear an iron ring—which the tribe regards as a mark of disgrace—in token of bondage, until they have freed themselves by the slaughter of an enemy'. The iron finger-ring[1] symbolized a bond or fetter (*vinculum*), and so was a badge of servitude; hence the wearing of it was *ignominiosum*. By wearing it the Chattan warriors declared themselves slaves of the war god, pledged to his service, from which they could only be released by slaying a foe. Cp. *vinculo ligatus*, c. 39, 3.

---

[1] Some have taken *anulus* to mean an arm-band, such as was worn in the Middle Ages by insolvent debtors and others in token of servitude, but it is highly improbable that Tacitus would have used *anulus* in the sense of *armilla*.

Among the Romans, on the other hand, finger-rings of iron, and later of gold, were a mark of distinction and rank; according to Pliny (*N. H.* 33, 8 ff.), the iron ring was originally *virtutis bellicae insigne.* Aristotle mentions an old Macedonian law which required that a leather band (φορβεία, 'halter') should be worn until an enemy had been slain (*Pol.* 7. 2, 6).

insuper = *praeterea*, besides the long hair. id = *anulum gestare*: the warriors wear the symbol of *ignominia* as a sign that they are under a bond to the god. *Ferreum anulum . . . velut vinculum gestat* recalls Pliny's *ferreum anulum . . . vinculum id, non gestamen* (*N. H.* 33, 8, a *locus classicus* for rings).

§ 4. plurimis, etc. 'Very many of the Chatti favour (take pride in) this appearance, and even grow grey with this mark of distinction, conspicuous alike to enemies and to compatriots.' What follows shows that Tacitus is here describing a warrior caste, a class of devotees, who after slaying a foe lay aside their *squalor* only for a moment; they let hair and beard grow wild again even in time of peace, and so when war breaks out they present a terrifying appearance to the foe. *Plurimis* is an exaggeration, as they formed only the front rank in battle; and naturally a large unproductive class could not have been supported by the tribe, as these men were. They bore some resemblance to the Berserker, the wild Norse warriors known to English readers from Kingsley's *Hereward*, ch. 12 ff. It is strange that nothing is said of any means of distinguishing these heroes from the cowards, and a gap in the text after *habitus* has been suggested (Robinson, *Germ.*, *ad loc.*), the lost words describing some distinctive difference from the ordinary *habitus*. But this is not the only difficulty involved in Tacitus' description (see below).

habitus refers primarily to the long dishevelled hair and beard, but includes the ring.

monstrati, 'pointed out' with the finger, then 'marked out' (*Agr.* 13, 5, etc.).

penes hos, 'rest with them', i.e. these old heroes.

haec, 'composed of these'.

nova, 'unusual' and so 'strange', 'startling', as in c. 43,5.

nam ne in pace quidem, etc., '(they are always available for war) for even in peace they do not mitigate their fierceness by a milder aspect'. *Vultu* seems preferable to *cultu*: it is their fierce aspect (*visu nova*), not their mode of life (c. 43, 1; 46, 1) that is in question; cp. Lucan, 4, 238 *mansuevere ferae et vultus posuere minaces.*

§ 5. aliqua cura, 'occupation of any sort'.

prout, with weakened sense, equivalent to *ut*, 'whenever'.

They lived on the hospitality of those who had house and land. Their entertainment was a burden (*prodigi alieni*), but we are not told whether it was law, religion, or force that obliged their hosts to feed them.

contemptores sui, 'scornful of their own' (*sui* is adjective, not pronoun), is in contradiction with *nulli domus aut ager*, but the contradiction is condoned for the sake of the antithesis. It might conceivably mean 'scorning the property they had before taking to this mode of life', hardly 'scorning to have any property of their own'. The whole phrase is perhaps imitated from Sallust's *alieni adpetens, sui profusus* (*Cat.* 5, 4). Similar contrasts between *alienum* and *suum* are common.

exsanguis senectus, perhaps a reminiscence of Lucan, 1, 343.

tam durae virtuti, 'such hardy heroism'.

The description given in this chapter involves difficulties. One has been mentioned, that the warrior heroes voluntarily retained through life the *squalor* which is said to have been the mark of *ignavi et imbelles*. The explanation of this may be that the statement about the latter is really an inference which Tacitus himself drew without noticing the inconsistency. Another difficulty is that, pitted as the Chatti would be against foes of equal calibre (whether German or Roman) and by no means at constant warfare, it could never have been possible for more than a minority to fulfil their vow, so that at any given time *squalor* would have been the condition of the majority of the population, and so the custom would have been meaningless. Hence it has been suggested that there must have been some alternative method of release from the vow, perhaps by giving some other proof of courage, e.g. by killing a boar or a bear single-handed (as among the Taifali, Ammianus 31. 9, 5), or by fighting in the first instance without a shield (as among the Heruli, Procop. *Bell. Pers.* 2, 25); Much, *Germ.*, 297 f.

CHAPTER XXXII

THE USIPI AND TENCTERI

The description now follows the course of the Rhine, as Tacitus himself says in c. 41, 1, proceeding downstream and beginning with the Usipi and Tencteri, who were neighbours of the Chatti.

§ 1. **certum iam alveo**, 'which has now a definite channel'. The contrast intended is usually believed to be the upper Rhine, which has often changed its bed down to modern times; but

such change, even if known to Tacitus, would not affect the
adequacy of the river as a boundary. It seems better therefore to take the contrast to be to the divided Rhine of the
Batavian district, with which the description began (c. 29),
iam implying a reversion of thought to the starting-point,
from which he was led on to the Mattiaci because of the
similarity of their political condition and then to the Chatti
as their neighbours (after parenthetical mention of the *Decumates agri*: cp. on c. 30, 1 *ultra hos*).

The phrase has been supposed to be a reminiscence of Mela,
who, after speaking (3. 2, 24) of the descent of the Rhine
from the Alps and its passage through Lake Constance, adds
mox diu solidus et certo alveo lapsus, but it is extremely
unlikely that Tacitus used Mela's jejune summary, which
contained little or nothing of value to him.

quique ... sufficiat, for the more usual *et qui*, 'and such as
to be fit'. For the subjunctive, cp. *Agr.* 43, 3 *securus iam
odii et qui facilius dissimularet*; *H.* 2. 25 *et cui ... placerent*,
etc.

Usipi ac Tencteri. Usīpi (with long middle *i*, Mart. 6. 60, 3)
or Usipetes with Celtic termination (Caes. 4. 1, 1; *A.* 1. 51, 4,
etc.). The two tribes are regularly associated from their first
appearance in 55 B.C., when under the pressure of the invading Suebi they attempted to cross into Gaul and were
severely defeated by Caesar near Coblenz. The remnants
found a home in the northern part of the territory of the
Sugambri, the Usipi between the lower Lippe and the Yssel,
the Tencteri to the east of them; and, when the Sugambri
were transplanted to the left bank of the Rhine by Tiberius
in 8 B.C., the Tencteri inherited their land. In the time of
Tacitus the Tencteri lived opposite the Ubii (c. 28, 5), whose
chief centre was Cologne (*H.* 4. 64), extending southwards
from the river Ruhr. Under the earlier Empire the Usipi still
adjoined them in the region of the lower Lippe, but some time
after A.D. 58 they had moved southwards into the district
bordering the Rhine gorge on both sides of the Lahn (details
in Appendix I to *Agricola*, p. 170 f.; cp. Schumacher, i. 145).
There they became subject to Rome early in Domitian's reign
(a fact about which Tacitus is studiously silent) and were
forced into Roman military service (*Agr.* c. 28). From Rhein-
brohl near Hönningen to the Lahn the *limes* ran through their
territory (cp. Schumacher, ii. 129).

colunt for *accolunt* (*H.* 1. 51), here alone in Tacitus, while
ripam colere (c. 28, 4; 29, 1) is common. The simple verb is,
however, used by poets (Verg. *Aen.* 7, 714; etc.), and may
stand here.

§ 2. **solitum**, usual among the Germans generally. *super* = *praeter* (c. 30, 3).

equestris disciplinae arte, 'in skill of horsemanship'. In 55 B.C. 800 horsemen of the Usipi and Tencteri by a sudden attack scattered right and left 5,000 of Caesar's Gallic cavalry (*B. G.* 4, 12).

Tencteris, varied to dative instead of repeating *apud*.

§ 3. **sic . . . imitantur** ('follow their example') is rhetorical for 'this is an ancient custom which is kept up'.

hi for *hoc* (i.e. riding), attracted, like *haec*, by a common idiom to the following noun.

§ 4. **inter familiam**, etc., 'horses are bequeathed along with the slaves, the home, and the rights of inheritance: they pass, not, like everything else, to the eldest son, but to the son who is the most warlike and the better soldier'.

inter, 'together with', indicates one category of inherited property, in which the Tencteri, contrary to the usual custom, included horses. Consequently, among other German tribes horses figured in another category, which probably included other animals (cattle, sheep, etc.), utensils, weapons, garments, etc. These two classes of property are clearly defined in the Folk Laws of the period following the invasions, which still exclude women from the first, because the solidarity of the family forbade the removal of property from it, and a woman could not become the head of a family. The second category may have been divided among the brothers, but Tacitus gives no details.

familiam, the slaves, who must have been exceedingly few (if they existed at all) in the primitive household of the ordinary German (cp. c. 20, 2; 25, 1); but here, as so often elsewhere, Tacitus probably had in mind the upper class. *Familia* can hardly mean 'patrimony', as F. de Coulanges understood it (*familiam suam, id est patrimonium suum*, Gaius, 2, 102), since a German would have no patrimony beyond the movable and immovable property mentioned above.

penates, the dwelling-house with the plot of ground surrounding it (c. 16, 2).

iura successionum, the rights attaching to every succession, e.g. the authority exercised by the head of the family (later called *mundium*) corresponding to the Roman *patria potestas* (c. 18, 2), the right to blood-money (*Wergeld*, c. 21, 1), etc., all of which had a pecuniary value and could therefore be classed as part of the inheritance. Some interpret 'and other legal (customary) objects of inheritance', but it is questionable if *iura* could bear that sense and, if it could, the definition of the things inherited would be comprehensive and would therefore include *equi*.

excipit, 'succeeds to them' (cp. c. 34, 1; *Agr.* 14, 3).

maximus natu. It is uncertain whether it is implied that the custom of primogeniture was peculiar to the Tencteri or common to all German tribes. The latter is not impossible, as Tacitus is only concerned to explain wherein the Tencteran rule of inheritance differed from that of other Germans. No mention is made of a prerogative of the eldest son in c. 20, 5, but there the rule of inheritance is only broadly stated. Nor is the right of primogeniture found in the Folk Laws, but by that time several older customs had changed or weakened. Where the right existed, the brothers, while unmarried, would continue to live with the eldest under his headship and share the enjoyment of the property of which he was the legal heir.

prout, i.e. the one who is most so. Who decided which son was the better warrior is not stated, nor what happened if a man left daughters only.

bello goes also with *melior*. Cp. *ferox bello* (Hor. *Carm.* 1. 32, 6), and the normal use of *ferox* and *ferocia* in a good sense (*Agr.* 27, 1; 31, 4; *H.* 1. 51, etc.).

CHAPTER XXXIII

THE BRUCTERI, CHAMAVI, AND ANGRIVARII

The scantiness of the material at Tacitus' disposal for cc. 33–34 is in striking contrast with the abundance of his information about the Chatti.

§ 1. **Iuxta,** next to them on the north, takes the place of the dative with *occurrebant*, which is used in a geographical sense (cp. *occurrit ei* (sc. *Euphrati*) *Taurus mons*, Pliny, 5, 84).

The **Bructeri,** settled in the region of Münster between the Lippe and the Teutoburger Wald, their natural boundary towards the Cherusci, had been one of the most powerful of the west German tribes. They had been allies of the Cherusci against Varus (*A.* 1. 60, 4) and against Germanicus (*A.* 1. 51, 4, etc.). After A.D. 58 they spread into the district left vacant by the migration of the Usipi southwards. They joined the rising under Civilis in A.D. 70, in which they took a prominent part owing to the influence of their prophetess Veleda (c. 8, 3). Some years later, between 75 and 78, they gave trouble again and were reduced to dependence by C. Rutilius Gallicus, who captured Veleda (Stat. *Silv.* 1, 4, 89 f.; Dessau, 9052).

The **Chamavi** (whose name has the same Celtic termination as their neighbours the Batavi) were formerly settled in the district between the Vecht and the Yssel, but moved across the latter river into the Dutch province of Oberyssel when Drusus turned their land into a military zone to protect his canal; there they became neighbours of the Bructeri.

Angrivarios, first mentioned in connexion with Germanicus' campaign of A.D. 16, when they dwelt on both banks of the middle Weser south of Bremen, bordering on the Cherusci, from whom they were separated by a broad *agger*, now identified with that which runs between the Weser and Steinhuder Meer north-west of Hanover (*A*. 2. 19, 3; *Præhist. Ztschr.* xvii, 1926, p. 100 f.). Their name probably means 'inhabitants of the Anger' (O.H.G. *Angar*), i.e. meadow lands. They reappear in the time of Charles the Great, under the name of Angrarii or Engern, higher up the Weser. Their name possibly survives in that of Enger near Herford.

immigrasse. At least part of the Bructeran territory was occupied. It was probably at this time that the Chamavi spread into the old home of the Usipi between the Yssel and the lower Lippe, where their name survived in the medieval district of Hamaland (its limits are defined in Schmidt, *Gesch. d. deutsch. Stämme,* ii. 423, n. 1). The Angrivarii also extended their territory south-westwards, or moved south-westwards, if c. 36, 1 correctly states the southward limit of the Chauci; while the Bructeri were perhaps, as a result, pressed across the Lippe, where they are found at a later time (see next note).

narratur, rarely used with accusative and infinitive.

pulsis . . . ac penitus excisis, apparently in A.D. 98: the report had recently reached Rome in an exaggerated form. The Bructeri were by no means utterly annihilated. They are mentioned in Roman documents down to the early fifth century, and they can be traced into the Middle Ages in the region between Lippe and Ruhr, where their name survived in the district called *Borahtra.* Later they amalgamated with the Tencteri and both were absorbed into the Franks.

With the internecine conflict here described was connected, probably as a sequel, a military promenade conducted by Vestricius Spurinna who 'by force of arms set the king of the Bructeri on his throne and by a threat of war terrified a most warlike tribe into subjection' and was awarded the honour of a triumphal statue on the proposal of the emperor (Pliny, *Epp.* 2. 7, 2). As Tacitus says nothing of this event, it probably took place late in 98 or in 99 (Müllenhoff, iv. 9 ff.). As Spurinna was at that time 70 years of age or more, it has been argued that he was too old to hold the governorship of Lower Germany and that the honour conferred on him was a belated one for an operation carried out in Domitian's reign (Dessau, *P.I.R.*,s.v.; Ritterling-Stein, *Fasti*,p. 61 ; etc.). But in that case Pliny would not have missed the chance of vilifying Domitian. Spurinna was a man of remarkable vitality (Pliny, *Epp.* 3, 1), and there are several instances under Nerva, Trajan, and Hadrian of old men holding military and other offices (*Klio*, i. 314 n.; von Premerstein, *Sitz. Bayer. Akad.*, 1934, 3, p. 12). Moreover, a comparison of § 2 and § 3 of the first of Pliny's two letters shows that Spurinna's honour and his military operation must be dated to one and the same time (W. Otto, *Sitz. Bayer. Akad.*, 1919, 10, p. 31).

odio, etc., causal ablative joined to the instrumental *consensu* ('by the common action').

ne spectaculo quidem, etc., 'they did not even grudge us the sight of a battle'. The Roman army of Lower Germany (under Spurinna) was watching the issue of the conflict. *Spectaculo* is probably ablative, as in *A*. 1. 22, 2, where *nobis* is to be supplied, as here. The dative of the thing is used in *A*. 13. 53, 4: elsewhere the case is doubtful. The ablative is specially common in Pliny's Letters, and indeed Quintilian (9. 3, 1) mentions it as one of the conceits of his day.

§ 2. **super sexaginta milia,** a great exaggeration. *Armis* is ablative of instrument, followed by a dative of purpose. The terrible inhumanity of the sentiment is due to the sense of security to the empire which was given by the quarrels of its foes: cp. *Agr.* 12, 2; *A*. 2. 26, 3; 62, 1. A similar thought is expressed by Livy, 2. 40, 13.

sed quod ... oculisque (sc. *Romanis*), 'but, grander still, for the delight of Roman eyes'. The datives are datives of purpose; the abstract *oblectatio* is more closely defined by the concrete *oculis*, as in Cicero's *delectationis atque aurium causa* (*De orat.* 3, 173). *Magnificentius*, because the conflict cost not a drop of Roman blood (*ingens victoriae decus citra Romanum sanguinem bellandi, Agr.* 35, 2), and took the form of a brilliant gladiatorial show, of which the Romans were delighted spectators.

maneat, so used in aspiration or prayer in *A*. 3. 55, 6. The addition of the synonymous *duretque* heightens the passion of the prayer.

gentibus, probably not limited to German tribes but equivalent to *exterae gentes* (cp. *more gentico, A*. 6. 33, 3), though those on the European frontier are specially in mind. *Gentes* in the sense of foreign, barbarian peoples is used by Cic. *Phil.*

14, 32; *Bell. Hisp.* 17, 3; Lucan, 1. 93, etc. (Löfstedt, *Syntactica*, ii. 466).

quando, 'since', as often in Livy and occasionally in Cicero and Sallust.

urgentibus imperii fatis, 'while the destinies of the empire drive it on'. The phrase *urgentibus fatis* is common from Virgil's time (*Aen.* 2, 653 *fatoque urgenti*; 11, 587 *fatis urgetur acerbis*), e.g. Livy, 5. 22, 8 *iam fato quoque urgente*; 5. 36, 6 *iam urgentibus Romanam urbem fatis*; 22. 43, 9; Lucan, 10, 30 *fatis urgentibus actus*. Here Tacitus, like Livy in the second passage, might have said *urgentibus imperium fatis*, without altering the sense. In itself the phrase might be neutral: the goal towards which the empire is being driven might be either world-rule or destruction (or at least calamity). But the context leaves no room for doubt that the *fata* are, as usual, *acerba*: 'it has come to this, that Fortune can vouchsafe no greater boon than discord among our foes'. Tacitus, always conscious of the uncertainty of human things, is expressing anxiety lest the immense fabric of the Empire may not always be able to withstand the assaults of its foes; and in fact, when he penned these lines, Trajan was still absent from Rome, busily engaged in looking to the defences on the Rhine and Danube fronts. It is noteworthy that in all three passages where Livy uses the phrase he is speaking of a threatening calamity and in two of them *iam* is used. This interpretation (well argued by Andresen in *Woch. kl. Phil.*, 1915, 755) is not in any way affected by the fact that the Druid prophecy, that the burning of the Capitol in A.D. 69 portended the approaching end of the Empire, is described as *superstitio vana*, which in fact it had proved to be (*H.* 4. 54). The suggestion *finem adesse imperio* is stated to have been one of the arguments used by the ringleaders in the Pisonian conspiracy in Nero's reign (*A.* 15. 50, 1). On this passage, cp. *Introd.*, p. xviii f., and (for the MSS. variations) *J. R. S.* xxvi. 274.

CHAPTER XXXIV

THE DULGUBNII, CHASUARII, AND FRISII

§ 1. **a tergo** can only mean on the south (or south-east), since the following *a fronte* means on the north (or north-west); but the statement is inaccurate (see below).

Dulgubnii, mentioned only here and in Ptolemy, 2. 11, 9. Their situation may probably have been between the Cherusci and Langobardi on the middle Aller and its tributary the Leine, which flows through Hanover. The name of the tribe, corrupted in the MSS. of Tacitus, is to be restored as *Dulgub-nii*, which is related to Ptolemy's *Dulgumnii* as *Cogidubnus* to *Cogidumnus, Dubnovellaunus* to *Dumnovellaunus*, etc.

Chasuarii. It has long been recognized that the name means 'dwellers on the Hase' (an eastern tributary of the Ems), just as Am(p)sivarii (who are not mentioned here, because they had been driven out of their home and partially exterminated; *A.* 13. 55–6) means 'dwellers on the (lower) Amisia' (Ems); cp. also Angrivarii (c. 33, 1). Consequently their district lay to the north of Osnabrück, behind that of the Chamavi.

claudunt: *cludunt* is written here by most MSS. but not in c. 43; nor is this form used elsewhere except in c. 45. It occurs twice in *Dial.* and once (apparently) in *H.* and *A.* As the *-au-* spelling is otherwise universal and is alone found in the Hersfeld MS., it is uniformly adopted in the text of this edition.

haud perinde memoratae, 'not much spoken of', 'not very notable'. For *perinde*, see note on c. 5, 4. This meaning is preferable to 'not so notable', since the Dulgubnii and Chasuarii were not famous. What tribes are meant is quite uncertain.

a fronte, to the north (or north-west). The *frons* is the boundary towards the sea, as in *H.* 4. 12 the *frons* of the Batavian 'island' is the side washed by the ocean. The whole sentence involves a geographical misconception, for *a tergo* was true only of the Dulgubnii in relation to the Angrivarii, while *a fronte* was true of the Frisii only in relation to the Chamavi.

Frisii. The oldest historical home of the Frisians, to which they have clung throughout the ages and which still bears their name (Friesland), was the coastal stretch of north-west Holland from the Old Rhine, the northern boundary of the Batavian 'island', to the Ems, where they bordered on the Ampsivarii until this tribe was driven out by the Chauci in A.D. 58 (*A.* 13. 55); their neighbours on the west were the Cannenefates (not mentioned in the *Germania*), who were closely related to the Batavi. The division into *maiores* and *minores* is also found in the case of the Bructeri (Strabo, 7. 1, 3 and Ptolemy) and of the Chauci. The boundary between them cannot be fixed: it may possibly have been the Yssel. The Frisii *minores* are generally identified, on the basis of Pliny, 4, 101, with the Frisiavones, who supplied an auxiliary cohort to the Roman army; but the identification is not certain, for a little later (§ 106) Pliny's text includes the Frisiavones among the Germanic tribes in Belgium (Tungri,

Sunuci, etc.), and this is thought by some to be supported (though the support is dubious) by a military diploma, *CIL.* vii. 1195. (Cp. Schmidt, ii. 74 ff.)

In 12 B.C. the Frisii were won over by Drusus and rendered valuable service to Rome until the arbitrary behaviour of tax officials drove them to revolt in A.D. 28 (*A.* 4. 72, 1). They were again reduced by Corbulo in A.D. 47 (*A.* 11. 19, 1), but they joined the revolt of Civilis (*H.* 4. 15; 79). Then they became again dependent on Rome (Dessau, 1461) and furnished troops to the Roman army as late as the third century (*cunei Frisiorum* in Britain, Dessau, 2635, 4761).

excipiunt, 'follow on, come next to'. In this topographical sense the verb is already used by Caes. *B. C.* 1. 66, 4 and often by the elder Pliny.

ex modo, 'according to the measure of'.

utraeque nationes for *utraque natio*: so with collective nouns in *A.* 13. 34, 5 and *H.* 2. 26, and not uncommonly of a pair of individuals.

praetexuntur, 'are bordered' (i.e. on the south); used in the same geographical sense by Pliny, *N. H.* 6, 112 (*montes*) *qui omnes eas gentes praetexunt*.

ambiunt, 'dwell around'.

insuper = *praeterea*, besides the Rhine bank. The lakes are those which were merged in the Zuyder Zee by a great inundation towards the end of the thirteenth century; they are mentioned in three passages of the *Annals* (1. 60, 3; 2. 8, 1; 13. 54, 2). The two largest of them formed the main part of the waterway engineered by Drusus in 12 B.C. from the Rhine to the ocean: these are the *duo praecipue lacus* of Pliny, *N.H.* 16, 5. One was Lake Flevo, which had an outlet to the sea, *Flevum ostium*, which Pliny calls the third mouth of the Rhine (4, 101); it is still recognizable as Vlie Strom between the islands of Vlieland and Terschelling. The other was a smaller lake which Drusus connected with Flevo when he constructed the *fossa Drusiana* (by canalizing the Vecht, which branches off from the Old Rhine at Utrecht). Pliny's description in his *German Wars* was probably Tacitus' source of information (Norden, pp. 298 ff.); with it is to be compared that of Mela, *Rhenus . . . iam non amnis sed ingens lacus, ubi campos implevit, Flevo dicitur, eiusdemque nominis insulam* (Schokland and Urk) *amplexus fit iterum artior iterumque fluvius emittitur* (3. 2, 24).

Romanis classibus (dative of agent), those of Drusus in B.C. 12, Tiberius in A.D. 5, and Germanicus in A.D. 15–16.

§ 2. Oceanum illa temptavimus, 'we have essayed, made trial of, the ocean in that quarter', i.e. ventured to explore it. Cp.

Sen. *Nat. Quaest.* 6. 23, 3 *omnia Oceano tenus vicit (Alexander)*, *ipsum quoque temptavit novis classibus.* Oceanus is personified, as in § 3. For *illa = ab illa parte*, cp. *H.* 3. 8; 5. 18; *A.* 2. 17, 6.

superesse adhuc, 'still remain to be explored'. Others explain 'still exist', but there appears to be no parallel in Tacitus for this use of *superesse* applied to things in the sense of *adhuc extare* (c. 3, 3).

Herculis columnas. The reference is no doubt to some natural feature resembling the 'Pillars of Hercules'(Abila and Calpe) in the Straits of Gibraltar. *Herculis columnae* also existed in the Black Sea (Servius on *Aen.* 11, 262). The German pillars of Hercules, if such actually existed, may have been the twin red and white rocks of Heligoland as they were before the latter was washed away by a great storm in 1721 (as Detlefsen suggested, Norden, p. 470). On the significance of *columnae*, see note on c. 3, 3 *(aram Ulixi consecratam)*.

in claritatem eius referre, 'to ascribe to (set down to the credit of) his renown'.

consensimus, we Romans.

§ 3. **Druso Germanico.** The brother of Tiberius is so called in *H.* 5. 19. The surname was not given till after his death, and was borne by his posterity. Suetonius describes him as the first Roman who sailed the North Sea *(Claud.* 1), and it is the daring of the first explorer that Tacitus is commemorating here (see below).

obstitit, here alone with the infinitive, like *prohibere* in *H.* 1. 62; *A.* 1. 69, 1; 4. 37, 4. The Ocean is conceived to resent the inquiry as an intrusion. The sentiment is similar to that of Pedo Albinovanus in his account of the voyage of Germanicus in A.D. 16 (Sen. *Suasor.* 1, 15):

> *Di revocant rerumque vetant cognoscere finem*
> *Mortales oculos: aliena quid aequora remis*
> *Et sacras violamus aquas divumque quietas*
> *Turbamus sedes ?*

With *in se inquiri* cp. Sen. *Nat. Q.* 3. 30, 7 *reiectus e nostris sedibus in sua secreta pelletur Oceanus.* For *simul atque = et . . . et* see c. 12, 3 ; 30, 1.

mox nemo temptavit, sc. *in Herculem inquirere,* as the following words indicate, not *Oceanum* (as above). The latter would make a surprising statement in view of the voyage made by the fleet of Tiberius in A.D. 5 *usque ad fines Cimbrorum,* in the words of Augustus (note on c. 1, 1), and of the voyages of Germanicus in A.D. 15 and 16. Hence various emendations of *Druso Germanico* have been suggested (see crit. note), but they are all unacceptable: the introduction of the name of Germanicus is inappropriate, as his voyages had no exploratory purpose.

sanctiusque ac reverentius, 'more in accordance with piety and reverence'. The closing epigram is perhaps ironical: another allusion to the greater enterprise of the Augustan age occurs in c. 41, 2. Cp. Horace's playful expostulation about travelling by sea as an instance of man's audacity: *audax omnia perpeti gens humana ruit per vetitum nefas* (*Carm.* 1. 3, 26).

actis, with reference to *adiit* and *magnificum*. *Credere de* is used elsewhere by Tacitus and occasionally by earlier authors, including Cicero.

CHAPTER XXXV
THE CHAUCI

§ 1. Hactenus . . . novimus, 'thus far we have learnt about Germany towards the west'. The emphasis is on *in occidentem*, as contrasted with *in septentrionem*; *novimus* is a true perfect. *Hactenus*, local, 'to this point'; cp. Mela, 3. 1, 11, *hactenus ad occidentem versa litora pertinent, deinde*, etc. The meaning can hardly be 'up to this point we have good knowledge of Germany towards the west', no indication being given that the districts about to be described were less known (though such was the fact).

in septentrionem . . . recedit, 'towards the north it falls back with a huge bend'. Cp. Mela, 3. 1, 8 *in illam partem quae recessit ingens flexus aperitur*. The reference is to the peninsula of Jutland, which was supposed to begin farther westward than it does and, after running north for some distance, to turn eastwards. The *flexus* is the *sinus* of c. 1, 1; 37, 1. All the MSS. read *redit*, which many editors retain, giving it the same meaning as *recedit*, but *redit* appears to be impossible without an indication of the starting-point, which is given in passages quoted as parallels: Verg. *G.* 3, 351 *quaque redit medium Rhodope porrecta sub axem*; Mela, 1. 9, 56 *tantum redeunte flexu quantum processerat*; Caes. *B. G.* 2. 8, 3 (*collis*) *paulatim ad planitiem redibat*, etc.

Chaucorum. The Chauci were one of the more important German tribes: Velleius, who served in Germany under Tiberius from A.D. 4, speaks of the large number and the fine physique of their fighting men (2, 106). They occupied the coastal region from the lower Ems to the Elbe, and were divided into *maiores* and *minores* (Pliny, 16, 2; *A.* 11. 19, 3), parted by the Weser, the former apparently (despite Ptolemy) on the west of that river (*A., l. c.*). They were won over by

Drusus in 12 B.C. and remained loyal to Rome until the revolt of the Frisii in A.D. 28. Later, despite Tacitus' eulogy, they made piratical descents on the Gallic coast in A.D. 41 (Suet. *Cl.* 24; Dio, 60. 8, 7) and 47 (*A*. 11. 18), and fought on the side of Civilis in the revolt of 69–70. Thereafter they perhaps forced their way up the Weser at the expense of the Angrivarii and the Cherusci (see below).

Tacitus had obviously little information about the Chauci and confines himself to their general qualities, which he idealizes at the expense of truth. He makes no use of Pliny's first-hand description of the dwellers on the extreme coast, who lived on hillocks or artificial platforms of earth, which were surrounded by the sea at high tide, gaining a miserable subsistence by fishing in the receding waters. Pliny had taken part in Corbulo's campaign in A.D. 47, and his account, preserved in *N. H.* 16, 2–4, was no doubt repeated in his *Bella Germaniae*, which Tacitus used freely not only for the *Germania* but also for his *Annals* and *Histories*. The name Chauci contains the German stem *hauh-*, 'high', used perhaps as a title of honour (*superiores*, § 4).

quamquam incipiat: for the subjunctive, see on c. 28, 5.

omnium . . . lateribus obtenditur, i.e. extends opposite, faces, the (eastern) frontiers of the tribes described in cc. 32–4. *Obtenditur* in the geographical sense, as in *Agr.* 10, 2. *Omnium* cannot be understood literally, since the Chauci did not border on the Usipi or Tencteri, but was perhaps intended to mean the group of tribes, taken as a whole, which were (wrongly) supposed to lie between the Frisii and the Chatti, viz. the Chamavi, Chasuarii, Angrivarii, and Dulgubnii.

donec . . . sinuetur, 'till it makes a bend (southwards) as far as the Chatti'. Such a southward extension of the Chauci is not elsewhere attested and may (as is usually believed) be based on a misapprehension or on exaggerated reports of recent changes in tribal boundaries in this part of Germany. If the statement be correct, we should have to suppose that the Chauci, who had shown an aggressive tendency in driving out the Ampsivarii (c. 34, 1, note), had pressed up the Weser at the expense of the Angrivarii (c. 33, 1) and driven them against the Bructeri, while the Chatti had extended their territory northwards after their victory over the Cherusci (c. 36, 2). So Schmidt, ii. 36. The Cherusci, however, may have been conceived to lie farther to the east than they actually did.

§ **2. sed et implent.** *et = etiam* (c. 15, 3, etc.). Velleius, 2, 106, says of them *iuventus infinita numero, immensa corporibus*.

nobilissimus, explained by what follows. *Quique = et talis ut.*

§ 3. **sine . . . impotentia,** 'without greed, without ungovernable passion', a periphrasis for non-existent negative adjectives. *Impotentia, ἀκράτεια,* 'ungovernableness'; often used in this sense, as is also *impotens* (e.g. c. 36, 1).

quieti secretique, 'peaceful and secluded': the Romans could only reach them through several other peoples or by sea; *situ locorum tutissima,* says Velleius (*l. c.*).

raptibus aut latrociniis, 'rapine or robbery', usually in inverse order and connected by *et* (but see c. 5, 2 note). The statement is contradicted by Tacitus himself in *A.* 11. 18 (see above); see also *A.* 13. 55.

§ 4. **praecipuum,** 'chief', see note on c. 6, 6.

quod, ut, etc., 'that it is not by aggression that they secure their superiority'. *Agere* in the sense of *se gerere* is common.

exercitus, plurimum, etc., 'an (organized) army, men and horses in abundance': *exercitus* (cp. c. 30, 2) as distinct from *arma, plurimum* in apposition to it. This, the reading of the MSS., may perhaps stand, though *plurimum ⟨enim⟩* would be an improvement. *Plurimum virorum* is a novel expression but has its analogy in *plus propinquorum* (c. 20, 5) and *plus feminarum* (*A.* 14. 36, 1) and in Livy's use of *multum, plus, nimium hostium* or *hominum* (23. 12, 17; 24. 40, 14; 23. 17, 12). Gudeman reads *plurimorum,* which is an easy emendation but produces a cacophony. It is perhaps not absolutely impossible to take *plurimum* as genitive plural, like *posterum* in *A.* 3. 72, 2 (as Gruber long ago suggested). *Exercitus* cannot be object of *poscat,* as *res poscit* is a regular formula (c. 44, 1, etc.); some editors cut out the word as a gloss on the following words (which needed no gloss) or as an interpolation to supply an object to *poscat* (which is improbable).

et quiescentibus, etc., 'and while they are at peace they have the same reputation (for strength as in war).

CHAPTER XXXVI

THE CHERUSCI AND FOSI

§ 1. **In latere,** 'on the flank', i.e. on the east; actually they lay north-east of the Chatti.

Cherusci. They dwelt on both sides of the middle Weser, from the Teutoburger Wald eastwards to the Elbe, extending northwards to the neighbourhood of Hanover (c. 33, 1, note) and southwards to the Harz: on the north-east they bordered on the Langobardi. Tacitus mentions them only in passing (as the opening words of the next chapter themselves show), and at the time of writing seems to have had inadequate knowledge about them: the cause to which he ascribes their downfall is wide of the mark. Under their leader Arminius the tribe attained prominence in the period A.D. 9–17, when they took a leading part in destroying the legions of Varus and so helping to bring about the abandonment of the Roman policy of conquering Germany, and in breaking up the confederacy of Suebic tribes under Maroboduus (c. 42). After Arminius' death in 21 the Cherusci were torn by internal feuds, which ended in the destruction of all their nobles save one, who had been brought up at Rome and whom they received as king in 47 (*A*. 11. 16). They were also weakened by constant warfare with the Chatti (*A*. 12. 28). About 85 their king Chariomerus, driven out by the Chatti on account of his Roman leanings, appealed to Domitian and received financial help but no military assistance (Dio, 67, 5). There the curtain falls on their fortunes.

marcentem, 'languorous', i.e. 'enervating', effect for cause: so *marcentia pocula*, Stat. *Silv*. 4. 6, 56.

diu, with *nutrierunt*, 'they have long cherished'. For the real causes of the downfall of the Cherusci, see note above.

inlacessiti, by their neighbours, as is clear from what follows, not by the Romans (with whom they had been at peace for 80 years). The verb is used only here and in *Agr*. 20, 3.

impotentes: see note on c. 35, 3. The reference is to the Chatti, while *validos* applies to the Chauci.

falso quiescas, 'devotion to peace is wrong-headed'. They should at least, like the Chauci (c. 35, 4), have kept up a strong defensive force.

modestia ac probitas, etc., 'moderation and righteousness are titles of the stronger', terms applied only to them, i.e. their conduct is so called by the outside world: might is right, *id in summa fortuna aequius quod validius* (*A*. 15. 1, 5). That the meaning is *modestus ac probus vocatur superior* is shown by the answering clause *qui olim boni aequique* (= *probi ac modesti*), sc. *vocati sunt*. For a similar use of *nomina*, cp. *sub nominibus honestis confessio vitiorum* (*A*. 2. 33, 6), *pluribus ipsa licentia placebat, ac tamen honesta nomina praetendebant* (*A*. 14. 21, 1), etc. The MSS. reading *nomine*, retained by a few and interpreted, on the analogy of *feminarum nomine* (c. 8, 1), etc., 'exist only for the sake of', as a claim of the stronger, is not tolerable Latin and does not suit the context. The correction *nomina superiori*, 'are mere names to the stronger', is likewise unsuitable to the following sentence.

§ 2. **ita**, 'and so'.

olim, sc. *vocati sunt* (cp. c. 2, 5), before their defeat.

Chattis victoribus. This victory perhaps took place about A.D. 85, when the Cheruscan king Chariomerus sought Roman aid against the Chatti (Dio, 67, 5, see above).

in sapientiam cessit, 'luck went for, was counted as, wisdom'. *Sapientia* is contrasted with *stulti*. The sentiment is a commonplace in Latin and Greek. The phrase is used by Sallust, *id illi in sapientiam cesserat* (*Hist.* frag. ii. 42 Maur.): cp. *cedere in solatium* (*H.* 2. 59), *in gloriam* (*A.* 14. 54, 5).

§ 3. **tracti,** 'dragged down'. This reading is supported by *quae . . . ruina sua traxit* (*H.* 3. 29), and *Agrippinae pernicies . . . Plancinam traxit* (*A.* 6. 26, 4). *Tacti*, the reading of most MSS., is used by Tacitus only in the sense of 'struck by lightning' (*de caelo*).

Fosi, only here mentioned. It has been thought that they lived on the Fuse, a small tributary of the Aller, on the northeast of the city of Hanover, but the identification of the two names is not accepted by philologists.

ex aequo, 'equally' (ἐξ ἴσου), as often in Tacitus and Livy: they shared equally in adversity, although in time of prosperity they had been in an inferior position (*minores*).

CHAPTER XXXVII

THE CIMBRI AND THE WARS OF ROME WITH THE GERMANS

Tacitus closes his description of West-German peoples with the Cimbri, a remnant of the formidable tribe which had been the first to come into conflict with Rome. But he tells us nothing about them. Their name serves merely as a peg on which to hang a historical survey of the long and stubborn resistance of Germany to Rome from the time of their invasion to his own day. Through it all runs one note, *tam diu Germania vincitur*: the German problem had not been solved—*urgentibus imperii fatis* (c. 33, 2). This excursus is a notable departure from the rule of limiting the historical element in the narrative to what was necessary for the comprehension of the ethnographical facts: indeed, for Tacitus the Germans had no history save in so far as they came into contact with Rome. Cp. *Introd.*, Sect. I.

§ 1. **Eundem . . . sinum,** the same projecting bend of land (cp. c. 1. 1; 29, 4), the *ingens flexus* of c. 35, 1 (the peninsula of Jutland). Tacitus had turned aside from the geographical order of mention to bring in the Cherusci, and now returns to it.

proximi Oceano, i.e. in the extreme north of the peninsula where it projects farthest into the ocean. The home of the Cimbri was discovered by Tiberius' fleet in A.D. 5 (Aug. *Res Gestae*, c. 26; Vell. 2, 106; Pliny, *N. H.* 2, 167 *Germaniam* *classe circumvecta ad Cimbrorum promunturium*). The name of the tribe survives in that of the Danish province of Himmerland, formerly called Himber-syssel (i.e. 'district'), in the north-east of the peninsula. (The change of the initial consonant from *H* to *C* was due to Gallic mediation.) Tacitus, however, had evidently no knowledge of the topography of the peninsula, being unaware that between the Cimbri, who are not reckoned as Suebi, and the mainland end of the peninsula lived most of the Nerthus-worshipping tribes enumerated in c. 40, 1, which he classes as Suebic. He apparently used two sources, neither of which brought the Cimbri and the Nerthus group into relation with each other, so that he was left entirely vague about the geographical position of the latter.

Cimbri, a remnant of the tribe which had not emigrated with the rest. They were discovered by the commander of Tiberius' fleet in A.D. 5 (see preceding note), and sent envoys to Rome to ask for the friendship of Augustus and the Roman people. Augustus (*l. c.*) says: *classis mea per Oceanum ab ostio Rheni ad solis orientis regionem usque ad fines Cimbrorum navigavit, quo neque terra neque mari quisquam Romanus ante id tempus adit, Cimbrique et Charydes et Semnones et eiusdem tractus alii Germanorum populi per legatos amicitiam meam et populi Romani petierunt.* The Charydes (Harudes) were their neighbours on the west coast south of the Limfiorden, where their name survived in medieval times in that of the district Har-(or Harthe-)syssel. Strabo (7. 2, 1) adds that the Cimbrian envoys presented to Augustus the tribe's most sacred cauldron (λέβης); such vessels were used to catch the blood flowing from the throats of slaughtered prisoners (*ibid.* § 3).

It is curious that Tacitus makes no mention of the Teutoni, the neighbours of the Cimbri in Jutland and their comrades in the great invasion, whom Marius destroyed in 102 B.C. at Aix in Provence; for though they had disappeared from history, their name, with that of the Cimbri, remained for centuries a name of terror and *Teutonicus* was a poetical synonym for *Germanicus* (Lucan, 1, 255 *furor Teutonicus*; Mart. 14, 26). The Cimbri and Teutoni were at first regarded as Celts, but their true nationality was recognized from Caesar's time (see *Introd.*, p. xxxviii f.). For the Teutoni in Jutland, cp. Mela 3, 32.

parva nunc civitas. They fade altogether out of subsequent history.

gloria is ablative (of respect), as the rhythm confirms (Norden, p. 220, n. 2). Cp. *regreditur ingens gloria* (*A.* 11. 10, 5).

lata vestigia, 'widespread traces', i.e. traces to be seen at various points over a wide area. *Manent* and *nunc quoque* imply that Tacitus is using the account of an eyewitness who had seen the remains more or less recently, and (as Norden has shown) this witness can hardly have been other than the elder Pliny, who served in Upper as well as in Lower Germany and whose *Natural History* abundantly attests his keen interest in archaeological remains, as in many other things.

utraque ripa. It is disputed whether this means 'both banks of the Rhine' (the course of which Tacitus' description has been following, as he himself states in c. 41, although the land of the Cimbri is far removed from the river) or 'on both sides of the river-boundary' of the empire (see note on c. 17, 2). The latter seems preferable, even though there is little doubt that it was the Rhine valley that his authority referred to (see next note).

castra ac spatia, equivalent to *castrorum spatia* (*H.* 4. 32), 'vast encampments', shows that more than one is meant. *Lata vestigia* makes it plain that the reference is not to one definite point of the bank, on both sides of which there were remains of *castra*, but to various places on both sides. The most probable view is that these *castra* were some of the many prehistoric forts (*Ringwälle*) to be found in the valley of the Rhine. They were mostly hill-forts of Celtic origin, but they were popularly attributed to the redoubtable Cimbri, just as 'Schwedenschanzen', which have nothing to do with the Swedes, are still pointed out in many parts of Germany. Norden's objection (p. 244) that the position and construction of these forts make them quite unsuitable for the role assigned them has no weight: all that was necessary was that they should be imposing enough to stir popular imagination. What particular forts were meant naturally cannot be said. Norden has withdrawn (p. 506) his suggestion that the *castra* lay on either side of the Rhine at Zurzach, anc. Tenedo, a little above the junction of the Aare, where the Cimbri probably crossed the river, and concedes that they may not have been on the upper Rhine. Yet they may have been there: prehistoric forts exist between the Lake of Constance and Bâle, some of them actually on the river, e.g. the Schwaben at Rheinau below Schaffhausen, where across a tongue of land formed by the Rhine runs a rampart of stones covered with earth, which stands 16–18 feet high (*Mitt. d. antiq. Ges. in Zürich*, 1853, pp. 179 ff.).

metiaris molem manusque gentis, 'one may gauge the mass, multitude, of the tribe and the (number of) hands at work': *moles* as in *A.* 2. 17, 8 *moles ruentium*, including men, women and children, *manus* of the able-bodied warriors, cp. *A.* 1. 61, 3, where the camp of Varus is said *trium legionum manus ostentare.*

exitus, 'emigration', here alone perhaps in this sense, though *exire* or *exire finibus* is commonly used of nations leaving their home.

fidem, 'the credibility': cp. c. 39, 1.

§ 2. sescentesimum et quadragesimum. The 640th year, reckoned by the Varronian era (which placed the foundation of Rome on April 21, 753 B.C.), was not quite completed when the first news of the Cimbrian invaders reached the capital (*audita sunt*) in the early spring of 113 B.C., the year of the consulship of Metellus and Carbo. The Cimbri had then made their way into Illyricum (Livy, *Epit.* 63, see § 5 below). The Varronian era is followed in *A.* 11. 11.

ex quo, sc. *anno.*

alterum . . . consulatum, i.e. the year A.D. 98, when Trajan was consul ordinarius for the second time with Nerva, who died on Jan. 25. The date is important as fixing the year of the composition and publication of the *Germania*.

ducenti ferme et decem, 'about', i.e. not quite, 210 years, reckoning to the beginning of the current year, for the first battle with the Cimbri took place in the spring of 113 B.C., while Trajan's second consulship began on Jan. 1, A.D. 98.

colliguntur, 'are counted, summed up'; so *centum et viginti anni . . . colliguntur (Dial.* 17, 3).

tam diu Germania vincitur, 'so long have we been conquering Germany', so long does the 'conquest' take: *vincitur* with ironical reference to the many triumphs celebrated, the repeated assumption of the title *Germanicus*, and Domitian's recent claim expressed in the coin legend *Germania capta*, the present tense implying that the conquest is as far off as ever. Cp. § 6 *triumphati magis quam victi.*

§ 3. medio . . . spatio, 'during this long period', within the space of it.

multa in vicem damna, sc. *fuerunt. In vicem* has the force of an attributive adjective (*mutua*): cp. *magnis in vicem usibus (Agr.* 24, 1), *multae in vicem clades (H.* 1. 65, 1).

Samnis, etc. In such enumerations Tacitus varies the wording, as here by change from singular to plural and from peoples to countries and back again. The most notable episode of the three Samnite wars of the later fourth and early third centuries B.C. was the disaster of the Caudine Forks in 321.

Poeni, in the Hannibalic War, which opened so disastrously for Rome.

Hispaniae, during the war with Hannibal and the revolts of the Lusitanians and Celtiberians (154-133 B.C.).

Galliae. As Caesar's campaigns are mentioned later, the reference is probably to older events, such as the battle of the Allia and the sack of Rome (390 B.C.), the defeat at Clusium in 225, etc.

saepius admonuere, 'have given us more frequent warnings, lessons', by inflicting severe defeats.

regno Arsacis, 'the Arsacid despotism'. Arsaces was the legendary founder of the kingdom of the Parthians, established in 248 B.C., and the name was borne as a title (like that of 'Caesar') by his descendants till their fall before the Sassanians in A.D. 226.

acrior, 'more energetic': cp. *acri* ('in full vigour') . . . *libertate* (*A.* 13. 50, 3); *vigor animi* . . . *acrior* (*A.* 3. 30, 5).

libertas. Even kingly governments in Germany were not such *regna* as those in the East (cp. c. 7, 1, etc.).

§ 4. Crassi, M. Crassus, the triumvir, who lost his army and his life at Carrhae in Mesopotamia in 53 B.C.

amisso et ipse Pacoro = (*Oriens*) *qui et ipse amisit,* 'which itself lost Pacŏrus'. *Et ipse* = *ipse quoque,* as in *Agr.* 25, 4 *diviso et ipse . . . exercitu incessit*; the pronoun is used of *Oriens* as if the Parthian monarch had himself been spoken of, and as if *amisso Pacoro* had been an active past participle in the nominative, with an accusative (καὶ αὐτὸς ἀπολέσας Πάκορον). Pacorus, son of the Parthian king Orodes, was defeated and slain by Ventidius in Syria, 38 B.C.

infra Ventidium deiectus, 'cast down beneath the feet of a Ventidius'. The antecedents of their victor are conceived as adding bitterness to their ultimate defeat. P. Ventidius Bassus, a Picenian, in early life led in triumph in the Social War, and forced to earn his living as a muleteer, had been advanced by Caesar, became consul in 43 B.C., and gained a triumph in 38 for driving the Parthians out of Syria and Asia Minor, which they had occupied as conquerors for nearly two years.

obiecerit, 'with what else can the East taunt us?'

§ 5. Carbone et Cassio. Cn. Papirius Carbo was heavily defeated by the Cimbri at Noreia in Carinthia in 113 B.C. (Livy, *Epit.* 63). Their next victory, that over M. Junius Silanus, the consul of 109 B.C., in the Rhone valley (Livy, *Epit.* 65), is omitted by Tacitus, who has wrongly substituted Aurelius Scaurus as one of the five commanders of consular armies. The disastrous defeat of L. Cassius Longinus, the consul of 107 B.C., which took place in the valley of the Garonne, was at the hands of the Helvetian Tigurini, who were allies of the Cimbri.

Scauro Aurelio. M. Aurelius Scaurus was consular legate of Mallius (see next note) commanding an advance-guard, which was destroyed before the main battle; he himself was taken prisoner and put to death (Livy, *Epit.* 67).

Servilio Caepione Maximoque Mallio. *Maximoque* is a very probable correction of the manuscript readings *Marcoque* and *Marco quoque*, which were due to the wrong expansion of an abbreviation. In 105 B.C. Cn. Mallius Maximus, consul of the year, and Q. Servilius Caepio, consul of the preceding year and then proconsul, were in command of two armies on the Rhone, but were prevented by jealousy from effectively co-operating, and their forces were cut to pieces in succession at Arausio (Orange). The Romans are said to have lost 80,000 soldiers and 40,000 camp-followers, and to have sustained a greater material and moral defeat than even that of Cannae.

quinque. The number is right, but for *Aurelio Scauro* we have to substitute *Iunio Silano* (see above).

simul, 'all together': the losses were spread over nine years, but they are regarded as incurred in one war, as happening 'at the same period'. Cp. Livy, 6. 4, 1 *Camillus . . . trium simul bellorum victor*; Quint. 10. 1, 76 *cum decem (oratores) simul . . . una aetas tulerit.*

populo Romano, from the Republic, in contrast to *Caesari.*

Varum, destroyed by the Cheruscans and Arminius in A.D. 9 (*A.* 1, 61, Vell. 2, 117–20, etc.).

Caesari, Augustus, as every Roman reader knew.

impune, 'without loss'.

in Italia, on the Raudian plain, near Vercellae, in 101 B.C. His colleague Catulus is not mentioned, nor is anything said of the defeat of the Teutons and Ambrones, who took part in the same movement, at Aquae Sextiae in Gaul, 102 B.C. The reason for these omissions was no doubt stylistic, to secure an exact balance to *divus Iulius in Gallia.*

in Gallia, alluding to his defeat of the German king Ariovistus in 58 B.C. (*B. G.* 1, 30–54), and his expulsion of the Usipetes and Tencteri in 55 B.C. (4, 1–15). His expeditions across the Rhine (4, 16–19; 6, 9 ff.) are omitted, and were really unimportant.

Drusus, the brother of Tiberius, 12–9 B.C. In these campaigns, carried out in pursuance of Augustus' plan of conquering Germany as far as the Elbe, he subdued a considerable territory and reached that river.

Nero, the name of the later emperor Tiberius before his adoption by Augustus. The nine campaigns which he claims

to have conducted in Germany (see *A*. 2. 26, 3) fall between
9 B.C. and A.D. 11.

Germanicus, the son of Drusus and adopted son of Tiberius:
his campaigns in A.D. 14–16 are fully related in *Ann*. 1 and
2. His successes were indecisive, and involved much Roman
loss (*nec impune*).

mox ingentes . . . versae. The reference is to the expedition of
the emperor Gaius to the Rhine in the autumn of A.D. 39.
Tacitus speaks similarly of the *Gaianarum expeditionum
ludibrium* (*H*. 4. 15, 3): cp. also *Agr*. 13, 4 *ingentes adversus
Germaniam conatus*. Suetonius speaks of a sham fight in which
the emperor's own German guard represented the enemy, and
of Gauls dressed up to represent German prisoners (*Cal*. 45, 47).
The second statement has its counterpart in the tale told of
Domitian (*Agr*. 39, 2), which was undoubtedly false. The
most recent interpretation of Gaius' military operations on
the Rhine sees in them mainly military manœuvres designed
to restore discipline and efficiency (Balsdon, *The Emperor
Gaius*, pp. 76 ff.). *In ludibrium versae*, 'became a laughing-
stock': cp. *A*. 12. 26, 2 *novercae officia in ludibrium vertebat*,
and *A*. 15. 19, 4.

§ 6. **otium,** sc. *fuit*. Tacitus does not think it worth while to
mention Corbulo's doings (*A*. 11. 18–20) and other slight
interventions (*A*. 12. 29; 13. 53–7).

discordiae nostrae, etc., during the year of the four emperors, A.D. 69. The rising headed by the Batavian Julius
Civilis broke out in the autumn of that year. He assumed
at first the character of a partisan of Vespasian, and then
threw off the mask. The fortress of the legions taken by him
(*expugnatis hibernis*) was that of Vetera (castra) near Xanten
on the lower Rhine. The organizers of a revolt of some important Gallic tribes, who aimed at the establishment of a
Gallic Empire (*imperium Galliarum*), made common cause
with him. The whole history of the rebellion is related in
Hist. 4 and 5.

adfectavere, 'aspired to the Gallic provinces'. The verb is
used by Tacitus only in the sense of 'seek to win'. Civilis
declined to recognize the 'Gallic Empire', the sovereignty
of which he intended to secure for himself: *fisus Germanorum
opibus et, si certandum adversus Gallos de possessione rerum*
('of power') *foret, inclutus fama et potior* (*H*. 4. 61).

pulsi, by Petilius Cerialis in A.D. 70. For the omission of
sunt, cp. *Agr*. 26, 3 *donec pulsi hostes*.

nam, with a common ellipsis of thought: '(I do not speak
of later reputed victories), for'. The variant *inde* is either
an arbitrary correction or an accidental repetition from

the beginning of the sentence (Robinson, *Germ.*, pp. 113, 313).

proximis temporibus, 'in recent times', under Domitian, whose expedition against the Chatti in A.D. 83 is elsewhere spoken of contemptuously (*Agr.* 39, 2; Dio, 67. 4, 1; Pliny, *Paneg.* 16) and deliberately underrated: see note on c. 29, 4.

triumphati. The use of this passive originates with Augustan poets (Verg. *Aen.* 6, 836; Hor. *Carm.* 3. 3, 43, etc.).

II. THE SUEBIC TRIBES OF THE EAST AND NORTH (CC. 38–46)

CHAPTER XXXVIII

GENERAL CHARACTERISTICS OF THE SUEBI

§ 1. **Nunc de Suebis dicendum**, an intentionally prosaic formula of return from the emotional heights of the historical retrospect to sober ethnographic narrative. *Suebi* was, as Tacitus says, a generic name, but here he gives it an abnormally wide extension, making it include all the tribes mentioned from this point onwards to the end of c. 45, i.e. all the German, or supposedly German, peoples of the east and north. That vast region is *Suebia* (c. 46, 1), and the Baltic Sea is *Suebicum mare* (c. 45, 2). This account is at variance with the statements of other ancient authors, including the authorities quoted in c. 2, 4, and with the general division of Germans into Ingaevones, Herminones, and Istaevones (*ibid.*), since the Suebi are made to include tribes belonging to the first two of these groups. The actual Suebi were the Semnones, Hermunduri, Marcomani, Quadi (in all probability identical with Caesar's Suebi), probably also the Naristi, and to the same stock belonged the Triboci, Vangiones, and Nemetes (c. 28, *Introd.*, p. xlv ff). Their original home was the Mark of Brandenburg round Berlin, between the middle Elbe and the Oder, which was still occupied in Tacitus' time by the Semnones, the parent stem, of which the other tribes were offshoots. The 'Suebi' of the *Germania* embrace all the German tribes which remained free when Augustus extended Roman rule to the Elbe, and this wide extension of the name is most simply explained as a survival from that time: the Suebic tribes bordering on Roman territory formed the core of the great empire of the Marcomanic king Maroboduus, and their name was extended to the non-Suebic tribes, such as the Langobardi and the Lugii (cc. 40, 43), which were incorporated into that empire, and to the tribes beyond them, in accordance with the process which is illustrated in the note to c. 2, 5. It is to be noted that in his later historical works Tacitus limits the name *Suebi* to the Marcomani and Quadi (specially striking is the contrast in *A*. 12. 29 between Suebi, Hermunduri and Lugii). The collective name still survives as Schwaben (Swabians), the designation of the people of Württemberg (see below on Semnones).

maiorem . . . partem, all beyond the Elbe and down to the Danube.

adhuc, probably best taken as 'further', 'besides', 'moreover', giving a second reason (see note on c. 10, 3) To give it the meaning 'to this day' would imply that specific names gradually gave way to generic, whereas the reverse was the case (though Tacitus may not have realized this).

in commune, 'generically', see note on c. 27, 3.

§ 2. **insigne,** 'a characteristic', as in c. 43, 6.

obliquare, 'to comb back the hair sideways and tie it in a knot below'. The description is elucidated by the monuments, which show that the knot was usually made on the right temple above the ear (see figs. 21–4). Seneca makes the hair-knot a characteristic of Germans generally (*de Ira*, 3. 26, 3; *Ep*. 124, 22; cp. Juvenal, 13, 165), Martial attributes it to the Sugambri (*Epigr. liber*, 3, 9), who were not 'Suebi', and monuments assign it to non-Suebic Germans. Tacitus himself goes on to modify substantially the statement which he makes here, and it is probable that the custom had once been common to many German tribes.

servis: German slaves generally had close cropped hair.

§ 3. **rarum** (= *usurpatum raro*, c. 31, 1), sc. *est*, 'the practice exists, but is rare, and confined to the period of youth'. What was really characteristic of the Suebi was its universality, among all free men and at every time of life. The causal ablatives *cognatione* and *imitatione* give reasons not for the practice being rare but for its existence elsewhere.

apud Suebos, etc., 'among the Suebi, till their heads are grey, the bristling hair is twisted back and is often knotted on the very crown of the head'. *Horrentes* is perhaps used proleptically, 'so that it bristles', as the result of being drawn backwards against the natural direction and made to stand on end: cp. Quint. 11. 3, 160 *capillos a fronte contra naturam retro agere, ut sit horror ille terribilis*; the word does not seem to denote merely 'unkempt', 'wild', 'shaggy'.

The meaning is clear, but the text is uncertain. The MSS. reading *apud Suebos usque ad canitiem horrentem capillum retro sequuntur* is plainly corrupt, for *apud Suebos* cannot be conjoined with an active verb which has *Suebi* as its subject (as Gudeman has rightly insisted), nor can *retro sequuntur* mean 'draw backward' with hand or comb. There are three possible ways of dealing with the crux. (1) The minimum of change would be to punctuate with a comma after *spatium* and a colon after *canitiem*, and to correct *retro seq.* to *retorquent* (cp. Mart. 6. 39, 6 *retorto crine*) or *retrorsum agunt* (on the analogy of Quint., *l. c.*). This requires the idea of *usurpatur* to be supplied from *rarum* with *usque ad canitiem*, with an explanatory asyndeton following; but the asyndeton is stylistically unsatisfactory, and it is not merely explanatory but adds a new fact. (2) *Horrentem capillum* may be emended (with Gudeman) to *horrentes capilli*, the corruption being due to the assimilation of *horrentes* to *canitiem*, which brought in its train the alteration of *capilli* to *capillum*—a common cause of error in MSS. But *retro sequuntur* cannot be retained and interpreted (with Gudeman) 'the hair runs backward, giving a dishevelled appearance' (*horrentes* proleptically): *sequuntur* has no object, and 'runs backward' is an unnatural expression to use of the hair being forced backwards. *Retorquentur* gives the sense required, and if it had been miscopied *retosquentur*, *retro sequuntur* might have been an infelicitous correction, as Frahm suggests (*Hermes*, 69, p. 439); a parallel is furnished by *oppugnase* for *oppugnare* in the Hersfeld codex, *Agr.* 25, 3. (3) Andresen has suggested a lacuna after *Suebos*, to be filled up on the model of *in consensum vertit* (c. 31, 1) and followed by *nam* (*Jahresb. phil. Ver. zu Berlin*, 48, 1922, p. 61). But after what has been already said *in consensum* would need no explanation by a *nam*-clause, and *nam* would be used unnaturally to introduce what is in fact an amplification of the previous description.

in ipso vertice. Some MSS. read *in ipso solo v.*, while others have *solo* as a variant or omit it. *Solo* is not wanted, as it is very unlikely that the hair was ever knotted both at the side of the head and on the top: it probably arose from a dittography of the second syllable of *ipso*.

§ 4. principes, etc., 'their chief men adorn their heads (sc. *verticem*) yet more elaborately', in the manner explained by *in altitudinem*, etc. The allusion is probably to the custom of arranging the hair in twisted tufts resembling horns or plumes: Juvenal, 13, 165 *caesariem . . . madido torquentem cornua cirro*. These peaked tufts were formed with the aid of a greasy soap, described by Pliny as made *ex sebo et cincre . . . apud Germanos maiore in usu viris quam feminis* (*N. H.* 28, 191). A fashion of this sort is shown in fig. 25. A still more elaborate head-dress is described by Sil. Ital. 5, 134 *cui vertice surgens triplex crista iubas effundit crine Suebo*. Cp. Ammian's description of king Chnodomar at the battle of Strassburg, *cuius vertici flammeus torulus* ('a flame-coloured tuft') *aptabatur* (16. 12, 24). The following words refer to the *principes* only; the simple knot of ordinary men being too small for any imposing effect.

ea cura formae, 'in this point they care for their personal appearance'.

innoxia, 'harmless', explained by the following words.

neque enim ut, etc., 'for it is not to make love or to inspire it that they adorn themselves, but for the eyes of their foes, dressing their hair when about to go to battle in such a way as to make themselves look taller and terrific'.

ut . . . amenturve = *feminarum oculis* and is balanced by *hostium oculis*. They adorn themselves for the eyes of their enemies (for *primi in omnibus proeliis oculi vincuntur*, c. 43, 5), not (as Romans) for those of a lover or mistress.

in altitudinem, etc., 'but to add to their height and strike terror'. The asyndeton is adversative, and the preposition expresses result, as in c. 24, 2, etc. *Et terrorem* is explanatory.

compti [ut]. The balance between *hostium oculis* and *ut . . . amenturve* requires *compti* to be taken with the preceding words *in altitudinem*, etc. *Ut* seems therefore to be an intrusion. If it be retained, it must be taken with *compti* in some such sense as 'as seems to them suitable (for the eyes of their foes)', but it can hardly bear this meaning, and the construction overlooks the balance of the sentence. The latter objection applies also to the conjecture *comptius*, which should follow *oculis* (*comptius ornantur* being common to both clauses); moreover, *comptius ornantur* is tautological.

CHAPTER XXXIX

THE SEMNONES

§ 1. Semnones (with long *o* in Strabo, but short in Dio and Ptolemy). They are first mentioned in connexion with Tiberius' campaign in A.D. 5 (Velleius, 2, 106-7), after which they sent envoys to seek the friendship of Rome (*Res. Gest.* c. 26, quoted on c. 37, 1). Their territory lay between the middle Elbe and the Oder, in Brandenburg and Lausitz. They were one of the tribes which formed the confederacy of Maroboduus, but revolted from him in A.D. 17 (*A.* 2. 45). They are mentioned again under Domitian when their king Masyus, accompanied by the prophetess Ganna, paid court to him in Rome (Dio, 67. 5, 3), and are last heard of under their old name about A.D. 179 in the time of the Marcomanic war (*id.* 71. 20, 2). In the third century they migrated south-west into the region between the Main and the upper Danube, where they appear under the new name of Alamanni. From them are descended the Swabians of Württemberg.

memorant: the subject is general, the authorities whom Tacitus is following, as in c. 3, 1; 43, 4. The verb is used by Tacitus most frequently of literary statements. The variant reading *vetustissimos se*, which would make *Semnones* the subject of *memorant*, has suggested that the source of information was the embassy which visited Domitian in A.D. 91-2 (see above). But *se* was probably a correction of *seu*, given by other MSS.; this may well have been an old misreading of *Sueu(orum)*, which retained a place in the margin after the true reading had been restored and then became incorporated in the text (Robinson, *Germ.*, p. 99). What the Semnones believed about themselves is stated at the end of the chapter, where it is said that they based their pre-eminence on their large numbers, not on *religio*.

fides, 'credibility', the belief in their antiquity: cp. c. 3, 4; 37, 1.

religione, 'a religious institution', 'rite', equivalent to *ritus* in the next sentence. The fact that this worship was held in their territory confirms the tradition of their antiquity.

§ 2. **stato tempore,** 'at a fixed time' (cp. *certis diebus*, c. 9, 1), perhaps in what was later called the holy week at the end of September and beginning of October (Müllenh. iv. 459).

silvam, possibly the Spreewald, Ptolemy's Σημανὰ ὕλη. On such sacred groves, cp. c. 9, 3 with the note.

auguriis, etc., 'hallowed by the auguries (dedicatory rites) of forefathers and by ancient awe'. The *silva* is *augurata*, consecrated after taking auguries: cp. *in augurato templo*, Cic. *Vatin.* 24; Livy, 8. 5, 8. Tacitus slips into a hexameter which shows reminiscences of Virgil (*tectum . . . horrendum silvis et religione parentum*, Aen. 7, 172; *religione sacrae et saevi formidine Martis*, 7, 608; *lucus . . . religione patrum late sacer*, 8, 598). The hexameter, though more noteworthy for its rhythm than others found in Tacitus, is unlikely to have been anything but accidental, like the verses or parts of verses noticed in other authors, although some have taken it as a quotation from a poet, whom Lundström would identify with Ennius, holding that it is only necessary to alter *sacram* to *sacras* in order to recognize that this verse belonged to his seventh book and followed the famous lines *postquam discordia taetra belli ferratos postes portasque refregit* (*Eranos*, xv, 1915, pp. 21-4). Against this view, Norden, *Ennius und Vergilius*, p. 54.

eiusdem nominis, etc., the Suebi proper (see note on c. 38, 1). The received reading *omnes eiusdem sanguinis populi* would mean that representatives of all the Suebic tribes, as Tacitus conceived them, met together, which is incredible.

FIG. 25. Bronze figure of a German noble with hair gathered into horn-shaped tuft (*bracae* furnished with woollen shoes (?), hands outstretched in prayer).

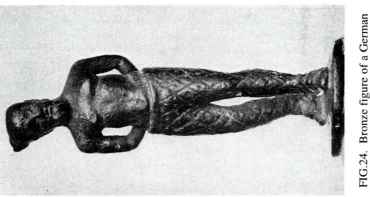

FIG.24. Bronze figure of a German with hands tied behind back, hair knotted over r. temple, close-fitting *bracae* (with diamond pattern).

FIG. 27. Relief from Tübingen, now in Stuttgart, showing Castor and Pollux at either end of the lower zone.

FIG. 28. The Nydam boat (4th cent. A.D.).

Such common worships were the only bond of union for tribal groups (cp. c. 40, 2 ; 43, 4 ; *A*. 1. 51, 2).

legationibus, 'by means of representatives'.

caeso, aoristic, like *vectam* in c. 40, 3.

publice, 'in the name of the whole group' (of *populi*).

barbari, not merely 'foreign', but 'barbarous', as in Cic. *Font*. 31 *illam immanem ac barbaram consuetudinem hominum immolandorum*.

primordia seems to mean simply 'the opening rite' of the religious ceremony: with the sacrifice of a man they begin in gruesome fashion the celebration of their barbarous ritual. Some interpret *primordia* as equivalent to *initia* in the sense of initiation into the sacred mysteries (cp. Norden, p. 127, n. 3), but no parallel is quoted, and *initia* means the sacred mysteries themselves which were the beginning of a new life. Others explain the meaning to be the 'establishment', 'foundation' of the cult (*horrenda* belonging in sense to *ritus*), which is far-fetched. For human sacrifices, cp. c. 9, 1, and note.

§ 3. **vinculo**, 'a cord' of some sort, a token of bondage, like the ring of c. 31, 3.

minor, sc. *deo*, 'an inferior', 'a subject': cp. c. 36, 3.

prae se ferens, 'outwardly acknowledging'.

attolli and **evolvuntur**, in middle sense: they must not get up, but roll themselves out.

§ 4. **eo . . . respicit, tamquam**, sc. *sint*, 'the whole superstition is based on the belief that', see note on c. 12, 2. The interpretation is that of Tacitus, not of the Semnones. Tacitus uses *superstitio* of all barbaric religions, in fact of all save Greek and Roman ; so of Christianity (*A*. 15. 44, 4), Judaism (*H*. 2. 4), and Druidism (*Agr*. 11, 4).

inde initia gentis, 'from this wood the tribe derives its origin', here is the cradle of the race, with reference to the legend of the divine ancestry of the race (c. 2, 3).

regnator omnium (neuter) **deus**, θεὸς παγκρατής or παντο-κράτωρ. From the fact that the later Swabians were entitled *Ziuwari* (*Cyuuari*), worshippers of Zīu or Tīu, and Augsburg was called *Ziesburg* (*Ciesburc*), it is generally inferred that the deity in question was Tīu (originally the equivalent of Juppiter-Zeus, later the war god), who had not yielded supremacy to Wodan among the conservative Suebi, as in western Germany (see notes on c. 9, 1) ; cp. Swabian *Ziestag* for *Dienstag*, Tuesday. But the correctness of the reading of the first two names is denied (J. Miedel, *Blätter f. d. bair. Gymnasialwesen*, 52, pp. 270 ff. ; Schütte, *Our Forefathers*, ii. 101). In any case Tacitus can hardly have thought of the god as other than Wodan (Mercurius), who was the supreme deity among the western Germans and to whom alone human sacrifices were regularly offered (c. 9).

adicit auctoritatem, 'gives them also prestige' (among the Suebi), i.e. makes them *nobilissimi*, as their religion shows them to be *vetustissimi*. Not 'adds to their prestige' (= *auget*), a sense which the context gives to the verb in *A*. 13. 46, 1.

centum pagis habitant. Caesar states the same fact of his Suebi, a single tribe (note on c. 38, 1)—adding that each *pagus* could put 2,000 men into the field, which is quite incredible (1. 37, 3; 4. 1, 4). It has been thought that the *pagus* was really the 'hundred', or that the statements of Caesar and Tacitus were based on a misunderstanding of reports which really referred to the 'hundreds' (so also the *centeni* of c. 6, 5 and 12, 3). But there is no evidence whatever of the existence of these political and territorial divisions till a very much later date: on this question see *Introd.*, p. lviii ff. Possibly the reports followed by Caesar and Tacitus used 'a hundred' in the sense of a very large number, a meaning which *centum* often bears. Possibly also *centum pagi* really applied not to the Semnones alone but to the whole group of Suebic tribes proper which sent representatives to the joint festival.

magno corpore: the Semnones considered themselves the leading tribe (*caput*) of the Suebi on the strength of their numbers. For the use of *corpus*, cp. *corpus ... Germaniae* (*H*. 4. 64), *unius populi corpus* (Livy, 1. 8, 1), etc.

CHAPTER XL

THE LANGOBARDI AND THE NERTHUS TRIBES

§ 1. The **Langobardi** were destined to play an important part in European history. According to their own tradition, recorded in the seventh century, their original home was a Scandinavian island (*Origo gentis L.* 1, Paul. Diaconus, *Hist. Lang.* 1, 1), which in all probability was Gotland; and the tradition is confirmed by archaeological and other evidence. They crossed the Baltic to the coast between the Oder and the Vistula, where they are said to have fought a successful battle with the Vandals, and then they moved westwards to the right bank of the lower Elbe, spreading later across the river. Their first contact with the Romans was in A.D. 5, when they were attacked by Tiberius and retired to the right bank of the river (Vell. 2, 106; Strabo, 7. 1, 3, p. 291), but after A.D. 9 they reoccupied their former territory, where their name survives in that of Bardowiek, older Bardauwich.

near Lüneburg in north-eastern Hanover. They were bordered
on west and south by the Chauci, Cherusci, and Semnones.
They joined the league of Maroboduus (c. 42, 2), but deserted
him in A.D. 17 to fight on the side of his enemy Arminius
(A. 2. 45, 1). According to their saga the name *Langobardi* was
substituted for that of *Vinnili* ('warriors') after the battle
with the Vandals when they placed their women in the line,
with their hair let down over their faces in the fashion of a
beard, to deceive the enemy about their strength. The occasion may be legendary, but the etymology of the name may
be correct (*fertur nominatos prolixa barba et numquam tonsa,*
Isidor. *Etymol.* 9. 2, 95): it may have been given them by
their Saxon neighbours, who wore short beards. The importance of their name in south Germany dates from the
middle of the fifth century, and their kingdom in Italy lasted
for two centuries from A.D. 568.

paucitas nobilitat, in contrast to the Semnones, whose *magnum corpus* made them *nobilissimi.* The Langobardi owed
their distinction to the fact that, though few, they had the
spirit to hold their own among more numerous peoples. They
afterwards increased their numbers by admitting slaves and
strangers.

valentissimis nationibus accords with the facts, but hardly
with the account which Tacitus has given of the peace-loving
Chauci and the decayed Cherusci.

proeliis et periclitando, alliterative. Velleius, who first mentions them, calls them *gens etiam Germana feritate ferocior*
(2. 106, 2).

Reudigni deinde, etc. Next to the Langobardi (*deinde,* as
in c. 42, 1) come the Reudigni and six other tribes, which
formed a religious union for the worship of the goddess
Nerthus. They are apparently enumerated in a geographical
order from the Elbe northwards but, as there is hardly room
for all of them in Schleswig-Holstein and Jutland, the last
two are perhaps to be placed in Mecklenburg. The Reudigni
must be located in Holstein, north and east of Hamburg; and,
as that is precisely where Ptolemy places the Saxons, whom
Tacitus does not mention, it is generally inferred that the
Reudigni were either the Saxons under another name or one
of a group of two or more tribes which were collectively called
Saxons. 'Saxons' indeed is not a very old name, being derived from the short one-edged sword (*sachs*), which came to
west Germany from the east (see note on c. 43, 6). The true
form of the name was Reudingi, for which Tacitus wrote
Reudigni, like Marsigni (c. 43) for Marsingi, under the influence of the Latin suffix -*ign*- (as in *Paeligni, privignus,*

etc.): for the common patronymic suffix -*ing*-, cp. note on Hermunduri (c. 41).

Aviones. The name means 'islanders', whence they are supposed to have lived in the North Frisian islands off the coast of Schleswig, and to have been descendants of a remnant of the Ambrones left behind when the main body joined the Cimbric migration. In Anglo-Saxon poetry (Widsith) they appear as Eówan.

The **Anglii** (double *i*, as in *Vandilii*, c. 2, 4), who invaded Britain in the fifth century with the Saxons and Jutes, dwelt in Schleswig, where they have left their name to the district of Angeln between Flensburg and the Schlei: it was from there that they crossed the sea to Britain (Bede, *Hist. Eccl.* I, 15). Ptolemy wrongly places them east of the Langobardi on the middle Elbe (2. 11, 8).

Varini, the *Warni* of later time, were evidently neighbours of the Angli and are subsequently found associated with them. If Tacitus is strictly following the geographical order, their home would lie to the north of the Angli, and with this agrees the occurrence of the name *Warnaes*, i.e. *Varna naes*, 'the promontory of the Varni', mod. Warnitz, for the north-east corner of Sundewitt. In the age of the migrations part of the tribe moved southwards in company with a section of the Angli to Thuringia, as is shown by the medieval names Werenofeld and Engilin for districts between the rivers Saale and Elster and between the Saale and Unstrut, as well as by the title of a ninth-century code *Lex Angliorum et Werinorum, hoc est Thuringorum*. Their original home seems to have been in Scandinavia, where the name Warnaes is also found and whence a portion of the tribe migrated, probably by sea, to the east bank of the Oder: these are the Varinnae of Pliny, *N.H.* 4, 99, a tribe of the Vandili (see note on c. 2, 4). Some, however, connect the Varini of Tacitus with the river Warnow in Mecklenburg on the basis of the evidence of Ptolemy and Procopius (Chadwick, *Origin of the Eng. Nation*, pp. 108 ff., 199; Much, *Germ.*, p. 348).

Eudōses, the same tribe as the Eudusii who furnished a contingent to the army of Ariovistus (according to the generally accepted emendation of Zeuss based on Orosius, 6. 7, 7, who reproduced *B.G.* I, 51). They lived in south Jutland, where their neighbours were the Harudes (Charydes, *Res Gestae*, c. 26, see note on c. 37, 1), who also furnished a contingent. The name of the latter survived in the medieval district Harthe-syssel between Limfjord and the Ringkjöbing-fjord: the Eudoses appear therefore to have dwelt on the east of them, though Ptolemy, 2. 11, 7 (who calls them Fundusii, misreading a Latin source) reverses the position. Their name is connected with that of the Jutes (*Iuti* or *Iutae* in Bede) through the intermediate forms Eutii, Eutiones, which are found in Frankish sources (Chadwick, pp. 106 ff.; Schmidt, *op. cit.*, ii. 25; Much, p. 349).

Suarines et Nuitones. Of these tribes nothing is known: even their names are doubtful. The former (for which there is a variant Suardones with poor MSS. authority) is explained by some as Su-Varines (*su = bene*), which would imply a relation to the Varini analogous to that of Su-gambri to Gambrivii (note on c. 2, 4). The name Nuit(h)ones is corrupt, for *ui* is an impossible combination in German unless *u* stands for *w*, in which case it must be preceded by *H*. Huitones is explicable as 'the White' (Much). There is hardly room for these two tribes in north Jutland, where a remnant of the Cimbri still survived, and some would place them on the Mecklenburg coast: Chadwick suggests that the name of Suarines may survive in the modern Schwerin (med. Lat. *Swerinum*).

fluminibus . . . muniuntur, short for 'next come the Reudigni, etc., who are protected'. The phrase is merely an antithesis to *proeliis ac periclitando tuti*. Tacitus had evidently no definite knowledge of their position.

§ 2. nisi quod. We should have expected *in commune autem*. All the seven are united by this Ingaevonic worship.

Nerthum. From the (Roman) identification with *Terra mater*, Mother Earth, conceived as the source of all life and the giver of fertility, and from the features of her cult it is clear that Nerthus was a Nature goddess, comparable to the Greek Demeter (γῆ μήτηρ) and the Mother Goddess worshipped in Asia Minor under various names, above all as Cybele, the *magna mater, mater deum*, whose worship, introduced into Rome in 204 B.C. and spreading widely over the Roman provinces, gave new life to the cult of *Terra mater* (Lucr. 2, 657, etc.). Indeed, the two main features of the Nerthus cult, the procession of the goddess in a chariot drawn by cows and the ablution of her symbol and her chariot, so exactly reproduce the ritual of Cybele worship at Rome as to raise the suspicion of borrowing. But the procession (to fructify the fields and animal life) and the immersion (to produce rain by sympathetic magic) are features of other popular festivals of this type (cp. H. Graillot, *Le culte de Cybèle*, p. 136; Chadwick, *op. cit.*, ch. x, which gives a discussion of the Nerthus cult).

The name of the goddess is connected with Celtic *nerto- (Welsh *nerth*), 'power', and is philologically identical with that of the Norse god Njǫrdh, a god of fertility and prosperity, who ruled wind and waves for the benefit of fishermen and traders. Nerthus was also worshipped in Sweden, as place-names indicate, and she was probably his sister-consort; but her functions are those attributed to Njǫrdh's son Frey, the great god of Upsala, and to some extent to his sister Freyja, a goddess of love, whose worship displaced that of Njǫrdh in Sweden. Like Nerthus, Frey made journeys through the land in a wagon to spread his fructifying influence. In western Germany Frīja (Freyja, old Norse Frigg) appears as consort of Wodan (c. 9, 1), whose worship came to be amalgamated with that of Frey in Sweden; she was equated with Venus and gave her name to *dies Veneris*, which was translated *Frīatac*, mod. Germ. *Freitag*, English *Friday*.

intervenire, so used with the dative in *H*. 4. 85, 4.

invehi is not elsewhere followed by a dative of the person (here used to balance *rebus*). The *populi* were probably represented by delegates who went to the island for the festival (cp. c. 39, 2), which perhaps took place in spring, like that of Cybele (end of March), though Chadwick argues for a date in late autumn.

insula, not identifiable, though many guesses have been made, such as Alsen, off the east coast of Schleswig, or Zealand.

castum, probably not only 'untouched by the axe' (cp. Ovid,*Am.*3.1,1; Lucan, 3, 399) but generally free from human profanation.

vehiculum, no doubt similar to the cult wagon in La Tène style found in the Dejbjerg Moor in Jutland (fig. 26).

veste, 'a cloth'. There must have been a roofed building of some sort to protect the wagon against the weather.

sacerdoti: a male priest, probably regarded as united with the goddess in holy wedlock (the ἱερὸς γάμος of Greek cults). So the god Frey had a priestess who accompanied his chariot and was called his bride. It is plain from § 5 that during the ceremonies the slaves also touched the chariot.

§ 3. **penetrali,** 'the innermost shrine', the holy of holies, by which seems to be meant the covered chariot kept in the sacred precinct in the dark depths of the forest.

intellegit, 'he perceives the presence of the goddess', i.e. he can tell the moment of her entrance. How he could tell was known only to the priest; the approximate time at which the festival would take place must have been known to all.

bubus feminis, the usual expression for cows (instead of *vaccis*) in sacred formulae. The cows were a symbol of fertility.

FIG. 26. Cult Wagon from Dejbjerg in Jutland. National Museum, Copenhagen.

laeti, sc. *sunt*, as also with *festa.*

adventu hospitioque, 'by visiting them and becoming their guest': so *A*. 4. 74, 7 *quos non sermone, non visu dignatus erat*, elsewhere with an infinitive. Cp. c. 2, 1 *adventibus et hospitiis.*

§ 4. non bella ineunt, etc. At every festival reigned a truce of God, any breach of which was severely punished: cp. note on c. 44, 3 *arma clausa sub custode*, and c. 11, 4 note.

pax with other tribes, quies among themselves.

tunc tantum amata, i.e. at other times peace and quiet were disliked, the result of the warlike character of the people and their habit of always carrying arms (c. 13, 1; 22, 1).

conversatione, 'intercourse': cp. *intervenire rebus hominum* (§ 2).

templo: the holy precinct (τέμενος) in the wood is what is meant, for (apart from the fact that according to c. 9, 3 the Germans did not build temples) goddess and chariot would not be replaced under cover until after the ablution in the lake. It is generally supposed that here and in *A*. 1. 51, 2 (*templum Tamfanae*) the word bears its older and proper sense of a space marked off and consecrated; but in literature it had come to be used (incorrectly, Varro, *Ling. Lat.* 7, 10) as a synonym of *fanum* or *aedes sacra*, and as Tacitus everywhere else uses it in this sense, it is better to regard the word as applied in these two passages somewhat loosely to the precinct in a wood, furnished with an altar (consisting of a stone or a heap of stones) and surrounded by a fence or wall, which linguistic and archaeological evidence shows to have been the form of a German sanctuary (cp. Wilke, *Arch. Erl.*, p. 74 f.). Cp. *Introd.*, p. xxxvi.

§ 5. numen ipsum, probably some rude symbol or a fetish in the shape of a stone or a block of wood, but according to popular belief 'the divinity herself' (hence *si credere velis*). The Germans made no images of their deities (c. 9, 3 and note).

secreto lacu 'in a secluded lake', which lay within the *templum.*

abluitur, to purify the goddess from human contact was probably the reason Tacitus would have given. The *lavatio* of the image and chariot of Cybele took place on March 27. Purificatory washing or sprinkling of statues had a place in Roman ritual: cp. *A*. 15. 44, 1. The real purpose of the washing was to induce rain (see above).

quos . . . lacus haurit. This may have been not only to ensure secrecy (as in the case of the massacre of the prisoners who had dug the grave of Alaric in the bed of a diverted river, Jordanes, *Getica*, 30, 158), but as an expiatory sacrifice.

arcanus, etc., 'hence a mysterious fear and pious ignorance concerning the nature of that which', etc. The noun *ignorantia* takes the construction of a verb.

illud, what is inside the chariot.

CHAPTER XLI

THE HERMUNDURI

§ 1. **Et haec,** etc. Tacitus passes to those Suebic tribes which were nearer and better known to the Romans.

secretiora Germaniae, 'the more secluded, remoter, parts of Germany'.

quo modo ... **sic** for *ut* ... *sic* is often used by Tacitus; here *ut* has immediately preceded.

propior, to the Romans.

paulo ante, viz. in cc. 28–34. With *Rhenum* sc. *secutus sum* from *sequar*, cp. c. 2, 5.

Hermundurorum. The Hermundŭri ('Ερμόνδοροι in Strabo, 'Ερμούνδουροι in Dio) extended from the region of Regensburg on the Danube northwards through Franconia into Thuringia. On north-west and north their neighbours were the Chatti, the Cherusci, and the Semnones. The southern Hermunduri owed their lands to L. Domitius Ahenobarbus, who in the course of a march from the Danube to the Elbe between 7 and 2 B.C. found a portion of the tribe wandering about in search of a new home and settled them in the territory recently evacuated by the Marcomani (c. 42, 1; *Introd.*, p. xlviii), thereby winning their goodwill for Rome and bringing them into friendly relations with the Empire (Dio, 55. 10ᵃ, 2). It is suggested that their territory included the strip of country between the Danube, east of Regensburg, and the source of the river Moldau (cp. Hist. Aug. *Vita Marci*, 22, 1; 27, 10; Gnirs, *Röm. Schutzbezirke an d. oberen Donau*, p. 4); but this is improbable. The western boundary of the tribe is uncertain. The only evidence is the account in *A.* 13. 57 of a successful battle which they fought with the Chatti in A.D. 58 for the possession of salt springs, which are usually supposed to be those of Salzungen on the river Werra (or of Kissingen on the Frankish Saale). A recent view which would place them at Franzensbad near Eger in the north-western corner of Bohemia (Gnirs, *l. c.*) is not tenable.

In A.D. 5 the northern section of the tribe seems to have retreated before the advance of Tiberius across the Elbe, which according to Velleius (2, 106) then formed their western boundary (*qui Semnonum Hermundurorumque fines praeterfluit*; cp. Strabo, 7. 1, 3). The southern section remained friendly to Rome till the later second centu·*r*, despite the part they played in A.D. 51 in deposing the unpopular Vannius, whom the younger Drusus had installed as king of the Danubian Suebi (*A*. 12. 29 f., see note on the Quadi, c. 42, 1). In the great Marcomanic war in the reign of M. Aurelius they joined Rome's enemies. Thereafter nothing more is heard of the tribe till it reappears in the fifth century under the name of Thuringi (*Düringe*), which is generally recognized as another form of the old name, with the same stem *dura*, 'bold', and the patronymic suffix -*ing* instead of the intensive prefix *ermun* (*ermin*), 'great', which appears as a stem in Herminones (c. 2, 3). From the Thuringi are descended the modern Thuringians.

non in ripa . . . sed (= *non solum . . . sed etiam*), not merely on the Danube bank but *penitus*, 'far within the frontier'.

in splendidissima . . . colonia. It is plain that Augusta Vindelicum (Augsburg) is meant, but it was not a *colonia*. Founded by Drusus after the conquest of Raetia (15 B.C.), the town was raised to the rank of *municipium* by Hadrian, as the titles *Aelia Augusta* and *municipium Aelium Augustum* in inscriptions show. The date of its foundation is given by a scholion on Hor. *Carm*. 4. 4, 17 *his devictis* (sc. *Raetis et Vindelicis*) *facta est civitas Augusta Vindelica apud Raetos*.

§ 2. **passim sine custode**, 'everywhere (instead of at stated points only) and without a guard set over them'. *Passim* might mean 'in large numbers', a sense which it bears in Tacitus (e.g. *A*. 14. 15, 1; 15. 46, 3; 57, 4, etc.); but this meaning does not suit the context. The Hermunduri enjoyed a privilege denied to the Rhine Germans, who were not allowed to cross the river except under strict supervision. In A.D. 70 the Tencteri complained to the people of Cologne that they could not have dealings with them except 'unarmed and almost stripped, under guard, and under payment of dues' (*H*. 4. 64). When Tacitus wrote, the Raetian section of the Danube had long ceased to be an open frontier. The military occupation of the southern bank, begun by Claudius, had been completed by Vespasian and Titus; and Domitian had advanced the frontier well to the north of the river and secured it by forts. Hence it has been argued that the statement made by Tacitus was taken from an older source (perhaps Pliny), which referred to the period before the river crossings were controlled (Barthel, *R.-G. Komm. Bericht*, vi, 1913, p. 167; approved by Fabricius, Pauly-Wissowa, xiii, 606, and Norden, *op. cit.*, p. 274 ff.). It should, however, be remembered that the frontier was an open one from the river Altmühl, west of Regensburg, as far as Pannonia, a distance of about 250 miles—a gap in the military defence of the Danube which can only be explained by the dependent relationship of the tribes on the northern bank of the river, viz. the southern Hermunduri and the Suebi of the kingdom of Vannius.

cum, 'whereas' (as in c. 36, 3).

ceteris gentibus, those of free Germany. Cp. note on c. 33, 2.

non concupiscentibus, 'without their hankering after them', in the way of plunder, as Germans generally would.

Albis. The Elbe rises in north-eastern Bohemia, which was certainly not within the territory of the Hermunduri (see c. 42, 1). It is usually supposed that the Elbe is here confounded with its tributary, the Thuringian Saale, a confusion which may be involved in Vell. 2, 106 and Dio, 55. 10ᵃ, 2 (referred to above) and also in *A*. 4. 44, 3. Another (improbable) suggestion is that Tacitus' authority took the point where the Elbe emerges from the Bohemian mountains as its source. Tacitus' statement would need no correction if the territory of the Hermunduri extended to the source of the Moldau and if that river was taken to be the main arm of the Elbe, as Ptolemy apparently took it to be (Müller, p. 248; Gnirs, *op. cit.*). But it is improbable that the Hermunduri reached to the Moldau. Much (*Germ.*, p. 365) suggests that the statement is an anachronism dating back to the time of Domitius Ahenobarbus, when the tribe still dwelt east of the Elbe on the north-eastern edge of Bohemia.

notum, known by exploration. Tacitus refers to the expedition of Drusus in B.C. 9, and those of Tiberius in A.D. 4, 5 (see on c. 1, 1; 34, 1), and of L. Domitius between 7 and 2 B.C. (*A*. 4. 44, 3). It had been the plan of Augustus to make the Elbe the frontier, but the effort was abandoned after the destruction of Varus in A.D. 9.

auditur, 'known by hearsay'. The name of the Elbe evokes a sigh over the failure of a great scheme, but Tacitus would not have favoured a forward policy in Germany.

CHAPTER XLII

THE NARISTI, MARCOMANI, AND QUADI

§ 1. **Naristi.** The position assigned to them by Tacitus places them in the Oberpfalz, on the west of the Bohemian Forest. That they were a section of the Marcomani which remained behind when the rest of the tribe migrated to Bohemia, is a conjecture devoid of proof. The only historical fact known about them is that they took part in the great Marcomanic wars of the second century (Hist. Aug., *Vita Marci*, 22, 1). The form Naristi (Naristae in Dio, 71, 21), philologically explicable as 'the most manly, warlike', is confirmed by *CIL*. iii. 4500; but there is a variant Varisti(-ae), found in Hist. Aug., *l. c.*, and Ptolemy, which also has an etymological meaning, 'the most prudent', and is regarded by some as an alternative name of the same people.

Marcomani et Quadi. *Marcomani* is the earlier spelling both in Latin and in Greek writers, while after the first century *Marcomanni*, already used by Velleius, is the more common and is philologically more correct (Ger. *mann*). The Roman pronunciation was apparently *Marcómăni*, as the short *a* in Stat. *Silv.* 3. 3, 170 and the spelling *Marcommani* in Strabo (7. 1, 3), Dessau, 2747, etc., indicate. The Marcomani are first mentioned by Caesar as furnishing a contingent to the army of Ariovistus (*B. G.* 1. 51, 2). They were one of the Suebic tribes, perhaps the most westerly of them, which towards the beginning of the first century B.C. broke through the wooded mountain girdle of northern Germany (Hercynian Forest) and flooded the region of the Main and Rhine (see *Introd.*, p . xlv). They settled on the middle and upper Main, in Franconia, extending southwards to the Danube. Their name was originally merely an appellative, meaning 'the men of the Mark', i.e. the unoccupied march or borderland separating them from the Celts (cp. Caes. *B. G.* 6, 23); it was probably borne by them before their arrival on the Main. Soon after their defeat by Drusus in 9 B.C. they migrated under the leadership of Maroboduus to Bohemia, where he made them the nucleus of a great empire, which was a cause of alarm to Rome (see § 2).

With them were closely associated the **Quadi,** who in all probability were identical with Caesar's Suebi. They migrated eastwards with the Marcomani and settled beside them in Moravia. They are first mentioned in A.D. 19, when Tiberius planted the followers of the exiled Marcomanic kings, Maroboduus and Catualda, on the left bank of the Danube west of the river March and placed them under the rule of a Quadian prince, Vannius, who appears to have become king of the Quadi (or of the Marcomani and Quadi: Mommsen, *Röm. Gesch.* v. 196, E. T. *R. Prov.* 1, 215) and to have amalgamated the two states (*A.* 2. 63). From this time both Quadi and Marcomani passed into Roman clientship and remained in it, despite Domitian's campaigns, until the wars of A.D. 166-80, when they joined with other tribes in invading the Danubian provinces and even Italy itself—the first of the great German offensives against the Empire.

agunt, 'dwell', as in c. 43, 3, etc.

praecipua (see c. 6, 6), sc. *est*, as also with *virtute parta*.

pulsis olim Boiis. It is usually supposed either that Tacitus made a mistake here, since the Boii appear to have been driven out long before the immigration of the Marcomani (see on c. 28, 2), or that the Marcomani had helped in the expulsion of the Boii (*c.* 60 B.C.) but did not claim their land till half a century later—a view most improbable in itself and hardly consistent with the fact that they were then supporting Ariovistus in Gaul. The most probable explanation is that the exodus of *c.* 60 B.C. was only partial and that *c.* 8 B.C. the Marcomani found Boii still in occupation of Bohemia. Cp. Franke in Pauly-Wissowa, xiv. 1611; Kahrstedt, *Gött. Nachr.*, 1933, p. 266 f.

nec ... degenerant, 'do not fall below them' in prowess.

eaque ... velut frons, 'these tribes are as it were the front presented by Germany' to the Romans. *Frons* in contrast to *terga claudunt* (c. 43, 1), but coloured by the military sense: these warlike tribes confront the Empire.

praecingitur, 'it (sc. Germany) is girdled', a correction of the MSS. *peragitur*, which several editors retain, supplying *frons* as subject and translating 'so far as it is formed by the Danube'. *Frons peragitur* would thus be the passive of *frontem agit* (c. 44, 1), strengthened by *per*. But it is the tribes, not the Danube, that form the *frons*, and elsewhere in Tacitus *peragere* means 'to carry through to the end', as opposed to *incipere*. Nor can the phrase be translated 'the front stretches along the Danube' (Gudeman). The emendation supposes a mis-reading of *pcīgitur* as *pagitur*.

§ 2. Marobodui. Established in Bohemia, this prince founded by war and negotiation a powerful empire such as Germany had never seen, capable of putting into the field a force of 70,000 foot and 4,000 horse (Vell. 2, 109). It reached from the Elbe to the Vistula, including such tribes as the Semnones, Langobardi and the large group of east German peoples called the Lugii (c. 43, 3). The Augustan policy of an Elbe frontier required the incorporation of Bohemia, and in A.D. 6 an attack on it on two fronts was planned, but was frustrated by the rebellion of Illyricum. But the king's attitude of neutrality in the fight of the western Germans for freedom led to a coalition against him, headed by Arminius and joined by the Semnones and Langobardi, which brought about his downfall; he fled to Tiberius, who kept him in honourable custody at

Ravenna, where he lived till A.D. 36 (Vell. 2, 108; *A*. 2. 45 f., 62 f.; Strabo, 7. 1, 3).

Tudri. The context shows that he was king of the Quadi, but nothing is known of him.

iam et, as in c. 15, 3; *et* means that their kings were sometimes, but not always, of foreign extraction.

externos, from other German peoples, opposed to *ex gente ipsorum*. *Patiuntur* implies that they were set up by Rome. The change of dynasties may have been a result of Domitian's campaign of A.D. 92 or of Nerva's *bellum Suebicum* in 97 (Dessau, 2720, 277; Pliny, *Paneg.* 8). In the second century the appointment of a king of the Quadi is celebrated by coins of Antoninus Pius with the legend *rex Quadis datus*.

vis et potentia, nearly synonyms, 'material force and ascendancy'.

ex auctoritate Romana, 'rest on Roman influence'.

armis nostris: no instance is recorded.

pecunia, cp. c. 15, 3.

nec minus valent, their kings are no less powerful than if helped by arms.

CHAPTER XLIII

EASTERN SUEBIC TRIBES

As the Romans never came into contact with the tribes mentioned in the last four chapters (except the Peucini-Bastarnae and two or three of the tribes bordering on the Marcomani and Quadi), Tacitus' information must have been derived from the reports of merchants engaged in the amber trade, who traversed the route from Carnuntum on the Danube through Poland to the mouth of the Vistula and the East Prussian Samland (see on c. 45, 2).

§ 1. **Retro,** really superfluous with *terga claudunt*, means 'to the north'; but the position of the Cotini and the Osi is misconceived: they were *in latere*. The forest and mountain tract which all these tribes are stated to have occupied is that between Bohemia and Silesia (the Riesengebirge and Sudeten), and the watershed between the Oder and some northern tributaries of the Danube, the Waag, Gran, and Eipel.

Marsigni, for Marsingi (see note on Reudigni, c. 40, 1). The name occurs nowhere else. As the other three tribes were neighbours of the Quadi, the Marsigni are to be placed behind, north or north-east, of the Marcomani. Their name points to a connexion with the Marsi (c. 2, 4) and suggests that they were a portion of that tribe which had migrated eastwards.

Cotini. The mention of iron mines in § 2 has led to the

location of this tribe on the upper Gran, anc. Granua, a
northern tributary of the Danube, where iron mines were
worked until recent times (Müllenhoff, ii. 324 ff., 334 f.). But
iron was also worked in the mountains north of the river
Thaya, a tributary of the March, anc. Marus (Gnirs, *op. cit.*,
p. 10), which accords with the position of the iron mines
mentioned by Ptolemy on the south of the Quadi (2. 11, 11)
and suits better the statement in § 2 about the payment of
tribute. They were a remnant of the Celtic population which
had remained behind when their compatriots retired before
the Germans (*Introd.*, p. xlviii). The correct form of the name is
assured by Dio, 71. 12, 3; *CIL.* vi. 32544 *g*, 32557; and Dessau,
8965, an inscription which shows that towards the end of
the first century B.C. a governor of Illyricum brought the
Cotini and other tribes in the adjoining Hungarian mountains
under Roman influence or control, with the object of securing
the middle Danube and preventing the extension of Maroboduus' empire towards the east (von Premerstein, *Jahreshefte*,
vii. 215 ff., xxviii. 140 ff.; Syme, *Class. Quart.* xxvii. 142 ff.).
In the Marcomanic war they promised but failed to give
assistance to the Romans (Dio, *l. c.*).

Osi. See c. 28, 3, where they are stated to dwell on the
German bank of the Danube opposite the Pannonian Aravisci,
to whom they were closely related; here they bordered on the
Iazyges. These facts point to the region of the river Eipel as
their home.

Buri. Ptolemy's description of their position 'under the
Asciburgian mountain (Gesenke) as far as the source of the
Vistula' (2. 11, 10) would place them in the Silesian borderland of Moravia. He calls them one of the Lugian group of
tribes (§ 3 below). They are mentioned in connexion with
Trajan's first Dacian War (Dio, 68. 8, 1) and the Marcomanic
war (*id.* 71, 18).

terga . . . claudunt, 'close in the rear', equivalent to *a
tergo claudunt* in c. 34, 1 and with the same military colouring
as *frons Germaniae*, with which it is contrasted.

cultu, 'mode of life', as in c. 46, 1.

referunt as in c. 20, 3, 'reproduce', 'are exactly like'.

Gallica, i.e. Celtic.

et quod . . . patiuntur, 'and the fact that they submit to',
co-ordinated with *lingua* as the subject of *arguit*.

§ 2. **partem tributorum**, i.e. the one (the Osi) were tributary to
the Sarmatae (the Iazyges noted on c. 1, 1), the other, the
Cotini, to the Quadi. The sentence is generally taken to mean
that tribute was exacted from the two tribes both by the
Sarmatae and by the Quadi, but it is very improbable that

each of these small tribes was subject to the two larger ones. Furneaux gave the right interpretation.

quo magis pudeat, 'more to their shame', because they have the material ready to hand which should make arms to win their freedom, and which was scarce in Germany (c. 6, 1).

ceterum, 'but mainly', 'but particularly': cp. *A*. 12. 59, 2.

montium [iugumque]. The latter word is usually bracketed as a repetition from the next sentence, probably rightly, as the *saltus et vertices* form the *iugum* of the mountains. *Vertices* is not to be taken quite literally, as the highest peaks were certainly uninhabited. *Insederunt,* from *insīdēre*.

§ 3. **Suebiam:** the name is found only in Tacitus, here and c. 46, 1, and in Dio, 55. 1, 2. Cp. *Suebicum mare*, c. 45, 2.

iugum, the mountain range separating Bohemia and Moravia from Silesia and that formed by the western Carpathians.

ultra quod, i.e. in Silesia and Poland as far as the Vistula.

agunt, as in c. 42, 1.

Lugiorum nomen, used like *nomen Latinum* or *nomen Germaniae* in *H*. 4. 64, in the sense of 'people', 'nation'. The correct form of the name is *Lugiorum* (Strabo, Ptolemy, *CIL*. xii. 4468), but the MSS. readings here, in c. 43, 6, and in *A*. 12. 29–30, may indicate that Tacitus wrote *Lygiorum*. Λύγιοι is the form used by Dio (67. 5, 2).

The name is a collective designation of the southern group of east Germans, which Tacitus distinguishes from the northern group consisting of the Goths, Rugii, and Lemovii (c. 43, 6). The region which the Lugii occupied is precisely that in which must be placed most of the tribes designated by the generic name of Vandals, the *Vandilii* of c. 2, 4, the *Vandili* of Pliny, 4, 99, who represent the east German tribes known to him (but include the Goths, whom Tacitus excludes from the Lugii, and the Burgundians, about whom Tacitus is strangely silent). 'Vandalic mountains' is the name given by Dio (55. 1, 3) to the range between Bohemia and Silesia, and the Silingi, who are attested as Vandals, have left their name, in Slavonic form, to Silesia (see note on c. 2, 4). Hence it is generally believed that *Lugii* and *Vandili* are designations of the same tribal group, the latter an extended ethnic name, the former probably a cult-title (note on § 4).

The Lugii are first mentioned as members of the confederacy of Maroboduus (Strabo, 7. 1, 3). In A.D. 50 the southern tribes took part with the Hermunduri in expelling the king of the Danubian Suebi (note on c. 41, 1), and about A.D. 91 they received support from Domitian against the

Marcomani and Quadi (Dio, 67. 5, 2). Thereafter the name *Vandali* begins to come into prominence, while nothing more is heard of the Lugii (save for the mention of a section of them, the Logiones or Longiones, with whom the emperor Probus fought successfully in A.D. 278).

plures = *complures.*

Harios. Of the individual Lugian tribes little or nothing is known. The Harii are probably identical with Pliny's Charini, a subdivision of the Vandili (*N. H.* 4, 99). Being the strongest tribe of the group (§ 5), they are presumably to be identified with what was subsequently the leading Vandal tribe, the Hasdingi, which derived its name from its ruling family (Cassiodor. *Var.* 9, 1; Jordanes, *Get.* 22, 113). This tribe is first mentioned in the Marcomanic War as invading Dacia and afterwards aiding M. Aurelius (Dio, 71, 12): they are the Vandali of Hist. Aug., *Vita Marci,* 17 and Eutropius, 8, 13. Their invasion of Dacia suggests that their home was in the southern part of the Lugian area. Harius occurs as the name of a *frumentarius* in an inscription of Rome (*CIL.* vi. 3052).

Helveconas, usually identified with the Aelvaeones of Ptolemy, 2. 11, 9 (Αἰλουαίωνες, where αι represents ε and a κ has fallen out), though he does not include them among the Lugii. He places them on the north of the Burgundians, who dwelt between the Oder and the Vistula in the region of the rivers Warthe and Netze (*ib.* 8–10) but are not mentioned by Tacitus: like other east German tribes, they were immigrants, their original home being the island of Bornholm, formerly called Borgundarholm.

Manimos. These correspond to Ptolemy's Omanoi, whom he describes as the southern neighbours of the Burgundians.

Helisios. The Harii and Nah(an)arvali are mentioned first and last because there is something definite to be recorded about them. If the other three are enumerated in geographical order, the Helisii would lie to the south of the Manimi; but some connect the name with the Polish town of Kalisz, Ptolemy's Καλισία, between Breslau and Warsaw.

Naharvalos (or *Nahanarvalos*). The sacred *lucus* of this tribe is generally believed to have been the wooded Zobtenberg in Silesia, south-south-east of Breslau, an isolated hill, visible from afar and destined to play an important part in popular religious belief, like such mountains in other lands. Hence the Naharvali are placed in Silesia and are considered to be the same people as the Silingi (note on Lugii, above), in whose territory the Zobtenberg certainly lay. The Tacitean name was perhaps a cult name (the ending -*vali* means 'mighty', 'powerful', but the first part is unexplained).

§ 4. **antiquae religionis,** 'of an ancient worship', 'with an ancient ritual'; *religioni* is supplied with *praesidet*. The worship was probably common to all these Lugian tribes, the grove being the centre of an amphictyony, like the sanctuaries of the Semnones, the Nerthus tribes, and the Marsi (c. 2, 4, note). One derivation of the name *Lugii* makes it mean 'comrades', connecting it with Gothic *liugan*, 'marry', and old Irish *lu(i)ge*, 'oath' (Schönfeld).

ostenditur, i.e. is pointed out, foreigners not being allowed to enter the *lucus*.

muliebri ornatu, a flowing robe and a long head-veil (cp. Girke, *Mannusbibl.* 24, p. 95). At Antimacheia in Cos, as Schwyzer has pointed out, the priest of Herakles wore what seemed to Greeks a female dress (Plut. *Quaest. Graec.* 58, cp. Paton-Hicks, *Inscr. of Cos*, p. xiii, 1). *Ornatus* refers to dress (as in *H.* 1. 30; 2, 20; etc.), not to the mode of wearing the hair, as Müllenhoff understood it, conjecturing that the priest was a member of the royal family of the Vandals, the Hasdingi, a name which he explained from old Norse as meaning 'men with women's hair': the later Frankish kings wore their hair long as a mark of their high nobility (*reges criniti*).

sed. The point of contrast seems to be that the gods are male.

interpretatione Romana, see note on c. 9, 1 (*Mercurium*).

Castorem Pollucemque. The worship of Twin Brethren, *Dioscuri*, who help warriors in battle and (among seafaring peoples) sailors in storms, was so widespread—from Gaul (Diod. 4. 56, 4) and Scandinavia to India— that it may justly be regarded as an old Indo-European cult. The Roman identification, evidently based simply on the fact *ut fratres venerantur*, is illustrated by a relief of much later date, now at Stuttgart (fig. 27), representing twelve Roman-German deities and showing the Dioscuri with their horses flanking the central group, Mercury (in double size), Mars on his right and Hercules on his left (Haug-Sixt, *Die röm. Inschriften u. Bildwerke Württembergs*, ed. 2, no. 331). The German Dioscuri had different names in different parts, *Hartunge, Harlunge*, etc., the latter derived from the name of the Harii.

memorant (cp. c. 3, 1; 39, 1), with indefinite subject, 'they', i.e. Roman traders.

ea vis numini, i.e. *ea* (*quae Castori Pollucique*), 'such is the character of their godhead': *vis* opposed to *nomen*.

Alcis is in all probability dative, balancing *numini*, as Roman readers would naturally take it to be. The dative with *nomen* is used in *A.* 1. 31, 2 (where, however, it is an

adjective) and probably in some other passages where the
name ends in the ambiguous -ae (Gerber-Greef, *Lex.*, s.v.
nomen, p. 850) ; so with *vocabulum* in c. 34, 1. In Tacitus the
nominative with *nomen* is far more common, and accordingly
some take *Alcis* as a Germanic nom. plur., but it is hardly
credible that Tacitus would have retained a plural ending in
-*īs*. The most probable explanation of the name connects it
with Gothic *alhs* ('sanctuary') and Lettish *elks* ('idol'), in
which case it would simply mean 'gods'.

peregrinae, i.e. non-German (c. 9, 2), by which is meant
Graeco-Roman: a foreign element would be shown by
images, etc.

ut fratres . . . ut iuvenes, i.e. though there are no images,
the fact that they are worshipped as youthful brothers justi-
fies the identification: the cult is in fact a counterpart of the
Roman.

§ 5. ceterum, returning after the digression to the tribe first
mentioned.

super, 'besides' (c. 30, 3).

truces, to be taken with *super vires*: fierce as they are by
nature, besides having a strength superior to other Lugians.

arte ac tempore, 'by the help of art and the choice of time',
referring to the black shields, etc., and the night attack.

lenocinantur, in a weakened sense, 'enhance', 'add to the
effect of'. So in *Dial.* 6, 5 (*lenocinatur voluptati*).

nigra, sc. *sunt*. tincta: the (naked) upper part of their
bodies is painted black for the occasion (probably with soot).

atras . . . noctes legunt: cp. *electa nox atra* (sc. *a Germanis*),
H. 5. 22, 1.

ipsaque formidine, etc., 'by the mere terrifying and
shadowy appearance of a spectral host' (apart from their
fighting qualities). For the force of *ipsa*, cp. c. 13, 4.

feralis exercitus is best taken with *umbra*, and in the sense
of 'an army of spectres', which is clearly the meaning conveyed by *infernum* below, and is supported by *feralibus . . .
tenebris*, 'the darkness of death', in *A.* 2. 31, 2. Some would
translate *feralis* 'funereal', considering (with Wölfflin) that a
new and distinctly stronger figure is introduced by *velut*, and
that *feralis exercitus* should mean 'an army like a funeral
procession': cp. *feralem introitum* (*H.* 1. 37, 5). But *feralis
exercitus* can only mean an army of ghosts, and *velut infernum* means that they look as if they had really come up
from the underworld (to drag their foes down with them).
The Harii got themselves up to resemble the host of the spirits
of the dead which rages through the air under the leadership
of Wodan (note on *Mercurius*, c. 9, 1), and from this custom

was derived their name, which is related to Gothic *harjis*, 'army', *the* army being the spectral host. The passage bears a certain resemblance to the description of the defence of Anglesey against the attack of Suetonius Paulinus, when the women *in modum Furiarum veste ferali . . . faces praeferebant, Druidaeque circum . . . novitate aspectus perculere militem* (*A*. 14. 30, 1).

nullo hostium, an instance of the frequent Tacitean and poetical quasi-partitive genitive, without any partitive idea. Cicero would have said *nullo hoste*.

velut infernum, 'as it were hellish', as though they had come from the underworld—a somewhat stronger expression than *feralis*. For *novum*, 'startling', cp. c. 31, 4.

nam primi, etc., a true statement, supported by Plut. *Mar.* 16 and Caes. *B. G.* 1. 39, 1, but not reconcilable with the dark nights. The terror was due to the invisibility of the attacking army.

§ **6. Gotōnes,** the Goths (Gothi) of later fame, lived at this time on the east of the lower Vistula, extending to the Pregel, probably the Guthalus of Pliny. According to their own tradition (Jordanes, *Get.* 4), they were immigrants from Scandinavia, and probably from Götaland in south Sweden, as the similarity of the archaeological remains in both regions shows, rather than from the island of Gotland, although its inhabitants also bore the Gothic name (Schmidt, *op. cit.*, i². 196). They are first mentioned in connexion with the fall of Maroboduus, but the fact that the usurper Catualda, who had been exiled by the king, found refuge among them (*A*. 2. 62) makes it doubtful whether they belonged to his confederacy. About the middle of the second century they expanded southwards at the expense of the Burgundians and the Lugian tribes, and the pressure of these on their neighbours set up a general tribal movement, the first effect of which was the Marcomanic war, the prelude to the invasions of the Empire. At the beginning of the third century they had reached the country between the Carpathians, the Don, and the Black Sea, and soon thereafter they began their attacks on Roman provinces.

regnantur (cp. c. 25, 3): the expression is concise (they live beyond the Lugii, and are ruled by kings).

iam, like *nondum*, marks a stage in a progressive series: limited monarchy in west Germany (c. 7, 1), less limited among the Gotones, absolute among the Suiones (c. 44, 2, where the adverb is similarly used). It may be rendered by 'here'. So in c. 45, 2 and 46, 6 it marks a stage reached in the description.

adductius, 'more strictly', a metaphor from a tightened rein: cp. *adductius . . . imperitabat* (*H.* 3. 7). The reason for the growth of a stricter form of monarchy in the east was that most of east Germany was conquered land, and conquest makes for the development of a strong central power.

nondum . . . libertatem, 'but not yet to such a degree as to overpower freedom', as in the case of the Suiones, c. 44, 2.

protinus ab, 'immediately bordering on', in contrast to *ipso in Oceano* below. By *Oceanus* is here meant the Baltic.

Rugii et Lemovii. The evidence of Tacitus combined with that of Ptolemy (2. 11, 7 and 12) places the Rugii on the west of the lower Vistula in Pomerania. Whether the island of Rügen derives its name from them or (as Zeuss believed) from a Slavonic tribe, the Rugiani, is uncertain. The Lemovii, nowhere else mentioned, dwelt between the Rugii and the Oder. The Rugi (Tacitus wrote double *i*, as in the case of the Angli and Vandili, c. 40; 2) were the most easterly tribe on the Baltic before the arrival of the Goths, who displaced them from their home in the country round the mouth of the Vistula (Jordanes, *Get.* 4). Jordanes calls them Ulmerugi, i.e. Holm-rugi, 'the island Rugi' of the delta of the river. There were Rugi also in south-west Norway in the region of Stavanger, where a people called Rygir and Holmrygir and a country named Rogaland are mentioned in old Norse literature. If the name Rugi is rightly explained as meaning Rye-eaters (or -growers), they would have acquired the name on the Baltic, for the Germans learnt the use of that cereal from their eastern neighbours, and in that case the Norwegian Rugi either immigrated from the Baltic or owed their name to the remigration of a part of the tribe to their original home. The Baltic Rugi are not heard of again till the fifth century, when they established a kingdom on the middle Danube which after a time became merged into the Ostrogothic empire.

insigne (cp. c. 38, 2), 'a characteristic'.

rotunda scuta: on the shapes of German shields, see on c. 6, 2. Round shields doubtless prevailed, but oblong shields are also found in Gothic graves.

breves gladii, short one-edged swords. These were primarily Gothic and Burgundian weapons, but they spread gradually over western Germany: see notes on c. 6, 1; 40, 1.

et . . . obsequium. The conjunction after an asyndeton introduces a characteristic of a different kind and of greater importance.

CHAPTER XLIV

THE SUIONES

§ 1. Suiŏnum. Suiones (i.e. Sviŏnes) was the ancient name of the Swedes, *Svéar* in Swedish (A.-S. *Swéon*). Tacitus conceives them as a group of tribes (*civitates*) ruled by a king whose power was absolute. Originally the Swedes were one of a number of tribes in the province of Uppland, but in the time of Tacitus they had evidently attained a predominant position in relation to their neighbours on the north, and perhaps the south, of Lake Mälar; the nature of this predominance is explained below. They are the only representatives of the Scandinavians known to Tacitus, but the common view that he uses their name as a collective name for all the Germanic peoples of the peninsula is unacceptable (cp. Kemp Malone, *Am. Journ. Phil.* 46, 1925, pp. 170 ff.). Scandinavia (*Scadinavia*) was known to Mela (3, 54) and to Pliny as a large island of unknown size—a belief that prevailed till the eighth century—lying in a part of the Ocean called *sinus Codanus* (the western part of the Baltic) and inhabited by the large tribe of Hilleviones (*N. H.* 4, 96). But the name was attached to the southern end of the peninsula, which is still called *Skåne* by the Swedes, and was apparently unknown to Tacitus, whose information about the more northerly Suiones was based on the reports of Romans trading between Carnuntum and the mouth of the Vistula: some of them had probably made the voyage from the Vistula to Upsala (see further below).

hinc, looking northwards from the coast of the Rugii and Lemovii. The expression *hinc ... valent* is concise, like *trans Lugios regnantur* above: next on this side come the Suiones, who have strong fleets.

ipso in Oceano: contrasted with *protinus ab Oceano,* 'in the midst of the Ocean'. Lake Mälar covered a larger area than it does to-day, and so the whole territory of the *civitates* seemed to be islands of an archipelago (G. Schütte, *Our Forefathers,* ii. 403). The reading *ipsae* for *ipso* would mean 'by themselves', but is merely due to attraction to *civitates.*

praeter, as in c. 2, 2, 'besides', 'not to mention'.

classibus valent. The reference is primarily to ships of war. Their sea-power is doubtless exaggerated, but they were seafaring and trading people, whose commercial connexions were mainly with the mouth of the Vistula (for the Baltic sea trade, *J. R. S.* xxvi. 196, n. 13). The existence of this trade route was no doubt the cause of Ptolemy's error in

placing Scandinavia (the largest of the four islands called
Σκανδίαι, the other three being the Danish islands) opposite
the mouth of the Vistula.

differt, from the Roman.

utrimque, used adjectivally with *prora*, like *cominus* in
c. 8, 1: 'a prow at either end presents a front always ready
for putting to land'. Cp. Verg. *Aen.* 5, 158 *iunctisque fronti-
bus*, 'with bows abreast'. Such vessels, known to the Greeks
as ἀμφίπρυμνοι or δίπρωροι, were in use among other
peoples, e.g. the pirate tribes of Pontus (*H.* 3. 47) and the
natives of Ceylon (Pliny, *N. H.* 6, 82), and still survive in the
coast districts of Norway. So Germanicus built ships fitted
with rudders at each end (*A.* 2. 6, 2). The object was to
avoid the necessity of turning them in narrow waters, *ne per
angustias alvei circumagi sit necesse*, as Pliny says. A large
boat of this form, belonging to the fourth century A.D., and
found in a peat bog at Nydam in Schleswig, is shown in fig. 28.

velis ministrant, abl. instr., 'work, manage them with
sails', a reminiscence of Verg. *Aen.* 6, 302; 10, 218. The
Nydam boat had no sails: it was propelled by fifteen pairs
of oars.

in ordinem, 'so as to form a regular row'. This final use
of *in* is common. The statement implies that Tacitus conceived the boats to be worked by paddles (as boats still are
on the Danube), not rowed—an impossible method of pro-
pelling sea-going craft.

adiungunt, 'fix' to the sides, as in the case of Roman
triremes, in contrast to *solutum*.

solutum, 'the oars are loose', so as to be shifted easily, not
secured to the boat.

quibusdam fluminum = *quibusdam fluminibus* (cp. c. 43, 5).

mutabile . . . hinc vel illinc, 'can be shifted, as circumstances require, from one direction to the other' (i.e. are
reversible), so that the vessel may be rowed either way. The
rowlocks of the Nydam boat were secured to the gunwale
only by ropes and could be reversed for rowing the opposite
way. The expression is explained by the description of the
Pontic boats (*H.* 3. 47), *pari utrimque prora et mutabili
remigio, quando hinc vel illinc appellere indiscretum et in-
noxium est* ('with a similar prow at both ends and oars that
can be shifted, since they can put in to land with equal ease
and safety at either end'), and by *A.* 2. 6, 2 *converso ut repente
remigio hinc vel illinc appellerent*. 'Oars which can be shifted
from side to side' is a possible translation, but gives no suitable meaning in relation to the propulsion of the boat: there
is no question of turning it.

ut res poscit: cp. c. 35, 4, etc.

§ **2. est . . . et opibus honos,** 'among these people even wealth is held in high esteem', in contrast to the small value set on it by Germans generally (c. 5, 2–4).

eoque unus imperitat, i.e. because he is pre-eminently rich. The king's power seems really to have rested on a religious ground (see next note).

nullis iam exceptionibus, etc., 'here with no limitations, no claim to obedience based merely on sufferance'. For *iam*, see on c. 43, 6. There are no such restrictions of the king's sovereignty as existed among western Germans and even among the Goths (c. 7, 1–2; 11, 5; and 43, 6). *Iure parendi* for 'the right to be obeyed' is a strained expression.

The Swedish royal power was not really unlimited, though it might seem so to outsiders. The facts may be gathered from later records. The kingship was of a sacral character: the king was also priest of the national god Frey, a deity of fertility, prosperity, and peace (cp. note on Nerthus, c. 40, 2), from whom the royal house traced its descent; and his chief function was to ensure peace and prosperity by due sacrifice. For this purpose he levied taxes on the whole people and so he was called 'monarch' (*einvaldr*), but apart from this he had little power. Olaf's saga (tr. Morris and Magnusson, c. 76) says that it was an ancient custom that the chief sacrifice should be at Upsala in February–March of every year: 'then should be done blood-offering for peace and victory to their king. Thither folk should seek from the whole realm of Sweden, and there at the same time withal should be the Thing [Assembly] of all the Swedes. A market and a fair was there also, which lasted for a week'. Visitors to Upsala at the time of this festival and fair or the nine-days' festival held every nine years at the vernal equinox (Adam of Bremen, 4, 27, eleventh century) would naturally carry away exaggerated impressions of the king's wealth and power. Adam says that in his time the power of the Swedish kings *pendet in populi sententia . . . nisi eius decretum potius videatur, quod aliquando sequuntur inviti* (4, 22).

§ **3. in promisco,** 'in every man's hands'. So used of what is universal in Livy, 29. 17, 14 *in promiscuo licentiam*. On the German habit in this respect, see c. 13, 1, etc.

clausa sub custode. The idea that disarmament was a permanent rule designed to guard against revolution is a misconception of Tacitus or his informants. It was limited to the period of the religious festivals, when a truce of God always reigned: *clausum omne ferrum*, c. 40, 4.

et quidem servo, parenthetical, not explained till *enimvero,* etc. The slave was probably keeper of the royal treasury (*Ynglinga saga*, c. 26), and it would be natural that arms should be consigned to him for safe-keeping during the festival.

quia, etc. The first cause shows why they need not be armed at all times, the second, why it is not thought desirable that they should be. The explanation is that of Tacitus himself. He overlooks the possibility of a sudden attack by pirates or by a hostile tribe. For German piracy, see *A*. 11. 18; Pliny, *N. H*. 16, 203.

manus, 'hands' (personified), as in c. 37, 1.

enimvero, 'and indeed', adding an explanation of why a slave is chosen as custodian.

regia utilitas, 'a king's interest', concisely and boldly used for *regibus utilitati*. See note on *nec rubor*, c. 13, 2.

CHAPTER XLV

THE SEA OF THE EXTREME NORTH. THE AESTII AND THE AMBER TRADE. THE SITONES

§ 1. Trans, 'to the north' of the Swedes, as in c. 43, 6.

aliud, i.e. different from the *Oceanus* of c. 44, 1, which is itself the *exterior Oceanus* of c. 17, 2. Perhaps the Gulf of Bothnia is meant.

pigrum ac prope immotum. A similar description is given in *Agr*. 10, 6 of the sea between Britain and Shetland (Thule): see the note there. These accounts rest ultimately on Pytheas of Massilia (*c*. 330 B.C.), cited by Strabo (1. 4, 2; 2. 4, 1). He placed this 'sluggish and almost motionless' sea one day's sail from Thule (by which he perhaps meant the middle part of the Norwegian coast round Trondhjem), describing it as πεπηγυῖα θάλαττα, a coagulated or stiffened (not frozen) sea, over which ships could make no progress. This is the *mare concretum* of Pliny (4, 104; 37, 35) and the sea which the Cimbri called by the Celtic name *Morimarusa*, 'dead sea' (*id*. 4, 94). Cp. Solinus 22, 9 *ultra Thylen pigrum et concretum mare*. The idea, born perhaps of the experience of sailors who found themselves battling with contrary currents in a windless and foggy sea, lived on through the Middle Ages under the name of *Lebermeer*, i.e. *mare coagulatum*. (Cp. Müllenhoff, *D. A*. i, 410 ff.; Nansen, *In Northern Mists*, ch. ii; Hennig, *Von rätselhaften Ländern*, 95 ff.; art. *Thule* in Pauly-Wissowa.)

quo cingi, etc., 'by which the world is girdled and bounded, as may be (*or* is) believed on the ground that the last radiance of the setting sun lasts till dawn with such brightness as to dim the stars'. The belief implied (which Tacitus himself strangely shared) is that the earth is a convex disk, surrounded by the ocean, and that at the edge of the world the shadow cast by the setting sun is so low as not to reach the sky. A similar account respecting north Britain is given in *Agr.* 12, 3–4 (where see the notes). In neither passage does Tacitus say anything of the corresponding darkness of winter, although Caesar (*B. G.* 5. 13, 3), Strabo (2. 1, 18, quoting Hipparchus), and Pliny (2, 186) had some information about the long winter nights as well as the long summer days. Nor is it noted that the night-long sunlight is limited to two or three months. The midnight sun had probably not been seen by any Greek or Roman mariner, although the phenomenon is reported by Mela, 3, 57.

sidera hebetet, a poetic phrase: *dies hebetarat sidera* (Ovid, *Met.* 5, 444).

emergentis, 'rising out of the ocean', opposed to *cadentis*. The popular belief that the setting sun made a hissing noise as it dropped into the ocean, like red-hot iron plunged into water, is first mentioned by Epicurus and later by many writers, e.g. Posidonius (*ap.* Strabo, 3. 1, 5), Juvenal (14, 280), etc.; but no other classical writer connects the belief with the rising sun. On the other hand, later German folk-lore associated the dawn ('day-*break*', Tages*anbruch*) with a noise: *tönend wird für Geistesohren schon der neue Tag geboren* (Goethe, *Faust*, ii. 1). Cp. J. Grimm, *Deutsch. Mythol.* ii⁴. 618 ff., iii. 221 (E.T. pp. 741 ff., 1518). The stillness of night does in fact end at dawn. It is unlikely that there is any allusion here to the Aurora Borealis, which in northern latitudes may have been (as it still is) supposed to give forth sounds but would not be associated with the rising sun.

formasque equorum et radios capitis. The sun-god with radiate head, driving a horse-drawn chariot, is an idea that belongs to Greek and Roman mythology but is not found in German, although sun-worship among the Germans is mentioned by Caesar (*B. G.* 6, 21) and is attested by some archaeological evidence belonging to the older prehistoric periods, especially the sun-wagon of Trundholm in Zealand, bearing a disk and drawn by a horse, which dates from the early Bronze Age (G. Wilke, *Arch. Erläuter. zur Germania*, p. 73 f.; Shetelig-Falk, *Scand. Archaeology*, pl. 25 and p. 156).

persuasio, 'popular belief', which Tacitus evidently did not share. The word is contrasted with *fama vera* and with *fides* above.

illuc usque . . . natura (sc. *est*), 'thus far only (and report speaks truly) extends the world'. *Natura* stands for *rerum* *natura*. It seems better to regard *et fama vera* (sc. *est*) as a parenthesis—although it separates *tantum* from *illuc usque* in a most awkward way—than to take *fama vera* as ablative, 'up to that point, and by true report thus far only, extends the world', which gives an even more unsatisfactory sentence (*illuc usque* having to be repeated with *tantum*). Some rather violently alter *et* to *si*, comparing Verg. *Aen.* 3, 551 and Livy, 25. 16, 25 and considering that a modestly expressed doubt is more appropriate than a confident assertion. But the confidence may have been inspired by Agricola's circumnavigation of Britain and his report of the *mare pigrum et grave* near Thule: he himself is made to call Caledonia *terrarum et naturae finis*. With this passage may be compared the elder Seneca's description of the Ocean (*Suas.* 1, 1), *stat immotum mare et quasi deficientis in suo fine naturae pigra moles . . . Ita est rerum natura: post omnia Oceanus, post Oceanum nihil.*

§ 2. **ergo iam**, 'so now', i.e. since here the world ends, I pass on from the left (c. 43, 6–44) to the right shore of the Baltic. For the force of *iam*, see note on c. 43, 6.

dextro, the eastern shore, so called from the Roman standpoint. The ablative is local.

Suebici maris, the Baltic, only here so named. Cp. *Suebia*, c. 43, 3; 46, 1.

Aestiorum gentes. *Aestii* was the name given by the Germans to their north-eastern neighbours, a group of Indo-European tribes living along the east coast of the Baltic and perhaps extending to the Gulf of Finland, the ancestors of the so-called 'Baltic' or 'Balto-Slavic' group of old Prussians, Lithuanians, and Letts. The name has been inherited by the modern Esthonians (Ger. *Esten*, old Norse *Eistr*), who are a Finnish people, descended from the Finns who adjoined the Aestii in Tacitus' time (see on Fenni, c. 46, 1). According to the evidence of grave finds their western boundary was the river Passarge in East Prussia (W. La Baume, *Vorgesch. v. Westpreussen*, 1920). The name *Aestii* is Germanic, but its meaning is uncertain: according to Müllenhoff, 'the estimable' (from Gothic *aistan* = *aestimare*) on account of their peaceful disposition (Jordanes, *Get.* 5; Adam of Bremen, 4, 18), while Much suggested 'the men of the (grain-drying) kilns' (A.-S. *ást*, Eng. *oast*, Dutch *eest*), which they used as winterquarters—an explanation consonant with their energetic practice of agriculture.

adluuntur: so Mela, 2, 6 *Borysthenes gentem sui nominis adluit*, and frequently in the elder Pliny.

ritus habitusque, 'their customs and outward appearance'. *Habitus*, of their general appearance, as in c. 46, 1.

lingua Britannicae propior. This statement is undoubtedly erroneous: the Baltic language must have had more resemblance to German than to any form of Celtic. It no doubt reproduces the impression of Romans, or more probably a Roman, engaged in the amber trade, who had also travelled in Britain (for Tacitus does not say *lingua Gallica*, as in c. 43, 1, though he knew that the Gallic and British tongues were not very different, *Agr.* 11, 4). The author of the statement may very well have been the Roman knight who travelled to the east Baltic coast in Nero's reign and *commercia* (= *fora*, ἐμπόρια) *ea et litora peragravit* (Pliny, *N. H.* 37, 45: see note on § 5). The language of the Aestii appeared to him not to be German, and seemed to sound like British. With this information before him, Tacitus still includes the people among his Suebi, although he was aware of the importance of language as a criterion of race. Cp. note on *sermone*, c. 46, 1.

§ 3. **matrem deum.** The goddess was evidently a deity of the Nerthus-Freyja type (see on c. 40, 2). The Roman identification of her with Cybele, the 'Mother of the Gods', probably rested mainly on the fact that her votaries wore as a talisman a figure of the boar, the symbol of the goddess or her consort, just as the worshippers of Cybele wore as amulets the figures of various animals (though not of the boar, which was not sacred to her).

formas aprorum. The boar was also sacred to the Swedish god and goddess Frey and Freyja (see on c. 7, 3; 40, 2; 44, 2), and was a common form of ornament on Scandinavian helmets (cp. Chadwick, *op. cit.*, p. 248); it figured also on Anglo-Saxon helmets, where it was rather a symbol of impetuous courage. Cp. Shetelig-Falk, *op. cit.*, 402.

hominumque tutela, 'human protection', is an easy correction of the MSS. *omniumque* and is recommended by the contrast with *deae*. The alternative emendation *omnique tutela*, 'protection of every sort', is palaeographically less easy. The MSS. text might be interpreted 'protection against everything', but this does not suit the context, and that against which protection is afforded is indicated by *etiam inter hostes*.

rarus ferri, etc. The statement is not quite in accord with the grave finds of the early imperial period in this region (M. Jahn, *Mannusbibl.* 16, Tafel ii), but wooden clubs were still used by Lithuanians as late as the fourteenth century.

§ 4. **ceterosque fructus,** 'and the other products of the soil', probably vegetables (see on c. 23, 1).

patientius, 'more perseveringly'. On the German *inertia*, sce c. 14, 4; 15, 1; 22, 1; 26, 2. The Aestii are thus reckoned as Germans despite their *lingua Britannicae propior*.

laborant for *elaborant*, 'cultivate' (as in *Dial.* 6, 6). The transitive use of the simple verb was originally poetical, but was finding its way into prose. The abundance of simple for compound verbs in the present chapter (*legunt* for *colligunt, clauduntur* for *includuntur, sudantur* for *exsudantur, labuntur* for *delabuntur*) is in keeping with its poetizing tone.

sed et mare scrutantur, i.e. not only do they work the land, but they also search the sea. The same phrase, *mare scrutantur*, is used in *Agr.* 30, 5. The reference may be to fishing, including perhaps seal-fishing; but the following *ac* may be taken as explanatory.

soli omnium, sc. *Germanorum.* Tacitus is speaking of his own time. The Aestian coast, the promontory of Samland in East Prussia, on the north of Königsberg, was (and still is) the chief amber-producing region, but it was not the only one. Amber was found in other parts of the Baltic coasts, and also on the shores and islands of the North Sea (Pliny, *N. H.* 37, 42). The early Greek explorer, Pytheas of Marseilles, heard of its being gathered in one of the islands off the coast of Jutland for use as firewood and for sale to the neighbouring Teutoni (*ibid.* 35); and the Roman fleet under Germanicus found it in one of the West Frisian islands (*ibid.* 42). In earlier time it had been exported from the North Sea to southern Europe, but this trade had evidently ceased before Tacitus' time (see following notes).

sucinum, the pure Latin term for amber, used by Pliny, Martial, and Juvenal, and expressing its character as an exudation (*sucus*). Earlier writers borrowed the Greek term ἤλεκτρον, and (like the Greeks) used it both of amber and of electrum, a metallic compound of gold and silver. This ambiguity affects the interpretation of several passages, but it is certain that amber was known and prized for decorative purposes by the Greeks of the Homeric Age, as is shown by Hom. *Od.* 15, 460 and 18, 296 and by the finds at Mycenae and in the domed tomb of Menidhi. It came to be worked into the myth of the sisters of Phaethon as early as the time of Aeschylus (Pliny, 37, 31). But from the time when Greek art began to develop it ceased to be used to any considerable extent, being an unsuitable artistic material. In Italy it appears in the fifth to fourth century in the Po valley and in Etruscan graves, but the Roman demand for it dates from the last period of the Republic, and there was no great import of it into Italy till Nero's time. Pliny gives an elaborate account of it (37, 30-51), bringing together apparently all

that was known down to his own time (see further below).
glesum, a word denoting brilliancy, from the same root as
'glare', with which 'glass' (A.-S. *glaes*) is cognate. It was a
German—not an Aestian—term, which the Romans learned
during the operations of Germanicus in the North Sea, as we
know from Pliny (*l. c.* 42), who states that the soldiers gave the
name *Glaesaria* to an island which the barbarians called
Austeravia (cp. 4, 97 and 103). The Aestian term is represented by old Prussian *gentars*, Lithuanian *gintāras*.

§ 5. **quae natura** (sc. *sit*), etc., 'being barbarians, they have
not investigated or discovered its character or the process
by which it is produced'. *Barbaris* is dative of agent; for
ut, cp. c. 2, 4, etc. They were enlightened by Cassiodorus, who
in writing (A.D. 523–6) to thank them for a gift of amber
which they had sent to his king, Theodoric, quoted (*Variae*,
5, 2) the explanation given by Tacitus. Amber is in fact
a fossil resin exuded by certain species of pines in the brown
coal (tertiary) epoch and found as irregular nodules in sub-
marine sand. Pieces torn from the sea-floor are cast up by
the waves (*eiectamenta maris*); it is now mostly obtained by
mining.

diu quin etiam . . . iacebat. Tacitus speaks from the Roman
standpoint. The statement is not historically exact. Amber
had been much used for ornaments and the decoration of
utensils both by the Aestii and by west Baltic tribes as early as
the later Stone Age, as is proved by grave finds, and it had
been imported into Greece and northern Italy (see on *sucinum*
above). But the great direct trade with Italy was recent.
Pliny states that the locality whence amber came had only
recently been discovered and records the mission of a Roman
knight still living who had been sent by one of Nero's officials
to get a supply and brought home an enormous quantity
(*l. c.* 45). His journey by way of Carnuntum in Pannonia,
Moravia, and Poland to the Samland started a brisk trade,
which reached its zenith about A.D. 150, thereafter declining
with the tribal unrest in Germany. In this trade a large part
was played by German tribes along the route: *adfertur a
Germanis in Pannoniam maxime provinciam*, says Pliny (*l. c.* 43).
The development of the amber trade from the later part of
the first century onwards is abundantly confirmed by numismatic evidence: along the course of the trade route through
Upper Silesia Roman coins have been found in increasing
numbers from Trajan's time, while those of the early Empire
are very rare, and Republican issues are practically absent;
and the same is true of a westward route from the Samland
through Pomerania to the lower Elbe (Blümner in Pauly-

Wissowa, iii. 302; C. Fredrich in *Ztschr. d. Hist. Ges. d. Prov. Posen*, xxiv. 193 ff.; see also *J. R. S.* xxvi. 200 f., where further references are given).

eiectamenta, 'refuse', used only here and in Apuleius, *Apol.* 35, a more refined expression than Pliny's *maris purgamentum* (*l. c.* 35).

nomen, 'reputation': cp. c. 13, 4.

ipsis in nullo usu. In earlier time the Aestii, like the natives of the other amber-producing regions, had used it for making articles of adornment (necklaces, amulets, etc.), but the Roman demand for it made it more profitable to sell it and use bronze, silver, and gold instead.

rude . . . informe, 'rough . . . shapeless'.

perfertur, it is brought to the market.

mirantes accords with what is said in c. 5, 4 of German indifference to the precious metals, which was certainly an exaggeration; but the Aestii may well have been surprised at the great demand for amber in the later first century and at the price paid for it.

§ 6. sucum . . . arborum: see on § 5.

tamen, i.e. though the people themselves know nothing of it.

terrena . . . volucria animalia, 'creeping and winged creatures'. This is a well established fact. Pliny instances ants, gnats, and lizards (*l. c.* 46), Martial adds bees and vipers (4, 32; 59).

plerumque, 'often' (c. 5, 1; 13, 4, etc.).

mox, 'subsequently'.

clauduntur = *includuntur*; on the use of the simple for the compound verb, see on *laborant* above.

§ 7. sicut Orientis secretis, 'as in the secluded, remote, regions of the East'.

tura balsamaque. Frankincense came only from the Arabian Sabaeans (Verg. *G.* 2, 117), balsam or balm from Palestine (*H.* 5. 6, 3).

sudantur for *exsudantur*, originally a poetic use (Verg. *Ecl.* 8, 55; Ovid, *Met.* 10, 308).

quae . . . expressa, etc. With the manuscript reading of this sentence, *quae . . . expressa* is an anacoluthon: instead of *quae* is required *quorum suci* (the antecedent being *nemora lucosque*). The slip seems to be due to Tacitus himself. Various emendations have been suggested, none of them convincing. The best is the insertion of *et* before *sicut*: 'I should believe that the woods are more than usually fertile (sc. *esse* from the following *inesse*), and that, as in the remote parts of the East, so in the islands and lands of the West there are

substances which', etc. (*quae . . . exundant* being the subject
of *inesse*). But this involves the infelicitous statement that
the substances are in the lands instead of in the trees.
Furneaux's interpretation of the MSS. text, 'As in the East
there are more productive trees than elsewhere, so I would
believe that in the islands and mainland of the West there are
substances which', etc., is open to the same objection, and
involves an unnatural limitation of *nemora lucosque* to the
East. One cannot but feel that *fecundiora . . . crediderim* was
meant to form a single clause; and the rest of the sentence
shows no sign of corruption.

vicini solis (like Horace's *nimium propinqui solis* of the
torrid zone, *Carm.* 1. 22, 21) refers to the view expressed in
§ 1. The idea seems to be that at the edge of the world the
sun is so close to the earth that it produces an effect similar
to that of the hot climate of Arabia and Syria.

exundant, 'are cast up'.

§ 8. naturam, 'the substance', qualities: temptes, 'test'.

pinguem et olentem, 'thick and odorous' (heavy-smelling).

ut in picem . . . lentescit, 'it becomes a sticky substance like
pitch or resin': *lentescit* is so used of that which becomes
viscous in Verg. *G.* 2, 250.

§ 9. Suionibus, etc. The position of this paragraph is surprising:
it might have been expected to come at the end of c. 44, and
some have transposed it thither. Not only, however, is there
no intelligible reason for the misplacement, but the transposition would involve the serious change of *trans Suionas*
(c. 45, 1) to *trans Sitonas*, and the mention immediately after
subitos incursus prohibet Oceanus of a group of tribes living
in close proximity would make that statement ridiculous.
Tacitus seems to conceive the Sitones as dwelling between
the Suiones and the Aestii, so that he reaches them by going
northwards from the east coast of the Baltic, and yet he does
not connect them with the Aestii.

Sitonum gentes. According to Müllenhoff's generally accepted view this tribal group is to be identified with the
Kvaens, a Finnish people named in Norse sources *Kvaenir*
(A.-S. *Cvénas*), a Germanic transformation of the name
Kainu-laiset, 'Lowlanders', by which these people, dwelling
in the flat land of north-eastern Scandinavia, distinguished
themselves from the highland Lapps (*D. A.* ii. 9 ff.).
There are still Kvaens in north-west Finland, and *Kven* is
the Swedish name for the Finns. The name Sitones was
formerly explained by Much from old Norse as meaning
'magicians', an etymology which accords well with the claim
of Finnish Shamanism to possess the power of conciliating

hostile supernatural spirits; but he now adopts a derivation
from a German stem (*sīdha*) meaning 'low' and so denoting
the same as *kainu* (*laiset*). Either derivation would favour
the form *Sithones*, which appears in one MS., but the reading
is of no value, as the interchange of *t* and *th* is frequent in the
reproduction of German names.

continuantur, middle, 'join on to'. Strictly this should
mean that the Sitones dwelt in the same island as the Suiones
or at least in the closest proximity to them, which is inconsistent with the statement in c. 44, 3 that the disarmament
of the Suiones was due to the security which the ocean
afforded against sudden invasion. Tacitus evidently had a
very nebulous idea of the geographical position of the Sitones
and was chiefly interested in the development of the climax:
stricter kingship—absolute kingship— gynaecocracy.

quod femina dominatur. This is explained by Müllenhoff as
a fable due to popular association (among the Germans of the
southern shore of the Baltic) of the name *Kvaenir* with the
German word for 'woman' (Gothic *quinō*, *quēns*, Old Norse
kvaen, Anglo-Saxon *cvén*, English *quean*), whence arose the
legend of a Cvenland, an Amazon kingdom in the north (Paul.
Hist. Lang. 1, 15), which was still an article of belief in the
eleventh century, when Adam of Bremen wrote: *regnant
Sueones usque ad terram feminarum* (4, 14). This ingenious
explanation is usually accepted, but some think that a matriarchal state of society may have existed among the Sitones,
who were perhaps an isolated remnant of a non-Indo-
European population (which Much, *Germ.*, p. 409, thinks
possible).

in tantum, 'to such an extent'.

a servitute degenerant, 'fall below even slavery', i.e.
political slavery of the type prevalent among the Suiones,
where the ruler is at least a man (c. 44, 2-3).

CHAPTER XLVI

THE TRIBES OF THE EASTERN BORDERLAND AND THE FABULOUS
REGION BEYOND

§ 1. Hic Suebiae finis, referring back to c. 38, 1. Some would
transpose these words, as well as the preceding, to the end
of c. 44, but they are required here to point the contrast to
the names which follow.

Peucinorum. The description proceeds from south to
north, as from c. 42 onwards. The Peucini were a section
of the Bastarnae who took their name from Peuke, 'Pine',
the island formed by the two most southerly mouths of the

Danube, now called St. George's island (Strabo, 7. 3, 15, p. 305), which they occupied before 200 B.C. (Ps.-Skymnos, *Perip. Pont. Eux.* 797; Pomp. Trog. *Prol.* 28). But their name was sometimes applied, as by Tacitus here, to the whole tribe: whether Pliny so applied it when he says *quinta pars (Germanorum) Peucini Basternae* (4, 100) is not certain, but Ptolemy's Πευκινὰ ὄρη or Πεύκη ὄρος (3. 5, 5; 9) is identical with the *Alpes Bastarnicae* of the Peutinger Table, the eastern part of the Carpathians. The Peucini proper had long been included in the province of Lower Moesia.

Venethorum, the ancestors of the Slavs. They were neighbours of the Germans on the east of the middle Vistula, south of the Aestii and Gotones. Their name was applied in the (O.H.G.) form *Winidā* (*Winidae* in Jordanes), later *Wenden*, 'Wends', to all the Slavs with whom the Germans came into contact; and it is still used in a restricted sense for certain peoples of Slavonic stock. *Venedi* (or *-ae*) is clearly the right spelling (Pliny, 4, 97; Ptol. 3. 5, 7, and the Peut. Tab.). What form of the name Tacitus used, it is impossible to determine. The MSS. give *Venethi* or *Veneti*. The former would correspond to Gothic *Winitha-* and may have been used by Tacitus, but the *th* spelling has no certain value owing to the copyists' habit of writing *th* for *t* between vowels in German names. If he wrote *Venedi*, there would be a strong tendency to assimilate the name to that of the better known Veneti of north Italy.

In any case the names *Venedi* and *Venethi* or *Veneti* are identical, and it is probable that the identity is not accidental. The Adriatic Veneti were of Illyrian race, and there are good grounds for believing that the first inhabitants of east Germany were also Illyrians. Tacitus mentions an Illyrian tribe, the Osi, in the mountains north of the Danube (c. 28, 4; 43, 1). The occurrence of several place-names in Ptolemy's map of Germany which are certainly or probably Illyrian, and the similarity of the material culture of the Bronze Age in East Germany and in west and north Hungary, Lower Austria, and Moravia indicate that from their earliest home in Bohemia, Moravia, and north-west Hungary the Illyrian stock spread over the then empty region between the Oder and the Vistula (and even beyond these rivers). Thence they were gradually driven southwards or assimilated by the western Germans as they expanded eastwards, just as these Germans had subsequently to give way before the successive waves of immigration from Scandinavia(Vandals, Rugii, Burgundians, Goths). On this view the name Venedi, originally belonging to these north Illyrians, was transferred by the Germans to the Slavs beyond them, who replaced them as their eastern neighbours (see Kossinna in *Mannus*, iv. 176 ff., 287 ff., and *Deutsche Vorgeschichte*; Much in *Zeitschr. f. d. deutsch. Altert.* xli. 97, and Hoops' *Reallex*. iii. 393, iv. 509; Fluss in Pauly-Wiss., Suppl. v, s.v. *Illyrioi*).

Fennorum, the Finns, whom Ptolemy calls Φίννοι. This is the first mention of them. Those here referred to are not the ancestors of the present inhabitants of Finland, but are to be placed, in accordance with the order of enumeration, on the east of the Baltic, where they were neighbours of the Aestii. The original home of the Finns appears to have been in the region of Moscow, whence they spread up to the Gulf of Finland as early as about 1500 B.C., so that they may well have flowed into Esthonia and northern Latvia before the time of Tacitus.

Sarmatis, see note on c. 1, 1.

quamquam, 'and yet', 'however' (note on c. 5, 4), introducing the description of the Peucini (and therefore not belonging to the previous sentence, to which the ordinary punctuation assigns it).

Bastarnas, the first of all the German tribes to appear in history, as having been invited by Philip of Macedon in 182 B.C. to aid him against the Dardani (Livy, 40, 5) and in 179 against the Romans (*id.* 40, 57), with whom they often came into conflict in later time. They were a large tribe with many subdivisions, extending along the east side of the Carpathians from Galicia southwards. According to Pliny, they formed one of the five great groups of Germans (see on c. 2, 3). The most westerly section of them, the Sidones of Strabo and Ptolemy, occupied the hills to the south of the upper Vistula (Strabo, 7. 3, 17; Valer. Flacc. *Argon*. 6, 95; Ptol. 2. 11, 10). These were the Basternae who were routed by a legate of Illyricum towards the end of the first century B.C. (Dess. 8965, see note on Cotini, c. 43, 1).

sermone. The Romans knew something of their language, but nothing of that of the remote Venethi and Fenni. It is noticeable that the identity of language does not convince Tacitus of their German nationality; cp. c. 45, 2.

cultu, 'manner of life' (c. 43, 1).

sede ac domiciliis, 'mode of settlement and dwellings', i.e. in having fixed dwellings (*domos figunt*, § 2), *ac* being epexegetic.

ut Germani agunt (= *se gerunt*, as in c. 29, 3; 35, 4, etc.). They were thought to be Celts at a time when Germans were not yet known, and they were no doubt affected by Celtic influences coming from Moravia and Upper Hungary; but Strabo had already conjectured that they were Germans and

Pliny had no doubt about it. Their true nationality is assured
by the epitaph of one of the Peucini who had served among
the *corpore custodes* of Nero: *Nereus nat(ione) German(us)
Peucennus* (Dess. 1722). See Much, 'Der Eintritt d. Germanen in die Weltgeschichte', in *Germanistische Forsch.*, 1925,
pp. 7 ff.

sordes omnium (sc. *sunt*), etc., 'they are all squalid and
their chiefs are slothful'. The phrasing is harsh and the
sequence of thought is not too clear, but it seems plain that
omnium is contrasted with *procerum*, as in c. 11, 1 *omnes* is
opposed to *principes*. *Sordes* (not personal uncleanliness but
the squalor that results from poverty) and *torpor* (uncon-
cerned indolence) are apparently further points of resemblance to Germans, while the next asyndetic clause adds a
non-German trait (cp. c. 4, 1 *nullis aliarum nationum conubiis
infectos*), which might seem to tell against the Germanic
nationality of the tribe. For the *sordes* of Germans, cp.
c. 20, 1 (for their *inopia*, c. 28, 3; 5, 2; Caes. *B. G.* 6, 24);
and for the *torpor* of nobles when no fighting is on hand,
c. 15, 1; 22, 1; 45, 4. The asyndeton, however, is somewhat
awkward.

Some editors place a colon after *torpor* and insert before
procerum some such word as *ora*, a palaeographically easy
supplement, which has found fairly wide acceptance but is
by no means convincing. Against it is the ascription of *torpor*
to the whole people: no people sunk in *torpor* could possibly
have survived. The same objection applies to the emendation *torpor; ceterum conubiis*, etc., suggested by the feeling
that the separation of the *proceres* from the mass of the people
is out of place here; and the corruption would hardly be
intelligible, even if a dittography of *-por* be assumed.

nonnihil . . . foedantur, 'are to some extent getting the
debased appearance of the Sarmatians'; *habitus* as in c. 45, 2
(cp. c. 4, 2). The present tense means that the process is
steadily going on.

§ 2. **moribus,** sc. *Sarmatarum*, contrasted with the mere *habitus*,
as *multum* is contrasted with *nonnihil*. The insertion of *et*
before *ex* (Gudeman) would make Tacitus say that, besides
intermarrying with the Sarmatians, like the Peucini, they
have also contracted many of their habits. The addition is
unnecessary and therefore arbitrary. The contrast of the
mores of the Venethi with the *habitus* of the Peucini tells
against it. Intermarriage may have been common, but the
source followed by Tacitus evidently knew nothing about the
tribe except that they were like the Sarmatians in one respect
and unlike them in others.

montium. Ptolemy also speaks of Venedic mountains (Ούενεδικὰ ὄρη, 3. 5, 5). Nothing more than rising ground exists in this tract.

erigitur, 'lifts itself', i.e. 'rises', like Virgil's *insula* . . . *erigitur* (*Aen*. 8, 416).

latrociniis: Germans also had plundering habits (c. 14, 3), though they only occasionally practised them.

tamen, in spite of their Sarmatian habits.

domos figunt, 'they build permanent houses': so *fixerant domos* (*Frisii*), *A*. 13. 54, 3.

scuta gestant, which was not a Sarmatian practice (*H*. 1. 79).

pedum, taken also with *pernicitate*. The Sarmatae relied on the *pernicitas equorum*, and were most inefficient on foot, most formidable on horseback (*H*., *l. c*.).

Sarmatis, dative, abbreviated for *Sarmatarum moribus*. So *Agr*. 24, 2 *a Britannia differunt* ('from those of Britain').

§ 3. Fennis mira feritas. The description of the three tribes works up to a climax, which culminates in *fabulosa*: the Peucini-Bastarnae are somewhat below the German type, the Venedi more, the Fenni most of all. Very similar is Herodotus' account of the progressive barbarism of the Scythian tribes, which proceeds from south to north, like that of Tacitus, and then to east, and culminates in stories of men with goats' feet, one-eyed Arimaspi and gold-guarding griffins (4, 17 ff.).

The description of the Fenni, despite its rhetorical traits, is not an imaginary idealization of a primitive people. The style expresses the writer's feeling of marvel at the existence of such extreme barbarism. The facts were probably drawn from the report of a traveller who had spent some time in the amber country and had gathered information about the tribe, possibly the Roman knight of Nero's reign who *commercia ea et litora peragravit* (notes on c. 45, 2 and 5). In Latvia there is evidence of such a primitive form of material culture with implements made of bone and horn, and this may probably have persisted till the time of Tacitus at least in the inland region adjoining the coastal area. The account of Tacitus closely resembles that given five centuries later by Procopius of the Scrithifinni, the 'ski-ing Finns' (*Bell. Goth*. 2, 15), a designation of the Lapps of northern Scandinavia, who are still called Finns by the Norwegians; and some scholars believe that it really referred to these Finns and not to those of the east Baltic, who had developed a material culture of the Iron Age type long before Tacitus wrote. But the archaeological evidence, which belongs to the region between the Memel and the Gulf of Finland, is not so securely dated as to discredit the account of Tacitus (if the Fenni really dwelt in that region in his time). Cp. G. Ekholm in *Camb. Anc. Hist.* xi. 66 f.

non arma. The bows and arrows mentioned below are used to procure food and are not counted as arms.

non penates, 'no household' (cp. c. 15, 1), no regular dwelling-place, in contrast to *domos figunt* above.

victui, etc.: for these datives, cp. c. 23, 1.

herba, wild plants, *herbae sponte nascentes, quibus pleraeque gentium utuntur in cibis* (Pliny, *N. H.* 21, 86). These would be available only in summer, but that was the only season when traders or travellers would visit the country. The statement is not quite consistent with what is said of their hunting, but the meaning is that they had no agricultural produce.

cubile for *cubili* is an intentional variation at the close of the series. Cp. *mihi* (the Scythian Anacharsis) *est cubile terra* (Cic. *Tusc.* 5, 90).

solae in sagittis spes: the alliteration here and in the next sentence, *partem praedae petunt,* is notable. Tacitus uses *spes* in the plural even where there is only one thing hoped for.

inopia ferri: cp. c. 45, 3.

ossibus asperant, 'tip with sharp bones': *asperare,* 'sharpen', as in *A.* 15. 54, 1 *pugionem . . . asperari iussit.* Bone arrow-heads were used by Sarmatians in the time of Pausanias (1. 21, 5), and by the Huns in the fourth century (Ammianus, 31. 2, 9), and are stated to be still in use in Lapland and in parts of Siberia.

alit, 'supports'. The meaning is 'they support life by hunting, in which men and women alike take part', as the next clause plainly shows.

passim, 'everywhere', wherever they go: not 'in numbers' (c. 41, 2, note), a meaning unsuitable to the context.

comitantur, sc. *feminae viros.* The extreme form of the hunter's life is that in which women hunt as well as men.

partemque praedae petunt, 'they claim a share in securing the spoil' (not 'claim a share of the spoil', which would be an absurd statement when the game was destined for household consumption). *Praeda* is used in the active sense which it not uncommonly bears (like Eng. 'plunder'), e.g. *A.* 1. 60, 4 *inter caedem et praedam* ('killing and looting'), and so 15. 6, 6; 2 52, 2 *ad praedam et raptus congregare*; *H.* 1. 45 *caedis et praedarum* (= *praedationum*) *initium,* etc. So Procopius says that among the Scrithifinni (Lapps) hunting is an occupation which, like every other, the women share with the men (*l. c.*).

§ 4. **suffugium**, with objective genitives, as in c. 16, 4.

aliquo ramorum nexu, 'a sorry interlacement of branches'. Such seems to be the meaning of *aliquo*: the intertwined branches give just some sort of protection. For a similar depreciatory use, cp. *Dial*. 29, 1 *infans delegatur Graeculae alicui ancillae*, 'our children are handed over to some silly little Greek sewing-maid'. (Some take *aliquo* as equivalent to *quodam*, as in *Dial*. 39, 2, Cic. *pro Arch*. 18.) These hovels resembled those found among Laplanders, made of four boughs bent together and held in place by twisted twigs and covered with some sort of canvas or reindeer hide. Similar huts are described by Herodotus as used by the Scythian Argippaei, who dwell under a tree which they cover with a close felt-cloth (4. 23, 6), but with some distinction between summer and winter dwellings, which Tacitus here ignores, because his source described only summer conditions, as is plain from *herba—imbrium—agris*.

redeunt, i.e. from hunting.

receptaculum, 'their refuge' when they can hunt no more.

§ 5. **beatius arbitrantur**, etc. This section is an ironical allusion to the Stoic and Epicurean doctrine that the highest good is attainable only by freedom from material wants.

ingemere agris (dat.), 'groan over the tillage of fields', imitated from *bidenti, aratro ingemere* (Lucr. 5, 209; Verg. *G*. 1, 45).

inlaborare domibus. The verb was coined to answer to *ingemere* and produce a phrase balancing *ingemere agris*. It would seem therefore that it must take the same construction, and that the phrase must mean 'toil over house-building', in contrast to their rude shelter above described. *Ingemere agris* and *inlaborare domibus* are obviously the opposites of the two features of Finnish life just described, viz. no agriculture but only hunting, and no house-building; and this fact is decisive against taking the latter phrase to mean 'labour indoors', in reference to women's house-work.

versare, etc., 'to traffic with their own and other people's property under hope and fear', as all traders do. Cp. Suet. *Galb*. 9 *nummulario non ex fide versanti pecunias*, and *faenus agitare*, c. 26, 1.

securi, etc., 'having nothing to fear at the hands of men or gods', as they have nothing to excite either the cupidity of the one or the envy of the other. Poverty, says Seneca, holds out the promise of *perpetua libertas, nullius nec hominis nec dei timor* (*Epp*. 17, 6).

ne voto quidem opus esset, 'not to feel the need even of a wish', to have nothing to long for and pray for. *Illis* is emphatic, *they* unlike others. The sentiment was no doubt a commonplace in idealizing and moralizing descriptions; we meet it in the Augustan age in Pompeius Trogus' account of the Scythians, epitomized by Justin, 2. 2, 10: 'Gold and silver they spurn just as the rest of mankind covets them; they live on milk and honey; the use of wool and clothes is unknown to them ... but they wear the skins of wild beasts and martens. *Haec continentia illis morum quoque iustitiam dedit, nihil alienum concupiscentibus ... prorsus ut admirabile videatur hoc illis naturam dare, quod Graeci longa sapientium doctrina praeceptisque philosophorum consequi nequeunt'*, etc.

§ **6. cetera iam fabulosa.** 'all from this point is fabulous'. For *iam* see on c. 43, 6.

Hellusios et Oxionas. Neither of these fabulous peoples is elsewhere mentioned. *Hellusii* is explained by Much as meaning 'fawn-like' (Lith. *élnis*, Gk. *ἐλλός*), *Oxiones* as 'ox-like'; or, as both names may well have come from an old Greek source, *Oxiones* may have been a Celtic formation (like *Morimarusa* for the *mare pigrum* of c. 45, 1) and may be connected with Irish *oisin*, a young seal.

The variant *Etionas* (*Exionas* in two MSS.), probably a corruption of *et Oxionas*, was preferred by Müllenhoff, who by a forced etymology took it to mean 'greedy giants', probably giving the idea of cannibals or ogres, which does not suit the context.

ora ... vultusque, 'faces and features'.

corpora ... ferarum. From the time of Herodotus (§ 3, note) men's imagination peopled remote regions near the edge of the world with all sorts of such monsters: examples may be found in Mela, 1, 48; 3. 56, 88 and 103; Pliny, 4, 95; 5, 44. In those northern parts Mela and Pliny speak of men with horses' feet and others with enormous ears, which served to clothe their otherwise naked bodies. *Ambiguae hominum et beluarum formae* figured among the marvels 'seen or in their terror believed' by the soldiers of Germanicus shipwrecked in the North Sea (*A.* 2. 24, 6). Even in the eleventh century the far North was believed to be inhabited not only by Amazons (note on c. 45, 9) but by men with dogs' heads on their breasts, cannibals and giants, as Adam of Bremen narrates. Müllenhoff's suggestion that tales of creatures with the faces of men and the bodies of beasts may have arisen from seeing men wrapped in skins, with little but their heads showing, is hardly probable. It is more likely, as the passage of the *Annals* suggests, that they owed their origin to the same cause as the mermen and mermaids of popular fantasy.

incompertum seems to imply that Tacitus hesitated to call

such tales positively incredible, though he considered them
fabulosa.

   in medio, 'an open question': cp. Sall. *Cat.* 19, 5; Cic.
Cael. 20, 48. The MSS. read *in medium*, but it is very doubtful whether Tacitus, who in *H.* 2. 33 wrote *in incerto reliquerat*,
is to be credited with the accusative here, which may easily
have been due to assimilation of the ending to the preceding
incompertum. Gellius (17. 2, 11), quoting *in medium relinque-
mus* from Claudius Quadrigarius, a historian of Sulla's time,
admits that the expression, like *in medium ponere*, was
generally regarded as a solecism, but defends it (*set probabi-
lius significantiusque sic dici videbitur, si quis ea verba non
incuriose introspiciat*), quoting as an analogy θεῖναι εἰς μέσον.
This defence is by no means decisive in favour of *in medium*
in the present passage. Quadrigarius used many unusual
expressions which Tacitus would not have approved, nor is
it very likely that here he preferred an uncommon usage just
because it was uncommon.

I. INDEX OF NAMES

The references are to chapter and section.

II. INDEX OF SUBJECTS

The reference is to the page, except where 'c.' is prefixed.